D. J. Taylor

was born in Norwich in 196_ _____
School and St John's College, Oxford, where he read
modern history. A distinguished, sometimes controversial
critic, who reviews for several papers including the
Sunday Times and the *Independent*, his outspoken attack
on the literary establishment in *A Vain Conceit: British
Fiction in the 1980s* created widespread debate. He is also
author of two novels, *Great Eastern Land* and *Real Life*.
He lives in London with his wife and son.

D. J. TAYLOR

After the War

The Novel and England since 1945

Flamingo

An Imprint of HarperCollins*Publishers*

Flamingo
An Imprint of HarperCollins*Publishers*
77–85 Fulham Palace Road,
Hammersmith, London W6 8JB

Published by Flamingo 1994
9 8 7 6 5 4 3 2 1

First published in Great Britain by
Chatto & Windus Ltd 1993

The quotation used as an epigraph © Anthony Powell,
Hearing Secret Harmonies, Heinemann, 1975 is reproduced
by kind permission of the author and publisher.

ISBN 0 00 654753 2

Set in Garamond

Printed in Great Britain by
HarperCollinsManufacturing Glasgow

Rachel's

Contents

Irritated by what he judged the 'impacted clichés' of some review, Trapnel had once spoken of his own opinions on the art of biography.

'People think because a novel's invented, it isn't true. Exactly the reverse is the case. Because a novel's invented, it is true. Biography and memoirs can never be wholly true, since they can't include every conceivable circumstance of what happened. The novel can do that. The novelist himself lays it down. His decision is binding. The biographer, even at his highest and best, can only be tentative, empirical. The autobiographer, for his part, is imprisoned in his own egotism. He must always be suspect. In contrast with the other two, the novelist is a god, creating his man, making him breathe and walk. The man, created in his own image, provides information about the god. In a sense you know more about Balzac and Dickens from their novels, than Rousseau and Casanova from their Confessions.'

'But novelists can be as egotistical as any other sort of writer. Their sheer narcissism often makes them altogether unreadable. A novelist may inescapably create all his characters in his own image, but the reader can believe in them, without necessarily accepting their creator's judgment on them. You might see a sinister strain in Bob Cratchit, conventionality in Stavrogin, delicacy in Molly Bloom. Besides, the very concept of a character in a novel – in real life too – is under attack.'

'What you say, Nick, strengthens my contention that only a novel can imply certain truths impossible to state by exact definition. Biography and autobiography are forced to attempt exact definition. In doing so truth goes astray. The novelist is more serious – if that is the word.'

Conversation between X. Trapnel and Nick Jenkins, from Anthony Powell: *Hearing Secret Harmonies* (1975).

A book is written not in a vacuum but at a precise historical moment which will affect not only the stylistic dress in which it is clothed but its moral and political underpinnings.

Maureen Duffy, introduction to Virago Modern Classics edition of *That's How It Was* (1962).

Acknowledgements

The initial idea for this book came in an invitation from *The Guardian Weekend* to write on 'character' in the English novel since the war. My most immediate debt, consequently, is to Murray Armstrong, who commissioned the original piece and is in many ways the cause of all that followed.

An early version of Chapter 10 appeared in the *Guardian* ('Sex and the Singular Novel', 9 January 1992). Similarly, Chapter 12 began life in an article commissioned by the *Independent* in advance of the 1992 General Election ('Behind the Scenes in the Story Cabinet', 4 April 1992). I should like to thank Robert Winder, literary editor of the *Independent*, and Ian Mayes, then deputy features editor of the *Guardian*, both for their interest and enthusiasm and also for permission to reprint copyrighted material.

A number of people were kind enough to discuss their work with me, lend or suggest useful books or respond to enquiries. In particular, I should like to acknowledge the help of Malcolm Bradbury, Melvyn Bragg, A. S. Byatt, Nicholas Clee, Jonathan Coe, William Cooper, Martyn Goff, Anthony Powell and Harry Ritchie. My editor, Jenny Uglow, and publisher, Carmen Callil, were an invaluable source of advice, information (and debate). Among an extensive bibliography, I should like to acknowledge the particular influence of Harry Ritchie's *Success Stories: Literature and the Media in England 1950–59* (Faber 1988) and James Gindin's *Postwar British Fiction: New Accents and Attitudes* (University of California Press 1962).

My most profound debt, however, is to my wife Rachel, who

greeted a succession of lost weekends and desk-bound nights with an exemplary tolerance. This book is for her.

London, January 1993

Introduction

Whatever Happened to Lucky Jim?

Orwell maintained that no piece of writing above the level of a railway timetable could be wholly disinterested: what follows, consequently, has a personal explanation. I grew up on the Victorian novel of character. Queerly enough, I can date the beginning of this obsession exactly, to a single week in February 1978 when, with the demands of homework temporarily eclipsed by the aftermath of mock 'A' Levels, I established myself in front of the gasfire in my father's study with a copy of *Dombey and Son*. Even now, half a lifetime away, I can still recall the excitement of discovering Mr Dombey, Major Bagstock and Toots for the first time, something that I can only describe as an actual physical thrill. A collected edition of Thackeray, discovered a year or so later gathering dust in the college library, produced a similar effect. One of my more satisfactory memories of Oxford is of sitting in a low, shadowy room with the light fading away in the distance beyond Trinity Chapel, reading 'A Little Dinner at Timmins's'. Rhapsodies over the literary discoveries of one's youth are a particularly dreary form of reminiscence, but it would be accurate to say that for a long while the characters who populated these novels – Dombey, Reardon in Gissing's *New Grub Street* (a girl once said I reminded her of a character in *New Grub Street*, which I took as a compliment), the Timminses who *would* give their little dinner – were far more real to me than the undergraduates and, eventually, the business colleagues with whom I daily came into contact. There are literary precedents for this, of course: Charles Highway in Martin Amis's *The Rachel Papers* reads Dickens and Kafka 'to find a world full of the bizarre surfaces and sneaky tensions with which I was always trying to invest my own life'. At the same time this immersion in nineteenth-century literature had a tremendous effect on the contents of my own mental lumber room. Gissing once said that he could never walk past the Monument without thinking of Todger's boarding house in *Martin Chuzzlewit*. In the same way I have never been able to walk down Cursitor Street without thinking of Rawdon Crawley's imprisonment for debt in *Vanity Fair* or to cross Portman Square without remembering Phineas Finn's pursuit of Lady Laura Standish. If this book sometimes seems like a sort of hopeless love-letter to Thackeray, Trollope and Gissing it is because of this early grounding. The Victorian tree, as M. R. James remarked in a slightly different context, cannot but be expected to produce Victorian fruit.

Curiously, literary journalism – to which I gravitated in my mid-20s – had the effect of reinforcing this obsession, if only by providing continual examples of the bastard great-grandchildren of a once unsullied family. Reviewing thirty or forty novels a year is not a task calculated to preserve any illusions you may once have harboured about modern fiction. To say this is not to adopt the depressingly common *Guardian* line of modern British writers being unable to write, but to acknowledge the fact that nearly every critic who approaches the modern British novel does so in the consciousness of debasement and decadence, narrowed horizons and limited aims. We read Dickens and George Eliot at school and we know, we just *know*, that no modern writer – certainly no modern *English* writer – can hold a candle to them. Inevitably, the critic who maintains this position with any conviction will end up having to answer several awkward questions. There are a number of plausible replies to the type of cultural pundit who wonders whether the review pages of newspapers couldn't decently be filled with some other material: novels presumably have to be reviewed, and Orwell has some useful remarks on the necessity for spring balances capable of weighing both elephants and fleas. Sooner or later, though, anyone seriously interested in modern fiction will be forced to confront an enquiry which is more or less unanswerable: why devote so much attention to an art-form which nearly everybody admits is in a wretched state, and in which large numbers of intelligent people have lost interest?

Here the average critic, whose sincerest wish is not to jeopardise his own livelihood, is liable to become slightly evasive. It is not enough merely to say that novels have to be reviewed, for one sometimes gets the feeling that book reviewing in this country is simply an amiable conspiracy designed to pass third-rate goods off as second-rate. On the other hand, if novels are going to be reviewed, then it is a rather pointless exercise to write them all off as worthless. You and I know that the new Shirley Conran is tripe, and you and I might suspect that the new Graham Swift is tripe as well, but they are different kinds of tripe and need to be treated in different ways (a process by the way that does not automatically work in favour of 'serious' writers). In an atmosphere where quite ordinary books are regularly trumpeted as works of genius it is the critic's duty not simply to point out every now and then that Dickens can knock any modern writer into a cocked hat, but to define the nature of that superiority and account for it. A comparison between a 'modern' (i.e. post–1945) novel and one of Henry James's great baggy monsters from the Victorian age can be an eye-opening experience. Anyone who has ever read *David Copperfield* and *Lucky Jim* back to back, for example, will immediately recognise the similarities between them. Each derives from a much older tradition which goes back as far as Fielding, the novel of the young man making his way through society, searching for his fortune (which Jim Dixon would construe as 'a decent job') and romantic happiness. Here, however, the similarity ends, washed aside by a wave of discrepancies in scope, outlook, humour – if you wish to take the measure of a particular age, a good place to start is in establishing what it finds funny – and ambition. But the most important difference between Dickens and nearly every modern novelist lies in the field of character. One of the touchstones of the Victorian novel is the faith which we display in the characters who populate it, characters whose behaviour is always plausible, and somehow, owing to the underlying strength of the portrait, that much more plausible when they behave out of character. Compared to David Copperfield and Lucy Snowe, Jim Dixon and his descendants seem pale, pallid creations, the 'people in paper houses' of Graham Greene's essay on Mauriac of 1961. Greene ascribed the frailty of modern fictional characters to a decline in religious belief, but there is more to it than this. The gulf between Jim Dixon and David Copperfield, Gissing's Godwin Peak and many another a Victorian hero is a moral one, a matter of scrupulousness, and ultimately a social gulf. The society through which Jim is making his way has fundamentally altered, grown simultaneously more and less complex. At the same time Jim is both more and less able to deal with the challenges imposed on him by this new and uncertain environment. The explanation of his inferiority to what came before him lies not in any creative failure but in the prevailing social circumstance. Jim and his own fictional descendants are victims of their time. My aim in writing this book has been to investigate some of the links between modern English fiction and the historical process, in the conviction that the latter not only helps to explain the concerns of the former but also most of its inadequacies.

Considering literature in its social context is not a newfangled technique. Most of us at some point in our academic lives have examined Blake's lyrics in the light of the Industrial Revolution or the relationship of Kingsley's *Alton Locke* to Chartism. However cursory their application, and however obtuse some of the linkages between cause and effect, these approaches have deep roots. It is over a century since the appearance of the French critic Hippolyte Taine's fundamental doctrine that 'we must study the organism in connection with the medium', or Leslie Stephen's claim that 'the literary history of any period gains by being seen as one strand in a complex social tissue'. Taine's *History of English Literature*, published in 1873 and excoriated by Stephen in a famous review, and Stephen's own early work are perhaps the first signposts on the long road of what might be called English literary sociology.

Taine and Stephen were pioneers, although more narrowly engaged descendants might want to envy their breadth of sympathy. As John Gross has pointed out, Stephen might have been the gentleman in the library, content in the last resort not to ask too many embarrassing questions, but his achievement was to demonstrate just how formidable a force the gentleman in the library could be. It took a later generation of critics to establish some of the more subtle ways in which literary consciousness might be transformed by environment, for example Ian Watt's exemplary study *The Rise of the Novel* (1957). The principle divined by Watt and other critics from Paul Fussell to Samuel Hynes – that books are no more than reflections or amplifications of history – can occasionally seem so obvious as to be scarcely worth stating. Surely we all *know* that, whatever the theorists might tell us about literature ultimately reducing itself to the mechanics of language, books are not simply matrixes of words but the product of a particular mind writing at a particular time. The contemporary reader might regard the modern movement in textual criticism as a gigantic exercise in wool-pulling, designed to exclude ordinary people from literature, but surely, he or she reasons, it is not such a swindle as that?

If academic criticism sometimes seems rather a soft target – the jargon, the opinion masquerading as fact, the dons who talk about 'sequential, realism-based narratives' when they mean realistic stories – this is not to ignore the significant effect it has had on modern literary interpretation. The academic, at least, has some claims to professional status, whereas the hack merely makes his or her living from writing about books. To the modern critical theorist the tools of social and historical analysis are infinitely suspect, always ripe for relegation at the expense of language on the grounds that language created them. The newer type of campus critic will tell you, consequently, that Taine's 'medium' – which he defined as '*race, milieu, moment*' – is only words after all, a sort of historical smokescreen obscuring a book's true function as a component in a vast, endless fictional game carried on solely for the reader's sake. As Roland Barthes put it in *The Death of the Author* (1968), writers cannot use writing 'to express themselves' but only to draw upon a hidden dictionary which is 'always already written'. The author therefore is himself a concept, the creation of his work rather than the creator of it. A quarter of a century on from Barthes, there is something uniquely depressing and at the same time faintly unfair about all this. On the one hand it imposes a set of rules on people who don't know that the rules exist. On the other it defies a very common assumption, here breezily expressed by Simon Raven, that 'if you hang on long enough, if you pin it down to what it is, it [the novel] feels obliged to answer your questions about society'.

At the most basic level, regarding a novel as merely another brick in the high, gloomy wall of critical theory also ignores the fact that many books are written in a very mundane way and for very mundane reasons. It tends to be forgotten, for example, that Johnson wrote *Rasselas* to defray the expenses of his mother's funeral, or that Dumas's terse, interrogative dialogue was the result of his being paid at so many centimes a line. The same point can be made of literary collusion in pursuit of some luminous aesthetic aim, which is frequently deflated by the most cursory investigation of the wider background. Malcolm Bradbury might hazard the existence of a 'certain and self-asserting movement that made up the spirit of modernism', but, set against this, detailed work on the social history of the English novel before 1914 shows only how fragmented and random was the new wave of early twentieth-century novelists. Many of the changes in artistic direction were provoked by commercial considerations. The collapse of the three-volume novel, for instance, though long desired by novelists, came about largely because the libraries decided that the format was no longer economically viable, and if there is a single material factor linking Joyce, Woolf and Conrad it is that they all at one time or another in their literary career submitted work to *Titbits*. The 'causes' of modernism were quite as much historical – social and economic – as aesthetic, and it was at least as much a social revolution as a 'revolution of the word', to borrow the title of Colin MacCabe's alarmingly clever book on Joyce. If the most satisfactory explanation of modernism is an historical one, then so is an explanation of the disconnected, self-referring writing which we now automatically describe as 'post-modernism', and so, necessarily, is an explanation of the particular types of novel which we find being written in England in the period after 1945.

Inevitably, too, any critic examining the writing of a particular historical period is forced back to the narrower question of personal motivation, Orwell's 'Why I Write'. The aesthetic movement view of literature, in which everybody has their sights fixed on some glamorous artistic deal, ignores, or partly obscures, some of the more blatant social forces that prompt any sort of artistic composition. Maintaining that literature reflects the aspirations of the people who write it and the characters who embody those aspirations might not seem an altogether startling claim, but it can look markedly original when matched against the latest textual scrabblings from Yale. What we categorise conveniently enough as 'aspiration' can range from the idiosyncrasies of a particular temperament to the prejudices of a particular class, can be conveyed through transparent idealism or bruising satire, but behind it generally lies a conception, however vague, of how the world ought to work. Even fiction as profoundly disillusioned as the later novels of Evelyn Waugh expresses idealism of a sort. Waugh might regard nearly every manifestation of the post-war world as an unfortunate mistake, but the principles and values that he cares about – however unpalatable they might be to a contemporary audience – are always present as a stick with which to beat modern depravity.

Naturally enough, notions of how the world ought to work are usually centred on the private aspirations of fictional characters. Smollett's Roderick Random, Dickens's David Copperfield and even Gissing's Godwin Peak are united by their status as young men on the make. Again, the sprawling collection of post-war fictional heroes, from Jim Dixon and Charles Lumley to Keith Talent and Morgan Leafy, are drawn together by the fact that they want things from the society which created them. Billy Fisher in Keith Waterhouse's *Billy Liar*, who hankers after a new life as a radio comedy scriptwriter, Jim Dixon with his gaze fixed on the best job and the prettiest girl, differ in degree from Roderick Random, voyaging after his beloved Narcissa, or Godwin Peak, attempting to square his rationalist principles with his love for a conventionally devout young woman, but not in kind. If they seem diminished figures when matched against the great Augustan and Victorian exemplars, it is because the social and moral environment in which they operate has undergone such a radical transformation.

To say that the mechanisms of fiction are predominantly social rather than aesthetic also has the advantage of illuminating a period of literary history in which domestic writing defies easy categorisation and the over-convenient taxonomy of 'modernism' and 'post-modernism' no longer seems helpful. The 'elusive' and 'pluralist' qualities of the novel since 1945 have not escaped the attention of contemporary critics. There are some regretful sentences, for example, in Bradbury's essay 'The Novel No Longer Novel', noting that 'the post-war novel has been with us long enough for us to see that there is not one single flavour of fiction, but in fact a variety of directions in a variety of phases'. As a summing up, or a confession of bafflement, this is difficult to dispute. Random, eclectic, in many cases blatantly hostile to the traditions it supplanted, the great corpus of post-war writing in this country owes much of its randomness and eclecticism to the variety of social factors to which it has been subjected. At the same time, these factors give it a particular and sometimes very definite focus. Though it is possible to oversimplify the links between social cause and literary effect – Stephen's complaint about Taine – I believe that the novel becomes more coherent to us, as social beings, if we see it as formed in this crucible of social influence. However much the representatives of more transient media might dispute it, the novel is still a part of our lives, even here at the tail-end of the twentieth century, still a repository for what we know as 'value', still a connecting point between a world and a generally sceptical individual intelligence. This isn't to say that the novelist is always 'right' about society. In fact he is generally wrong, or at best misguided. All the same, by examining the post-war novel in its social context, as opposed to its narrower role as one of several meagre blooms in a windswept literary garden, we not only learn something about the relationship between Art and Society; we learn something about ourselves.

Inevitably, much of the foregoing may look like special pleading. Theme, environment, society: all this might be germane enough to the 'development' of the novel – always a slightly suspect term – but it is not obviously central. The reader of fiction tends to see novels in terms of their characters. I remember *Pendennis* for the old Major and Captain Costigan, not for its portrait of a landed aristocracy infiltrated by an emergent bourgeoisie. It is here, in the portrayal of character, that the transformations which have overtaken the novel in the past forty years are most immediately apparent. The difference between Jim Dixon, the hero in Kingsley Amis's *Lucky Jim* (1954), and John Self, the protagonist of his son Martin's *Money* (1984), is so vast as to seem unbridgeable. The same point could be made of the gap between a Rosamond Lehmann heroine and a woman in a Fay Weldon novel. Each inhabits not merely a distinct environment, with its shifting constraints and freedoms, but almost a separate mental atmosphere.

Behind the distinctions of individual quiddity lie more powerful forces. The symbolic importance of fictional heroes and heroines has long been appreciated by book publishers. The jacket of a recent paperback reprint of *Lucky Jim*, for example, carries the confident assertion that Kingsley Amis gave post-war fiction 'a new and enduring figure to laugh at', and that the book is 'the comic novel of our time'. While the second claim is questionable – Jim Dixon's 'time', given the novel's roots in the late 1940s, is nearly half a century ago – the first is undoubtedly correct. If a novel's popularity can be measured by the number of people who have tried, however unconsciously, to imitate it, or by the number of critics who have adjudged other novels to be derived from it, then *Lucky Jim* must stand as one of the most successful novels of the post-war era. Even now it remains an enduring reference point and a source of invidious comparison. Tom Sharpe, William Boyd and a host of minor novelists of the 1980s were at one time or another promoted as heirs to the Amis tradition.

Though it would be foolhardy to pretend that Jim Dixon is a hero for our time, there is something in the suggestion that each decade throws up a new type of fictional hero or heroine, a representative who might be thought to epitomise some of the aspirations and anxieties of the age. The novels of the 1930s, or some of them, were populated by young, mildly upper-class, metropolitan men, Waugh's young men, Powell's young men: not particularly well-off (though there was often money in the background), not exclusively heterosexual. Jim Dixon and his coevals – Joe Lunn in William Cooper's *Scenes from Provincial Life* (1950), Charles Lumley in John Wain's *Hurry On Down* (1953) – were different, tending to live outside London (though they were later to gravitate there by means of a sort of natural law), their social affiliations more obviously located in the middle class, unambiguously pro-women. But they too were quickly supplanted, changed out of all recognition by the ensuing thirty years. If one wanted a male fictional stereotype of the 1980s, he exists as the fat, beery incompetent who adorns the jackets of novels by William Boyd and Tom Sharp (and it is significant that the 1990 Penguin version of Jim Dixon now looks very like Boyd's Morgan Leafy, such is the degree of cross-fertilisation that attends book-jacket portraiture).

Beneath these dramatic alterations to the outward look of fictional characters, let alone the changes forced upon their interior lives, have come more lasting transformations in scope and theme. Like many of the issues that have animated post-war public life, these have often had a profoundly retrospective focus. The post-war novelist who writes about class or the loss of imperial power, to take two salient examples, is generally conscious of a pontoon bridge extending from his or her current vantage point deep into the 1930s. This long-term perspective is understandable in the context of the post-war novelist's chief public theme, which might be summed up as the long, slow course of national retrenchment. From the promontory on which society and the novel come together, the outlook has invariably been gloomy, the occasional ray of light (enthusiasm for Attlee, Mrs Thatcher as a saviour) swiftly obscured by gathering clouds. If the post-war English novel has a public theme, that theme is decline. Whether the writer was a disillusioned 1950s liberal, grimly acknowledging the arrival of a world in which liberalism had no place, a 1970s Conservative distressed by the Wilsonian slide, or a 1980s progressive who regarded Mrs Thatcher as a genuine manifestation of evil, the effect is the same: an unspoken assumption that present circumstance is of no account when compared to the agreeable playgrounds of the past.

Predictably this interest in the public consequences of decline has an intense private corollary. The most sentient post-war novelists tend to be concerned with 'value' in a way that is simultaneously more committed and more uncertain than their predecessors'. Their search to discover appropriate and salutary ways of living is no less intent, but it is accompanied by a widespread awareness of moral diaspora, of standards which are no longer standards but merely points of view, contending styles in a world where moral superiority seems to be based on distinctly *un*moral criteria. Occasionally these intimations of public and private distress come together beneath a single banner. When they do so, it is invariably under the flag of 'Englishness'. 'English' – never 'British', a word that scarcely exists – is a characteristic adjective of disapproval in the post-war domestic novel, a kind of byword for hypocrisy and archaism, capable of describing anything from a limp handshake to class hatred. Its reiteration by novelists, discussed in Chapter 2, has the cumulative effect of suggesting that the question of national identity had by 1945 become a fictional obsession. The public debate about England's role in a post-war world whose concerns seemed fundamentally opposed to English interests, which fizzes on throughout the post-war period, is consistently reflected in the fiction of the time, occasionally manifesting itself in unexpected ways but always providing a thin current of dissatisfaction flowing beneath the surface of individual lives.

The average post-war novelist might seem unreasonably concerned with the fact of his or her nationality. He or she was also liable to be exercised by some more obvious changes which would have a decisive effect both on novelists themselves and on the national life which their books purported to reflect. Post-war novelists were, for example, the first generation of writers afforded a more or less decent standard of living, permitted to deal openly with questions of sex and gender, and allowed a wider medium for the expression of their opinions than the confines of the printed page. More often than not the effect of these relaxations was contradictory. The post-war novel of working-class life which crows over newly achieved mass affluence generally concludes with some elegiac glances back to a pre-war world in which there were fewer material goods but a greater awareness of the moral advantages of a communal life. Similarly, the arrival of sexual explicitness, though it produced a large number of sexually explicit novels, rarely seems to have enhanced the novelist's ability to write convincingly about sex. Writers, if they have any opinion of the wider environment, are likely to greet these facts with weary resignation. They know that it is a bad age for the novel. Scarcely a week passes without a Sunday newspaper taking up that original theme. They will have been told repeatedly that the truly intelligent person now becomes a stockbroker or a video producer and regards novel writing as a pointless and rather antiquated hobby. None of this is liable to increase their self-esteem or their confidence in the particular art-form on which they have staked the greater part of their lives. In these circumstances a glance at the history of the past fifty years is likely to depress them even further. At any rate, they are likely to be highly distressed by the implications for the novelist's task.

One talks confidently enough about 'the novelist'. In fact there are only novelists. Something like seven thousand novels get published in this country every year, a category which includes everything from Ms Shirley Conran's latest opus to the severest experimental text ever brought out by a fictional co-operative working from somebody's back bedroom. Multiply that figure by fifty – the chronological span of this book – and you are left with a total which at the very least approaches half a million books. Naturally I have not read even a hundredth part of this material. What I have read, too, has been biased by the existence of canons and the exclusion of interesting but uncanonical work from the bookshops and the library shelves. In *Success Stories*, his study of the conditions of literary production in England in the 1950s, Harry Ritchie makes the point that backscratching and the convergence of critical interest elevated a handful of novels and a handful of novelists to a position which they have occupied for nearly forty years. The 1950s, whatever the uncommitted onlooker might feel, is the decade of Amis, Wain and Co., and it would take a very ambitious critic indeed to suggest that they were not a dominant force and that the whole thing was got up by a group of impressionable hangers-on. Despite the straitjackets imposed by critical orthodoxy, which I have tried to compensate for by bringing in the work of less well-known writers, nearly every reader will be conscious of the absence of a number of famous names. Surely a study which omits extended discussion of, to take only the most obvious absentees, Golding, Spark, Burgess and Murdoch, cannot claim to be a survey of the post-war English novel?

To which I can only reply that this is a study of a particular type of book and a particular, though more often than not unconscious, literary response, whose development is best illustrated by concentrating on a particular collection of writers. We may dislike categories, but trying to work outside them frequently causes more problems than it solves. In much the same way, many people who note the references to 'women novelists' and the 'women's novel' will retort that there is no such thing as the women's novel, only novels – not enough of them, and seldom given their proper due at that – written by women. This is true, of course, but while the 'women's novel' is an absurdly elastic category, capable of including at least half the books which get written, there is a type of novel, very common in post-war English fiction, concerned with what might be called the condition of women, which loses something if it is not seen in isolation and on its own terms.

In the end, any discussion of dominant names and traditions takes us back to Kingsley Amis. As it happens, I don't care for Amis's novels. I find them slackly written and intellectually disingenuous, locked into that peculiarly English mental world in which cleverness or seriousness is seen as an unforgivable display of bad taste. Yet the fact remains that no discussion of the post-war novel can journey very far without acknowledging Amis's enormous importance. In many ways this proceeds out of sheer longevity. Like Mr Jingle in *The Pickwick Papers*, Amis is *always there*, popping up in the mid–1950s with his stories of army life, surfacing a quarter of a century later to present Mrs Thatcher with a copy of *Russian Hide and Seek*. Similarly, in any discussion of the link between intellectual and political life in post-war England, Amis is a figure of monstrous symbolic interest, a representative of all those earnest young Bevanites who fell out with the Labour Party over education, the unions or Russia – to name only three sticking points – and regarded the Conservative election victory of 1979 as a national deliverance. For these reasons, whether we like it or not, *Lucky Jim* is a key post-war English novel whose resonance – both as a social and a literary artefact – endures even forty years after its first publication.

So whatever happened to Lucky Jim? Why did he turn into Morgan Leafy, or John Self, or Keith Talent, or any other of the heroes and anti-heroes of the 1980s? The answer is, perhaps, that he grew up, enjoyed a better standard of living, acquired a different morality, watched television, stopped voting Labour and bought shares in a newly privatised public utility. The answer is, perhaps, that his wife went to university, had affairs, discovered Germaine Greer and natural yoghurt. The answer is that he became a different creature, living in a different world, and if we wish to understand him and his motivation, we need first to understand the milieu in which he, and the writer who created him, currently operates.

I

Unconditional Surrender

The result of the 1945 General Election, announced on 26 July after a three-week delay to accommodate the service vote, occasioned widespread bewilderment: 'a prodigious surprise', Evelyn Waugh recorded in his diary. Waugh, who had not voted, began the day at White's Club in St James's, watching the details come in over the ticker-tape machine. Within an hour and a half the extent of the Conservative defeat became apparent. A dozen ministers had lost their seats. Even the Prime Minister, unopposed by the major parties, could not escape the groundswell of anti-Tory feeling: '10,000 votes against Winston in his own constituency for an obvious lunatic.' Subsequently Waugh attended a party convened by Lady Rothermere in the anticipation of victory – 'A large, despondent crowd joined later by a handful of the defeated candidates. Watered vodka, exiguous champagne, rude servants, a facetious loudspeaker.' There was something ominous about these minor privations. 'There are many people puzzled about their future,' Waugh concluded. On this occasion the premonitions of a single arch-conservative did no more than reflect general unease.

The scope of the Labour victory – a majority equalled only by Margaret Thatcher's triumph in 1983 – was quite unheralded. Though primitive opinion polls had put Labour an average of eight points ahead, they had not been expected to win: at worst, political commentators had predicted a reduced Tory majority. Kingsley Amis's short story 'I Spy Strangers' (1962), written in the 1950s but set in the occupied Europe of July 1945, reflects the prevailing air of complacency, tempered by a suspicion that all might not be all right on the day. The letters which Major Raleigh's wife sends from England 'said that nobody knew anybody in the whole town who was a Labour supporter and that everybody felt very sorry for poor Mr Jack, the Labour candidate'. Though momentarily cheered by the news, the Major is uneasy:

> Something monstrous and indefinable was growing in strength, something hostile to his accent and taste in clothes and modest directorship and ambitions for his sons and redbrick house at Purley with its back-garden tennis court . . .

The Major's suspicions are abruptly realised when friendless Mr Jack wins an 18,000 majority.

Hindsight, a creeping teleology that was to envelop chroniclers of both Right and Left, is characteristic of the fiction of the Second World War. Even at the time the election and its immediate aftermath were seen to symbolise an ineradicable transfer of power. Much of this, naturally enough, came in slightly stagey attempts to *épater les bourgeois*: Labour MPs singing 'The Red Flag' in the Commons chamber, Sir Hartley Shawcross, shortly to achieve celebrity as a Nuremberg prosecutor, informing the cowed rump of Conservative members that 'We are the masters . . .'. A more formal but equally deliberate statement of intent could be found in Major Freeman's moving of the address in reply to the King's speech:

> We have before us a battle for peace no less arduous and no less momentous than the battle we have lived through in the past six years. Today the strategy begins to unfold itself. Today we go into action. Today may rightly be regarded as D-Day in the battle for the New Britain.

Oddly, perhaps deliberately, the military imperatives contained in Major Freeman's address tended to be concealed in a fog of parliamentary civility. Hansard records that it was greeted as 'an admirable speech' and 'a model parliamentary performance'. As Anthony Howard has observed, nobody appeared to think that it was seriously meant.

At any rate Major Freeman's martial metaphors had set one

question in sharp relief. Labour's victory, inevitably, was connected with the war that had preceded it, to the extent that it could be assumed that the one had caused the other. 'Only a socialist nation can fight effectively,' George Orwell had suggested at an early stage in the conflict. England had won – the hammer blow to national prestige and influence which the war had brought about would become apparent only later. Did that mean it had become a socialist nation? Orwell rather thought not. In fact his comments on the possibility of social and political revolution grow progressively more gloomy. In a 1944 letter to the American magazine *Partisan Review* he recalled his early hopes for major social change:

> I wanted to think that we would not be defeated, and I wanted to think that the class distinctions and imperialist exploitation of which I was ashamed would not return. I overemphasised the anti-fascist character of the war, exaggerated the enormous strength of the forces of reaction.

A later article, written in the wake of the election, linked the Attlee government with expectations of material benefit rather than ideological fervour. The drift to the Left, Orwell concluded, had not been accompanied by any strong revolutionary yearnings or by any sudden break-up of the class system:

> In the popular regard the Labour party is the party that stands for shorter working hours, a free health service, day nurseries, free milk for schoolchildren, and the like, rather than the party that stands for socialism.

And, he might have added, the Conservative party was the party that stood for dole queues, appeasement and pre-war stagnation. Churchill's detachment from mainstream Conservative thinking was well-known: the Churchill who led the Conservative party in July 1945, with his talk of socialist 'Gestapos', cut an incongruous figure. As a party politician, rather than a war leader, he seemed unconvincing. Orwell's emphasis on England's unaltered state is all the more revealing in the light of his earlier work, written during the lead-in to the war. In *Homage to Catalonia* (1938) and *Coming up for Air* (1939) he had imagined that Hitler's bombs might finally disrupt the national slumber (the image recurs in a war-time novel by J. B. Priestley), that the English body politic – 'a family with the wrong members in control' – might be sharply rearranged. The forecast had been sadly inexact. 'Neither would I have prophesied that we could go through nearly six years of war without arriving at either Socialism or Fascism, and with our civil liberties almost intact.' Orwell maintained that the British people continued to exist in a state of 'semi-anaesthesia'. He was unable to decide if this was a sign of 'decadence' or whether 'it is a kind of instinctive wisdom'.

Orwell exaggerates the degree of national quietism, of course, just as a cadre of left-wing journalists exaggerated the prospects for a socialist Jerusalem. It is fatally easy to assume, on the strength of selective written evidence, that the major issues of the day were debated solely by a committee headed by Kingsley Martin and Harold Laski, convening thrice-monthly in the back office of the *New Statesman*. Yet the potential for social revolution, or at any rate a wide-ranging reform of the nation's institutions, was undoubtedly present in the England of 1945. The war might have preserved the stately homes and the ancient universities, albeit in mothballs, but it had reduced the public schools to evacuated shadows of their former selves, demolished the caste system in the civil service – a process reflected in the novels of C. P. Snow – allowed infiltration of government departments at almost every level by the humbly born, and in the words of Anthony Howard 'eroded practically every traditional social barrier'.

At the same time more deliberate initiatives were well in hand. The Beveridge Report of 1942 had established the foundations of the Welfare State. Prolonged government interference in industry had cleared a path for nationalisation. The 1944 Fleming Report's concern over the divisive nature of the educational system had produced a scheme for the voluntary association of the public and state-aided schools. There had even been faint attempts to democratise the army – very faint, according to Orwell's essay, yet Field Marshal Montgomery, whose attitudes were thought to exemplify this levelling down, was much resented by the stiffer sort of field officer. In short, six years under arms had produced a kind of socialism in embryo of which the most exacting 1930s ideologue might have been proud. The conviction that this process had begun before 1945, that it had been authenticated by Attlee's election victory, and that it was bound to continue into the late 1940s, if not beyond, is perhaps the single most important theme of post-war English society, and – the two are not necessarily connected – the immediately post-war English novel.

'For God's sake don't let's talk about the war,' advises Ada Leint-wardine, the literary siren of Anthony Powell's *Books Do Furnish a Room* (1971), 'such a boring subject.' Few post-war novelists, had they been present – and the *roman à clef* element of Powell's work abets the possibility – would have paid her much heed. War gave an unavoidable focus to the fiction of the post-war era. The whole tendency of the post-war novel, a few disagreeable projections excepted, is retrospective. Even the landmark novels of the 1950s have a habit of looking backwards, lie trapped in a sort of no-man's-land between the battlefield and the beckoning utopia beyond. David Lodge has noted that *Lucky Jim* (1954), widely advertised as a novel about a post-war generation and a post-war ethic, has roots extending far back into the 1940s. Jim Dixon's enthusiastic student Mr Michie commanded a tank troop at Anzio, in painful contrast to Dixon's own tenure as an RAF corporal in western Scotland. Dixon keeps his lecture notes in an old RAF file, and visualises the streets and squares of London by remembering a weekend leave spent there during the war. The same point could be made of Alan Sillitoe's *Saturday Night and Sunday Morning* (1958), with its memories of draft-dodging and bygone family solidarity. 'There was a war on then,' Arthur Seaton recalls, 'and they were fighting the Jerries, and Churchill spoke after the nine o'clock news and told you what you were fighting for, as if it mattered.' Deep into the fiction of the 1960s the war continued to be invoked to provide psychological explanations of contemporary behaviour. 'Authority, the war, Truby King,' the narrator of Margaret Drabble's *The Millstone* (1965) recalls. 'I was reared to believe that the endurance of privation is a virtue, and the result is that I believe it to this day.' The shadow cast by traditionally conceived war fiction was even longer. The literary critic Daniel George had predicted in 1945 that it would take ten years to produce a war novel of any consequence. The post-war epics had long gestation periods. Waugh's *Sword of Honour* trilogy was not completed until 1961. *The Military Philosophers*, the last of Anthony Powell's novels to deal specifically with the events of 1939–45, appeared in 1968, and Powell's interest in the social consequences of the conflict is apparent throughout *Books Do Furnish a Room*.

Few of these post-war writers shared Orwell's assumption of inertia. The majority of the fiction of the post-war period is animated, or cast down, by a conviction that nothing – family life or even physical surroundings – would ever be the same again. Colin in Philip Callow's *Going to the Moon* (1968) remembers his father's escape from a bomb blast that destroys the family home: 'the dirt blinded him. His jaw was splintered and fractured, nothing else. Only it was. The old life was smashed to bits that night, and for good.' Examining the Sussex village in which she resides, Laura in Mollie Panter-Downes's *One Fine Day* (1947) concludes that 'something had happened here, so that the substance in which Wealding had been embalmed for so long... had very slightly curdled and changed colour, as though affected by an unprecedented spell of thundery weather. Its perfect peace was, after all, a sham.' To literal destruction and the figurative assumption of decay could be added the scent of social flux. Traditional social values and hierarchies were everywhere called into question. 'Loyalty to families is going to be a thing of the past if my newspaper is anything to go by,' Simon Raven's Mrs Gray remarks, announcing her decision to sell the late Mr Gray's business. In a dozen novels of the kind made popular by Angela Thirkell, landed families find themselves having to sell their estates and squander the family patrimony by converting dower houses into grain silos. There is a memorable scene along these lines in *Books Do Furnish a Room*, in which Nick Jenkins attends Erridge's funeral at Thrubworth. The majority of the house is not in use; barbed wire-enclosed Nissen huts are visible from the drive.

Allied to this decline were the consequences of social mobility. Patrick Hamilton's *The Slaves of Solitude* (1947), set in a seedy

Maidenhead boarding house in the winter of 1943, makes this point with some force:

> In the war everywhere was crowded all the time. The war seemed to have conjured into being, from nowhere, magically, a huge population of its own – one which flooded into and filled every channel and crevice of the country – the towns, the villages, the streets, the trains, the buses, the shops, the houses, the inns, the restaurants, the movies.

Hamilton's characters, marshalled in the living hell of the Rosamund tea rooms under the thrall of its resident Lucifer, Mr Thwaites, are the English refugees, flotsam adrift on a tide of bombed-out houses and dispersed families, the diaspora of the Blitz and the call-up. Their attempts to retain a precarious hold on their social position – all that they possess, with the exception of a handful of belongings – are further undermined by the arrival of officers from the local US army base. The free and easy Americans are not so much contemptuous as unaware of prevailing social constraints and conventions. Consequently Miss Roach, meeting 'her' lieutenant in a crowded bar, is introduced to two girls who work in the town's shops and 'were not as one's mother would have said "in her class".' The meeting is therefore 'embarrassing', for all Miss Roach's good nature, and quickly brought to a close. There are half-a-dozen similar infringements of this invisible etiquette. Ultimately Miss Roach judges her American lieutenant to be 'inconsequential', but he is no more inconsequential than her present surroundings or her way of life: drinking too much in noisy pubs, living cheek by jowl with people one neither likes nor respects, above all the terrifying inability to foresee one's destiny. If nothing else, *The Slaves of Solitude* is a reminder that some of the worst privations of the war were experienced by civilians.

What Hamilton's novel makes plain, in addition, was the war's ability to disrupt every area of social life, a disruption that transcended the demarcations of class or professional status. ' "What lax morals people have these days. The war, I suppose" ' – Stringham's comment in *The Soldier's Art* (1966) on hearing of Moreland's liaison with Mrs Maclintick – is quite as applicable to

Virginia Troy, knocked up by the ineffable Trimmer, as to the ruined doxies in Pamela Hansford Johnson's *Winter Quarters* (1943).

A restless, rackety atmosphere colours nearly every aspect of writing about the war, a succession of chance encounters and sudden departures, incongruity and fear mixed with unconquerable boredom. Trimmer and Virginia meeting in the Glasgow hotel; Jenkins discussing Trollope with General Liddament; Guy Pringle's *accidie* – these are the images that remain from English war fiction, once the surface debris has been cleared away. Move a little further back into the literature written while the war was actually taking place and the air of fragmentation becomes even more evident. One leaves the pieces assembled in the anthology of Woodrow Wyatt's *English Story*, an influential 1940s annual, with a confused impression of half-finished conversations, troops on leave lamenting the shortage of cigarettes, petty deprivations, snatched repartee, 'tables over which smoke thickened, round which khaki melted into the khaki glow'. It was the time of MacLaren-Ross's telegraphic short stories, Henry Green's evocations of life in the London Fire Service. Fiction possessed a queer, documentary quality – even the finest short pieces of the period have a tendency to shade off into reportage.

Yet this exactitude over dress, detail and atmosphere co-exists with a characteristically blurred chronology. Many war novels give the impression that they take place in a void where all is dislocation and uncertainty. Time and the immediate past telescope into unquantifiable space. Nick Jenkins reflects: 'the odd thing was how distant the recent past had now become, the army now as stylised in the mind as the legionaries of Trajan's columns'. Timelessness is a deliberate Powell technique, but the sense of dislocation is a feature of novels written at a much shorter remove from the events they affected to describe. Thus Laura Marshall, trying to harden her grasp on the details of life before the war, can recall only 'the long, warm Sunday afternoons into which all that time seemed to have condensed when one looked back on it'. The past has become fugitive, inchoate, grasped at to provide a yardstick in the face of present imprecision but ever liable to disappoint, furnishing the Proustian twitch on the thread but seldom an ally. ' "It's pre-war," ' says one of the protagonists in Elizabeth Bowen's elegiac story from the 1940s 'Songs My Father Sang Me' after his companion has become agitated by the strains of a familiar dance tune. ' "It's last war," ' the girl replies. ' "Well, last war, pre-war." ' Continuity, persistence, while welcome, seem infinitely suspect. So Nick Jenkins, meeting Moreland during a war-time leave in the Café Royal, decides that he is 'an improbable survival from pre-war life'. Moreland's talk shows the characteristic signs of fracture:

> When he dwelt on the immediate past, it was as if that had become very distant, no longer the matter of a year or two before. For him, it was clear, a veil, a thick curtain, had fallen between 'now' and 'before the war'.

Powell is writing with hindsight, in his case a transparently prejudicial hindsight. Yet the assumption of unalterable change goes back a great deal further, into the depths of the war itself. Its most obvious by-product was the evolution of a politically and socially committed literature at a relatively early stage in the war's development. The concept of a 'People's War' is by now an historian's cliché, and so intimately bound up in the fabric of the novels written to support the conflict that it is difficult to prise the two apart and establish whether literature was an impetus or a vehicle. Its origins are post-Blitz. The fiction of the first two years of the war is predominantly conventional, documentary, propagandist in the narrow, patriotic sense. Analysing early war fiction over a two-year period in *Horizon*, Tom Harrisson of Mass Observation found that it fell into distinct and progressively more redundant categories: war in the country and evacuation novels (Evelyn Waugh's *Put Out More Flags* (1942) extracts a great deal of snobbish fun from the antics of working-class evacuee children), Dunkirk novels, RAF novels, Blitz novels. One factor alone unites them: they were right-wing. Priestley's *Out of the People*, published in 1941, was an early corrective to the view that the war could be fought without damage to traditional social arrangements: 'Go to the nearest ARP post and you find there people, not members of classes. The bombs kill people, not classes. Nevertheless, they may blow classes clean away.' This is essentially Orwell's message, given an immediate focus. In Priestley, however, the People's War movement had a spokesman of far greater influence. His radio broadcasts rivalled only Churchill's in popularity, to the extent that at one point Churchill tried to have him taken off the air.

In *Daylight on Saturday* (1943), subtitled 'A novel about an aircraft factory', Priestley's message becomes more explicit. Set over a four-day period in October 1942 immediately preceding the decisive battle of El Alamein, it dramatises the argument that, because the war was stagnating, morale in the factories was low and production falling. The result is ominously prefigurative. 'Where these factories are, there is power.' The narrator goes on to remark that they will remain power-houses in the post-war period. 'What we don't know yet is for whose sake their power will be operated. We can only hope.' Later in the novel, a couple marry in the expectation that their children will be brought up in a world of 'socialism and engineering'. Less outwardly committed but equally potent People's War novels peddled a similar message. Monica Dickens's *The Fancy* (1942), for example, set in an aircraft factory in the London suburbs, depicts a communal war effort which ignores class boundaries and brings people from different backgrounds together over the machines. Ledward, its central character, is portrayed as the average conscientious man, diligently working overtime out of a sense of duty, pleased that his hobby – backyard rabbit breeding – can play a small part in the further-ance of the war. His wife Connie, alternatively, is implicitly criti-cised for her reluctance to undertake war work. Her eventual departure with a man subsequently exposed as a profiteer may not be presented as an act of villainy – generally the novel manages to avoid outright propaganda of this sort – but the reader is left in no doubt as to where his sympathies ought to lie.

The theme of impending or actual social change underpins the fiction of the post-war period. Here, however, the assault was liable to come from the opposite end of the political spectrum, from the type of right-wing writer who found Priestley anathema, whose energies had been trammelled by the war – both Waugh and Powell were serving officers – but for whom the accession of the Attlee government allowed a welcome opportunity to luxuriate. Whatever defenders such as Andrew Sinclair may assert, the late 1940s was not a period of literary innovation. *Horizon* was not alone in wondering where the new novelists were, an absence confirmed by novelists themselves. X. Trapnel, the saturnine autodidact of *Books Do Furnish a Room* – by Powell's admission, a projection of MacLaren-Ross – is promoted to Nick Jenkins as 'one of the few promising talents thrown up by the war, in contrast to the previous one, followed by no marked luxuriance in the arts'. As literary life struggled back into some sort of genuine existence and the war-time constraints of paper shortages and censorship were gradually overcome, its tone was markedly reactionary. As David Pryce-Jones has put it:

> in so far as literature tried to come to terms with social and political change, to assess what sort of feeling was abroad among the unobserved, it had assumed a peevishness. Not so much at what was new, as what survived of the old.

The occasional Leftist might strike a satirical note. The hero of Raymond Williams's 1940s story 'A Fine Room to be Ill in', noting the existence of gardeners and domestic staff at an adjoining property, reflects that this is 'a pretty prosperous household these days ... Obviously film stars or crooks. Who else could afford it?' This is ironic, a send-up of the view of the average *Daily Telegraph* reader beset by punitive taxation, but there were plenty of novelists prepared to deplore the success of those who had done well out of the war, and the official interference that had supposedly promoted the interests of one section of society at another's expense.

Consider, for example, the career of Angela Thirkell (1890–1961). If Miss Thirkell is ever allowed her paragraph in the literary histories these days it is to be disparaged as an inferior Trollope whose tendency to repetition would have put Trollope himself to shame, but in her time she was an enormously prolific and successful writer whose portrayal of English life in 'Barsetshire' won her a loyal following among the middle-class readership of the circulating libraries. The Royal Family was known to admire her and she received an invitation to the wedding of Princess Elizabeth to Lieutenant Philip Mountbatten. As a chronicler of the post-war era Thirkell laboured under a single, implacable resentment. As her biographer remarks: 'It was the Conservative defeat in the general election that marked a turning point in her work.'

The reader who takes the trouble to leaf through a copy of *Love among the Ruins* (1948) or *The Old Bank House* (1949) might feel that 'turning point' is putting it mildly. Miss Thirkell's assault on what she imagined to be a new social order begins in her 1946 novel *Peace Breaks Out* (titular signposting is a feature of her work) in which the socialist Sam Adams defeats Sir Robert Fielding MP for the Barsetshire seat. Sir Robert tries to put a brave face on it: ' "there's nothing so conservative as a good Labour man" '. Mrs Moreland cannot share his optimism. She feels that ' "it's really goodbye to everything nice for ever" '. A year later came *Private Enterprise*, whose jacket copy, devised by the author, noted that 'the first post-war summer, with its strong resemblance to a winter of discontent, is providing a full helping of the horrors of peace'. There followed *Love among the Ruins* and *The Old Bank House*. ('The prevailing note is still kindliness spliced with wit, though it must be admitted that the note tends to tremble at the mention of "them" '. 'Them', of course, refers to the Labour party).

Inevitably Thirkell had her revenge. Her 1952 novel, written in the wake of the 1951 General Election, is titled – predictably enough – *Happy Returns*. Judging by the sour tone that invests her later books, it was a fairly hollow victory. Not even Anthony Eden or Mr R. A. Butler, apparently, was capable of resurrecting the kind of lost decencies elegised by the author of *The Duke's Delight* and *Enter Sir Robert*. With hindsight it is easy enough to see Thirkell's career as being all of a piece – the juvenile lampooning of 'Kripps', the characters who are made to say 'I daresay that there is a dictaphone behind the wainscot and whoever is in charge of liquidating labourers taking it down in shorthand', the fury over practically every enlightened measure of the post-war era – and to mark the whole down as bourgeois hysteria in the face of minor inconvenience. To do so would be to ignore an earlier note of kindliness progressively snuffed out by what seemed, to the author at any rate, very real grievance. Certainly there are things to be said in Thirkell's defence. Approaching her later novels one tries to remember that their author was ill and insecure, one tries to take into account the degree of genuine provocation – the note of class hatred in some of Bevan's speeches of the period alarmed many a less excitable onlooker – only to stumble upon a statement of the kind attributed to a character in *Private Enterprise*:

> 'What I really mind is their trying to bust up the *Empire* ... I mean like leaving Egypt and tr ing to give Gibraltar to the natives. If they try to do anything to Gibraltar, I shall put on a striped petticoat and a muslin fichu and murder them all in their baths, because TRAITORS ought to be murdered.'

In any case, the shrillness, the urge to defend bygone tradition at whatever cost, was an integral part of her appeal. Or as a Canadian reviewer of one of her war-time novels put it:

> If England is to be completely changed, as we are assured it will be, why do so many people want to read books about an aspect of English life which would not survive a revolution? Second, if county society and old families are objects of mockery to the young Britons of today, why do they lap up these books which glorify these things? ... Mrs Thirkell knows what she is doing better than the post-war planners.

Thirkell continued to produce novels throughout the 1950s, although her popularity was in decline by the end of her life. But by this time the torch had passed to other, more powerful hands. Evelyn Waugh and Anthony Powell were quite as interested in post-war social arrangements, or to be accurate their pre–1945 prefiguration (it is significant, surely, that both Waugh and Thirkell should produce a novel with the same title, *Love among the Ruins*). The tone of their fiction – Waugh's *Sword of Honour* trilogy, volumes seven to nine of Powell's *A Dance to the Music of Time* – is profoundly disillusioned, the standpoint rarely disinterested. The supposition that the conflict of 1939–45 had been a

'People's War' is a marked feature of Waugh and Powell's writing, and the conviction that they and their contemporaries had won the battle but lost the argument underlies every overt display of political consciousness. Almost without exception, the heroes of the post-war *romans-fleuves* – Nicholas Jenkins, Guy Crouch-back, Olivia Manning's Guy Pringle – are emasculated, ineffectual, fatally upper-class figures, carefully deployed to mock the prospect of a better post-war world. Predictably, the most explicit criticism comes from Waugh. His 'common man' characters – Trimmer in *Sword of Honour*, Hooper in *Brideshead Revisited* (1945) – are invariably repellent prefigurations of a post-war archetype. Hooper, in particular, poor harmless Hooper with his middle-class accent and his innocuous personal habits, is 'a symbol of Young England' to Charles Ryder's wintry eye. But throughout their post-war fiction we can see both Waugh and Powell indulging in a sort of blatant teleology, endlessly dramatising their perspectives on the post-war landscape back into the early 1940s. There is a revealing scene in *Officers and Gentlemen* (1955) in which Colonel Blackhouse tells Guy sardonically that he is the Flower of England's Youth, 'and it just won't do'. Waugh notes that Blackhouse is 'prophetically drunk'. Olivia Manning satirises Guy Pringle's pro-Soviet views from the political standpoint of the mid–1960s. In much the same way Powell has Widmerpool (who has already contrived to have Jenkins's friends Templer and Stringham sent to almost certain death, thereby settling God knows what adolescent scores) remark in 1945: ' "We are going to see great changes. As you know, my leanings have always been leftward. From what I see round me I have no reason to suppose that my sympathies were mistaken. Men like myself will be needed." '

Doubtless many an aspirant Labour MP fresh from military service – Major Healey, Major Wyatt and Lieutenant Crosland spring to mind – was saying much the same thing. Yet for all their apparent anchorage in the war years, Waugh and Powell's novels do not have a single focus. Increasingly, what is being reacted to is not the actual events of 1939–45 but the alleged political consequences. Waugh's obsession with the enormities of the Attlee administration provoked several of his more memorable public performances during the next decade. As late as 1959 he could be found complaining of 'bitter memories of the Attlee–Cripps régime, when the country had seemed to be under enemy occupation'. An earlier controversy with J. B. Priestley – an inevitable target for Waugh's asperity, one might feel – reveals some of the assumptions on which Waugh's treatment of the 1940s was based. According to Waugh, Priestley was one of those authors who before 1939 'went to great lengths to suck up to the lower classes', foreseeing the present 'social revolution' and knowing who would emerge 'top dog'. This type of festering resentment goes some way towards explaining the very large number of passages in *Sword of Honour* written with the more or less deliberate intention of annoying the Labour party. Certainly there is more than a hint of self-consciousness in the outwardly panoramic, in fact absurdly narrow, scene-setting that introduces the war's outbreak:

> Everywhere houses were being closed, furniture stored, children transported, lawns ploughed, dower houses and shooting lodges crammed to capacity, mothers-in-law and nannies were everywhere gaining control.

(To which Kingsley Amis retorted: 'You know, everywhere, from South Shields to Llanelly.')

Waugh's retrospective fixing of the evidence is well-known, perhaps a little too well-known to bear repetition. A number of critics have documented his wilfully partial treatment of the guerilla warfare in Yugoslavia, whose pro-Catholic and anti-Tito slant is quite at variance with actual events. After Waugh's intrigues and his almost pathological snobbery, to turn to Anthony Powell can be a refreshing experience – this in spite of the fact that Powell is no less consistent in his view of the post-war world. *The Soldier's Art*, which covers the period from December 1940 to the German invasion of the Soviet Union in June 1941, gives a very fair idea of the technique Powell is prepared to employ in his depiction of war, a technique which simultaneously reduces and magnifies the conflict's importance, while managing to suggest that the consequences, both for the narrator and the social grouping to which he belongs, will be highly unwelcome.

A key element in Powell's treatment of the war is his opaque chronology. James Tucker, in his excellent study of the Powell novels, talks of their 'habitual imprecision'. *The Soldier's Art* refines this technique to the point where the war, and indeed the action of the novel, appears to be taking place in a kind of vacuum, set apart from pre- or post-war existence. Although only in its second year, the conflict has already stretched out to embrace – and extinguish – great swathes of past time. Thus Nick Jenkins's friend Stringham, asked at what stage in the proceedings he joined up, replies: 'too long ago to remember – right at the beginning of the Hundred Years War'. Jenkins experiences the sensation in reverse. An explosion at the London home of Molly Jeavons, which he remembers from the 1930s, effectively cancels out the intervening period:

> Reflecting on these things, it did not seem all that long ago that Lovell, driving back from the film studios in that extraordinary car of his, had suggested that we should look in on the Jeavons.

This vagueness about time is at its most barbed in any discussion of death, which consequently happens almost in parenthesis. Thus Jenkins records of Greening, General Liddament's ADC, that 'towards the end of the war, I heard in a roundabout way, that, after returning to his regiment, he had been badly wounded at Anzio as a company commander and – so my informant thought – might have died in hospital' (in fact Greening survives). Another officer's later career is sketched in with similar brevity: 'He led the Divisional Recce Corps, with a great deal of dash, until within a few days of the German surrender, then was blown up when his jeep drove over a landmine. However, that is equally by the way.' 'In a roundabout way'; 'So my informant thought'; 'That is equally by the way' – these are typical Powell approximations, of a kind common throughout the whole twelve-volume sequence. Applied to the subject of death on military service, even the deaths of people with whom Jenkins was only narrowly associated, their effect is rather horrible. Extended to take in Jenkins's intimate friends, they can seem chillingly laconic, as in the novel's final throwaway sentence: 'That same week the plane was shot down in which Barnby was undertaking a reconnaissance flight with the aim of reporting on enemy camouflage.'

This type of distancing is a deliberate artistic device in which emotion, kept outwardly in check, takes on an unquantifiable life of its own. At any rate this seems the only suitable reading of the Barnby passage. War's horrors are such, Powell seems to be saying, its personal cost – whether or not one survives – so exorbitant that the public display of emotion is meaningless, an unaffordable luxury. All the protagonist can do is to grit his teeth, set himself apart from the proceedings, leave others to haggle over his destiny in the hope that something will survive the wreckage. Nothing of Priestley's fortitude, the sense of a grim struggle in pursuit of a brighter future, can be found in *The Soldier's Art*. Its tendency is not heroic, but mock-heroic, a stance that can be glimpsed as early as the opening scene which gives the novel its title. Buying an army greatcoat in a shop which doubles up as a theatrical outfitter, Jenkins examines himself in a mirror, 'aware at the same time that soon, like Alice, I was to pass, as it were by virtue of these habiliments, through its panels into a world no less enigmatic.' The outfitter mistakes Jenkins for an actor and assumes that 'the war', for which he requires the coat, is a theatrical production. The image is to Jenkins's taste and he immediately sets about developing it:

> Now that the curtain had gone up once more on this old favour-
> ite – *The War* – in which, so it appeared, I had been cast for a
> walk-on part, what days were left before joining my unit would
> be required for dress rehearsal.

Subsequently the idea of war as artistic spectacle provides a con-tinuing theme for Jenkins's ruminations. The Blitz and the Allied withdrawal from Greece are 'noises off in rehearsals that never seemed to end', prompting him to wish that 'the billed perform-ance would at last ring up its curtain, whatever form that took'. Unfortunately, Jenkins notes, the date of the opening night rests 'in hands other than our own'. Meanwhile, 'nobody could doubt that more rehearsing, plenty more rehearsing, was going to be needed for a long time to come'.

The contrast with a novel of the Priestley school could scarcely be more marked. On the one hand heroism, purpose, resolve; on the other a perpetual, ironic deflation. In fact Powell's detachment from the war, his consistent ironic note, goes a great deal deeper than this. Its walking embodiment might be the character of Bithel, a bumbling drunk who intermittently propagates the myth of fraternity with an officer of the same name and regiment who won a VC in the 1914–18 war. Encountering Jenkins during the course of an air-raid, Bithel discourses on his childhood love of *Chums* and the *Boy's Own Paper*: ' "always imagined myself the hero *of those serials*" ' he confides above the clatter of the guns. Bithel's is an ignoble destiny, alas. After a final bout of drunkenness, he and his mobile laundry unit are dispatched to the Far East. Elsewhere Powell subjects both the physical processes of the war and those concerned with its prosecution to a continual diminishment or comic reinvention. General Liddament and his satellites, seen in late-night conclave, are compared to a Pharaoh and his attendants. Odo Stevens, persuaded to discuss the experience of hand-to-hand combat, remarks that it is ' "Difficult to describe ... You feel worked up just before, of course, rather like going to school for the first time or the morning of your first job." '

The cumulative effect of these techniques is to impart to the war a profound sense of unreality. The air-raid witnessed from Jenkins's divisional headquarters which takes up a proportion of the novel's opening section is a good example of the otherworldly air which Powell contrives to attach to a scene of presumably vigorous physical reality. Jenkins's observation of the tumult above him leads to all manner of suggestive comparisons. Flares descend 'like Japanese lanterns at a fête'. At ground-level knots of flames begin to blaze away 'like a nest of nocturnal forges in the Black Country'. All the world, Jenkins concludes, 'was dipped in a livid, unearthly refulgence, theatrical yet sinister, a light neither of night nor day, the penumbra of Pluto's frontiers' – which is perhaps nearer to art criticism than a description of a bombing raid (Waugh, in the opening scene of *Officers and Gentlemen*, where the skies erupt over the gentlemen's clubs of St James's, achieves a strikingly similar effect). The atmosphere, heightened by this Turner-like impasto, is then sharply lowered by the appearance of Bithel, lamenting 'a spot of bother' over a cheque.

This is an absorbing piece of writing, in which painterly description and near farce combine to produce an effect of curious unease, but the raid by this stage seems queerly remote. War, Powell apparently feels, is a tedious, unreal business, detached from time, involving the dispersal of one's friends and the disruption of one's pleasures. And yet – this appears to be the point of Powell's irony – it has unavoidable and potentially unsatisfactory consequences for all but a tiny minority of the people caught up in it. At the very least, for example, it provides an opportunity for the power-hungry and the unscrupulous to secure both advancement in their careers and the more doubtful gratification of power's exercise. Widmerpool is at this stage in his remorseless trajectory working in a very limited sphere, but he succeeds in having himself transferred to the War Office, with the promise of speedy promotion, while settling some personal scores along the way. Widmerpool's vendetta against Bithel provides a telling contrast. Bithel is inept, unreliable and self-indulgent, but at the same time well-meaning, reasonably enthusiastic and, the reader is encouraged to believe, fundamentally decent. Widmerpool's treatment of him is narrowly vindictive. ' "War is a great opportunity for everyone to find his level," ' Widmerpool tells Jenkins feelingly.

For Widmerpool the war is a welcome vehicle for self-aggrandisement. For another type of character it forms a kind of unbridgeable fissure. One remembers Moreland and the 'thick curtain' tugged down to cut off pre-war life. Together with this reckoning up of personal destinies comes any number of oblique glances at the notion of the 'People's War' and the incipient rearrangement of social hierarchies. After Stringham, Jenkins's friend from Eton days, resurfaces as a mess waiter, Jenkins makes tentative attempts to get him a better job. Widmerpool is unyielding. ' "Why should Stringham have some sort of preferential treatment just because you and I happen to have been at school with him? That is exactly what people complain about – and with good reason." ' Widmerpool continues in this vein for some time. Surely Jenkins must be aware that such an attitude of mind – 'that certain persons have a right to a privileged position' – causes ill feeling among those less fortunately placed? In reality this is the merest cant – Widmerpool's egalitarianism is simply a convenient weapon – but the imputation of a compromised exclusivity remains. On another occasion, discussing the restricted nature of officer material, he informs Jenkins that he ' "should not suppose for one moment that I presume that minority to come necessarily, even primarily, from the traditional officer class" '. In addition, much of Powell's dialogue draws its impetus from the thought of unwelcome post-war social change. ' "Cheques are always a worry. They ought to be abolished," ' Bithel sagely observes during the air-raid. ' "Perhaps they will be after the war," ' Jenkins replies. On another occasion Stringham tries to remember a sergeant-major's joke for use at dinner parties after the war, ' "if I'm asked to any again, indeed, if any are given *après la guerre*" '.

The Soldier's Art ends with the suicide of Captain Biggs, Staff Officer Physical Training, in the cricket pavilion – an inglorious conclusion, in keeping with the novel's tone. The irony that pervades each level of the text exists as an aesthetic device, but it is also there to make a political point, oblique, but none the less unignorable. It is, of course, possible to overstress the portrayal of Powell's novels as texts of reaction. Alan Munton's *English Fiction of the Second World War* (1989) carries some stern remarks on the 'repressive' interpretations of the war made by post-war epic fiction, a category in which Powell can be presumed to reside. Pigeon-holing of this sort begs several questions. One might begin by asking who or what in a novel like *The Soldier's Art* is being repressed? The working classes? The Labour party? Mess waiters? Teased, maybe, and occasionally in a rather mordant way, but *repressed*? More ominous, perhaps, is the not quite conscious assumption that right-wing novels about the war and the war's consequences (Munton predictably finds the politics of *Unconditional Surrender* to be 'an insufficient justification for Guy's disillusionment with the war') are unlikely to be very good novels. To which one is tempted to ask: where is a decent left-wing alternative? The average reader, asked to choose between *Men at Arms* and *Daylight on Saturday* as representative novels of the war, in nine cases out of ten settles for Waugh, however strongly he may be invited to cast his vote for 'truthfulness'. In any case how much 'truth' is there in Priestley?

Unsurprisingly, the Left, or the notional Left, was capable of behaving in a very similar manner. Amis's 'I Spy Strangers' takes as its focus a soldiers' parliament, whose debates reflect both the government policies which helped to cause the war and the remedial measures necessary to construct a better post-war world. ' "We're going to build a decent Britain," ' one speaker maintains:

'Fair shares for all and free schools and doctoring and hospitals and no class distinctions. The old school tie and the old boy network aren't going to work any more. To make sure of that we're going to abolish the public schools and Oxford and Cambridge, or at any rate change them so that anybody who's got the brains can go there.'

R. F. Delderfield's *The Avenue Goes to War* (1964) might be taken as a representative post-war People's War novel. Examining the experiences of a cast drawn from a single suburban London street, it involves a careful breaking down of pre-war social categories and attitudes, culminating in a double wedding whose participants are drawn from across the social spectrum. Looking back on the day, working-class Jim Carver, now married to the genteel Edith Clegg (Jim's daughter has married a squadron leader), imagines that it was a time 'when the majority of the Avenue's inhabitants became, for a few days at least, a closer-knit community than they had ever been in the past, even during the worst nights of the Blitz'. The day reaches its climax with the symbolic destruction of a high board fence separating two of the street's gardens. When the demolition is proposed by a neighbour, Jim immediately sees what he is getting at and approves. 'It matched his own feelings about the Avenue since Churchill had taken charge of the war.' The levelling of the fence 'would be symbolic of the unity of the British, of the sinking of party differences and social distinctions, of the Avenue's implacable determination to scotch German Fascism from the face of the earth'.

This sort of staginess was endemic both to the serious war novel and to those pitched at a slightly lower level. Inevitably it reaches its most conscious figurative height in descriptions of official or semi-official commemorations of the war's end: VE Day, VJ Day, the host of memorial services taking place in churches and school chapels up and down the country. Powell's account of the Victory Day service at St Paul's Cathedral, towards the end of *The Military Philosophers*, strikes a characteristically oblique note. Jenkins, musing on the Ingoldsby Legends – in which certain of the cathedral's monuments appear – feels that they serve to mitigate an atmosphere 'in other respects oddly frigid, even downright depressing'. What lies at the heart of Jenkins's unease?

> With a fashionably egalitarian ideal in view, those responsible for such things had decided no mere skimming of the cream from the top echelons, civil and military, should be assembled to give symbolic thanks for Victory. Everyone was to be represented. The congregation – except for those who had a job to do – had been picked from the highest official level to the lowest.

There follows a carefully weighted passage whose implication is that the mixing of ranks is somehow inappropriate for the nature of the ceremony:

> For some reason this principle, fair enough in theory, had in practice resulted in an extension of that atmosphere of constraint. Uneasy nervous tension, common enough in larger or smaller degree to all such ceremonies, the sense of being present at a Great Occasion – for if this was not a Great Occasion, then what was? – had somehow failed to take adequate shape, to catch on the wing those inner perceptions of a more exalted sort, at best transient enough, but not always unknown. They were, in fact, so it seemed to me ... entirely absent.

One looks eagerly for an unqualified statement in these ruminations, only to find a routine covering up of tracks. The principle of senior officers mingling with other ranks is 'fair enough in theory'. Nervous tension is in any case common to all such ceremonies. The type of personal exaltation Jenkins presumably wishes to experience is 'at best transient enough'. More prosaic factors are swiftly advanced to explain away the unsatisfactory nature of the proceedings. Everyone is very tired. 'The country, there could be no doubt, was absolutely worn out. That was the truth of the matter.' In a later passage Jenkins attempts to frame his unease over the public celebration of victory in an historical context. A rendering of the National Anthem, including its supposedly obsolete second verse, prompts him to reflect that there must have been advantages, 'moral and otherwise', in living in an outwardly less squeamish period, 'when the vestiges of high-thinking had not yet checked such politics as those put forward in the second verse, incidentally, much the best; when, in certain respects at least, hypocrisy had established less of a stranglehold on the public mind'.

Again, appropriate camouflage is rapidly wheeled into place. Jenkins concedes that his mental picture of the past is 'no doubt largely unhistorical'. But the implications are clear. Like Guy Crouchback, Jenkins yearns for an older and less sophisticated world, a humbler yet more satisfying patriotism. If there is an overriding complaint to be deduced from Powell's evasions and his conditional clauses, it is that government, officialdom, the whole pageant of public life, has redirected national sentiment in pursuit of narrower political ends. With Crouchback this awareness is expressed in the lament for a vanished 'honour'. Jenkins soberly acknowledges that he has fought the war together with and under the direction of a group of hypocrites. Whatever mild sense of nobility the victory over fascism might impart will soon be swallowed up in the return to mean-spirited party politics. 'Quite soon,' Jenkins predicts, 'people would . . . begin to say that the war was pointless, particularly those, and their associates, moral and actual, who had chalked on walls "Strike now in the West" or "Bomb Rome".' This reference to the advocates of the Second Front is, as Alan Munton notes, a curious one. The Left had striven for Hitler's defeat; the triumph over fascism was seen as the touchstone of Leftist unity. Few left-wingers in the post-war period could be found alleging that the war was pointless. But the expression of such views, however inaccurate, is typical of Jenkins's view of the world.

In other novels which dwell on the commemoration of victory the oppositions are more clear-cut. *Fielding Gray* (1967), Simon Raven's novel of public school life set at a thinly disguised Charterhouse, opens with an account of a service in memory of the dead held in the school chapel on the second Sunday after VE Day. After a collection of haughty officers has sat and sulked over an exhaustive roll call of the departed ('At the very least, they appeared to feel, the list could have done with some discreet editing') they are further antagonised by a militant sermon from the headmaster:

'I tell you again, as a Christian, that whatever happened cannot be dismissed as though it had never been. You cannot say, "the war is over, let us forget it and do as we did before." '

The sermon is greeted with resentful murmuring from the officers present: one makes an obscene gesture at the headmaster's retreating back. Significantly, the proceedings are linked with prefigurations of social change. Among the guests is the gloomy figure of Robert Constable, recently appointed senior tutor of the Cambridge college (an even less thinly disguised King's) where the 17-year-old Gray has won a minor scholarship. The senior master predicts that Constable is bent on egalitarianism of the most disquieting sort.

'Before you can turn around, he'll have that college changed into an *institution*. He'll put a cafeteria in Hall, he'll sell the port to endow bursaries for the sons of dustmen and he'll grow cabbages on the front lawn.'

And hats off to the senior tutor, one might think.

These opinions, as Raven's subsequent autobiographical writings make clear, are quite as much the author's as those of his characters. But the view of VE Day and its associated ceremonies as an expression of socialist triumphalism runs very deep. To balance it, perhaps, is the fact that more sympathetic accounts of the national thanksgiving display a similar, though less specific, unease, the feeling that there is something rather suspect and unwelcome in the tumult of popular rejoicing. Jim Carver in *The Avenue Goes to War* joins the VE Day crowds in Piccadilly expecting to find the spirit of Armistice Day reborn, only to be disappointed by a sense of 'extravagance and false gaiety', a 'lack of spontaneity'. Nicky Chapman in Callow's *Common People* (1958), whom one might expect to have some interest in communal celebration, chooses to spend VE night at home reading a book. 'The din outside sounded false and loutish and maggot-like.' There were other expectations of the war's end, apart from those of right-wing schoolboys and disillusioned officers, equally unsatisfied.

Powell's valediction to the war comes at the end of *The Military Philosophers*, when Jenkins arrives at Olympia for demobilisation. The venue imparts a final irony to the last rites of his military career. Here, as a child, Jenkins has watched a succession of Royal Tournaments. Now the memory of such stirring moments has been replaced by the sight of rail upon rail of grey flannel trousers. 'Was this the promise of a better world?' Jenkins muses. 'Perhaps we had reached that already and this was a celestial haberdasher.' Lurking in the bright, high corridors is Huxley's shade. But one can trace the development of these views – they are hardly views, insinuations would be nearer the mark – on into Powell's accounts of the post-war world. *Books Do Furnish a Room*, for example, finds Widmerpool – now a Labour MP – repeating Sir Hartley Shawcross's words 'We are the masters'. These are tiny details, but they are everywhere in Powell, in Bagshaw's tongue-in-cheek remarks about 'commitment', or on the occasion when Alfred Tolland, encountering Jenkins at Erridge's funeral, remarks on the absence of silk hats. ' "Quite right. Not in keeping with the way we live nowadays." '

The right-wing view of the war and the war's consequences, which we can see coming into existence before the war's end, which gathers steam throughout the 1950s and is still going strong a quarter of a century after the cessation of hostilities, is pervasive. It is ironic, then, that the picture of impending social revolution advertised by a novel like *Unconditional Surrender* should bear so little relation to fact. Waugh might imagine, probably did imagine, that he lived out his declining years in a socialist holiday camp.

The reality was markedly different. The conspicuous failure of the Attlee administration to bring about a lasting redistribution of wealth or a significant irruption of existing social arrangements has been well documented by historians. Anthony Howard points out that while Labour might be seen to have won the public battles – the debate over nationalisation, Bevan's conflict with the BMA – the struggle that really mattered was being fought below stairs, and largely to the Right's advantage. The public schools, with a few token nods in the direction of 'guinea pigs', survived unscathed. No Labour politician whose career had been assisted by a grammar school education was prepared to attack the concept of selection. University entrance procedures remained unchanged. In the arena of practical politics, the House of Lords consolidated its energies to the point where in the course of a single year it could bring down the bill to nationalise steel and the attempt to nationalise the gas industry. What might, in the hands of genuine ideologues, have become the seed-bed of socialist revolution perished in sleepy inertia. The period 1945–51 brought no significant institutional reform either of local government, industrial relations or the civil service. Bevan might denounce the upper classes as 'vermin' – a remark that he came very much to regret – but if one wanted an approximation of the spirit which motivated the Attlee cabinet, it could be found in Herbert Morrison's remark to the Liberal party leader Clement Davies *apropos* the undesirability of tampering with the House of Lords: 'We should not set up something different from the past.' Far from introducing a social revolution, the Labour victory of 1945 resulted in what Anthony Howard has called 'the greatest restoration of traditional values since 1660'.

Certain novelists of the Right were, to do them justice, dimly aware of this discrepancy. Waugh, in a preface to the 1959 edition of *Brideshead Revisited*, admitted that his threnody for the English stately home had been premature. 'It seemed then that the ancestral seats which were our chief national artistic achievement were doomed to decay and spoliation like the monasteries in the sixteenth century.' Yet the English aristocracy had maintained its identity to a degree that then seemed impossible; the advance of Hooper had been held up at several points. Much of *Brideshead*

Revisited, Waugh acknowledged, was a panegyric preached over an empty coffin. Ironically enough, Waugh had socialism to thank for one of the most crucial aspects of this salvation: the survival of many stately homes was a direct consequence of the Attlee government's National Trust Act. But uneasiness about the post-war achievement – of lack of it – cut both ways. If Waugh felt that the full horror of the socialist nirvana had been postponed, there were plenty of socialists who feared that something – humanity? *élan*? – was missing from the reconstituted post-war landscape.

Something of this disquiet can be seen in the contrasting fictional treatments of the Attlee government's last great symbolic action, the Festival of Britain. Outwardly Sir Gerald Barry's celebration of national heritage, radiating out from its South Bank nerve centre to hundreds of towns and cities around the country, divided opinion on party lines. The Beaverbrook press was hot against it, while the *Daily Telegraph* likened it to 'a moderately successful party, but one held on the wrong day and at far too great a cost – we are no more sadder for it, but one might have been wiser to have kept the money in one's pocket'. Waugh's epilogue to *Unconditional Surrender* is a fastidious variation on this approach:

> In 1951, to celebrate the opening of a happier decade, the Government decreed a festival. Monstrous constructions appeared on the south bank of the Thames, the foundation stone was solemnly laid for a National Theatre, but there was little popular exuberance among the straitened people, and dollar bearing tourists curtailed their visits and sped to countries of the continent, where, however precarious their position, they ordered things better.

Waugh at his most intransigent, though, would have hesitated to adduce a triumph of the proletarian spirit. With the exception of Herbert Morrison, who was responsible to the cabinet for the event's overall direction, the festival committee was drawn entirely from the *New Statesman* reading, third-programme listening radical middle classes. In some ways, of course, this is Waugh's point – Powell's point about the war as a whole: a supposedly national event had been hijacked by the progressive bourgeoisie in pursuit of its own sectional interests. Certainly the scent of uplift was in the air. Gerald Barry, the festival director, was editor of the *News Chronicle*, whose tone, Michael Frayn thought, extended to the proceedings themselves: 'philanthropic, kindly, whimsical, cosy, optimistic, middlebrow'.

The tensions which might be expected to have characterised this country-wide display of high-mindedness are reflected in Priestley's *Festival at Farbridge* (1951), a snapshot of the response of a single fictional town, published only a few months after the real event had ended. The plot is typical Priestley. Farbridge, thrifty and provincial, has decided not to stage a festival, on grounds that combine parsimony and insularity. To the town come various people – the faintly mysterious Commodore Tribe, a young man named Theodore Jenks and a girl called Laura Lacy – who resolve to organise the thing themselves. A good many strings are pulled, inertia and the vested interests of both Right and Left are overcome, fairy godmothers arrive to distribute bags of largesse and the event steams ahead.

The question of motive – why everybody should be so very enthusiastic – scarcely raises its head. When it does, it is to suggest that the festival is needed to drive away spiritual malaise rather than to celebrate national well-being. The opinion of old Mr Lacy, conveyed by his daughter, is that ' "the trouble with people now was that their energy was running away somewhere, as if it had a bad leak, so that most of them neither worked hard enough or played hard enough, and all the colour was draining away" '. Anyhow, Laura concludes, ' "if festivals will break this dreary routine, then let's have festivals" '. But there is also the question of what precisely the festival ought to consist. 'Uplift' rears its head in the persons of Ernest and Hilda Saxon, the couple with whom Laura lodges, socialists of the dreariest sort ('they had not a glimmer of humour between them'). Discussing the attractions of some sort of communal event, at the point where it is assumed that the festival will not take place, Hilda supposes that ' "it might have been very pleasant ... Some good drama, music, exhibitions of modern art, and lectures." ' In other words, everything calculated to drive the working classes into the nearest public house. What eventually emerges is a rather uneasy compromise – some good drama, a fashionable band leader and dancing *and* some lectures (their cynosure, the Cambridge don Mr Mortboy who expatiates on 'The Novel: A Revaluation', is an exact portrait of F. R. Leavis).

The festival is a success, the social classes are persuaded to intermingle with a fair degree of amity, but for all that there is something unsatisfactory about the atmosphere, and not merely because of the book's conspicuous inability to blow classes away. Priestley's shameless fixing, his twinkling pub landlords, his *deus ex machina*s scattering money on all sides combine to create an air of unreality. Much of this, of course, is a consequence of Priestley's failings as a novelist, and the habit of his characters to shade off into 'types' at a moment's notice, but it also has something to do with a profound uneasiness over his subject matter. More so than many a post-war chronicler, Priestley is conscious that the existence of sectional divisions and categories in society may be incompatible with the idea of an inclusive national interest, that the impresario who tries to activate a general consciousness may only stimulate a variety of independent consciousnesses, with sharply differing results. No doubt 'heritage' has always meant different things to different people, and the value of a phrase like 'the national fabric' will always be questionable in an advanced society, but the gap between the Festival of Britain and – say – the Diamond Jubilee was an awesome one, and Priestley knew it. He is trying too hard, and with inferior materials, to pin down something that resists easy taxonomy and the result is patchwork.

Powell, in the guise of Nick Jenkins, talks somewhere of the war's 'violent readjustments', a usage in which the personal and the social combine. Less embattled novels of the immediately post-war period, particularly those written within a year or two of the war's end, presuppose not so much a transfer of power as a more subtle shifting of social axes, an awareness of change accompanied by an acceptance of the personal consequences. Mollie Panter-Downes's *One Fine Day*, whose action encompasses a single twelve-hour period in a Sussex village in the first summer after the war, possesses an almost photographic quality – Panter-Downes was a journalist who reported the Blitz for the *New Yorker* – in its depiction of the reassessments and altered destinies which the war has brought about. Stephen and Laura Marshall, a youngish couple with a small child, are struggling to keep up a way of life that has all but disappeared, the old life of servants and tennis parties and dividend-bolstered leisure. Its disappearance is not so much the result of Cripps and Attlee – I doubt if you could find a single reference to the Labour party in *One Fine Day* – but the consequence of wider social changes. Young people, made restless by the war years, can't settle to rural inertia. The factory seems infinitely preferable to the old standby of domestic service. Some people, mostly sharp-eyed tradesmen, have done well out of the war. Others, notably the old *rentier* class whose fortunes had long been in decline, have not, and the manor house is being turned into an institution.

It is, of course, possible to insulate yourself from the war if you have sufficient money and maintain an ostrich-like refusal to face facts. Laura's mother, for example, has remained 'inflexible, following like a mesmerised hen, a chalk-line of behaviour which the years had laid down . . . The war had flowed past her like a dark, strong river, never pulling her into its current.' But such a luxury is open only to the very old, the very wealthy or the very foolish. For all their memories of unseen hands and nursery teas, the Marshalls accept the inevitability of compromise. There is a significant scene in which Stephen, alone in the house and awaiting his wife's return, comes to appreciate the absurdity of this bygone existence:

> it suddenly struck him as preposterous how dependent he and his class had been on the anonymous caps and aprons who lived out of sight and worked the stage. All his life he had expected to find doors opened if he rang, to wake up to the soft rattle of the curtain rings being drawn back, to find the fire bright and the coffee smoking hot as though household spirits had been working while he slept, and now the strings had been dropped, they all lay helpless as abandoned marionettes with no one to twitch them.

The solution would seem to lie in a slightly more modest bourgeois existence and getting your own shaving water. But the tone is never quietist. Laura returns ecstatic from her excursion in pursuit of the family dog, a state of mind which is bound up with her feelings about the war. National spirit, for once, has the capacity to heal and renew, the excuse not dubious political manoeuvring but an intense private epiphany. There is an inclusiveness about it, too, that can make Guy Crouchback's specialised concept of 'honour' or Jenkins's wintry detachment seem merely insipid.

Today we tend to take the pallid wraiths of *Officers and Gentlemen* and *The Soldier's Art* rather for granted, the predictable developments of much earlier tendencies in Waugh and Powell's fiction (Pringle in *Afternoon Men* (1931) and Lushington in *Venusberg* (1932) would not seem out of place in Nick Jenkins's regimental mess). What we tend to overlook is how directly they emerge out of the war and the prevailing conditions in which their creators imagined the war to have been fought. Here aesthetic and ideological imperatives slide effortlessly into one another. In purely aesthetic terms, the writers of post-war epics realised that conventional means were inadequate to describe the tumult and dislocation of war. This led them to take up positions in the very front rank of the avant-garde, a point which critics of Waugh the 'traditionalist' might care to ponder. But the choice of the aesthetic tool had a deeper ideological purpose. Crouchback might not 'do' as the flower of England's youth; he was even less effective as a hero. The unwritten thesis that Waugh and, less overtly, Powell wished to prosecute relied on creating characters who were at once remote and ineffective. One of the most remarkable things about Waugh and Powell's creations, given the conventions of the war novel, is their incapacity for decisive action. When we see Jenkins at work he is generally engaged on some fairly menial and pointless exercise – trying to conceal Bithel's drunkenness, smoothing out difficulties between foreign liaison officers. Crouchback's interventions are seldom anything more then mock-heroic. But to allow them to ascend to the heights of heroism would be to compromise Waugh's purpose: the circumstances of the war, the conditions in which it was fought, and the spoils of victory are not such as to allow for individual heroics. This was a communal, not an individual age. The members of the disillusioned patrician Right were in no doubt where they stood in relation to post-war Britain. From the standpoint of the immediate past they looked at the present and the future and found them wanting. Hooper and Widmerpool were the victors, not poor Guy Crouchback. The flower of England's youth was dead, at any rate from the point of view of fiction. He had been ailing throughout the 1930s, but the war finished him off. From the ashes was to emerge a different and perhaps more recognisable figure.

2

Figures in a Landscape

In his essay 'Notes on Nationalism' (1945) Orwell suggested that nationalism falls into two categories: on the one hand the habit of assuming that human beings can be classified like insects and that millions of people can be confidently labelled 'good' or 'bad'; on the other, the habit of identifying oneself with a single national or other unit, placing it beyond good and evil and recognising no other duty than that of advancing its interests. The majority of Victorian novelists might have shied away from the second of these contentions, but they would have had few qualms in endorsing the first. It is impossible to browse for very long in the writings of Thackeray, for example, before coming across something like the following:

> I say to you that you are better than a Frenchman. I would lay even money that you who are reading this are more than five feet seven in height, and weigh eleven stone; while a Frenchman is five feet four, and does not weigh nine. The Frenchman has after his soup a dish of vegetables, while you have one of meat. You are a different and superior animal – a French-beating animal (the history of hundreds of years has shown you to be so) ... (*Memorials of Gourmandising*)

It is odd that Thackeray, so sane and sensible when it comes to capital punishment and not living beyond your income, should harbour such a blind spot over the innate superiority of the English to any other European race. All that can be said in his defence is that such attitudes were deeply engrained. Read a century and a

33

half later, his insistence on the merits of the English diet may seem like the worst form of populist xenophobia, but there are things very like it in Trollope, whose French characters tend to smell of hair-oil and to capture heiresses on the strength of their prowess on the dance floor. Trollope's particular bugbear was Italy, an enduring source of moral contamination from *He Knew he was Right* to *Is He Popenjoy?*

With a few blatant exceptions, flag-waving of the 'England My England' variety has tended to disappear from the post-war novel. In fact most novelists have a habit of beginning their enquiries at the opposite end and assuming – for example in any work involving the Third World, secret-service collusion or nuclear disarmament – that England is guilty until proven innocent. In diluted form this attitude has proceeded a long way down the literary chain to the point where even the average blockbuster about imperial twilight seems uncomfortably aware of imperialist rapacity. R. F. Delderfield called one of his novels *God is an Englishman* (1970), something even Trollope would have balked at, but even in the 1960s praise of empire builders and Britain's industrial might is tempered by some eye-opening revelations of the seamier side of Victorian life.

Doubtless there will never be another fictional character who can cheerfully inform his sidekick that 'for sixty years ... we've been ruled by absolutely the finest sovereign the world has ever seen' (the speaker is E. W. Hornung's 'Raffles'): such a cast of mind is as out of date as frock coats or Raffles's own notions of 'playing the game'. At the same time 'Englishness' is still a topic of abiding interest to the novelists of the immediately post-war period. For all that, the writer who considers the idea of national consciousness invariably does so in the assumption of a radically lowered national morale. This awareness unites both sides of the political divide, from right-wingers going around proclaiming 'I told you so' over the post-imperial chaos, to parlour socialists convinced of the survival of a great deal of 'English hypocrisy' requiring extirpation, and it has the effect of setting alleged national characteristics in sharp relief.

What does an English novelist in the quarter-century or so after the war mean by the adjective 'English'? What does 'England' conjure up in the mind of the average writer? Which qualities or attributes are assumed to be important in any examination of English character? A trawl through even the most negligible literary novels of the period discloses a whole range of assumptions and beliefs about national prestige, individuality, private and public worth, all the various strands of behaviour and expectation that might be classified as the English experience. What was it like to be alive in England in the period 1945–70? No writer can ever provide a satisfactory answer – though the tendency to regard the novelist as a social historian manqué was and is extremely strong – but at the very least trying to determine what novelists mean by these words gives us a valuable context in which to discuss their work.

The assumption of a lowered national morale is unignorable. So is the thought that this impairment is the responsibility of the executive: a conviction that government is both corrupt and opportunist unites Right and Left. Thirkell's don who maintains that "we are living under a Government as bad as any in history in its combination of bullying and weakness, its bid for the mob's suffrage, its fawning on unfriendly foreigners who despise it, its efforts to crush all personal freedom" is an extreme case, but there exists throughout post-war fiction a widespread belief that political parties exist to promote not a vague but honourable 'national interest' but some narrower sectional or even personal programme. Frequently this feeling manifests itself in doubts over the promotion of government 'policy', at a time when manipulation of the public will seemed much easier to effect. In *Friends in Low Places* (1965), which touches on the political landscape of the late 1950s, Simon Raven has one of his characters quote from an analysis of practical politics, written by an aspiring Labour MP. Among other topics, the book examines the process of 'selling' policy:

'The sale can be effected by high pressure methods which ignore or obscure the real issues and insist on others which, while irrelevant, are plausible and attractive. This has always been true, but never so true as now, when techniques of publicity are quicker and slicker than ever before.'

This is a comment on the formidable Macmillan publicity machine – Vicky's cartoons are another – which harbours the assumption that politics is a cheap swindle, practised through dubious methods, and a vehicle for personal advancement. (Peter Morrison MP, Raven's 'decent man', is seen as a horribly compromised figure, morally hamstrung and unable to square his principles with the party diktats. Sent to an important trade fair in a later novel Morrison seems to have learned his lesson: he is now an enthusiastic practitioner of industrial sabotage.)

Political power is both weakened and corrupt. Decisively exercised on the international stage, it is invariably derided. Bumbo Bailey, the hero of Andrew Sinclair's *The Breaking of Bumbo* (1959), fits his disagreement with Suez into a much older tradition of, as he sees it, unprincipled interference abroad: ' "In goes bumbling, stupid, hypocritical old England. Pulling her punches. War with morals. I ask you. *War with morals.*" ' In some ways, Sinclair suggests, naked self-interest would be preferable to the veneer of gentlemanly principle which seemed to cover the Eden government's dealings with Nasser. But then England's attempts to preserve its old international prestige would always be liable to failure. Power in the developed world has moved westward across the Atlantic.

The official 'building up Britain' line which characterised government publicity campaigns in the early 1950s finds little echo in fiction. The journalist in *Festival at Farbridge* (1951) explicitly rebukes it.

'Fact is, Jenks, we've gone American; bound to happen – that's where the real power is. Our boys in the news know it, act on it, but it's too early yet for the paper to say so in its editorials. So we go on printing all the old nonsense about believing in Britain.'

Even in the continuing struggle for security, Britain is likely to be outwitted by competing allies who are simply more competent, basing their actions on a more realistic view of the world. The British intelligence men in Raven's *The Sabre Squadron* (1966), its subject the jostling for power in the occupied Europe of the early

1950s, seem amateurish when compared to the efficient, cynical Americans.

Belief in national prestige might still be recommended to a hoodwinked populace by politicians who had long ago acknowledged the passing of national power. The thought of 'England' – and it is nearly always 'England', seldom 'Britain' – stirs mixed emotions in the characters of the average post-war English novel. Seeing it from the decks of ships, reconnoitring it once more after long periods abroad, they are conscious of nostalgia battling inconclusively with feelings of unease and inadequacy. Simon Moffat, the returning naturalist of A. S. Byatt's *The Game* (1968), invokes Tennyson to quantify his dislike of England. ' "On the bald streets breaks the blank day," he said in his mind.' Walker in Malcolm Bradbury's *Stepping Westward* (1965) imagines a 'simple, comfortable hospital of a place'. Frequently an acknowledgement of the beauty of England and the charm of its landscape is coupled with the thought that these are somehow insufficient. Sarah in Margaret Drabble's *A Summer Bird-cage* (1963) returns from France to drive through the Warwickshire countryside: 'it looked unique and beautiful, not flat and deadly ... Oh it was beautiful, very much England and beautiful.' But this is a tarnished rapture. 'Why weren't they enough, why won't they do, things like that?' Even observers of the less cosmopolitan type, prone to praise England at the expense of 'abroad', are often pulled up short by the realisation that the country they value is drastically flawed. Garnett Bowen, the xenophobic narrator of Kingsley Amis's *I Like It Here* (1958), concludes such a comparison with an acknowledgement of the sheer inconvenience and bloodymindedness that attends many areas of English life. Praising London, Bowen concedes:

> Admittedly it, together with most of the rest of the United Kingdom, was the land of sorry-sir (sorry sir bar's closed, sorry sir no change, sorry sir too late for lunch, sorry sir residents only sir), but one couldn't expect to win all the time. Or any of the time, apparently.

Bowen's complaint is ingeniously framed. He dislikes the surliness and the ingrained unwillingness to please; he abhors the attendant banks of rules and regulations; he detests the unspoken assumption that the customer is always wrong; but what really seems to annoy him is the patina of deference. To be gleefully informed that the bar closed five minutes ago would be less unsettling if one didn't have to be called 'sir' into the bargain.

What a character in John Fowles's *The Collector* (1963) calls 'the great dead weight of the Calibanry of England' was to become a topic of absorbing interest to the post-war novelist. The impression of a straitened, constricted national landscape is confirmed by the descriptions of the people set down in it. Victorian novelists frequently supply page-long encomia of their characters' physical comeliness. The creations of their successors are unbeautiful, worn, anxious, watchful. Lumley in John Wain's *Hurry On Down* (1953), examining an old acquaintance from college days, detects 'the same immature, arrogant face. The same cold eyes behind glasses.' Jim Dixon inventories the features of his girlfriend, Margaret Peel: 'the tufts of brown hair that overhung the ear pieces of her glasses, the crease running up the near cheek and approaching closer than before to the eye-socket, and the faint but at this angle unmistakable downward curve of the mouth'. Billy Fisher in Keith Waterhouse's *Billy Liar* (1959) observes a typical Saturday morning in the Yorkshire town of Stradhoughton, 'the fat women rolling along on their bad feet like toy clowns in pudding basins, the grey-faced men reviewing the sporting pinks'. Much of this is nothing more than a straining after rather bitter comic effect, but it is lodged in genuine observation. In *Still Life*, a novel published in 1985 but depicting the England of the 1950s, A. S. Byatt includes a long passage which at once summarises and rationalises these complaints. Examining a row of faces at a church carol service, Stephanie reflects that 'the English are ugly . . . they were not outdoor faces, they were not easy faces. Nor were they suffering faces.' Stephanie attributes this unease to social self-consciousness, the pressures of personal or familial self-esteem. 'They were the faces of people concerned predominantly either with what people thought about their behaviour, property, social standing, or with their own judgment of other people's behaviour, property, social standing.' Their clothes are 'ugly carapaces', designed not to beautify them or even to fulfil practical criteria but 'to show the quality of the cloth and be decent'. Ugliness and ugly clothes, though, are only a small part of the definition of national identity. Later in the novel Stephanie's sister Frederica approaches a group of acquaintances on a French beach. She acknowledges that 'you could see they were English, though how this was, since they were mostly gleaming brown and both elegantly and scantily dressed, it was hard to say'. A pinker skin-tone under the brown, Frederica decides, 'and the pristine, non-domestic look this kind of English had'. Such descriptions are perhaps even more revealing when they are attributed to non-English observers. John Masters's *Bhowani Junction* (1954), set in the India of 1946, examines the relationship between half-caste Eurasian society and pukka English officialdom. Taylor, the Eurasian railway policeman, is desperately emulous of the English – he has invested a whole lifetime in an attempt to appear English – but he is still prepared to characterise their representatives as 'a typical square Englishman. He had a moustache and spoke gruffly' or 'pansy-looking, rather fat'. One may admire a race or feel that they are capable of offering protection – a strong emotion in Taylor's case – without wanting to share their physical character-istics.

Inevitably external features have an inward projection. 'English' as an adjective is rarely used to convey approbation. When it does, the exact meaning is generally elusive, linked to vague suggestions of 'naturalness' or 'joy'. Thus the soldier in Alun Lewis's 1940s story 'They Came', hearing the sound of someone behind him on the road, imagines that the footsteps are 'natural and English'. Alexander Wedderburn, waiting outside the church for Stephanie's wedding in Byatt's earlier *The Virgin in the Garden* (1978), feels 'happy and English'. Usually, however, the emphasis of the adjec-tive is negative, shorthand for a crippling shyness or reserve. At the same wedding the church-goers try to avoid each other's eye 'in a truly English way'. Colin in Philip Callow's *Going to the Moon* (1968), having shaken hands with someone, notes that it was 'an English handshake, frosty'. Frequently, this reserve mani-fests itself in a dislike of physical intimacy. Nicky Chapman in Callow's *Common People* (1958) curses the fact of his nationality, as 'it seemed to me that no people in the world were as shrinking and self-conscious as the English, or so ashamed and in fear of their bodies'. Later in the same novel, during a walk in Greenwich Park, Nicky's mistress tells him ' "that's an English sun ... No passion in it." '

Elsewhere 'inhibition' is regularly employed by foreigners as a weapon with which to belabour their English acquaintances. Miss Roach in Patrick Hamilton's *The Slaves of Solitude* (1947) is cruelly mocked by the German Vicki Kugelmann as 'the English miss', 'Miss Prim'. More often it is used to suggest a wholly disabling reserve. Two incidents in *Still Life* convey this sense of inadequacy. In the first Winifred Potter sits talking to the wife of the headmaster at the school where her husband teaches, a conversation dominated by the unspoken acknowledgement of Mrs Thorne's private tragedy, the early death of her son. 'They sat in Mrs Thorne's chill drawing room, two stiff, grim, tall Englishwomen, unable to drop their English shield of cautious silence.' Winifred thinks that she could 'fling myself about. How she would hate that.' In the second Alexander finds himself at the centre of an improbable *ménage à trois*, living with his friends Thomas and Elinor Poole as the father of their child. 'What did Thomas know, or guess, or think, or feel?' It is possible, Alexander realises, that 'simply because they were English, all would silently go away, because raising a voice, or commenting energetically, were in moral bad taste'.

A little more warmth, you feel, a little more personal resonance would go some way towards solving these problems. Invariably, though, attempts to ameliorate complicated emotional situations are weakened by what Stephanie defines as 'the infinite English capacity for underplaying drama, pretending things were normal'. Byatt's novels, in particular, provide a devastating critique of 'Englishness'. Their effect is to suggest that many time-honoured English characteristics – stoicism, reserve, the fatal tendency to conceal everything beneath a smokescreen of 'good manners' ('a horrible thing', Stephanie thinks) – are not so much unappealing as downright dangerous. Significantly, Byatt places these warning signs in the most crucial departments of personal life – birth, death, family relationships. In hospital, waiting to give birth to her son, Stephanie is left alone in a room with a bell but no instructions as to when she might need to ring it, or when, 'as the English require, she must be silent and uncomplaining'. Subsequently, Stephanie hears the noise of a woman screaming. She thinks 'it would be helpful, but not English, not good manners, to make a noise like that'. This is perhaps only inconvenience. Earlier Stephanie has seen a woman miscarry merely out of a reluctance to draw attention to herself. She rails at the doctor: ' "the English. Are so damned. Polite ... Mrs Owen. Lost her baby – I know – because. Because no one would let her tell them." '

A similar indifference surrounds the aftermath of Stephanie's death in a freak electrical accident. 'So quickly, so quickly, the English stop speaking of grief,' her bereaved husband reflects. He resents the 'inadequate words they had spoken'. Daniel's subsequent physical decline and psychological disturbance go unremarked. Worse still, perhaps, is the hypocrisy that this sort of concealment brings to any sort of personal relationship. An important strand of *The Virgin in the Garden* is taken up by the sinister association between Marcus, Stephanie's brother, and his schoolmaster Lucas Simmonds. Marcus, a pale, obsessed adolescent in the typical Byatt mould, makes various attempts to unburden himself. One of his potential confidants is Alexander. But the older man is careful to keep the boy at arm's length. When evidence of Marcus's disturbed condition becomes unignorable, Alexander, thinking seriously about him for perhaps the first time, decides that 'their few meetings had all consisted of choked attempts by Marcus to tell him, or show him, something'. At the time, Alexander wanted to discourage this 'out of an English feeling that endemic hysteria was best kept at bay'. Shortly after this Stephanie comes across Lucas Simmonds in the church. Confronted by obvious signs that the man is insane, she realises that she should ask what is terrifying him, should offer – this is, after all, a church, and Simmonds's troubles have a religious aspect – to kneel down and pray with him. But Stephanie is transfixed by inanition: 'I should say Marcus is sick. I cannot. I cannot.'

Plenty of novelists have laboured the effects of reticence on English family life. Few have woven it so determinedly into a fictional structure. Byatt is a psychological novelist, but it is a national psychology, a silent conformism wrapped up in a deference to 'manners, the English panacea', a mass conditioning whose grasp is inescapable. But reticence, it might be said, is only an effect. Searching for an explanation of English diffidence, several novelists have sought refuge in sexual conditioning. Colin in *Going to the Moon* thinks that his is 'the old, old story of sons in England, coddled and comforted by the mother who yearns over them like a lover, all artificial, till the spunk's sucked out of them'. When Gunn Goater in Ferdinand Mount's *The Clique* (1978) claims to like women, his friend Antic is mildly puzzled: ' "It's quite rare, you know. Most Englishmen don't. We are oddballs in that way, you know." ' Whatever the explanation, the singularity of the English seems in no doubt when set against other nations. Sarah in Drabble's *A Summer Bird-cage* contrasts what she sees as her own conformism with the less constricted approach of her French friend Simon. The latter lives 'a wholly willed, a wholly undetermined life . . . She lacked an instinct for kitchens and gasmeters and draughts under the door and tiresome quarrels.' Irony, and its extension 'the English sense of humour', provide a further stumbling block. The American Restarick's comment in Raven's *The Sabre Squadron* (after Daniel Mond has lent him an Anthony Powell novel) that, ' "I didn't realise you English could be so oblique," ' is a compliment of a sort. Set against this is the scene in Malcolm Bradbury's *Stepping Westward* in which James Walker introduces his class of American students to Swift's *A Modest Proposal*. Its satirical suggestion that the problem of mass starvation could be solved by eating babies is greeted with horrified incredulity, only the class anarchist hazarding that ' "maybe we should re-evaluate our whole attitude to cannibalism" '. A similar confusion worries two of the characters in *Bhowani Junction*, who overhear a conversation between the English Colonel Savage and the Indian, though Oxford-educated, District Collector. ' "Why were they speaking in that funny way?" "It is a joke. An English joke." '

Such a concentration on at least the vestiges of an interior life is rare. In seeking to establish the salient features of their characters, English novelists generally rely on externals – accent, dress, real or imagined status. In particular, the way in which people speak is an automatic guide to social position, bearing with it all manner of assumptions about future behaviour. When Fielding Gray and his companions arrive at a bathing-place at the same time as a party from a local girls' school, the gym mistress accompanying them sighs with relief at hearing the 'safe public school voices'. Jane Graham in Lynne Reid Banks's *The L-Shaped Room* (1960) considers Toby, her fellow-lodger, to possess 'a very nice cultured accent'. Dr Earley in Angus Wilson's story 'Learning's Little Tribute' (1950) is expertly pinned down: 'His voice with its over elocutionised vowels ill concealing their cockney origins sounded like some 18th century radical priest.' Accent, inevitably enough, provides valuable evidence for a snap social judgement. The assumption that to drop an aitch is on the one hand unspeakably vulgar and on the other uproariously funny persists well into the 1970s. Conversely, differences in speech patterns supply an important contrast in many of the deliberately class-conscious novels of the 1960s. Clegg in Fowles's *The Collector*, for example, who graduates from trapping butterflies to holding a young woman captive in his cellar, imagines that, 'It's the way people speak that gives them away, not what they say.' For her part, Miranda is in no doubt about Clegg's social origins: 'He's got one of those funny inbetween voices, uneducated trying to be educated.'

Quite as important a defining role is played by the clothes characters wear and their personal appearance. Jim Dixon's contempt for Bertrand Welch's lemon-coloured coat and his beard are well known. Unexceptionable in themselves, these items infuriate Jim because of the social and cultural affiliations they display, immediately revealing Welch as an arty bohemian of the painting, third-programme listening type. A similar set of assumptions, in this case directed from the other side, emerges in John Wain's *Hurry On Down*. Visiting his girlfriend's home, Charles Lumley realises that her relations' objections to him derive in a large measure from his failure to wear 'a uniform', a type of dress that announces 'his status, his earnings and his ambition'. Dressing the part, Lumley reflects, is a 'sacred duty'.

Frequently personal appearance joins with domestic circum-

stance to extend one character's grasp on another. Jenny Bunn in
Kingsley Amis's *Take a Girl Like You* (1960) conducts an exhaustive examination of her landlord, Dick Thorpe, designed to 'place'
him within her own terms of social reference. Dick is 'obviously
a nice enough man'. However, 'she did wish she understood more
about him and about how he had come to be as he was'. For a
start, Thorpe is too kind and cheerful:

> and not badly dressed enough (he was wearing a collar and a
> self-colour tie even though his trousers were that very dark grey
> flannel kind), and not really old enough either, to be the kind
> of man to take in lodgers. He had treated her almost like a
> guest, or at least a relation.

Thorpe's job as an auctioneer is an additional source of confusion.
'Chalking or sticking the numbers on, reading out about dinner
services, and getting through the going-going-gone part was not
enough to count as a full-time job for a grown man,' according
to Jenny's strict notions of respectable male employment. Jenny
moves through a world whose significance consists of minute
social gradations. One of the first things she notices about Patrick
Standish, her eventual seducer, is that his hand bears a ring, 'gold
or getting on that way, on its little finger'. To Jenny, rings on men
have 'something flashy and foreign and common about them'.

To 'place' a character in this way is to arrive very speedily at a
social judgement. This need not be as clear-cut as Jenny Bunn's
homely assumptions, or Billy Fisher's characterisation of the
approach and demeanour of his employer Shadrach as 'that of
the second-hand car salesman'. In fact upper-class fiction of the
period is awash in barely perceptible nuances, capable of being
decoded only by a small group of the socially and linguistically
competent. Thus in Laura Talbot's *The Gentlewomen* (1953), an
authentic backs-to-the-wall defence of threatened gentility, Lady
Rushford warns her daughter of the dangers of marrying into a
neighbouring family:

> 'The Barnsleys are not quite . . . not quite . . . but I hardly need
> tell you that; you were always perceptive, Roona.'

'Not quite what, mother?'
'Well, rather deuxième. Not quite out of the top drawer.'

'Not quite'; 'Rather deuxième'; 'Not quite out of the top drawer'. This is the stuff of the *Punch* cartoon and the drawing-room comedy. None the less, it expresses a very genuine sense of social distinction, and one can believe that Lady Rushford's conviction of the Barnsleys' unsuitability is built on a much more solid foundation than, say, her belief in God. But this sort of camouflaging of a moral judgement is evident a good deal further down the social scale. In *Hurry On Down*, Lumley attends a party at the digs of an acquaintance. His opinion of the premises is that the landlady 'probably kept Cairn terriers or a Labrador'. It is a tiny detail, but a whole range of Lumley's social assumptions and prejudices is thereby propelled to the surface.

The assumptions are generally a good deal plainer – and a great deal more vocal – than this. At the party, for instance, Lumley is rebuked by his fellow guests for having taken a job as a hospital porter. His offence is that he has been false to their expectations of him, or as one character puts it: ' "You had some sort of education, some sort of upbringing, though I must say you don't bloody behave like it." ' One of the striking features of the average post-war novel is the intensity of social judgements of this sort. Rosamund Stacey in Margaret Drabble's *The Millstone* (1965), so mature in her analysis of Elizabethan sonnet sequences, is reduced to paroxysms of rage by the thought of her brother, who 'went and married a ghastly girl whose father was a Colonel and now he lives in Dorking and spends all his time having absolutely worthless people to dinner and playing bridge'. Absolutely worthless from the point of view of your average Hampstead-residing, *Guardian*-reading socialist, that is. Peter in Thomas Hinde's *Mr Nicholas* (1952), asked by a neighbour what he thinks of the Surrey town in which they both reside, considers and rejects 'provincial' and 'suburban' before settling on the adjective 'smug'.

The degree of hatred which invests the use of a word like 'provincial' or 'suburban' in the English novel of the 1950s and 1960s is startling. It is as if moral worth were attainable only by people living in city tenements or on blasted heaths. Angus Wilson is a good example of a post-war novelist obsessed by the codes of social status and position. The result is a series of delicate nuances, accurately reflecting upper-class speech patterns of the time, simultaneously mocking and indulgent. The following passage from *Hemlock and After* (1953), which describes Bernard Sands's attitude towards what he regards as his father's self-deception in defending an unpopular neighbour from unkind gossip, is fairly typical:

> He and Sonia were perfectly well aware of the vulgar stupidity of the greater part of these local people, quite as well aware as his father, but they were capable of a little civilised tolerance. It was typical of his father's endless self-deception. All this universal understanding, this Dostoevskyian emotional brotherhood, and, at bottom, he had nothing but utter contempt for nine-tenths of humanity; as for the other tenth he probably hated their guts for not being susceptible to his patronage.

Disentangling the opinions of each participant – Bernard, Bernard's father and Wilson himself – is a complex business. The elder Sands is plainly being skewered as a *faux bonhomme*. Bernard's fastidious remarks – 'vulgar stupidity', 'these local people', 'a little civilised tolerance' – are sufficient to compromise his own professed humanity. But at bottom, it may be suspected, Wilson is playing the game himself, making his own highly critical assessments of father and son. Elsewhere in the novel judgements tend to be firmly ascribed to the character pronouncing them. For example, Bernard considers the young man who makes homosexual advances towards him in Leicester Square to be 'vulgar' and 'second-rate'. Several other unfortunates who stray into his orbit are marked down as 'second-rate failures'. Yet it is always difficult to separate Wilson's stance from that of the characters he is allowing to condemn themselves. The short stories in *Such Darling Dodos* (1950), to take an obvious reference point, are spattered with judgemental language – 'socially pretentious', 'undeniably extravagant', 'under-bred', 'suburban'. Obviously Wilson is mocking the sort of people who find their neighbours 'vulgar', but it seems clear that there are others whom Wilson himself wants to convict of this failing.

These authorial concealments and ironies are perhaps no more than a reflection of actual circumstance. There is a significant moment at the beginning of Anthony Powell's *The Acceptance World* (1955) – significant, at any rate, from the point of view of Powell's art – in which Nick Jenkins muses on the complexities of writing a novel of precisely the genre in which Powell himself, not to mention Wilson, resides. 'Intricacies of social life make English habits unyielding to simplification, while understatement and irony – in which all classes of this island converse – upset the normal emphasis of reported speech.' This goes some way towards explaining the very strong feeling one obtains from a novel of the Angus Wilson/Laura Talbot type that the whole thing is being written in an immensely subtle and sophisticated code, whose solution presupposes a highly developed social, as opposed to literary, sensibility on the part of the reader.

The implications of this close, sequestered, status-conscious society for wider areas of national life are profound. Ominously perhaps, no novelist worth speaking of finds much to praise in the arts as practised in post-war England. For Philip Callow's autodidact Nicky Chapman, 'English writers hardly existed in my world, they were a class apart, right out of it with their noses in the air.' Chapman prefers Faulkner and Hemingway: 'at least they had a living, warm quality'. Miranda in *The Collector* tempers her praise of a few exceptional artists with an acknowledgement of the depressing conditions in which they work: 'the real saints are people like Moore and Sutherland who fight to be English artists in England, like Constable and Palmer and Blake'. The English artist's spiritual home lies across the Channel. 'It's all because there's so little hope in England that you have to turn to Paris or somewhere abroad. But you have to accept the truth – that Paris is always an escape *downward*.' This is not to disparage Paris, 'but you have to face up to England and the apathy of the environment'. To apathy can be added a naïve provincialism, a fatal willingness to settle for second-best. Raphael Faber, the fastidious German-born don in *Still Life*, expands his instinctive dislike of 'clotted English nature mysticism' by sharply criticising Alexander's play about Van Gogh: ' "Van Gogh knew Rembrandt and understood impressionism. He was not English. It is so *easy* for the English to get excited about corn and blossom in a rather intense way. It is a provincial art." ' An amateurish, genteel art, too. Malcolm Bradbury's *Eating People is Wrong* (1959) contains some deft evocations of the poetry-reading/glee-singing/literary lecture side of English cultural life, as does *Lucky Jim*. Predictably, lack of professionalism in the arts extends into other areas where rigour and aesthetic discrimination are badly needed. Frederica's request that Faber should supervise a proposed Ph.D. thesis provokes a gloomy prognosis of the chances of her ever achieving anything: ' "the English respect for amateur muddling through is a major reason for the few successes there have been" '.

Diminished, impoverished, ingrown and self-obsessed, 'Englishness' can be seen in clearer relief through comparisons with 'abroad'. With minor exceptions the attitude to foreign countries, their customs, landscape and representatives, is deeply insular – an ingrained suspicion that frequently borders on outright hostility. The RAF men in J. L. Carr's war-time novel *A Season in Sinji* (1967) remain fundamentally incurious about their exotic surroundings: 'Bridlington is as remote as Lourenço Marques and that sounds about as far as they could post you.' Above all, this indifference takes in food. Invited to dine with her *echt* English boyfriend, Rosamund Stacey asks what type of cuisine the restaurant offers. ' "I'm not sure," Roger replies, ' "but they said it was quite clean for foreigners." ' Rosamund cannot determine whether this is intended as a joke. The odds are that it is entirely serious. But the tendency to judge anything non-English unfavourably even extends to language. Simon Raven's *The Survivors* (1976) opens at an international writers' conference in Venice. Here Captain Detterling, mortally offended by a rendering into English of some ideological reflections from a Bulgarian delegate, adjusts his headphones to see what it sounds like in other European languages. An Italian translator is going at full pelt, causing Detterling to reflect that Italian is a degenerate tongue: 'its constant juxtaposition of the diminutive with the grandiose transposes everything, whether the most noble utterance or this jargon which we are hearing now, to the same level of trivial hysteria'. No wonder, he concludes, that the Italians 'are at once so conceited and so futile; their language compels them to live a libretto'. Subsequently Detterling turns the arrow to French. Here he finds only silence: 'French, a precise and civilised language, had no equivalent for this rubbish, so the translator, one assumed, had simply given up.' Detterling makes a final effort with German. The result is 'great throatfuls of congested inflection, ejaculated in a tone at once whining and aggressive'.

America, the alleged bumptiousness of whose inhabitants animated many a Victorian novelist, might be thought a prime target for this type of graceless patronage. In fact, attitudes towards America and American culture are a great deal more complex than this. On the one hand, Americans are often targets for heavy-handed satire: one thinks of Evelyn Waugh's novels or Nancy Mitford's Hector Dexter. Alternatively, they are frequently used as a means of working off English liberal grudges. Often this is no more than parenthetic. Catching sight of a pair of tourists in the Soho restaurant, Rosamund Stacey cannot resist a swipe at these 'fat Americans, both bulging from their ill-chosen clothes', and their ability to make conspicuous nuisances of themselves. At the same time the much more serious absurdities of American political life in the immediate post-war era do not go unremarked. John Bowen's first novel, *The Truth will not Help Us* (1956), which purports to be an account of the unjust execution of three English sailors on piracy charges in a Scottish port early in the eighteenth century, is actually a satire on the McCarthy trials, in which the characters speak in American accents.

What no novelist is in any doubt over is the gradual infiltration of American culture into English social life. Jim Dixon's frame of cultural reference is dominated by jazz and gangster movies. Similarly, Billy Fisher's speech patterns are crammed with expressions derived from American cinema. When Billy assembles his financial reserves in anticipation of departure from Stradhoughton, he imagines himself to exist 'in the tradition of American writers, driving lorries, sweeping up, South American revolutionary, soda jerk, newspaper boy'. Little wonder that Jenkins, the sociology professor in *Eating People is Wrong*, is unsure whether he is glad to be back from his exchange year: ' "It's like coming back home, looking for England, and finding America again." ' The degree of American influence is a mixed blessing. Bowen's *The Centre of the Green* (1959) is an early send-up of the world of American advertising and its deathless jargon. Alternatively, the Americans seen at large in Europe in the aftermath of the war – for example in *The Sabre Squadron*, David Lodge's *Out of the Shelter* (1970) and Anthony Powell's *Temporary Kings* (1973) – possess a definite vitality, a glamour sufficient to set them apart from the representatives of an exhausted and uncertain backwater.

Europe emerges in a much less ambiguous light. Detachment from European culture and anything that might amount to European statehood is a feature of the protagonists of the average postwar English novel. Jim Dixon notes bitterly of his professor's wife that 'she liked to think of herself as a Western European first and an Englishwoman second'. To Dixon this is simple affectation, cultural posturing of the most pretentious sort. Walker in *Stepping Westward* is characterised by his lack of interest in Europe. On board a transatlantic liner he examines the luggage of a party of American girls returning from a continental tour, 'garish with the labels of hotels in Vienna and Rome, Brussels and Paris, places he scarcely knew at all'. Subsequently Walker tells an American girl, ' "I'm not European, I'm English." ' Isn't England in Europe, Miss Snowflake wants to know. ' "Yes, in a way," ' Walker concedes.

But Englishness can seem a prized possession when matched against certain emanations from the continent. Kingsley Amis's ritual disparagement of European – specifically French – culture is well-known, but its origins probably lie in resentment of the pre- and post-war Connolly/*New Statesman* cult of Europe. In railing against the Welches' decision to name their sons Bertrand and Michel, in abusing Bertrand's beret and inveighing against French food, Amis is mocking what he assumes to be English cultural pretensions rather than their raw material. Elsewhere, though prone to equate France with effeteness and homosexuality, Amis is rather more even-handed in his forays abroad. *I Like It Here* is a resounding titular statement of intent, but as Garnett Bowen concedes 'here' can have profound disadvantages. In *Take a Girl Like You* Jenny Bunn's native saws and homespun wisdom seem threadbare when compared to Anna le Page's enviable sophistication. In any case, whatever the efforts of Amis and a handful of like-minded compatriots, the highbrow pro-European tradition was far from extinguished. It takes only a glance at a novel by Iris Murdoch or A. S. Byatt to establish that the really serious action is taking place on the other side of the Channel. Murdoch's first novel, *Under the Net* (1954), for example, though initially misappropriated by the Angry Young Man lobby, is saturated with contemporary French philosophy; not the least among its conspicuous marker flags can be found in the dedication to Raymond Queneau. Elsewhere Doris Lessing is capable of making the reader's judgement of her characters turn on their patronising attitude to 'foreigners'. In *Retreat to Innocence* (1956), Julia Barr recalls travelling through Spain with her mother. After a peasant has mended a puncture and the two women have spent several hours talking with the man's family, all the mother can find to say concerns the need for 'a sensible English town council and a birth control centre'; smug English complacency at its worst. However, 'abroad' continues to serve one very important function for nearly every English novelist of the period: it is somewhere you go for sexual adventure. Sarah in *A Summer Bird-cage*, Clara Maugham in Drabble's later novel *Jerusalem the Golden* (1967), allowing herself to be fondled by a strange young Frenchman in a cinema – the role of France as a haven from English repressiveness (an alternative venue is the Israeli kibbutz) survives into the 1960s and beyond. It is, for example, a theme of Nigel Williams's *My Life Closed Twice* (1977) and Julian Barnes's *Metroland* (1981). 'Abroad' might for many novelists be crammed with frightful foreigners, noisome food and influences guaranteed to make a particular type of loathsome and culturally impressionable Englishman yet more loathsome still, but it is at least a place where one can achieve a sexual relationship.

A diminished international status; a venal and self-interested executive; a populace animated by fussy social judgements, repressed, insecure and inward-looking – of such, at least according to the novelists, does 'Englishness' in the third quarter of the twentieth century consist. It would be strange if this perception of a radically lowered national morale failed to stray into another key area of fictional consciousness: the novelist's view of the past. The national entity might seem directionless and without purpose now. How, with the benefit of hindsight, had it seemed then? History as presented in the post-war British novel is, according to the American critic Margaret Scanlan, 'neither glamorous nor consoling'. The post-war years brought an immediate vogue for nostalgic evocations of past time, evident for example in the popularity of novelists such as L. P. Hartley, Nancy Mitford, Rosamond Lehmann and Anthony Powell. But it is a wistful view and a suspect heritage, built on an awareness that the past had changed out of all recognition, that any reconstruction of a bygone world would carry with it the seeds of its own demise. 'The past is a foreign country. They do things differently here' – the opening lines of L. P. Hartley's *The Go-Between* (1953) – operate as a kind of shorthand for all the fond re-creations of Edwardian summers, Georgian cricket fields and inter-war social life. It is rare for a novelist of this kind to escape the scent of prefiguration. Powell's young men at their deb dances, Hartley's squires – there are bombs and gelignite coming to blow them away and the chronological void in which they appear to exist is pre-ordained by the certainty of eventual destruction.

Primed by fashionable critical notions of diminishment and uncertainty, many critics in recent years have argued for the predominance of a certain kind of historical novel, at once sceptical and critical, based on assumptions of national decline and a loss of confidence in the conduct of public life. Its characteristics have been analysed by Margaret Scanlan in her exceptionally interesting study *Traces of Another Time*. The sceptical historical novel, Ms Scanlan suggests, looks back to a public past, to a world war or to conflicts in former colonial outposts such as India or Ireland. Rather than displaying a triumphalism of thin red lines and white man's burdens, the particular moments chosen for fictional recasting are mostly inglorious or violent. Similarly, such novels are more likely to evoke defeat than victory, stupidity and arrogance rather than heroism, a sense of private consciousness intersecting with public events in a highly unsettling way. The techniques of these fictions, Scanlan goes on to suggest, abet their themes. The oblique, the fabular and the post-modern replace the central, the realistic and the representational. J. G. Farrell's *Troubles* (1970), for example, examines the years of De Valera, Michael Collins and the Black and Tans through a group of Irish men and women who sit out the national revolution in the backwater of a seaside hotel. Frequently the novel's action will emanate from some deeply disturbing incident about which the truth remains uncertain: the murder of the child in Francis King's *Act of Darkness* (1983), the rape in Paul Scott's *The Raj Quartet* (1966–75) (itself a throwback to *A Passage to India*). Throughout, one can observe a painstaking deconstruction of attractive and longstanding myths: the superiority of 'English civilisation', benign colonialism, Ireland the beautiful mother, native regret of imperialist retreat – a deconstruction made all the more powerful by its allusions to earlier literary justifications of the imperial ethic. No post-war novel about India, it seems fair to say, can function without its obligatory and disparaging nod towards Kipling. Ultimately there remains only the sense of a loss of shared history – the thought that the past is both readily explicable and collective – and a forfeiture of confidence in the scrupulous conduct of public life: bare, arid landscapes stalked not by heroes but by the flawed and duplicitous. A touchstone of the post-war historical novelist's interest in this sort of moral ambiguity can be found in the obsession with Kim Philby and his conversion into a metaphor by which to dramatise increasingly uncertain concepts of 'patriotism', 'loyalty' and 'the national interest'.

As a theory, this is highly seductive. There are any number of modern novels which seem to bear it out. William Boyd's *An Ice-cream War* (1982) examines the events of 1914–18 not from the vantage point of Passchendaele, but through the clouded lens of colonial East Africa. In Carr's *A Season in Sinji*, World War Two increasingly retreats to the edge of the stage, leaving the centre clear for an examination of personal rivalry. Iris Murdoch's novel about the Easter Rising of 1916, *The Red and the Green* (1965), which Scanlan subjects to an exhaustive analysis, has a similarly oblique focus. Here the historical relationships between England and Ireland are reflected in the relationships between members of the Anglo-Irish family to which the major characters belong; the literary allusions – Yeats, Joyce and others – come thick and fast;

and the novel's conclusion suggests that motives for political action are inseparable from individual psychology, that the impact of a political crisis is largely personal, that there is in the last resort no communal grasp of an historical event. *Troubles* falls into a similar category: an anatomy of conflict is achieved by way of allegory. Most obviously, there is the story of the hotel's cats. In early sections of the novel numerous dogs are seen milling around the outbuildings, whose British names and hunting skills clearly invite the reader to associate them with the Ascendancy. Subsequently, however, they are put to flight by a gang of cats. The leader is a ferocious orange female with 'bitter green eyes' – Mother Ireland, in other words, exacting her revenge for centuries of suppression.

The Red and the Green and *Troubles* are complex, difficult novels, whose allusions are not always easy to unravel – just the sort of books, one might say, to lend themselves to high-powered critical analysis. But the type of diminishment or 'de-centring' which Scanlan detects in Iris Murdoch's densely figurative pages can be found in many a more popular and less self-conscious work. For example, a novel such as John Masters's *Bhowani Junction*, published in 1954 and set in an Indian town on the Bombay-Delhi rail link in the year before Independence. Unusually, the conflict between Indian nationalism and British colonialism is seen from a vantage point somewhere between them. Masters's principal characters – Patrick Taylor, the traffic department officer, Victoria Jones, the engine-driver's daughter – are Anglo-Indian, Eurasian half-castes whose lives are lived out in a dreadful sub-world of keeping up appearances and despising the 'natives'. Perhaps the strongest theme to emerge from Masters's novel is the sheer horror of having to live halfway between an oppressed community and the people who are doing the oppressing: hated by the English, the Eurasians are of course held in even greater contempt by the native population. Anglo-Indian society, here carefully outlined by an old India hand, is revealed as a ghastly parody of 'Home', parents referred to as 'Pater and Mater', the house reeking of roast lamb (Mrs Jones, being three-quarters Indian, is not allowed into the kitchen as she knows only native dishes). Lurking beneath the fiction of 'Englishness' and the struggle to maintain prestige – 'When we are on our jobs we are real men, as good as any

Englishman,' Patrick proclaims – is a dreadful consciousness of their true position: 'We didn't look like English people. We looked like what we were. Anglo-Indian, Eurasian, cheechee, half-caste, eight-anna, blacky-white.'

Stuck in this unenviable no-man's-land between governor and governed – characteristically, the Eurasians occupy subordinate positions in the colonial hierarchy – Patrick and Victoria are consequently placed at an oblique angle to the novel's activity, a ferment of local nationalist feeling whose severity is such as to require a military presence. The English, represented by Colonel Savage and Lieutenant Macaulay, arouse conflicting emotions. Old Mr Jones, enraptured by a social visit, considers the Colonel to be a 'real English gentleman'. Victoria finds him brutal, boorish, devious and careless of the sensibilities of the populace over whom he has authority (when nationalist protestors lie down on the railway line, Savage's response is to have his Gurkha soldiers urinate on them). Patrick is caught in the dilemma of needing to respect the upholders of law and order while fearing their designs on Victoria. Matters come to a head when Lieutenant Macaulay attempts, unsuccessfully, to rape Victoria. For the girl this is an event of huge personal significance. Previously she has 'always admired the English, like the rest of us, pretended to be more English than I am'. Macaulay's clumsy assault 'broke that chain. I was free.' Subsequently she realises that Colonel Savage, with his studied English mannerisms and his contempt for the environment in which he finds himself, 'was pulling me farther away – from the English, from Patrick, from all the stagnation of the past'. When Macaulay is unwise enough to make a second rape attempt in a deserted railway siding, she stabs him to death and conceals the body with the help of nationalist friends. The Rubicon is crossed. Later she abandons Western dress for the sari, moves in nationalist circles and decisively rejects Patrick by taking up with an Indian boyfriend.

Victoria's quarrel with the English centres less on the round of petty humiliations to which she is intermittently subjected than on her realisation that through them she has lost her identity. Even her name, after all, symbolises imperial power. Considering her upbringing, environment and uncertain destiny, she reflects that, 'this I could have loved: this the English have spoiled for me; sneering at me, they have brought me up to sneer at myself'. Later Victoria attempts to establish a position in a more significant historical context:

> Perhaps no one but a Jew could understand what it was like to be my sort of Anglo-Indian, and not even a Jew could really know, because the Jews are there in the history books before the English.

This is one of a number of passages which hammer home the novel's theme. To balance this heavy-handedness Masters supplies a careful framework of literary and historical allusions (naming the English lieutenant 'Macaulay' is perhaps the most notable), and the neatly laid out imperial past provides a sharp context for this deviation from the paths of heritage.

At other times, though, the whole deconstruction/decentring process – the rending apart, for example, of imperial superiority – can seem much less clear-cut, the rabbit drawn out of the hat a rather familiar animal pulled from other hats long before Derrida. To say of *The Red and the Green* that it demonstrates the inseparability of political and psychological motive, and shows that the impact of a political crisis is largely personal, is unexceptionable, but could not the same be said of *A Tale of Two Cities* or *Barnaby Rudge*? Again, there are plenty of right-wing, One Nation novels about India; an example might be Simon Raven's *Sound the Retreat* (1973), in which an acknowledgement of imperial deviousness when the going gets tough mingles with a clear implication that India without the British will be a mess and that no Indian with any intelligence imagines otherwise. It is easy, too, to talk of the subversion of agreeable but unsustainable myths, but equally easy to argue that the truly agreeable myth of the post-war era is that of the wicked colonial oppressor. Even a socialist, I suspect, would have difficulty in denying that a great deal of what passes for Third World history is simple guilt transference.

Amid these well-meaning attempts to redress the imbalances of history, it can be argued that the really subversive novels come from the Right – books which seek to deflate an anti-colonial myth rather than to discredit further a supposedly threadbare imperialism. Here left-wing assumptions of the moral worth of subject nations are gleefully overturned, the 'freedom fighter' becomes an opportunistic thug and 'national self-determination' a swindle practised in the name of a handful of native autocrats. A good example would be Raven's *The Judas Boy* (1968), in which Fielding Gray, retired from the army after losing an eye in the Cyprus disturbances, is sent back to the island by a sympathetic television producer with instructions to prove that its inhabitants are not ' "the sturdy freedom lovers of liberal legend, but just a pack of cruel and treacherous bastards" '.

There is also the habit of what looks at the outset to be a deflation and diminishment of imperialist pretension to transform itself imperceptibly into something a great deal friendlier. John Masters, for example, in addition to *Bhowani Junction*, wrote a series of extremely conventional novels about the First World War. Something of this transformation emerges from a study of George Macdonald Fraser's Flashman novels, historical re-creations written at a lower level than, say, those of J. G. Farrell, but equally capable of being read as exposés of the imperialist sham. The Flashman books follow an invariable pattern. Their hero, formerly the villain of Thomas Hughes's classic Victorian morality tale *Tom Brown's Schooldays*, now an officer in the British army and a very nasty piece of work indeed, has a habit of turning up at the centre of key events in Victorian history. He fights in the First Afghan War, and is present at Balaclava. The Indian Mutiny (*Flashman in the Great Game*, 1975) finds him working as an undercover agent. He serves in the Chinese campaign of the early 1860s (*Flashman and the Dragon*, 1985). In each of these passages Flashman behaves with maximum discredit, saves his skin with appalling displays of cowardice, and yet – this is the novels' running joke – takes advantage of enormous strokes of good fortune to emerge as a hero. In passing he manages to let innumerable cats out of the imperialist bag: the Crimea campaign, to take only one episode that was to print itself indelibly on the Victorian consciousness, is treated as an ignoble fiasco, characterised by criminal mismanagement and military incompetence.

On the face of it no irony is left unexplored: there are even scenes in which Flashman encounters the boys he knew at Rugby – Tom Brown and East – and derides them as fools and hypocrites. But somehow the atmosphere, from the point of view of those exercised by imperial 'myth', is never quite satisfactory. Set Flashman down in the midst of the Indian Mutiny, show him the brutality practised by insurgents on defenceless women and children, and he is suddenly clamouring for revenge. Introduce him to any situation involving the French and he will outdo Thackeray in his contempt. His sketches of Victorian generals and imperial trailblazers (with the notable exception of Cardigan, who bears him a grudge and lusts after his wife) are a shade more approving than they should be. Flashman's verdict on the triumphalist pageant of which he is a part might be that it was a dirty, hypocritical business – but if we hadn't got there first, somebody else would have bullied the natives with equal vigour.

As an exposure of British hypocrisy, the Flashman books are fatally flawed – and aesthetically satisfying, it must be said, for the same reason. No doubt this is a way of saying that theories of decentring and deconstruction seem much more attractive when applied to individual books rather than affixed to whole swathes of literature. Still more suspect, perhaps, is the critical high ground which books of this sort occupy. One of the most widely advertised themes of Ms Scanlan's work is her assumption that the boundaries between fact and fiction are ceasing to exist. Taking her cue from Derrida – 'il n'y a pas de hors texte' (which might be translated as 'there is no such thing as objectivity') – she suggests that:

> Every written history must to some extent reconstruct the always absent past, and the most sophisticated historian's hypothesis about if and in what sense Minoan culture was matriarchal differs in degree, but not in kind, from a fictional hypothesis, accompanied by imagined characters and invented dialogue, that we might find in a novel by Mary Renault.

At the very least this ignores some powerful distinctions between history and fiction which would be immediately apparent to a professional historian and an historical novelist, if not to a

Yale-reared literary critic. The message of the Flashman novels, for example – fantasies, perhaps, but supported by the most rigorous footnotes – is that there is such a thing as historical evidence, and both historians and novelists ignore it at their peril. Oddly, one emerges from the Flashman books, which might be described as the adventures of an unreal man in a real world, believing very strongly in them both. But this sort of assertion is all of a piece with the lurking ulterior motive. Like many another study of its kind, *Traces of Another Time* contains routine references to 'our greatly diminished sense of the importance of western culture in the world'. There must be a very large number of cultural commentators – and ordinary people – to whom this diminishment has not yet become apparent. Even in the narrower field of literature, to talk of 'a diminished sense of the importance of western culture' has its dangers. The Egyptian novelist Naguib Mahfouz might be the first Arab to win the Nobel Prize for Literature, but the *Cairo Trilogy*'s (1956–7) influences start with Galsworthy. Deconstruction might make a useful tool with which to excavate post-imperial guilt in a handful of modernist historical novels, but the English novel's view of the English past is a complex one, containing several questions of national self-awareness which works like *Traces of Another Time* are signally unable to answer.

There is another type of 'Englishness' on display in the novels of the immediately post-war era, unobtrusive perhaps, yet as important as the fussy, socially judgemental side of English life. Orwell remarks that one of the more attractive features of English life is our habit of not killing each other. A marked feature of the English novel of the 1950s and 1960s – a few brutal dystopias excepted – is its gentleness. The braggart, sub-Hemingway novel of male posturing, in which the hero's ability to hand out socks on the jaw at a second's notice is somehow a sign of moral worth, simply has no equivalent here. When at the tail-end of the 1950s transatlantic publishers began to produce 'Angry Decade' anthologies, juxtaposing for example the work of Amis and Wain with 'tough' American writers such as Kerouac and Nelson Algren, the effect was notably incongruous: compared to Algren's *A Walk on the Wild Side* (1956), *Lucky Jim* seems a model of sweet reasonableness and gentle comedy. A belief in 'decency', 'live and let live' – virtues that are typically ignored by the jump-on-his-testicles type of urban US practitioner – shines through the 1950s English social panorama, for all the occasional frigidity of the social attitudes that are on display. One of the agreeable characteristics of the 'People's War' novel, however unalluring the reader may find its prognoses of a world of 'socialism and engineering', is a belief in the existence of a communal spirit, a commitment to the values of a calm, national life lived out at factory gates, in back kitchens or on village greens, far away from 'politics' or pressing national issues. This tradition survives deep into the 1950s. The working-class sections of *Hurry On Down*, in which Lumley pays court to Rosa, whom he has met while working as a hospital porter, are sentimentalised, but they testify to Wain's belief in the natural decency of ordinary people, adrift on a slow, unhurried current of English life that will persist whatever the manoeuvrings of the politicians.

This is a very Orwellian sentiment, of course – Orwell's influence on the Wain/Amis/Larkin group of writers was substantial – that cannot be allowed to stand without occasional qualification. In contrast, a novel like Sillitoe's *Saturday Night and Sunday Morning* (1958) implies that the fundamental decency of ordinary people is dependent on full wage packets. But lowered national morale is capable of existing side by side with a residual patriotism made all the more powerful by a sense of how near England has come to desecration. Amis's story 'I Spy Strangers' (1962), to take an obvious framing of national attitudes in time of crisis, is remarkable for the confidence with which representatives from both political camps face the future. Archer's hope for a world 'full of girls and drinks and jazz and decent houses and decent jobs and being your own boss' is predictable enough, but even Major Raleigh, massively discountenanced by the Labour election victory, nurtures a belief that all will be well:

Much of what he believed in would survive, and the guarantee of that was England. England had been up against it in 1940, in 1914 and no doubt earlier, with the Napoleon business and so on. She had weathered every storm, she had never gone under.

All that was needed was faith. Despite everything that Hargreaves and Archer and the rest of them might do, England would muddle through somehow.

Laura Marshall's feelings at the close of *One Fine Day* (1947) are similarly thankful and optimistic. 'She had had to lose a dog and climb a hill, a year later, to realise what it would have meant if England had lost.'

Together with this confidence survives a lingering belief in English capability, the English capacity to act in pursuit of some common good, of particular significance when compared to representatives of other countries. Le Carré in *A Small Town in Germany* (1967) can still contrast British decencies with the doubtful qualities of a restored European democracy. The American critic James Gindin has drawn attention to what he defines as the 'qualified nationalism' of Angus Wilson's early novels. The 'limited and perceptive rationality' displayed by the heroes of Wilson's work is a peculiarly British virtue. While this tendency never manifests itself in outright flag-waving, the man of intelligence and responsibility who finds himself exercising some control over the bestial and chaotic is, like Gerald Middleton in *Anglo-Saxon Attitudes* (1956) or Bernard Sands in *Hemlock and After*, invariably British. This theme reaches its apogee in Wilson's fable *The Old Men at the Zoo* (1961), an allegory of a future England realised in the successive administrations governing London Zoo. Sir Bobby Falcon's British Day party may be outmoded and faintly ludicrous, but it is infinitely preferable to the sinister (and foreign) Uni-European movement, and it is left to another Englishman, Simon Carter, to take the symbolic step of resistance. To say that one 'believes' in one's country is perhaps not worth a very great deal, but the conviction remains that a society which can produce such men as Carter and Middleton is, despite its obvious injustices and hypocrisies, more or less a fair one. The governments which plot England's shaky post-war course may be unprincipled and opportunistic, but they are not *obviously* corrupt. They may prostitute themselves in search of votes, but there is at least the consolation that they cannot be bought and sold over the counter. One remembers Orwell's comment about the hanging judge:

That evil old man in scarlet robe and horsehair wig, whom nothing short of dynamite will ever teach what century he is living in, but who will at any rate interpret the law according to the book and will in no circumstances take a money bribe, is one of the symbolic figures of England.

'Decency' and 'live and let live' are vague, talismanic phrases, but the outrage that English novelists were subsequently to express when it seemed that they might be in danger goes very deep. If nothing else, it is one of the distinguishing marks of the post-war English novel.

3

Cross-currents of the 1950s

The 1950s had no Angela Thirkell to chart the shift in its political alignment. Miss Thirkell hung on, of course, like some aged Sibyl, but her days as a political barometer were behind her. Perhaps it was simply that political pressure-gauging no longer seemed a relevant accomplishment for a novelist. The assumption of political consensus, which led quickly to the coining of the expression 'Butskellism' to describe the continuities between Hugh Gaitskell, the outgoing Labour Chancellor, and his Tory successor in 1951, R. A. Butler, was something of a joke at the time, more likely to provoke gentle satire than serious political analysis. Edward Hyams's *Gentian Violet* (1953), for example, one of the few political novels of the period, is a skit on the idea of a system in which opposing parties possess indistinguishable views; its hero, James Blundell, is a working-class man with a distinguished war record who contrives to be elected to Parliament simultaneously as a Conservative member for a rural constituency and as a Labour member for a working class area.

There were several youngish Conservative MPs in the House of Commons of the early 1950s whose career bore some relation to Blundell's meritocratic progress – Edward Heath, for instance. But the appearance of a grocer's son in the Whips' office did not mean that any profound change could be glimpsed in the composition of the parliamentary Conservative party. Still less did it imply that future conflict between the major parties would be a matter of principle edging out social class. Class divisions between the two parties had never been clear-cut, and the relatively exalted social background of certain Labour leaders was a byword.

If the Conservatives had their Heaths, Labour's upper-middle-class hierarchy still had the party firmly within its grasp. If anything Hugh Gaitskell (Winchester and New College), who succeeded to the leadership in 1955, was more reassuring to the floating Home Counties voter than Major Attlee (Haileybury and Univ.). Bevan and the 'Keep Left' group might make an occasional disturbance, but theirs was the conventional language of left-wing Labour protest: noisy, peripheral, frowned on by the leadership and unlikely to do lasting damage.

'Consensus' is perhaps too emollient a term for a period which saw its share of political in-fighting, but the reluctance of the incoming Conservative government of 1951 to tamper with Labour Trade Union law, the National Health Service and many of the nationalisation statutes was marked, and it would be foolish simply to ascribe this to political expediency. If we set the Suez crisis of 1956 down as the salient issue that divided British society in the immediately post-war period, we do so in the knowledge that Suez was assimilated into the national consciousness with rather startling ease; scarcely an issue by the time of the 1959 General Election and, as Labour leaders privately conceded, warmly approved of by most working-class Labour voters.

For all that, the 1950s inspired lasting confusion over the national role and the national identity, the first stirrings of a deep-seated unease that by the 1960s had developed into a full-blown neurosis. Amid all the talk of affluent societies, signs of national decay were not hard to detect. At bottom the 1950s were the years in which Britain was decisively worsted by its economic competitors. By 1955 West Germany had overtaken the UK as an exporter of vehicles. A year later Japan became the world's leading shipbuilder. These were harsh lessons for a country whose industrial reputation had been founded on heavy industry. Economic failings, quite as much as the political retreats over Europe, the Commonwealth and the Middle East, seemed to stem not from having been dealt the wrong cards, but from an engrained inability to face up to changing prospects.

Evelyn Shuckburgh, Eden's private secretary, attempted to quantify this attitude:

All those people who were the bosses in the Second World War found it impossible to believe that we didn't still have great influence . . . There had been so much of this going about as top people, deciding everything for the world.

The unreasonable expectations of the staff officer who returned to England to manage an industrial concern were reflected at the very highest level. For all his massive symbolic authority and his permanent seat at the councils of the great powers, Churchill carried no real weight. Moreover, Britain's attempts to secure influence nearer home were always likely to be compromised by an awareness of where its true interests lay. British entry into the European Economic Community was delayed for a generation, merely because De Gaulle had realised at an early stage in the negotiations that in any crisis Britain would always put the United States first. The gulf between public portrayals of Britain's supposed international status and private acknowledgements of what this status consisted is revealed in a document written for Churchill by his foreign secretary Eden in 1952: 'The more gradually and inconspicuously we can transfer the real burden from our own to American shoulders, the less damage we shall do to our position and influence in the world.'

But the damage was already done. To confusion about Britain's political destiny could be added uncertainty over personal status. The mid–1950s brought a general lightening of the post-war gloom: an end to rationing, the wider availability of consumer goods. While relative affluence was welcome to an older generation with grim memories of the 1930s, it did not obscure a widespread anxiety over the position of the individual in this new society. The degree to which 'class' had survived the war and taken on new guises and gradations to assimilate itself to the peace remained a topic of absorbing public interest.

A Mass Observation survey of 1949 sheds a revealing light on what could fairly be described as a national obsession. The professional women and housewives who constituted one of its main sampling groups disclosed simultaneously the great importance they ascribed to being able to 'place' themselves accurately in class terms, and the very different criteria by which that placing was achieved. Thus one woman, a civil servant, defines herself as 'middle class' on grounds of job, education and parentage. A second plumps for 'upper-middle-class' for financial reasons – she and her husband live on the income from investments – but also on grounds of 'culture': 'We know what is correct wear even though we may have to do with old clothes.' A third woman, the wife of a production manager in an engineering firm, locates her husband and herself in the lower middle class for the reason that education has separated them from the working-class people with whom they would otherwise have felt an affinity by furnishing them with superior taste. A fourth describes her family's status as 'professional' because 'our threadbare conditions seem at variance with the comfortable plumpness one associates with the term middle-class.'

Heritage? Attitude? Money? Education? Professional standing? Nobody seemed sure which of these elements contributed, and in what proportion, to one's class status. At the same time there was widespread agreement that most people fitted into one or other of the accepted social divisions suggested by sociologists and the compilers of surveys. In a 1948 opinion poll, for example, only 5 per cent of respondents were unwilling to insert themselves into one of the five categories on offer. These anxieties, and the wider unease that played a part in conceiving them, ran very deep. Both are reflected in the novels of the time.

To say that the fiction of the 1950s reflects some pressing post-war anxieties might seem a glib correlation. If so, it is a little less glib than many estimates of the relationship between life and literature made at the time. More so than the decades which had preceded them, the 1950s were a time when novels were thought accurately to reflect the social microcosm. A good deal of inferior social criticism proceeded from the assumption that the novel possessed a documentary value, sometimes to the exclusion of all other values. The mania for literary groupings – the Angry Young Men, the Movement, even tiny, fanciful offshoots such as the Beets – abetted what seemed at the time to be a straightforward equation. If one could define a group of writers with similar backgrounds, ambitions and beliefs then surely it was not unreasonable to expect those details to be reflected in their published work?

The effect of this type of attitude on middlebrow literary critics was alarming. In the past the heroes of novels had survived, prospered and obtained some hold on the popular consciousness by dint of their singularity; now it seemed they had to do so by dint of their ordinariness. This led to some highly questionable assumptions being made about characters from the major novels of the period. Jim Dixon, according to George Scott, was 'like hundreds and thousands of young men of the post-war world' – and Jim Dixon is a university don! But novelists, quite as much as their creations, were thought to repose in a common socio-intellectual stratum. 'Walker belonged, after all, to a generation of literary men all of whom, thanks to a common educational system and a common social experience, had exactly the same heads, buzzing with exactly the same thoughts,' runs a description of the protagonist of *Stepping Westward* (1965). Bradbury is joking, but other commentators were less sure. In fact, as Harry Ritchie has demonstrated in his persuasive study *Success Stories* (1988), conventional accounts of the period relied on extremely simplistic accounts of the relationship between fiction and reality; the publicity that surrounded the Angry Young Men did more to create the reality that the Angry Young Men were supposed to be reflecting than Amis and Wain themselves.

Publicity did more than impart phantom coherence to groups of writers whose members were in some cases scarcely aware of each other's existence. By focusing on a handful of texts – *Lucky Jim* (1954), *Hurry on Down* (1953), *Billy Liar* (1959) – and a handful of names, it both established a canon and effectively excluded large numbers of novels from critical consideration merely because they failed to conform to the prevailing orthodoxy. The novels of John Lodwick, for example, were highly regarded in their day – his admirers included Somerset Maugham and Anthony Powell – but their doomy romanticism sat queerly alongside the comic realism of an Amis or a Waterhouse: Lodwick's reputation did not survive the 1960s.

Like the 1930s, a decade which Evelyn Waugh alleged had been 'captured' by Spender, Auden and MacNeice, the 1950s seem in retrospect a time of cliques and subterfuges, inflated reputations, a media concentration on literature whose motives were not always literary. The need to categorise, together with the urge to fit works of the imagination into an over-narrow social theory, led to some pervasive myths. In Byatt's *Still Life* (1985), for instance, Frederica reads *Lucky Jim* on several occasions, progressively more mesmerised by the intellectual chatter that encircles it. By the time of the third reading, circa 1956, she is 'able knowledgeably to place Jim's antics as part of what was known as the "limited revolt of the intellectuals against the welfare state" '. Byatt, of course, would not believe this for a moment: she is merely being historically accurate, recording what a girl like Frederica (and presumably her own younger self) would have thought about Amis three decades before. To be fair, 'limited revolt of the intellectuals against the welfare state' is a resonant enough phrase, and no doubt some sociologists would still apply it to *Lucky Jim* with enthusiasm. All the same, it is rather like saying that *Little Dorrit* is a parable of an advanced society fatally compromised by a laggardly bureaucracy.

Little wonder then that Angus Wilson should complain that Jim Dixon was the victim of 'sociological gossip'. The revelation of their sociological importance and their status as a kind of social litmus paper came as a surprise to the majority of novelists caught within the columnists' nets. There are some good jokes in Bradbury's *Eating People is Wrong* (1959) at the expense of Carey Willoughby, an archetypal Angry Young Man supposedly modelled on John Wain, who turns up to lecture at a provincial university. Though appreciative of his success, Willoughby is mystified by its origins, particularly by the assumption that he represents some common and clearly defined thread of experience and opinion: 'he had thought himself a perfectly detached observer of the modern scene'. One can sympathise with Willoughby's resentment of this wilful misrepresentation, still more with the resentment of actual novelists who found their positions called into question in this way – Iris Murdoch, for example, marked down as an honorary Angry Young Man on the strength of *Under the Net* (1954) – but for all that, the documentary quality of many 1950s novels is undeniable. Large stretches of C. P. Snow's *Strangers and Brothers* sequence (1940–70) read very much like a sociological treatise, meticulous in its use of social detail, happy to promote milieu at the expense of character. Much of the humour in Bradbury's early novels derives from the author's amusement at the blanket literary categorisations of the time, but Bradbury who re-examined *Eating People is Wrong* on the occasion of its reissue two decades later was in no doubt that what he had written was, substantially, a report on the new England of the Welfare State.

There is also the fact that the similarities between a number of the major 1950s novels are a little too obvious to be explained away by nods towards comic convention. The narrator of Hilary Finch's *Felix Walking* (1958) characterises what he imagines to be the fashionable new fictional hero as 'an Angry Young Man with a provincial University degree, and nothing but obstinacy, low comedy and a sense of decency to face the world with'. This might be a gross exaggeration, but it does not invalidate the link between the heroes of early novels by Kingsley Amis, John Wain and Keith Waterhouse. The constraints of environment are such that each of the three protagonists, Jim Dixon, Charles Lumley and Billy Fisher, inhabits a sort of brightly coloured fantasy world in which the humdrum is rendered more pleasurable by a persistent under-current of invention. Dixon makes pseudonymous telephone calls and then devises plausible explanations of his innocence. We first see Charles Lumley on the steps of his lodgings, trying to persuade his landlady that he is a private detective. Billy Fisher's shaky progress through life is constantly impeded by falsehoods and evasions, most memorably the invention of non-existent relatives and his simultaneous engagement to two separate girls, neither of whom is aware of the other's existence. The circumstances of Billy's downfall, which occurs when the chain of deceit finally spirals out of control, are not unlike the accumulation of past transgressions that eventually topples down on to Dixon.

Inevitably, definition emerges out of negatives. Looking back, it is perhaps easier to demonstrate what the fiction of the 1950s was not. A common adjective of the time, for example, was 'provincial'. In retrospect this looks just as dubious as 'academic'. Undoubtedly William Cooper's *Scenes from Provincial Life* (1950) was an influence on the Amis–Wain generation – on hearing broadcast extracts from *Lucky Jim*, Cooper was immediately struck by the similarities in tone and approach – but Cooper's next novel, its publication prevented for many years by the libel lawyers, was entitled *Scenes from Metropolitan Life* (1982). While the early novels of Amis, Wain and Waterhouse have a provincial setting, London is invariably the protagonist's target; any anti-metropolitan bias is correspondingly faint. *Lucky Jim* has barely concluded its second chapter before Jim is contemplating 'packing a few clothes and catching the ten-forty for London'; it ends with him drooling over London place names, having secured a job in the capital. Charles Lumley ends up as a London-based writer of radio comedy scripts. *Billy Liar* is stuffed with visions of the hero 'coughing my way through the fog to the Odd Man Out Club, Chelsea, with its chess tables and friendly, intelligent girls'. London, then, is not somewhere to be avoided, but a potent lure, an escape hatch from provincial inertia, a source of better jobs and romantic involvement, 'full of good stuff' as Garnett Bowen in Amis's third novel, *I Like It Here* (1958), maintains.

Quite as suspect as this presumed dislike of London are two other common assumptions of the time: that the characteristic 1950s novel was both politically committed and class-based. Such evidence of political commitment as exists in Amis and Wain's fiction is extremely limited. Jim enjoys a brisk exchange of views with Bertrand Welch over the redistribution of income (' "If one man's got ten buns and another's got two, and a bun has got to be given up by one of them, then surely you take it from the man with ten buns?" '); Lumley at one point gets thrown out of a party for expressing 'red notions', but these are largely gestural devices, designed to offend individuals whom Dixon and Lumley dislike rather than to express a distinctive political viewpoint. Similarly, while Amis, Wain and Waterhouse's work displays a strong awareness of class – something it could scarcely avoid doing – suggestions of class conflict are rarely advanced. Dixon may be uncomfortably aware that his punctilious student, Michie, is his social superior, but the animosity between himself and the Welches has no grounding in class. The superiority which Billy Fisher feels towards his hapless fiancée, Rita, is expressed in class terms, notably by mockery of her accent. Lumley is conscious that greater educational opportunities are changing social patterns. At the same time he observes some of the cross-generational unease that this instils: for example, he despises his former fellow undergraduate Hutchins for the embarrassment the latter feels about his working-class parents. However, Lumley is not up to showing solidarity: meeting Mr and Mrs Hutchins unexpectedly on a train, he eventually takes refuge in the lavatory. Unusually for a 1950s hero, Lumley makes a polemical statement about class, when he informs another university acquaintance that his education ' "didn't leave me with any illusions about the division of human beings into cricket teams called classes" ', but this too is done largely to differentiate himself from people he despises. Lumley's general attitude to class is that of a neutral observer: he wishes to detach himself from the system rather than to combat or rearrange it.

If there is a clue to the genuine relationship between the fiction of the Cooper/Wain/Amis school, it lies in the distinctive literary context in which the books are framed. Almost without exception their tone is anti-modernist, self-consciously opposed to the 'serious' fiction of the pre-war era, its characters and the attitudes they espoused. Undoubtedly many of the writers of the immediately post-war era considered that modernism, here defined as the obfuscations of Woolf and Joyce, the 'highbrow' and 'committed' literature of the 1920s and 1930s, had had a wholly negative effect on the novel, destroying its accessibility and interest to the ordinary intelligent reader. William Cooper has said that after the war he and C. P. Snow had made a conscious decision to 'run modernism out of town'. *Lucky Jim* is crammed with anti-highbrowisms, digs against a powerful literary establishment which was presumed to have set itself up as an elitist cultural arbiter. 'No, not Bloomsbury,' Dixon decides in an early edition of *Lucky Jim* (later versions have 'Chelsea') as he runs through a list of London districts in which it might be appropriate for him to reside. On the novel's final page Professor Welch and his son are said to resemble 'Gide and Lytton Strachey represented in waxwork form by a prentice hand'. The strongest declaration of intent, though, comes from Wain, in a scene where Lumley – deliberately mocking the actions of a bygone generation of literary heroes – stands on a bridge watching the river flow beneath him. Here he reflects on:

all the expensive young men of the thirties who had made, or
wished to make, or talked of making, a gesture somewhat similar
to his own, turning their backs on the society that had pampered
them, and how they had all failed from the start because their
rejection was moved by the desire to enter, and be at one with,
a vaguely conceived People, whose minds and lives they could
not even begin to imagine, and who would in any case, had
they ever arrived, have made their lives hell. At least, Charles
thought with a sense of self-congratulation, he had always been
right about *them*, right to despise them for their idiotic attempts
to look through two telescopes at the same time: one fashioned
of German psychology and pointed at themselves, the other of
Russian economics and directed at the English working class. A
fundamental sense of what life really consisted of had saved him
at any rate from such fatuities.

This is more than a touch complacent. After all, how can Lumley
be so certain the he possesses 'a fundamental sense of what life
really consisted of'? Yet it strikes a note of genuine anger. Freud,
Marx, 'commitment' – most of the key 1930s icons are here, and
the shades of Connolly, Auden and Isherwood lurk in the middle
distance. Kingsley Amis's literary journalism of the period has a
similarly hostile tone. Reviewing Anthony Powell's *The Acceptance World* (1955), he welcomes the fact that Powell is not 'committed', except to an interest in human behaviour 'and to the duty
of irony and scepticism which confronts every chronicler of an
exclusive group'. A glance at some contemporary talents 'committed' in other directions would not show, Amis suggests, that
Powell had chosen wrongly. The 1950s 'rebellion' consequently
took the form of a deliberate literary opposition – several of its
exponents were university teachers – put to work in a relatively
downmarket cultural and social context. It was this characteristic
that so appalled contemporary observers from the older literary
generation, convinced that they were witnessing an assault on the
throne-rooms of culture. The heroes of *Lucky Jim*, *Hurry On
Down*, *Room at the Top* (1957) and *Billy Liar* are aggressively
'normal'. They have mundane jobs. Jim Dixon's academic appointment carries a certain amount of prestige, but it is a temporary

post and the university is clearly undistinguished. Lumley drifts from window cleaner to drug courier to hospital orderly. Billy Fisher works in a funeral parlour. At the same time their tastes and habits are profoundly ordinary. They drink beer rather than wine or spirits, are suspicious less of 'culture' than of the people who practise it, an attitude that verges on the disingenuous. Dixon, in particular, is much more culturally accomplished than he cares to admit – he claims to be able to read music 'after a fashion' – and frequently has to disguise his knowledge in a manner that can look simply Philistine.

Gesture, in a novel such as *Lucky Jim* or *That Uncertain Feeling* (1955) is all. Each of Amis's early protagonists votes Labour, but they do so largely to annoy the people with whom they are forced to associate. One looks for 'commitment' and finds only a desire – generally quite a reasonable desire – to settle a personal score. Even the working-class scenes in *Hurry On Down*, which are written with genuine interest and appreciation, fall a long way short of demonstrating the solidarity that a writer of an earlier or later generation might have favoured: they are simply a rather mystical form of prole worship, couched in vaguely anthropological terms, whose origins can be detected in the early writings of George Orwell. Wain's working-class scenes are interesting, in that they hint at a type of romanticism mostly absent from novels of this sort, but they are far from typical. In general Amis, Wain and Co. are determinedly anti-romantic. Dixon's intense concern with the pints, fags and hangover side of male life distressed many a contemporary reviewer. Billy Fisher amuses himself by mocking a journalist who under the pseudonym 'Man o' the Dales' composes self-satisfied eulogies of the local landscape and its amenities for the *Stradhoughton Echo*. 'I had a fairly passionate set-piece all worked out on the subject of rugged Yorkshire towns,' Billy reflects, 'with their rugged neon signs and their rugged plate glass and plastic fronts.' In contrast to the guardians of local civic pride, Billy knows that his home town is simply a dump.

Not only did many writers of the period frame their novels in a deliberately literary context; they performed the same service for the hero. Like the concentration on 'ordinariness', whether expressed in a preference for beer or heterosexuality, this too was a reversion, a return to the nineteenth-century fictional theme of the young man making his way through society. The majority of Victorian writers had ascribed individual human progress to a combination of nature and nurture. On the one hand they assumed that the social environment played a large part in conditioning the attitudes and responses of their characters. On the other, they were careful not to exclude the possibility of the heroic individual, the man whose ability, virtue and intelligence set him apart from his contemporaries and who is consequently not constrained by milieu. It is this quality that renders David Copperfield, Pip and Martin Chuzzlewit 'heroes' in the conventional sense. We know that on one level they are very ordinary young men, using not terribly conspicuous talents to progress through a world whose social barriers are a great deal less solid than they once were, but we also appreciate their singularity, their 'otherness' from the tribe of Heeps, Magwitches and Pecksniffs to the point where they seem creatures of infinite resource. This heroic quality is not, it should be stressed, always synonymous with traditional notions of 'virtue'. Godwin Peak, the protagonist of Gissing's *Born in Exile* (1892), is a good example of a late-Victorian hero. Brought up in genteel poverty by his widowed mother, he resolves to succeed through strenuous hard work. By studying obsessively and denying himself a social life he secures a position as an industrial chemist, which leaves him free to nurture his most coveted ambition – marriage to a cultivated woman. On almost any level of estimation, Peak is completely intolerable. He holds all those whom he imagines intellectually inferior to himself in contempt (including members of his own family), despises the working man and is not above straightforward deception. For example, his plan to marry Sidwell Warricombe, the woman of his dreams – which fails only at the final hurdle – involves passing himself off as a Church of England ordinand. Eventually Peak's imposture is exposed, when he is revealed to be the author of an anonymous magazine article advocating free thought. Sidwell declines to marry him, although not without extensive heart searchings, and he disappears to a lonely exile's death abroad.

We may not like Peak – and Peak would not much care if we did or not – but there is still something vital about him, something heroic in the dictionary sense of the word: a man who has definite goals, who will achieve them or quite literally die in the attempt. At the same time his background is sharply outlined – the widow's house, the fevered application, the despised plebeian relatives – as is his sense of personal destiny. This allows us to form a very clear idea of who Peak is and what he might be thought to represent, even here amid the late-Victorian social flux. He is the man who has succeeded by means of his intelligence, but also through an innate belief in his personal nobility, 'one of us' to the people with whom he sits down to dinner, but simultaneously more intellectually ambitious and less socially adept.

To compare Peak with his post-war equivalents is immediately to become conscious of a precipitous decline. The 1950s hero has ambitions, he believes, to use the catchphrase title of John Braine's novel, that there is Room at the Top, but he betrays a marked lack of assurance as to what the society he is travelling through and the people who inhabit it are really like. Apart from cases in which his personal comfort is involved, he has very few opinions. Godwin Peak would offer you his views on God, Darwin and Lyell at the drop of a hat. Jim Dixon, alternatively, seems merely incurious. Nature rather than nurture has ordained his responses and decisions. Above all, he is constrained by a tremendous feeling of uncertainty. He may be more socially mobile than his forebears, but he is less sure from what and to what he is moving. Education has taken him so far, but it may not have taken him far enough. It is certainly valueless in ministering to his sense of social insecurity. Dixon, like Lumley or Braine's Joe Lampton, cares how he behaves in pubs and at parties, and, more important, how he is seen to behave. Wishing to make a good impression at the Welches' ghastly cultural weekend, he even pretends to be able to read music.

Occasionally in the 1950s novel these anxieties transform themselves into a full-blown obsession with status. Treece in Bradbury's *Eating People is Wrong* frets about the position of a professor in the humanities in a small university in the provinces. 'It could not be denied that all the forms of social stratification, once solid, were liquefying in the torrid heat engendered by reforming zealots like himself.' Frequently status attaches itself even to romantic aspiration. Dixon, for example, is attracted to Christine, but rather fears that he may have to settle for Margaret, who is much closer to his concept of the social category in which he reposes.

With uncertainty comes an awareness of social limitations. By and large Dixon, Lumley, Lampton and Fisher have little room for manoeuvre. Decisions tend to be forced upon them. This makes them opportunists. They want the best job, the best girl, and they have a habit of getting them by accident. Dixon's simultaneous pulling down of Christine and a better job is a lucky chance, rather than a reward for virtue, persistency or superiority to the competition. In fact the distinguishing mark of Dixon and the others is their lack of heroic qualities. Many contemporary observers sought to attribute to Dixon an innate 'decency', but it is surprisingly difficult, forty years later, to establish of what exactly this decency consists. Jim tells lies. He behaves badly to his girlfriend Margaret – who, granted, is a manipulative neurotic, but remains deeply insecure and vulnerable – disliking her on the arbitrary grounds of bad make-up and arty skirts. He is described as 'hating' an old lady for wearing a peculiar hat. Dixon's speciality is a sort of infantile practical joking. Adept at exposing the pretensions and limitations of the people he runs up against, Jim is also notably good at exposing his own.

The hero of the Victorian novel demonstrated his superiority over the villain by being 'better' than him, often in ways that are highly questionable to a modern sensibility. Thus David Copperfield's superiority to Heep turns on the moral point of honesty (Heep is a hypocritical swindler) as well as on the fact that David is a fine young Christian gentleman whose love for Agnes is 'pure' and romantic, whereas Heep is merely a low-bred Jew who harbours base lusts. Dixon's superiority to, say, Professor Welch is a great deal more doubtful, to the point where there is little to choose between them. He is not even Welch's professional superior: a medieval historian who scarcely knows the meaning of the word 'scholasticism' and specialised in the medieval period as an undergraduate only because it was an easy option.

Billy Fisher, the protagonist of Waterhouse's *Billy Liar*, is an even nastier piece of work, who behaves abysmally to his various girlfriends, treats his family with contempt and is indirectly responsible for his grandmother's death. Most culpable of all, perhaps, is Billy's inability to make any connection between his actions and their consequences: the thought that he might be responsible for this chain of contingency scarcely crosses his mind. One of Billy's more spectacular failings concerns a large pile of calendars which his employer, Shadrach, instructed him to dispatch some months before the novel's commencement. This Billy has omitted to do – he keeps them hidden in his bedroom and has set about destroying them in a desultory way – with the result that Shadrach warns him that he intends to investigate their non-delivery. For some reason Billy is infuriated by his employer's questions: 'I was beginning to be possessed by the inward, impotent rage. What did the man want me to do? Atone for my sins? Work for another year as penal servitude? Pay for the calendars and the nameplate? Get the goodwill back?' But surely Shadrach's complaints are quite justifiable? No one could say, as in Victorian novels about harassed clerks, that Billy is being discriminated against. All he is rebelling against is his own inadequacy.

Very few of the archetypal heroes of the 1950s can escape strictures of this sort. Cooper's Joe Lunn is selfish and predatory, interested only in his writing and having sex with his girlfriend (and under no illusions as to which is the more important of these activities); Dixon has an eye for the main chance; Billy Fisher is a spiteful and mean-spirited fantasist. The best of an indifferent bunch is Lumley in *Hurry On Down*, and even he has a tendency to retreat from situations if he doubts his ability to deal with them. Significantly, this concentration on the anti-heroic is not simply a feature of comic or quasi-comic fiction. It can also be seen, for example, in the work of as sober an analyst of contemporary life as C. P. Snow. *The New Men* (1954), set during the Second World War, finds Lewis Eliot leaving his academic job to work in government. Eliot becomes aware of the high-level work being carried out on the development of the atom bomb. This involvement is strengthened when his brother Mark joins the team, a group of scientists led by a fellow of Eliot's Cambridge college. Together they constitute the 'new men' of the title – highly intellectual and powerful individuals whose lives combine scientific and political interests. Inevitably, ethical considerations intrude as the scientists become aware of the implications of their research work. This prompts Martin to draft a letter to the press protesting at British involvement in the Hiroshima bombing. Eliot, while largely agreeing with him, persuades him not to send it, if only to preserve his career. Subsequently it becomes known that one member of the team is passing information to the Russians. Again Eliot is consulted. Again he gives advice which differs from his personal views. The imperatives which govern the career of a Whitehall scientist in the 1940s – hang on to your job, don't rock the boat – seem to prohibit displays of personal virtue.

Why is this? To compare Trollope's novels of administrative life with the Lewis Eliot sequence, written less than a century later, is to reach some inexorable conclusions about the decline of individual effort, the sense of personal integrity making a difference. One can imagine the speed with which a Trollope hero would have settled on a moral position in the Bomb debate, and the relish with which he would have stuck to it (think of Phineas Finn throwing over his career for the sake of Irish land reform). It is not, perhaps, that Snow's heroes are less principled. It is, rather, that they are aware of the consequences for individual destiny of life in an advanced society, that the forces at work even within their own limited spheres of operation are too vast to be contained by a single person, however able or persistent. In much the same way, though less conspicuously, Dixon, Lumley and Co. are constantly aware of the constraints on their ability to act, the precarious nature of their hold on any sort of individual identity. Dixon has great trouble in persuading people to remember his name: the university porter refers to him as 'Mr Jackson'; Professor Welch has a habit of confusing him with his predecessor. Lumley drifts through a series of dead-end jobs calculated to reduce him to anonymity. Billy Fisher's mundane sequestration in Stradhoughton is made tolerable only by his lurid fantasy life.

The search for personal identity which these predicaments impose is dominated by a wish to confound other people's assumptions, to take up a position that is genuinely the character's own, even if this involves rebelling against middle-class notions of status and appropriate livelihood. Lumley is infuriated when his girl-friend's brother-in-law demands to know what he proposes to 'do'. Lumley wishes only to be his own man, to live life on his own terms, the implication being that he can accomplish this feat only if he escapes the straitjacket of class. Reflecting on the vagrant, drifting existence which he subsequently pursues, Lumley decides that:

> he must form no roots in this new stratum of society, but remain independent of class, forging roots only with impersonal things such as places and seasons, or, in the other end of the scale, genuinely personal attachments that could be gently prised loose from all considerations involving more than two people.

Peter in Thomas Hinde's *Mr Nicholas* (1952) finds himself in a similar predicament. Well-meaning people keep asking him what he wants to be. 'They would not realise that he might never know, or understand that he might not want to be anything. They could not imagine a person without an occupational label.'

The constraints placed by society on individual lives, and the ability of social forces to mould individual personalities to their own design, are a feature of two very odd minor novels of the period, Nigel Dennis's *Cards of Identity* (1955) and Michael Wharton's *Sheldrake* (1958). Both might be described as parables of, or fantasies on, identity. In *Cards of Identity* three members of the 'Identity Club' arrive from London to take over an abandoned manor house in the country. Merely by asserting themselves they establish a position in the community and are able to start administering the property. They recruit local people as domestic staff, persuading them that they are other, and have always been other, than their true selves. These deceptions are accepted without protest by those on whom they are practised. As Mrs Chirk, formerly Finch, puts it: ' "If I knew my name, sir, I would feel more myself than I seem to feel." ' When asked if there is any persona with which she would be happy, Mrs Chirk replies: ' "It's all the same to me, sir. I only want to work and be at peace with the world. I don't need no name for that." ' Eventually the house becomes the venue for a full-scale meeting of the club, at which learned papers are read demonstrating the vulnerability of shell-shocked modern man.

Sheldrake takes a slightly different tack, but its theme is the same: the susceptibility of the average man to suggestions about himself and his position, and the ease with which he can be duped. Major Sheldrake, an authority on Tibet, arrives in the Northern town of 'Borewich' to deliver a lecture. Here, to his surprise, he discovers a burgeoning independent state with its own government and religion. The Major's initial bewilderment is quickly replaced by a passionate sense of affiliation. This reaches its height when he is given control of the Borewich army in its struggle with the rest of Britain. Speeding off to the front line, the Major is assailed by doubt. 'A feeling of terror and emptiness rushed through his mind. Who was he, what was he doing here?' However, despair is swiftly replaced by a mood of exultation, the sense of a vibrant personal destiny about to be fulfilled: 'Yes, he was Sheldrake, and he Sheldrake would save Borewich, that was God's will.' Mysteriously, and without apparent military activity, a victory over the British army is achieved. Sheldrake, acclaimed as a conquering hero, finds himself appointed head of state by the High Priest and head of the 'College of Prophets'. Fearing civil war, Sheldrake tries to escape by the simple expedient of walking to the station and taking the first train to London. On arrival he is informed by a porter that the London train has just left; there will never be another. In despair Sheldrake leaves the station and jumps on a tram. 'It was going to nowhere.'

Cards of Identity and *Sheldrake* are satires, and right-wing satires at that. Michael Wharton wrote the 'Peter Simple' column of the *Daily Telegraph* for forty years; Dennis was, among other journalistic appointments, a joint editor of *Encounter*. Neither, for all their obvious dislike of large areas of contemporary life, could be described as Angry Young Men or, in political terms, as much distant from prevailing Conservative orthodoxies. Each, however, reveals a profound dissatisfaction with existing social and political arrangements. This was to obtain less sophisticated expression elsewhere. The idea of the 'Establishment', a vast, self-sustaining and exclusive organism by which the country was administered, was very much a 1950s concept. Coined by the political columnist Henry Fairlie, the term had by the end of the decade begun to inspire both lightweight media analyses and more considered investigations: an early example is Hugh Thomas's symposium of 1959, which contained, among others, Simon Raven on the army, Christopher Hollis on Parliament and John Vaizey on the City. Such analyses expressed a deep-rooted uneasiness over what was seen as national inertia, a failure to modernise antiquated social institutions, a feeling that the progress of the individual was liable to be frustrated by the closed doors of caste, education or background.

An 'anti-establishment' tendency – an antiphonal term which came into vogue at the time – is detectable in the English novel from about the mid–1950s onwards. Then and more recently it was seen as a source of motivation for writers of the Amis/Wain school. David Lodge, for example, in an afterword to a new edition of his second novel *Ginger, You're Barmy*, first published in 1962, maintains that the anger of the Angry Young Men was directed at the 'slow rate of change in British society'. The old rigid class society, in which inherited privilege was unquestioned by the vast majority of the population, 'had been, or should have been, swept away by egalitarian social, economic and educational policies'. However, the revolution was proceeding at a snail's pace. Applied to the first wave of 1950s novelists, Lodge's assumption seems highly questionable. Amis and Wain are ambivalent towards 'inherited privilege' – Dixon admires Gore-Urquhart, his eventual benefactor, from the start and is delighted to accept his offer of a job. Even in *Lucky Jim* the hostility towards progressive educational policies which was later to make Amis notorious is already evident. In fact Lodge's diagnosis seems much more applicable to writers of a slightly later generation, who began their careers in the late 1950s and early 1960s.

Amid the talk about 'establishments' and the opposition to them – fuelled, it must be said, as much by the contemporary satire boom as by concerted political action – it is tempting to see Suez as a watershed. Surely no writer with even the vaguest interest in politics could fail to be moved by the fight for Nasser's canal, or be in any doubt that it symbolised the loss of Britain's ability to exercise influence over its more powerful allies, and the collapse of the Butskellite consensus? In reality novelists do not seem to have been greatly concerned by Suez. Kingsley Amis attended a

Labour party meeting on the crisis, but played down its importance, for which he was roundly rebuked by a hot young radical
named Paul Johnson. A *Times Literary Supplement* editorial of the
time lamented the fact that young writers seemed too committed to
a sceptical and empirical attitude to be roused by political causes.
Such Suez novels as exist consequently adopt wildly differing
tones. Suez in Simon Raven's *The Rich Pay Late* (1964), which
centres on the activities of a group of youngish Tory MPs, is
merely a political problem, a mess to be tidied away as quickly as
possible: ' "trouble with every Blimp in the House and in the
country. Ex-corporal Blimp as well." ' The implications for
national prestige and influence come as no surprise to anyone who
has given the matter any thought.

The straight anti-imperial line, alternatively, is advanced most
vociferously in Andrew Sinclair's *The Breaking of Bumbo* (1959).
'Bumbo' Bailey is an interesting example of the 1950s hero who
has contrived to slip across the class barrier without attaching
particular importance to his transit, a middle-class young man
from suburbia doing his National Service in a fashionable London
regiment. Accepted by his contemporaries as a sort of licensed
jester, whose defence of strikers, oppressed races and other leftish
ragtag and bobtail forms an agreeable comic turn, Bumbo causes
unforgivable offence by announcing that: ' "I like Nasser. I think
he's a sound man." ' To him the effect of the crisis is to set Britain's
post-imperial dilemma sharply in context. At one point Bumbo's
brother officers are favoured with a tremendous harangue:

'Suppose we beat Egypt? We lose anyway, we've got to sell
ourselves to live, and who'll buy Johnny Bull, with a Boer War
musket in his hand? We don't want our Empire ... Give it
away, as long as you still buy British ... OK, we think we're
so damn wonderful still, and all we are is a lousy, punch-drunk
ex-champ between a couple of real big men, jockeying around
for the KO, not caring two damn hoots about us.'

But Bumbo's is not a typical reaction: writers were quite as
likely to line up on the opposite side. The anti-establishment views
of Simon Smith, the Foreign Office functionary of Hugh Thomas's

The World's Game (1958), are of a wholly different kind. Throughout the events leading up to the Israeli invasion, he is gravely disillusioned both by the anti-semitism of his Foreign Office superiors and by their refusal to comprehend what he diagnoses as Egypt's moral guilt. To Smith the issue can be reduced to a straightforward struggle between an embryo liberal democracy and predatory authoritarianism. Ultimately Smith resigns his post and plans to go to Israel, a gesture worthy of comparison with the attitudes of C. P. Snow's heroes, who, confronted with similar conflicts of private and public interest, tend to think in terms of self preservation.

Suez, then, is far from being a watershed, despite the fact that a large collection of anti-establishment fiction trails in its wake. The connection between the two can only be imagined. Many contemporary novels mention Suez only in passing; their targets are both disparate and localised. Nevertheless, their general effect is to present a comprehensive and impenitently jaundiced view of national institutions and society at the height of the Macmillan era. An inevitable focus was the political arena itself. Raven's *Friends in Low Places* (1965) describes Tory party chicanery about a confidential letter proving government connivance over Suez (the implication being that Eden encouraged the Israelis). Beneath a plot of cross and double-cross lies a bristling satire on politics in the television age, Macmillan's combination of moral uplift and consumerism and its 'sale' to the electorate by means of sophisticated manipulation of the media. The novel's funniest scenes concern the appointment of roguish Lord Canteloupe as 'parliamentary secretary for the Development of British Recreational Resources', an initiative designed to give the Conservative part a 'new look' in anticipation of a forthcoming general election. Canteloupe's promotion, which recognises his success in commercially developing his own stately home, is welcomed even by Labour sympathisers, one of whom thinks that ' "the PM has been rather subtle. The fact is that Canteloupe has shown a conspicuous talent for entertaining the young. He knows the kind of rubbish they want and he gives it to them in just the right packaging." ' Canteloupe's own view of his responsibilities is a ludicrous mixture of cynicism and political shrewdness:

'Now what about this? Government-sponsored caravan sites for holidays. Make a filthy mess of some well-known beauty spot – they'll love that – and then publish a lot of balls about The People enjoying Its Rights in The Countryside, that kind of blab. Jam the bloody caravans as close together as possible – you know how they love being crowded – make a song and dance about being good neighbours, give a prize for the best-behaved family, and perhaps throw in compulsory PT.'

Eventually a single such camp is constructed in the West Country, television cameras attend the arrival of the first coachload of holidaymakers (the majority of whom are out-of-work actors hired for the occasion) and the project is publicly accounted a great success, after which the site falls into disrepair and the few genuine visitors leave. But Canteloupe has achieved his aim: a convincing demonstration of the government's affinity with the interests of the electorate. An absolute contempt for ordinary people, a belief that the electorate responds only to material inducement, however heavily veiled in moral uplift, the triumph of expediency over principle – this would be a fair description of the practical politics of *Friends in Low Places*. In contrast the novel's minor depravities – the fixing of shortlists, the intermittent blackmailing – come as something of a relief, energetic moves in a game first brought to our attention by Trollope.

At least Raven's evocations of the political landscape allow for a good deal of incidental excitement. Alternatively, a novel such as William Camp's *The Ruling Passion* (1959), in which a civil servant falls in love with his minister's wife, emphasises only the dullness of the higher administrative life. Important decisions are made, or procrastinated over, by men of limited ability whose duties are in reality carried out by their underlings. At the constituency level politics is a matter of conciliating one's supporters, however reprehensible their views: the scene in *The Ruling Passion* where the Conservative minister is confronted by two party activists, one of whom wants tougher anti-homosexual legislation, the other of whom favours the withdrawal of state benefits from unmarried mothers, has a depressing ring of authenticity.

From politics, whether at Westminster or constituency level, it was but a short step downward to conspicuous social institutions. Several writers provide relatively scornful reports on the Mayfair/débutante world of the late 1950s. Roger Longrigg's *A High-pitched Buzz* (1956), for example, satirises a tight-knit group of almost half-witted young men and women, united by education, social background and the machinations of society hostesses, and the professions (notably advertising) that sustain it. *The Breaking of Bumbo* reserves some of its most scathing contempt for the London 'season', of which Bumbo is a half-hearted participant. 'A badly-organised, commercial marriage market, screened by a venial veneer of ex-aristos,' is Bumbo's verdict. Looking at the rows of girls assembled at a dance, he thinks that 'their parents should be prosecuted by the RSPCA for deliberate and protracted cruelty to pets'.

Other attacks avoided the empty-headed young men of the débutante ball to concentrate on their breeding grounds. David Benedictus's *Fourth of June*, which caused quite a stir on its publication in 1962, is a full-scale assault on Eton, focused on the school's efforts to admit middle-class pupils by way of a 'guinea pig' scheme. At bottom Benedictus's novel is an account of personal loyalties compromised by class affiliation. Scarfe, the 'guinea pig', strikes up a friendship with a polite, thoughtful boy named Phillips, based on the former's religious interests. Phillips, while despising Morgan and Pemberton, the bullies who make Scarfe's life hell, can never quite dissociate himself from them. 'Sick of their mockery, sick of their crudity, and sick too of the grace and flow of their eloquence,' Phillips is nevertheless seduced by their charm. Eventually he throws Scarfe over. Finally the bullies administer a ferocious beating to the hapless guinea pig on the grounds that he has infringed some trivial rule. Though Scarfe is seriously injured, their expulsion is forestalled by a parental connection with the school governors.

As an institution, Eton was perhaps rather too obvious a symbol for attack. In fact *Fourth of June* fits neatly into a long tradition of excoriations extending back to, and probably beyond, John Heygate's *Decent Fellows* (1932). David Lodge's *Ginger, You're Barmy* examines what might be thought a much more worthwhile target for anti-establishment criticism – National Service. As might be expected from a novel written by one of the last young men to proceed through the two obligatory years of service life, and whose academic career was temporarily impeded by this enforced sequestration, *Ginger, You're Barmy* is quite unforgiving. 'Two years of tedious serfdom' is the narrator's summing up of his army life. Jonathan Price has a number of complaints about the army, over and above the fact that it has deprived him of two years of his life. As an institution it is supremely anachronistic, built on privilege and out-of-date concepts, without relevance to the modern world. Price, whose career has so far proceeded by dint of academic ability, is immediately aware that he has no chance of shining in this new environment:

> I dimly perceived that I had been wrenched out of a meritocracy, for success in which I was well-qualified, and thrust into a small archaic world of privilege, for success in which I was singularly ill endowed.'

Among his complaints are class bias – the Etonians whose commissions are the result of their fathers' status as former officers; a disciplinary system that seems to create crime in order to punish it; and above all a pervasive air of officially sanctioned brutality. One of the novel's most distressing moments comes when a feeble and ineffectual boy from a Catholic public school is driven to shoot himself by a callous NCO. The tragedy is made to look like an accident; Price is happy to acquiesce in the army's desire to avoid a scandal, as a verdict of suicide would be incompatible with his own and the victim's religious beliefs.

Ginger, You're Barmy is a convincing demolition of a system built on outmoded principles. However, other contemporary novels of army life took a different line. The message of Simon Raven's *The Feathers of Death* (1959) is that the army is becoming over-democratised, its traditions ruined by zealous generals of the Montgomery school. Still, the final litany is impressive: the House of Commons, 'society', the army, the public schools – scarcely a single aspect of the higher national fabric stands revealed as anything other than corrupt, elitist and inert. Ask what all this amounts to, however, and the answer, strangely enough, is not very much. Invariably, what at first resembles a sharp stab in the underbelly of the establishment turns out to be an expression of personal irritation or simple ironic detachment. Simon Raven might adopt a number of fictional guises – a right-wing maverick, an exuberant fiddler while Rome burns – but he is not anti-establishment; he is amused by his characters' venality, not shocked by it. Roger Longrigg's credentials as a critic of the advertising profession are undermined by his narrator's willingness to discriminate, (' "Advertising does sound *odd*. Is every firm like yours?" "Oh no, I don't suppose so. They couldn't *all* be. Quite a lot of good advertising happens, after all." ')

Elsewhere, the force of a particular onslaught is often deflected by the writer's reluctance to move from the specific to the general. *The Fourth of June*, for example, is not a condemnation of the public school system as a whole, but an attack on an individual school. No doubt it could be argued that many of Benedictus's complaints apply elsewhere, but the concentration on Eton jargon, the harping on the school's singularity, give the novel an exclusive focus. Phillips would probably have behaved in the way he does at Harrow or Charterhouse, or half a dozen other places, but it is the specific cast of Etonian snobbery which make his treachery so unforgivable.

Other narrators exhibit an odd ambivalence towards the institutions they affect to despise, or at best a concern for personal interests which calls wider criticisms into question. Bumbo Bailey's status as a class warrior is fatally flawed. Though he might mock the moneyed ephebes of the Brigade of Guards, and live his real life with bohemian acquaintances from the Chelsea coffee bars, Bumbo is careful to instruct his parents to telephone him at the barracks only in the direst emergency: he is embarrassed by his suburban origins. Similarly, *Ginger, You're Barmy* is not so much an attack on National Service – though it contains some telling criticisms – as an attack on the indignities visited upon a single National Service conscript, in all probability the author himself. Lodge's narrator is notably uninterested in his fellow recruits, and openly contemptuous of those members of the 'vast, uncouth British proletariat' who sneer at his attempts to read Empson in public. His 'commitment' is merely to his sense of self-preservation.

The revolt of the novelists of the 1950s, then, was an extremely limited rebellion: the few battles that emerged along the way were indecisive and had more to do with characters' resentment of their own inadequacies than with outrage at a genuine collective hurt. The instinctive conservatism of the new breed of post-war writers, whether thought to belong to the Movement, the Angry Young Men or some other grouping, had in any case already become apparent. Angus Wilson, writing as early as 1959, marked Amis, Wain and Co. down as the 'New Establishment': such radical forces as existed in contemporary culture could be found in the theatre. But if Dixon, Lumley and Fisher had won a salient victory, it was over the old notions of character and the traditional upper-class hero. Guy Crouchback and Nick Jenkins – whose careers, it should be pointed out, were proceeding in parallel – retained a certain old world dignity, a faint resourcefulness in the face of changing circumstance. Their newer imitators looked supremely anachronistic. Peter Morrison MP in Raven's *The Rich Pay Late* is an upper-class hero of the old school, who tries to combine his instinctive distaste for Suez with loyalty to the Crown and regiment. When Morrison eventually resigns his seat he merely looks ridiculous, a man out of his time. The same outmoded morality characterises his unsuccessful attempt to re-enter Parliament in *Friends in Low Places*. Subsequent appearances in Raven's novels, alternatively, are marked by unprecedented deviousness: Morrison has learned his lesson. Bumbo, too, makes an attempt at an heroic gesture when he offers to pay for a girl's abortion. But each of Bumbo's gestures, from Suez to Sheila's pregnancy, is doomed to failure. Having drunkenly instigated a riot at a party in the Inner Temple, he is broken from the service.

However noble their aims, Morrison and Bailey are, as much as Dixon, Lumley and Fisher, very much less the hero when compared to the shining exemplars of the past. If one had to draw a single distinction between Gissing's Godwin Peak, with his fiery dreams of intellectual and romantic triumph, and Jim Dixon, with his soft options and his saloon-bar reveries, it is that Jim has had to struggle less. This, inevitably, has made him less of a hero. He is merely a 1950s man with a job he doesn't particularly like and a girlfriend he would like to replace, but he is subject to neither overwhelming fear nor overwhelming ambition. For all his conspicuous failings, one would rather have had Godwin Peak.

4

Reading the 1950s

A. S. Byatt's *The Virgin in the Garden* and *Still Life*

The Virgin in the Garden (1978) and *Still Life* (1985) represent the most sustained attempt by any modern novelist to recast the 1950s in fictional form. The first two volumes in a 'planned series' which is likely to reach at least the 1970s (both books carry a substantial cargo of prefigurative ballast), they show every sign of developing into a weighty *roman-fleuve* of English life in the second half of the twentieth century. Like many other *romans-fleuves*, most obviously works by Powell, Snow and Simon Raven, their genesis is in some degree autobiographical, the North York-shire and Cambridge settings running in parallel to Byatt's own career, but at the same time each novel is capable of tugging free from the anchorage of lived experience in unexpected and imaginative ways. Certainly the account of a provincial ado-lescence that takes up the majority of *The Virgin in the Garden* is no more a re-creation of Byatt's early life than *A Question of Upbringing* (1951) provides an accurate picture of Powell's schoolboy years at Eton.

While the Powell connection cannot be ignored in any consider-ation of Byatt's work – and Byatt's admiration for *A Dance to the Music of Time* is made plain in her extensive critical writings – it would be easy to exaggerate its importance. Like Powell, Byatt's angle on the past is never fixed, and she is fond of the retrospective hypothesis, but the deliberateness of intent is that much more unfeigned, the chronology that much more distinct. Powell's novels, it has been frequently pointed out, exist in a vacuum where past and future slide away into a mythical hinterland in which the reader struggles to find any fixed point of consciousness, any yardstick for measuring a loosely sketched present against whatever vague historical tableau may have preceded it. In contrast, there is a concreteness about Byatt's view of history, a sense that human beings operate in fixed and assimilable periods of time – even if that assimilability may be called into question by knowledge subsequently acquired, intellectual equipment that was not formerly to hand. Powell's hindsight is vague and equivocal; Byatt's exact. *The Virgin in the Garden*, for example, which covers the period 1953–4, begins fifteen years later with a reconvention of its main characters at the National Portrait Gallery. *Still Life* (1954–9) has a similar post-dating in 1980. Each of these perspectives gives a deliberate colouring to the consideration of past time. ' "Funny, the fifties," ' Frederica remarks to Alexander Wedderburn from the vantage point of 1968. ' "Everybody thinks of it as a kind of no time, an unreal time. Just now. But we were there, it was rather beautiful, the Play and the Coronation, and all that." ' The reference to 'just now' is significant. A characteristic Byatt theme is that cultural judgements of this sort are bound by their very nature to be provisional, liable to be altered by mental baggage picked up along the way.

Nevertheless, the tone assumes a conscious authority. At the very least Byatt is suggesting that her own and her characters' judgement of history should be given serious consideration. Frederica's claim to 'understand the fifties' is perhaps only a comment on Frederica's exaggerated notions of her status as a cultural pundit; other observations are less firmly attached to character. Later, for instance, Frederica will remember the 'innocence of that time', choosing to base her assumption on memories of the revival of the musical *Salad Days*. Grown-up singing children in swinging skirts and 'nice pullovers' – all this suggests the expectation of a happy-ever-after which is 'all the more possible and imaginable because the failure of their parents to live happily-ever-after could be attributed to the accident of Hitler and the war.'

The Virgin in the Garden, if not its successor, seems at times to be taking place in a sort of prelapsarian gap, embedded in the 'quiet, forgotten, static time of the middle fifties, after austerity, before hindsight', in which there is little to galvanise individual or collective passion. Politicians and social thinkers argue that there are no great issues left, only the practical problems of economic and social planning. Ideology is conspicuously absent. Byatt's summary of the prevailing attitude is:

> a broad consensus, no class conflict, only within reach, equality of opportunity. A time when most British people believed modestly and without excitement in better things to come as better things had come, bananas, oranges, the Health Service, the Butler Education Act, plans to expand higher education, motor cars for working men.

This is fictional background plucked from the textbooks, if you like, but it is remarkable how confidently Byatt's characters conform to what their creator imagines to be a broadly-based assumption of behaviour and expectation. The sense of a collective consciousness is not that of a novel by George Eliot – this is no longer possible – but at the same time 'society' has not yet become a rather questionable abstract.

On the strength of these and other passages it would be possible to mark Byatt down unhesitatingly as a 'social novelist' pure and simple. No doubt she would strenuously resist the imputation. One of the marks of her fiction is its ability to exist simultaneously on a number of different levels. *Still Life*, for example, is, among other things, an argument about signification. This much, at any rate, can be divined from the author's revelation – an odd intervention, towards the close – that:

> I had the idea, when I began this novel, that it would be a novel of naming and accuracy. I wanted to write a novel as Williams said a poem should be: no ideas but in things. I even thought of trying to write without figures of speech, but had to give up that plan, quite early on.

In much the same way, *The Virgin in the Garden* – notably in its account of Marcus Potter's psychological disturbance – occasionally looks less like a novel than a kind of symbolist pantomime. But the questions asked by both works are those with which the student of the Victorian social novel will be immediately familiar, even if the framing admits a degree of uncertainty unknown to a George Eliot or an Elizabeth Gaskell. Was there, at this point in time, given the inevitable artificiality of hindsight, such a thing as a shared culture, a collective life, a national existence even? Byatt knows that the writer, or at least her sort of writer, inhabits a post-modern world, and the debate about 'decentring' is never very far from her mind, but even so in the death of George VI, the Coronation of Elizabeth II, Suez, she addresses symbolic events which apparently function as spiritual touchstones, where the personal response may or may not shade into the communal. Disintegration is at hand, but the prefigurative signs that announce it tend to bolster present security. The pseudo-Elizabethan entertainment at the heart of *The Virgin in the Garden* takes place in the grounds of a stately home which will shortly become the site of a new university, the scene, we are given to understand, of student disturbances in the 1960s. Later Wedderburn will look back nostalgically to the 'shared certainties' of a 1950s BBC luncheon, relishing in retrospect a 'greyness' which at the time had faintly irritated him.

These oppositions are reflected in Byatt's largely domestic focus. Set predominantly in the North Yorkshire town of 'Blesford', with excursions to London and Cambridge, her novels are at the most basic level a study of 'ordinary' family life. Not that 'ordinary' is an adjective that could be applied with any conviction to the Potters – an irascible father who combines the teaching of English at the local grammar school with committed good works of the WEA lecturing sort, a kind, self-absorbed mother, two brilliant sisters, and dreary, ineffectual Marcus, a dislocated and disaffected adolescent of the kind in whom Byatt rather specialises. Each Potter, to a greater or lesser degree, advertises his or her superiority to humdrum circumstance, but it is Byatt's achievement to tether them unobtrusively to their native environment. Thus it is possible, in fact desirable, to consider simultaneously Frederica's estimate of herself as a genius in embryo and the nagging authorial hint that she is merely a foolish, if exceptionally clever, schoolgirl.

The Potters, particularly Stephanie and Frederica, are the books' organic core. Though the cast expands to take in Alexander Wedderburn, a colleague of Bill's and author of the Coronation play,

Frederica's Cambridge acquisitions, Daniel the dogged curate whom Stephanie eventually marries, the sisterly contrast remains paramount: Stephanie, who has confounded paternal expectations by settling for a schoolmistress's job and tongue-tied Daniel Orton; Frederica, who is determined to meet the physical and intellectual challenges of Newnham head-on. Throughout both novels the life of the mind and the familial hearth remain in sharp contention, to the extent that Stephanie's death at the end of *Still Life* – given the promise of succeeding volumes – seems a steely exhibition of authorial resolve.

Written nearly twenty years after the events they depict, both *The Virgin in the Garden* and *Still Life* are built upon a steady forward dynamic, the comparisons always those of an unseen future, the judgements those of a wiser retrospect, for all that they are dominated by an awareness of what went before, notably the war and the deprivations of a 1940s upbringing. The sisters' childhood games are a matter of Stephanie ordering 'unimaginable luxuries' from a make-believe shop. At quite a late stage in her adolescence, Frederica recalls a conversation with her mother, provoked by radio reports of casualty figures. ' "What will there be on the News . . . when we've won the war?" ' ' "Oh, I don't know," ' Winifred replies absently. ' "Cricket and things like that." ' This is period detail, perhaps, but its implications resonate throughout the accounts of family behaviour. Introduced to the splendours of Long Royston by its owner, Matthew Crowe, Frederica is unable, rather than unwilling, to be impressed. ' "I don't see it. I'm the austerity generation. Butter and cream and lemons are mythological entities for us, you know . . . All these carvings and hangings just make me uneasy." ' Alexander calls jokingly to Crowe, ' "Here's Frederica saying she has no feeling for your things because of the war," ' which is an over-simplification – Potter puritanism, one imagines, was engrained – but not much of one. Elsewhere there is a description of the family enjoying a frugal Christmas dinner: 'they had learned in the war to make do with the plain, avoid waste, make things go round'. Here, however, circumstance is abetting heritage. Three hundred years before, it seems safe to predict, Bill Potter would have been one of Winstanley's diggers. Set down in the mid-twentieth century, he is happy to allow government-inspired deprivation to reinforce the prompt-ings of temperament.

The death of George VI in February 1952 and the dawning of a new Elizabethan age provide a symbolic focus. Taking some of his pupils to hear the Crier proclaim the accession on the steps of Calverley Minster, Alexander reflects that the royal death marks 'a period to the first brief part of their existence, that must have seemed eternal – rationing, the end of a war, utility'. Alexander, an intensely private and self-contained man, attempts to frame his feelings in some sort of wider context. Focusing on memories of the King prodding bomb rubble on news-reels, a disembodied voice on the radio announcing the declaration of war, he visualises 'a nation attempting to imagine this known figure, dead alone in his bed, and failing in the attempt'. His own grief is 'both ludicrous and actual'. This is an important distinction. Alexander is lamenting the death of someone he could not know, a figure mediated to him through news-reels, photographs and radio broadcasts, but at the same time he realises that even remote royalty in uniform are ultimately reducible to flesh and blood, and that an awareness of what they represent makes it possible to mourn their passing.

The thought of external agencies imposing their interpretations of history on the private consciousness hangs over Byatt's treat-ment of the Coronation, which, with its accompanying celebra-tions – notably the staging of Alexander's play under Crowe's auspices at Long Royston – provides another chance to search for unity in the midst of disparate individual lives. Stephanie's col-league Miss Wells, who is co-ordinating Blesford's artistic efforts, sees herself 'at the spinning centre of endless threads of culture reknit, reknotted'. Stephanie herself, inspecting the mock-Eliza-bethan clothing laid out in the schoolmistress's room, acknow-ledges 'the ambition to embody here, in the present time and place, the sense of form, the cohesion lost, lost with the English golden age'. Miss Wells can only see continuities, coincidence, 'the super-imposition of past grandeur on present business'. Even Stephanie can make a connection between her friend's Elizabethan ruffs, the *Illustrated London News* picture of the Dean's collar, conceived in the age of Charles II, Daniel's own clerical neckwear. To balance this is the scent of a false opposition. After all, can any era have been quite so worked over by partial historians as the 'English golden age', any image quite as gilded and refined as that of the Virgin Queen? Matching the supposed frailty of the present against the imagined solidity of the past is always a dangerous exercise, just as it is naïve to credit the spectator of a bygone age with an 'authentic' perception. The late twentieth-century sophisticate knows that his outlook is irrevocably influenced by television, but the methods used to infiltrate the consciousness of the sixteenth-century peasant were quite as deliberate. Byatt knows this, of course, but the English golden age is to her a matter of symbolism rather than historical reality.

Whatever their own opinions of past and present artificiality, the cast of *The Virgin in the Garden* have difficulty in establishing exactly what the Coronation might be supposed to represent. Most of the principal characters assemble in the front room of the grammar school headmaster to watch the event on television and listen to the 'orotundities of Richard Dimbleby'. The national press, meanwhile, is using 'blandly lyrical, spasmodically archaic, uneasily hortative words about a New Elizabethan Age'. Anxious to supply a wider framework, Byatt then moves forward to 1973 and a television lecture given by Alexander in which he describes the Coronation as 'a true shadow of blood and state', ending with Low's much reproduced 'morning after' cartoon – a broken Union Jack, deflated or burst balloons, the party definitely over. Frederica, watching the broadcast, thinks that he oversimplifies: such a diminishment is characteristic of the medium's 'pervasive, receding narcissism'. There was, she feels, some sort of 'innocence' about the rejoicing at the time:

no duplicity, only a truly aimless and thwarted nostalgia, about the pious enthusiasms of the commentators, and the people had simply hoped, because the time was after the effort of war and the rigour of austerity, and the hope, despite the spasmodic construction of pleasure gardens and festival halls, had had, alas, like Hamlet's despair, no objective correlative. But they had been naturally lyrical. Their lyricism had turned out to be

wandering and threadbare, but nothing had replaced or succeeded it.

'A false beginning', then, as Alexander puts it, in another retrospective judgement. To the other members of the little circle of
television watchers, the Coronation prompts a series of private
epiphanies, bound up with particular views of society or public
purpose. The vicar and his wife are delighted and reassured, 'as
though the whole world wore, briefly and significantly, a Sunday
aspect'. Miss Wells, alternatively, is in a state of 'cultural ecstasy',
effortlessly combining the architecture of Westminster Abbey and
'the Queen's little white human face over her emblematically
embroidered robe' to produce a promise of renovation. For all this
contrivance there is something authentic about the proceedings,
something shared – on a very mundane level, for example, it is the
first occasion on which the majority of those assembled have
watched a television; doubts about the value of the medium are
temporarily eclipsed in the pursuit of spectacle. The view of the
past conveyed in Richard Dimbleby's highly coloured observations may be fundamentally imperfect, but the symbolism, in
both collective and personal terms, is inescapable.

The Coronation might briefly impose a sense of communal
awareness, make some vague gesture towards the thought of a
collective life. Elsewhere the ground is littered with the seeds of
cultural fragmentation; a tendency observable even in the highly
restricted milieu of Blesford itself, let alone the wider environments of London and Cambridge. Such formal 'culture' as Blesford might be thought to possess is personified in the prickly and
rebarbative form of Bill Potter. An inspired English teacher
and WEA lecturer, who proceeded to Cambridge via the relatively
well-trodden route of working men's institutes and night school,
Potter is the sort of working-class autodidact of whom Richard
Hoggart would have been proud, and indeed he epitomises many
of the arguments of *The Uses of Literacy* (1957): working to
promote his own version of Ruskin and Morris's popular socialism
'with dour respect for real workers and their lives and interests
more akin to Tawney's work in the Potteries'.

It takes very little investigation, however, to reveal that Ruskin and Morris are antiquated models. Thirty years before a man of Potter's calibre was content to remain in a provincial backwater, pleased to exercise his influence in a limited but definite sphere; his young modern equivalent seeks a larger, more brightly lit platform for his talents. The contrast between Potter and his former pupil, Wilkie, who turns up to watch the Coronation, is significant. Self-assured, confident, already a gossip columnist's standby, Wilkie has his sights fixed on London, television and celebrity. Bill, while not questioning Wilkie's ability, is deeply suspicious of its exercise. But cultural fragmentation is not merely a matter of clever young men forswearing their roots. Bill is similarly unimpressed by the new municipal developments which are springing up in Blesford, an initiative of which he might have been expected to approve. Such places, he feels, betoken rootlessness, absence of continuity, above all a want of affiliation:

> 'In Yorkshire we say our Nellie, our Ernie, our Cat, our Dog, our Street. But in that place it's *the* Estate and *the* everything else down. They hate it. Prowling kids and regularly sawn-off cherry trees. I've been there.'

Take away people's sense of community, Potter is implying – and there is nothing especially novel in the implication – and all that remains is an aimless selfishness. But the suspicion endures that his own cultural interventions are no more than surface glitter, a well-meaning but necessarily futile attempt to revive something which is already moribund.

Later Frederica, looking back on a 1950s holiday in the South of France, will make a damning comparison between the cultural landscape of North Yorkshire and its Provençal equivalent. Pound-saturated hindsight makes her see her hosts' 'easy educating communication about the land, the lore, the language in which she found herself, as a sign of real energy in his community which had been ersatz, or only wished for, in post-Festival of Britain Yorkshire.' Bill Potter has his local pride, his evening class students busy themselves in collecting local words which describe patterns of social behaviour and family interrelationship with a kind of Fabian zeal, 'but without the sun-saturated liveliness of M.

Grimaud's sense of what was shared and perpetual in his world'. There are points to be made in Potter's defence, of course – it does not need a Marxist to remind us that culture is ordinary; what in any case is 'real energy'? – but the fact remains that to Potter's daughters his cultural activities look simply like anti-quarianism.

Bill Potter himself would acknowledge the part played by social mobility in bringing about this fracture. His own career in any case is an example of the way in which people of intelligence can use educational opportunities to engineer an ascent through the social hierarchy. Frederica's progress is a magnification of this tendency, weighed down by an identical realisation that social mobility cannot confer social confidence. Frederica's educational accomplishments may have secured her a scholarship to Newn-ham, but they cannot render her socially adept. Assailed by upper-class suitors, she imagines that every part of her social armature – buttons, gloves, turn of phrase, lack of the right acquaintances and relations – is being 'as remorselessly weighed and found wanting as before her French grammar, Latin scansion, verbatim knowledge of Shakespeare, had on occasion been weighed and valued'. Freder-ica's extensive male acquaintance shares her unease. One young man, the son of a left-wing baronet, expensively raised and edu-cated, tries to give the impression that he comes from a working-class home in Battersea. The Glaswegian Alan, alternatively, is genuine working class, 'and would say so, if asked, though he created situations in which he was not asked'. Matched against this type of disguise and concealment, Crowe, who gives Frederica a part in Alexander's play and nearly seduces her into the bargain, is a figure of almost archaic solidity, moneyed, confident, a more adquately realised version of Gore-Urquhart, the *deus ex machina* of *Lucky Jim* (1954). But Crowe's day is over, and Long Royston about to become the site of a new university. While his intellectual self-confidence remains, the sense that the world now has a dimin-ished space for what he has to offer is never very far away.

If a single factor unites Byatt's characters, especially those forced out into the Cambridge charivari, it is uncertainty over role, assumptions, appropriateness to milieu. Frederica and her friends have the ability to jump through the approved intellectual hoops, but the assumptions on which they base their lives, and on which they presumably base their ideas of human conduct, are woefully vague. To this uncertainty is added painfully little exact information over the wider conduct of human affairs. Just as Frederica can stand near St Paul's watching the City crowds and reflect that 'she had *no idea* where they were going, or how they lived, or what they did', so she can only see a major national crisis such as Suez in vague storybook terms of Nasser the spirited rebel pitting himself against the school prefects. Frederica and her friends are deracinated and as such unpredictable, their identities as yet unformed. No assumptions of their collective behaviour could survive the individual qualification. As a consequence, their divisions over Suez and the Hungarian invasion of a few weeks later are often unexpected. There are those who believe in the British as a 'responsible' people, those who are afraid of the word appeasement, and those who see the 'action' as cynical opportunism or the product of an outdated vision of imperial glory. Byatt is quick to scotch the suggestion that support for or contempt of government action is divided along class lines. 'Ideas of national honour, mild or furiously xenophobic, pragmatic judgement of economic advantage exist in blank opposition in all parts of English society.' Whatever her initial ignorance of issues, motives or appropriate response, Frederica is forced to concede the unprecedented impact of Suez and the Hungarian crisis on individual lives. At Newnham she witnesses a screaming match between two gowned women standing on tables in hall: retrospect will convert this into 'her first close-up study of a real clash between opposed political visions'. Even more of an eye-opener, perhaps, is a meeting with her most elegant suitor's elegant relative, a woman now deeply involved with the care of Hungarian refugees. ' "This has changed my life," ' she explains. ' "This has given me a reason for living." ' Frederica, taken aback by such passion, is 'shocked and moved'.

These and other passages point towards the contradictions of Byatt's title: the 1950s are a 'still life', certainly, but one capable of being pushed aside by sharp, vigorous movement. In much the same way the narrower literary framework in which the second book operates is dominated by a continuing argument between opposing schools. Though written a quarter of a century later,

Still Life proclaims its affinity to the literary culture of the period by serving as a full-scale assault on the aesthetic values of *Lucky Jim*. Frederica is neither tolerant nor admiring of Jim Dixon. Instead she feels only a simple sexual distaste:

> There was a nice girl, whose niceness consisted of big breasts and a surprising readiness to find the lunatic Dixon attractive and valuable, and a nasty woman who was *judged* for bad make-up and arty skirts as well as for hysteria and emotional blackmail.

When a friend advances the standard theory of Dixon's decency and scrupulousness, his honest engagement with the snobbish pretensions of Bloomsbury or *Brideshead* cliqueishness, Frederica is unconvinced.

> If you were going to set up childish irresponsibility in a model of innocence she supposed she would rather have Charles Ryder and Sebastian Flyte in the garden from which they would inevitably be expelled, than the elementary school antics of Jim Dixon.

In the same way that E. M. Forster's relation to the novel is advertised by a personal appearance, so Amis turns up *in situ*, in this case as a speaker at the Literary Society. Although there is no means of knowing whether this scene records an actual event – and the balance is high on the side of probability – the author of *Lucky Jim* can be found taking a characteristic line, talking of the novel as primarily entertainment, deprecating the 'excessive seriousness' of *Mansfield Park*, speaking of the 'saving grace' of comedy as a way of destroying pretentiousness. Predictably this cuts no ice with Frederica, who maintains that the whole business makes her more sympathetic to Matthew Arnold and High Seriousness. To Bill Potter's daughter words like 'pompous' and 'pretentious' should always be looked at twice, in case you could substitute better ones, like serious or responsible.

Frederica is not alone in wanting maturity of response: her isolation stems from her inability to locate it. Jim Dixon and

Charles Ryder are perpetual schoolboys; Frederica wants men. A second suggestion to emerge from *Still Life* is that maturity of response is no longer framable in the old way, no longer a matter of plot, motive, character and resolution. One of the most sympathetically drawn of Byatt's people is Raphael Faber, an *émigré* don with whom Frederica is infatuated. Faber, who hates D. H. Lawrence, who rails against 'stories with character, against whining, against insularity, against verbal sluggishness', might be described as an *Ur*-post-modernist. This stance is firmly reflected in his creative work, notably in a poem which seeks to define the nature of the terror which hangs over his early life (his family was killed by the Nazis) while, characteristically, being unable to describe the experience in realistic terms. The techniques of art, Byatt suggests, change in response to historical imperatives, and to ignore this is to ignore one's responsibility as an artist.

On one level *Still Life* dramatises the battle between 'seriousness' and slapstick that has characterised the English literary aesthetic since the war, a battle convincingly won by the slapsticks, whatever their moral unfitness or changing and invalidating circumstance. Despite the forty years that have passed since his creation, despite cultural fragmentation, despite the fact that he exists as the representative of a wholly archaic social system, Jim Dixon is still 'a hero of our time'. Matched against these populist certainties, Dr Faber with his 'difficult' poems and his complaints about Lawrence can look simply a tiresome highbrow, but the suspicion lingers that his artistry is of a rather higher order. Byatt's own position lies somewhere between these extremes. *The Virgin in the Garden* and *Still Life* are meditations on past time, with all the subterfuge that this implies, arguments about signification perhaps, mental gouaches – but not works of realism. For all that, their sharpest effects – Stephanie giving birth, the Potter hearth – are conveyed by realistic means. Like the decade they purport to describe, these are transitional novels, open-ended and unresolved, whose explanations, if explanations they are, lie in another world and another time.

5

The Day of the Sardine

> Working men and women who read do not have the privilege of
> seeing themselves honestly and realistically portrayed in novels.
> They are familiar with wish-fulfilment images flashed at them in
> cliché form on television or in the press, and the novels they read
> in which they do figure are written by those novelists of the Right
> who are quite prepared to pass on the old values and who, unable
> to have any feeling for the individual, delineate only stock characters.
>
> Alan Sillitoe, *The Writer's Dilemma* (ed. Stephen Spender, 1961)

> We all need to remember, every day and more and more, that in the
> last resort there is no such person as 'the common man'.
>
> Richard Hoggart, *The Uses of Literacy* (1957)

The late 1950s and early 1960s were remarkable for the emergence
of a school of genuinely working-class fiction. Naturally, the
working classes had featured in fiction before. The majority of
Fielding and Smollett's novels carry their cargo of low-life 'types'.
Victorians such as Dickens and Thackeray recognised the comic
and criminal potential of the 'lower orders', while writers like
Kingsley, Mrs Gaskell, George Eliot and, slightly later, Beasant,
Gissing and Hardy made serious attempts to examine working-
class life in the round, to use a servant or a labourer not as a butt
for class-based humour, or to expose bourgeois pretensions, but
to describe him (or her) in their own terms, and in relation to an
inexorable social context. The Bank Holiday chapter in *The
Nether World*, Esther Waters on the station platform, Jude Fawley

struggling over his Greek Gospel – these are all characteristic images from the late Victorian novel, and they are trailed by a great deal of second- and third-rate moral earnestness. Much of the vast literature issued by the Religious Tract Society in the second half of the nineteenth century, for example, concerned the tribulations of the deserving or undeserving poor.

But these were novels about the working classes, not by them, their attitude towards the people they purported to describe – Gissing is an obvious case – notoriously ambivalent. Even Arthur Morrison's East End tales, which appeared in the 1890s and are the equal of Gissing in their portrayal of late-Victorian urban squalor, can seem merely the work of a clever journalist who has observed, observed very closely, and then retreated into a warmer, more comfortable life. Trying to establish who was the first modern English proletarian writer is not much of a literary parlour game – and do we count Lawrence? – but Robert Tressell's *The Ragged Trousered Philanthropists* (1907), an account of a group of Edwardian house-painters downtrodden and exploited by a particularly loathsome gang of local capitalists, must be a strong contender. Not very much is known about Tressell, who died in poverty having surrendered his copyright for a few pounds, but his knowledge of the painting and decorating trade and the lives of the people engaged in it is clearly based on first-hand experience. At the same time he is perhaps the first English novelist to examine the average working life from a Marxist economic and social perspective. Tressell sees how local cartels and employers' closed shops keep wages down, but he also sees the implications of this concentration of economic power – the swindle of early twentieth-century local government, with its backhanders and its deference to vested interests and the absolute powerlessness of the working people whose votes supposedly authenticated it.

The Ragged Trousered Philanthropists is a landmark on a faint and wavering path. Search for the proletarian literature of the 1930s, the decade of Jarrow, the PAC and the Unemployed Workers' Union, Orwell suggested, and all you are likely to find, with the exception of Walter Greenwood's *Love on the Dole* (1933), is a hole in the air. In fact this is a typical Orwell exaggeration. The 1930s produced, for instance, James Hanley, the work of the Birmingham Group, notably John Hampson's *Saturday Night at the Greyhound* (1931), and a mass of short stories of working-class life which appeared in left-wing magazines – but for every Greenwood one was equally likely to run up against a book like Alec Brown's *Daughters of Albion* (1935), wads of dutiful toeing of the party line written by a superannuated public schoolboy. Even Greenwood is very difficult to categorise as a 'proletarian novelist': *His Worship the Mayor* (1934), for example, perhaps his best later novel, is set rather higher up the social scale and features a struggling shopkeeper whose windfall legacy enables him to intervene in local politics. A much better exemplar would be Orwell's friend Jack Common, whose fictionalised account of a Tyneside childhood, *Kiddar's Luck*, was published in 1950.

Tressell, Greenwood and Common – and a handful of lesser writers – are not much on which to erect a tradition. They were writing at different times, and despite the evenness of the perspective – a society and a way of life viewed from the *inside* – the approach and the immediate concerns tend to vary. The clutch of late 1950s and early 1960s working-class writers – Alan Sillitoe, Sid Chaplin, David Storey, Bill Naughton and Philip Callow – are that much more homogeneous. To take a minor detail, it is surely not a coincidence that the heroes of the three greatest proletarian novels of the immediately post-war period, *Saturday Night and Sunday Morning* (1958), *The Day of the Sardine* (1961) and *This Sporting Life* (1960), have the same first name? Moreover, unlike many of those who preceded them, Sillitoe, Storey and Co. were genuine proletarians. Callow's working-class Midlands childhood is faithfully reproduced in his autobiographical novel *Going to the Moon* (1968). Chaplin may have ended his working life in a fairly exalted desk job at the National Coal Board, but he began it down the mine and his early books are rooted in the back-yard culture of the industrial North-East. Given their tenacity and their similarity, the sense one gets of fragments of experience chipped from the same block, it is a legitimate exercise to use these novels in an attempt to answer some of the questions which have always interested historians of post-war working-class life. Why did no genuine working-class political movement ever emerge in England? Why did the proportion of working-class people entering higher or further education remain broadly the same, despite greatly expanded opportunities? To what extent were traditional patterns of social and moral life breaking down in the post-war world, and, if so, what factors were assisting their decline?

Inevitably, there are dangers inherent in this approach. Orwell pointed out that the working-class man or woman who writes a novel is exceptional, and consequently no longer a member of the working class. Similarly, anyone who manages to rise above their milieu in this way is likely to harbour a series of prejudices which limit their usefulness as a social registrar. Sillitoe's Arthur Seaton is not typical – at least one hopes he is not – but by the same token he is not exceptional: if he were, he would not be where he is. In any case the historian of 'ordinary' working-class social life works in an area where statistics are of limited value, and prevailing attitudes more likely to be encapsulated in a fragment from a popular song than in a row of figures supplied by the Central Office of Information. In a world that tends to be re-created by means of anecdote and folk memory, whose physical lineaments have disappeared beneath a tide of municipal housing schemes, the novel takes on, more perhaps than is customary, the status of an historical artefact.

No discussion of the working-class novel, or working-class life itself in the immediately post-war era, can fail to take account of Richard Hoggart's *The Uses of Literacy*, first published in 1957. The work of an obscure lecturer in the department of adult education at the University of Hull, a working-class 'scholarship boy' in the classic mould, Hoggart's thesis about change in working-class life has occasionally suffered at the hands of reductionist historians. In particular, there have been attempts to reduce him to the level of the working-class intellectual who is merely horrified by the blandishments now being offered to the people he has left behind. As one of Hoggart's early summaries of his conclusions show, this is to oversimplify quite a complex position:

My argument is not that there was, in England one generation ago, an urban culture still very much 'of the people' and that now there is only a mass urban culture. It is rather that the appeals made by the mass publicists are for a great number of reasons made more insistently, effectively and in a more comprehensive and centralised form today than they were earlier, that we are moving towards the creation of a mass culture, that the remnants of what was at least in part an urban culture 'of the people' are being destroyed, and that the new mass culture is in some important ways less healthy than the often crude culture it is replacing.

Hoggart is careful not to make too many claims for working-class 'solidarity', but the society he defines is broadly homogeneous, tight-knit, centred on the family hearth, remote from considerations of public life, unambitious, easy-going, but infused with a queer spirit of 'decency' (to Hoggart, as to Orwell, a key word of approbation). Opposed to this, and relentlessly breaking it down, are not merely the hoodwinking cant of the ad-men and worthless literature, but less tangible factors such as affluence and educational opportunity: the scholarship boy, prised out of one class by intellect but denied any satisfactory position in another by social and intellectual uncertainty, and what one might call the trauma of his deracination, is one of the most finely observed of Hoggart's working-class types.

In the wake of a thousand sociological surveys on the effects of 'mass culture', many of Hoggart's conclusions can look merely obvious. Give people money and they have a regrettable tendency to spend it on what one scale of values will classify as rubbish. A gramophone record is a fine thing, but it will mean the end of the blind pianist at the working men's club concert. Affluence, as we all know to our cost, carries an enormous cultural time-bomb concealed beneath its skirts. At the time, though, Hoggart's thesis had a terrific impact, whose influence endures even today. No self-respecting social history of the period is without its four- or five-page redaction of Hoggart (see, for example, Arthur Marwick's *British Society Since 1945*). At the same time those historical novels which seek to encapsulate the attitudes of the late 1950s tend, consciously or unconsciously, to follow the Hoggart line: when the undergraduates Tony Watson and Owen Griffith in *Still Life* (1985) discuss working-class culture, they do so in terms established by *The Uses of Literacy*. Similarly, the elevation of 'working-class culture' to the status of a modish talking-point owes every-thing to Hoggart.

Contemporary fiction, too, confirms the accuracy of much of his observation. Thorpe, the declassed university lecturer in David Storey's *Flight into Camden* (1960), Billy Fisher's comic turn in the local pub's Saturday night variety show, Arthur Haggerston's mother in Sid Chaplin's *The Day of the Sardine* singing ancient popular songs as she goes about her household tasks, Arthur himself watching a group of small girls enact a mannequin parade – each of these snapshots of working-class life is more fully docu-mented in Hoggart, and the effect on the reader who strays from observation of actual circumstance to fictional re-creation and finds them identical can be disconcerting.

Such criticisms as can be levelled at Hoggart three and a half decades on are those of emphasis. For a start, his catchment area, his authentic working class, is uncomfortably narrow, consisting in effect of manual labourers and their dependants residing in the North of England. A quarter of a million agricultural workers living in the South and in East Anglia, and espousing very different social attitudes, presumably don't count. To this can be added a suspect chronology. Though devised in the 1950s, and purporting to deal with post-war developments, *The Uses of Literacy*'s essen-tial landscape, and much of its corroborating evidence, seems to belong to the 1930s: the most significant details and illustrations have a habit of coming from Hoggart's own, pre-Second World War boyhood. Of course cultural change does not happen over-night, but one has a feeling that the less fragmented working-class existence which he holds up as his exemplar is an older phenom-enon than he cares to acknowledge.

It is difficult, too, to exonerate Hoggart from a charge of mild sentimentalism. Certainly, he is strong on the 'crudity' of many aspects of working-class life, and there are any number of passages recounting genuine horrors of deprivation and wasted lives, but it is impossible to read him for very long before coming across a description of the average working-class existence as 'a good and comely life, one founded on love, affection, a sense of the small group if not of the individual'. To Hoggart the 1930s were a time of 'sacrifice, co-operation and neighbourliness', the hardships redeemed by a traditional urge 'to make life intensely human, to humanise it in spite of everything and so to make it not simply bearable, but positively interesting'. A human characteristic, surely, rather than one belonging exclusively to the working class? A novelist of the Sillitoe type would be disposed to sneer at this roseate vista, uncannily reminiscent of one or two of Orwell's evocations of working-class life in *The Road to Wigan Pier* (1937), and Sillitoe, on the strength of a novel such as *Saturday Night and Sunday Morning*, with its glimpses of an older world of dodging the rent-collector and the elder Seaton's face growing 'black from want of fags', can scarcely be gainsaid.

Perhaps, in the last resort, Hoggart is merely generalising about a subject on which it is impossible to generalise. This is certainly a point that can be made about his careful and deliberately circumspect views on the 'fragmentation' of working-class culture. After all, the corruption and trivialisation of working-class reading material goes back to the nineteenth century and beyond. In his short story 'The Spotted Dog', written in 1870, Trollope has a character visit the editor of a 'penny dreadful'. He reflects:

> We had not even known of the existence of these papers; – and yet there they were, going forth into the hands of hundreds of thousands of readers, all of whom were being, more or less, instructed in their modes of life and manner of thinking by the stories which were thus brought before them.

Similarly, one can shake one's head over the sensational and morally debasing American gangster magazines whose mass importation Hoggart regards as sinister while wondering if they differ in any vital respect from, say, *Varney the Vampire*, which beguiled the leisure of many a newly literate artisan a century before. Hoggart would argue that there are degrees of sensationalism, that watered-down Beckford Gothic belongs to a more wholesome tradition than sub-Chandler brutality, but we are dealing with a grey and mostly unexplored area of 'underground' popular literature, where everything but the artefact itself is uncertain, and ethical judgements not always sustainable. When watching a horror film of the *Omen* variety, for example, there is some consolation in discovering that the audience has a habit of laughing at especially gory moments.

Systematic deconstruction of a work such as *The Uses of Literacy* necessarily reduces itself to an exercise in point-scoring: when the dust has settled, Hoggart is still very much alive, and many of his conclusions stand firm. Perhaps the book should really be read as a sort of disguised autobiography, written by a Leavisite with a fairly exact notion of 'value' (how many contemporary cultural historians, one wonders, would care to use repeatedly adjectives such as 'healthy' or 'crude'?). This is not to say that his conclusions have no wider application, simply that the most illuminating touches tend to be autobiographical. Reading the account of the teenaged, scholarship-winning future author sitting next to a middle-aged bachelor miner who, whenever he bought a drink at the bar of the working men's club in which they were spending the evening, handed the boy half-a-crown with instructions to 'tek it lad, and use it for thee education', one is suddenly pulled up short by the realisation that half a century ago a decent education was a privilege, not a right, and that the odds were stacked against the average working-class child striving to achieve one.

Significantly, too, the sentimentality which occasionally colours Hoggart's generalised accounts of working-class life is absent from the memories of his own childhood. There is an unforgettable passage in which he describes his mother jealously guarding a rare 'treat' – a handful of shrimps or a few scraps of ham – from her children, and finally exploding in fury. Another of Hoggart's characteristics is his ability to provoke an intensely personal reaction: reading his early chapters I can detect a faint yet perceptible echo of my father's accounts of growing up on a Norwich council estate in the 1930s, three hundred miles away from Hoggart's juvenile romping ground, but with enough shared experience to establish a degree of consanguinity. In the end, however, it is Hoggart's lament over the encroaching tide of commercialism and lowbrow punditry, the 'shiny barbarism' of modern mass culture, that bears the strongest relation to our own circumstance. Anyone, for instance, who has ever imagined that the *Sun* or the *Daily Mirror* reflect popular opinion or harbour the qualities of 'robustness' or 'plain-speaking' occasionally associated with cheap journalism should read pages 204–5 of the Penguin edition of Hoggart's book, which contains one of the best condemnations of mass-circulation newspapers ever written. If nothing else, *The Uses of Literacy* is an exposure of the deceits practised on 'ordinary people' in the name of progress.

The two chief forces at work in Hoggart's world might be described as, on the one hand, creeping fragmentation, and, on the other, a resistant but already fractured homogeneity. It is not difficult to find elements of both in each of the major working-class novels of the period, most obviously in Sillitoe's *Saturday Night and Sunday Morning* and the short stories collected in *The Loneliness of the Long-distance Runner* (1958), in Callow's *Common People* (1958) and *Going to the Moon*, Chaplin's *The Day of the Sardine*, Storey's *This Sporting Life* and *Flight into Camden* and Bill Naughton's story collection *Late Night on Watling Street* (1959). Outwardly the similarities between them are very great. To the fact that their protagonists tend to be named Arthur can be added the almost identical nature of the emotional predicaments. In five of the six novels listed here, for example, the central character is a young man involved in some more or less illicit relationship with an older woman, either married or widowed (the only female protagonist, Margaret Thorpe in *Flight into Camden*, maintains the pattern by taking up with a married man).

Each exists at the core of a tiny but minutely known environment ('Robust, ugly, close' is the hero of *Going to the Moon*'s description of his upbringing) and a tight-knit family group. The Seatons' ability to close ranks if they feel that one of their number is threatened, by a drunken husband or an interfering neighbour, is a feature of *Saturday Night and Sunday Morning*. The Haggerstons in *The Day of the Sardine* are limited to mother and son, the absence of Arthur's father proving a hinge on which the novel will ultimately turn, but theirs is an intense, claustrophobic relationship, built on mordant but subtle wisecracking, oblique remarks flicked across the breakfast table, gallows humour congealing with the bacon fat. Here, as in Hoggart, it is the mother who reigns, balancing severity with indulgence and inspiring fierce devotion in her sons. Mrs Haggerston might occasionally hurl a teapot at Arthur, but she holds off from marrying the lodger for his sake. Old Mr Seaton is a cowed and faintly anonymous figure when set against his loud and matriarchal wife. Colin in *Going to the Moon* supplies several tributes to his mother's 'honesty' and 'simplicity'. On the first occasion that he leaves home he looks back from a moving vehicle and is overcome with emotion: 'Her small figure was perfectly motionless, as though frozen, and I could not bear to look at her.' If the heroes of the late 1950s are sometimes reluctant to leave home, settle down, conform to whatever is their own immediate circle's concept of responsible behaviour, it is because the ties that bind them are uncomfortably strong.

What sort of a world is it, this dense, stifling, exclusively Northern universe (with the partial exception of *Flight into Camden* none of these novels is set further south than Birmingham), composed of back-to-back streets, pubs, and fat, garrulous women hanging out washing in grimy back yards? The first thing to say is that compared to the world of the average middle-class novel of the time, where a raised fist or an overturned glass is a major event, it is extraordinarily violent. Arthur Seaton is always in fights, either fending off angry husbands or simply being bloody-minded. Arthur Haggerston is little more than a teenage gangster. Machin in *This Sporting Life* is a flashfisted bully both on and off the rugby field. Moreover, this is not an individual aggression, clinging to a particular psyche; it is liable to spill out without warning into collective uproar, as in the cinema punch-up in *The Day of the Sardine* or the street brawl that enlivens *Saturday Night and Sunday Morning*. The whole atmosphere of the Sillitoe/Chaplin/Storey novel is a throwback to the old-fashioned 'they went at it like good 'uns' type of novel which reached its height with Thackeray and Surtees and had a late flowering under Meredith and Charles Reade.

At the same time the novels depict a more prosperous world. Arthur Seaton reflects on one occasion how 'happy' his father is: a sit-down job, money for beer, holidays, a television set, steadily rising wages (it is typical of Arthur that he should conceive of happiness in wholly material terms). In a growth economy the advantage lies with the wage-earner:

> No more short-time like before the war or getting the sack if you stood for ten minutes in the lavatory reading your *Football Post* – if the gaffer got on to you now you could always tell him where to put the job and go somewhere else.

Arthur is keenly conscious that the war has done this: 'the difference between before the war and after the war didn't bear thinking about. War was a marvellous thing in some ways, when you thought about how happy it had made some people.' The average middle-class fictional sensibility of the immediately post-war era might have visualised 1939–45 as an impenetrable shutter brought down over a world of vanishing plenty, but for the workers on the morning shift it was a limitless window of opportunity.

However, prosperity has not changed some fundamental attitudes and uneasinesses. Chief among these is what might be called a dissociation from official or public forms of life. Few protagonists of working-class fiction, for instance, have any strong patriotic feelings. Arthur Seaton's memories of childhood include listening to Churchill's radio broadcasts on the progress of the war 'as if it mattered'. His father is quietly proud of the fact that he managed to evade military service by feigning poor eyesight. A middle-class writer would have sensationalised these attitudes: to Sillitoe they are merely routine. Flag-waving is, he seems to imply, a middle-class luxury. The law is as suspect as patriotism, an excuse for wool-pulling and obfuscation on the part of 'them' – that is, amorphous yet malevolent authority. Thus Mrs Haggerston wants a divorce from her absent husband, but fears the upheaval it will bring. 'That's us lower orders,' Arthur reflects. 'We'd rather keep the ball and chain than go to law.'

Above all, there is still the destructive influence of class, which is always on hand to disturb people who are keenly aware of their vulnerability to social slights, ready to jeopardise a character's view of himself and his integrity. In the war-time section of *Going to the Moon*, Colin and his family are evacuated from their bombed-out house to a dug-out home: the socially superior relatives who live nearby want nothing to do with this unexpected visitation. 'My mother burst into tears that first night in the cellar,' Colin remembers. 'I got it then in a flash, the bitter caste system, the up there and down here and half ways, and Christ knows how many graduations in between.' Machin in *This Sporting Life*, his confidence boosted by good wages and his position as a professional Rugby League player, is better equipped to deal with unwelcome manifestations of class prejudice, but he is still violently irritated by them. At one point he takes Mrs Hammond, the woman with whom he is emotionally involved, to Sunday lunch at an exclusive country restaurant. Infuriated by a patronising waiter, he gets his revenge by ordering the most expensive items on the menu, arguing over the bill and finally leaving a derisory tip.

If there is something familiar and immediately recognisable about the worlds created by Sillitoe, Callow, Storey and Chaplin, then there are strong links between the mental outlooks of their protagonists. Each is marked out by a tremendous sense of vitality, all the more remarkable in that it is purposeless, a tide of energy without obvious direction. Even Nicky Chapman in Callow's *Common People*, who stands slightly to one side of the main group on account of his artistic and bohemian leanings, burns with this vital force, in his case settled on literature. 'I turned to books. I bolted them down with real hunger, reading indiscriminately.' It would be dangerous to argue that Seaton, Chapman and the others are representative proletarians, which would ignore the obvious projections of the authors' younger selves that exist in their characterisation, but their vigour is in sharp contrast to the vacillations or inanition of a Jim Dixon or a Charles Lumley. The sack, for instance, holds no terrors for Arthur Seaton. Neither would someone like Professor Welch.

This vitality, however, coexists with overwhelming sensations of loneliness and insecurity. Nearly all of these protagonists feel hemmed in or threatened in some way. Arthur Haggerston, elevated through nepotism to a post in his Uncle George's municipal construction gang, is perpetually conscious of these pressures: 'Every day I jumped out of bed with a feeling of being trapped.' Arthur's isolation is compounded by his inability to connect with the people around him, his mother, the lodger, workmates or his fellow hoodlums. 'What I'm trying to say,' he discloses at one point, 'is that nobody knows anybody.' Arthur Seaton, for his surface cockiness, is quite as obsessed with these uncertainties:

> He felt a lack of security. No place existed in all the world that could be called safe, and he knew for the first time in his life that there never had been such a thing as safety, the difference being that now he knew it as a fact, whereas before it was a natural unconscious state.

The image of a young working-class man as a fish, either caught on a hook or netted and imprisoned in a tin, is common to *Saturday Night and Sunday Morning* and *The Day of the Sardine*. Seaton reflects that 'mostly you were like a fish: you swam about with freedom, thinking how good it was to be left alone, doing anything you wanted and caring about no one, when suddenly: SPLUTCH! – The big hook clasped itself into your mouth and you were caught.'

'Caught' has two meanings for Seaton. Specifically, it refers to his impending marriage, or at least to the prospect of a steady and non-illicit relationship. More generally, it describes his status as a tiny component in a vast machine whose revolutions he has no power to alter or even influence. Haggerston, alternatively, visualises himself as a sardine. 'Stiff and straight and swimming in the gravy, but that's no consolation when the lid's clasped.' In a final stroke of irony, Haggerston ends up working in a sardine factory. He leaves the novel as confused and dissatisfied as when he began it.

Beneath these affirmations of vitality and indomitable spirit coupled with deep insecurity lies a common attitude to life: quietist, fatalist, resigned, passive, reactive. Chance, rather than individual effort or supernatural agency, governs one's progress through the world. Seaton ascribes his good job, his wardrobe full of expensive clothes and his success with women to sheer good fortune. The Second World War, to which he constantly refers, is seen as simply another devastating stroke of fate, bringing suffering and heartbreak for millions, but prosperity and happiness for millions more. Conscious striving for betterment, consequently, will always be futile. Seaton values his own worth, but he doubts his ability to change anything:

> I'll never let anyone grind me down because I'm worth as much as any other man in the world, though when it comes to the lousy vote they give me I often feel like telling 'em where to shove it for all the good using it'll do me.

Amidst an uncertain present, the future is regarded with wary resignation. Arthur Machin is keenly aware of his probable destiny as a Rugby League player once his strength and speed have gone: an end to his considerable prestige, no more hobnobbing with the local worthies and back to factory wages. However, he is not particularly discomfited by this prospect: he can see it coming, which is an anaesthetic of a sort. *Carpe diem* is a maxim to which Seaton, Haggerston, Machin, Chapman and the others would swear unhesitating loyalty. Something might turn up. You never can tell. The catch phrases so lovingly assembled by Richard Hoggart recur with unfailing regularity in novels such as *Saturday Night and Sunday Morning* and *The Day of the Sardine*, bearing out Hoggart's observation that 'the working classes have been cheerful existentialists for centuries'.

In a world where progress of any sort depends upon chance, there is correspondingly little room for ambition. One looks for the ghost of Samuel Smiles in these accounts of 'ordinary life' lived out in the shadow of the factory gate, the self-bettering, 'improving' side of working-class existence satirised a century before by Matthew Arnold, and finds instead a handful of vague daydreams, simple exercises in wish-fulfilment. Arthur Haggerston hankers after a 'private plane, personal yacht, my own island and a regiment of personal slaves, including girls'. Even when Seaton manages a realistic assessment of his prospects, it is still couched in the faintly unreal, grossly materialist terms of the music-hall chorus's 'good time': 'me, I'll have a good life, plenty of work, plenty of booze and a piece of skirt every month until I'm ninety'.

Here, perhaps most obviously of all, Seaton and Co. emphasise their detachment from the conventional middle-class hero of the 1950s: Jim Dixon with his dead-end job in a ghoulish provincial university, Billy Fisher with his ambitions to be a radio comedy scriptwriter, Joe Lampton with his conviction that there is room at the top if you can take a few knocks and don't mind treading on the fingers of the man beneath you on the ladder. Seaton, Haggerston and Chapman do not want to 'get on'. They would like more money, certainly, but they would balk at taking a supervisor's job, a position that would take them out of the circle of ordinary workmen and seem a disloyal mingling with the 'bosses'. Such expressions of ambition as do arise, consequently, are mostly ironic. ' "Ah'm going to be someone," ' Arthur Haggerston declares. ' "Get filthy rich. Hob with the nobs." ' This is tongue-in-cheek, but one of John Braine's bustling young go-getters might have said it and actually meant it.

Rather than desiring to be 'taken up' by authority, whether the management of their place of work or some other echelon of the establishment, Seaton, Haggerston and Co. merely want to be left alone, far away from 'them' with 'their' tax demands, pettifogging regulations and bureaucratic bloodymindedness. If they have an ambition it is to preserve their integrity, their sense of who they are, in the face of what they have come to see as chaotic external forces. Not only does Haggerston fear the constriction of the sardine tin; he fears resembling everyone else. Machin sees the professional Rugby League game as a means of preserving his identity. His regard for Frank, the team captain, stems from the fact that 'by playing Rugby League he kept his head above the general level of crap and that to me was the main thing'. The result is a delicately balanced view of the future in which a hankering for material success, measured out in new suits and the ability to stand rounds at the bar, is balanced by an engrained wariness over the possible consequences of that success and, above all, a fervent desire to maintain a tiny but inviolable corner of personal space.

Practically applied, this collective mental outlook leads to a series of confused moral positions. The distinguishing feature of nearly all these protagonists is a passionate anti-authoritarianism, a dislike of officialdom that takes in the police, park-keepers, rent-collectors and almost everyone claiming some form of official status. There is a symbolic moment in *Saturday Night and Sunday Morning* when Seaton and his brother try to stop a woman in khaki from apprehending a confused middle-aged man who has hurled a stone through the window of a shop selling funeral headstones. The man's explanation is that he did it for his mother: ' "I buried her three months ago. I didn't mean no harm." ' Despite Arthur's encouragement – ' "Why don't you run mate? You'll be all right. I wain't stop yer, and my brother wain't" ' – the man is mesmerised by both his crime and the woman's authority, even though it would be a simple matter to push her aside. The incident reveals two things about Arthur: on the one hand a genuine compassion; on the other an intense hatred of women in uniform who attempt to enforce the law. In fact Arthur's whole life is shot through with moral ambivalence. He and his brother are quite happy to separate a drunk from his wallet or to plug an air-rifle bullet into the face of an interfering neighbour. At the same time he shows consideration towards women, is capable of considerable generosity, albeit a free-handedness which is born of a full wage-packet, and is able to cultivate warm, if guilt-ridden, feelings towards the man with whose wife he is having an affair. Arthur's attitude to Jack, Brenda's husband and his colleague at the factory, is complex. At one point he wants to 'shake his hand and tell him everything; tell him how good he thought he – Jack – was, that he had guts, and that he was all right, that he didn't like to see him suffer because of a looney thing like this . . .'

The majority of Seaton's fictional contemporaries share this fractured moral outlook. Arthur Haggerston will cheerfully steal newly-baked cakes left out to cool on an unguarded windowsill, and his chief complaint about the rackets practised at his place of work seems to be that he is not allowed to participate in them, but he is capable of intense loyalty, both to his mother and to his friends. Even in the violent world of gang warfare, Haggerston adheres to certain rules: he refuses to carry a knife, for example, and prefers 'a fair fight' – one against one – to a group attack on a single victim. Machin, in contrast, is an altogether nastier piece of work, arrogant, boorish, vengeful, capable, for instance, of contriving to have an opponent sent off the field of play by covertly striking one of his own team-mates. Machin can be generous, but never disinterestedly so. His attitude to women is simply disgusting. There is a teeth-grating scene in which, having publicly insulted Mrs Hammond, he is rebuked by a shocked friend: ' "You shouldn't say things like that to her. You talk as if you own the woman." ' ' "For the moment I do," ' Arthur replies, ' "and she doesn't like it." ' It is a far cry from Hoggart's intimations of 'decency', his promise of a 'comely life'. Only Philip Callow's heroes, Colin and Nicky Chapman – considerate, self-abasing, nervous – correspond to these standards, and they are exceptions, adrift from the mainstream of working-class life, Hoggart's 'solitaries', enflamed by the prospect of a bohemian existence lived out beyond the shadows of the factory gate and the back-to-back terrace.

The varying degrees of unpleasantness exhibited by Seaton, Haggerston, Machin *et al.* were not lost on other fictional commentators of the time. Reflexiveness of this sort is characteristic of the novels of the 1950s and 1960s, many of which sometimes seem to be fighting out private battles with other novelists rather than addressing themselves to that elusive creature, the general reader. If one wanted a gauge of the vast gap which separates Arthur Seaton from some of the tepid middle-class fall guys who populate the novels of the 1950s, it can be found in the diary kept by Miranda, the art student whose imprisonment by a deranged pools winner forms the basis of John Fowles's *The Collector* (1963). Miranda, with her exemplary left-wing views and her genuine, if somewhat imperious, concern for humanity, is appalled by Arthur Seaton.

I think *Saturday Night and Sunday Morning* is disgusting. I think Arthur Seaton is disgusting; and I think the most disgusting thing of all is that Alan Sillitoe doesn't show that he's disgusted by his young man. I think they think young men like that are really rather fine.

Presumably 'they' are working-class novelists of the Sillitoe/Chaplin type.

It is clear that Fowles is fascinated by Seaton's attitudes and their significance to a middle-class woman held captive by a newly rich class obsessive, as he allows Miranda to spend several paragraphs quantifying her dislike. Additionally she 'hates the way Arthur Seaton just doesn't care about anything outside his own little life'. He is 'mean, narrow, selfish, brutal'. Moreover, 'because he's cheeky and hates his work and is successful with women, he is supposed to be vital'. The only thing that Miranda can find to say in Arthur's favour is that she has the feeling that there is something within him that could be used for good if it could be got hold of. Perhaps, she muses, Sillitoe wanted to attack the society that produces such people. But he never makes his intentions clear. In other words, loathing mixes with fear, incomprehension and a lurking desire to patronise. In the end Miranda simply marks Seaton down as a fictional representative of the new 'Calibanry' epitomised by her gaoler, Clegg. Her most profound regret, one might say, is the inability of the working classes to match up to her expectations of them.

But then plenty of people at the end of the 1950s and the beginning of the 1960s had 'expectations' of the working classes, from the Labour party and the trades-union movement, with which they were indelibly associated, down to Kingsley Martin's *New Statesman*, with which they were not. The tendency to label this extremely large group of people – perhaps 25 million men, women and children – 'working class' and assume that the taxonomy was complete is symptomatic of the lack of curiosity shown by the average middle-class commentator. Harry Ritchie has pointed out that the critics who agonised over the exact place in the social scale occupied by Jim Dixon altogether failed to perform the same service for Arthur Seaton: he was merely working class, and there was an end to it. In fact the 60 or 70 per cent of the population logged by the census surveys as 'working class' were characterised by distinctive economic and social differences. Statistics reveal widening economic divisions, accentuated throughout the immediately post-war years. But to the effects of a selective affluence can be added a series of infinitely subtle and unspoken class gradations capable of separating one street from another or detaching a single family from the casual solidarity of the neighbourhood.

For all their strong similarities, the characters in Sillitoe, Chaplin and Storey's novels come from very different sections of the working class, each espousing slightly different collective standards. The Chapmans in *Going to the Moon*, for example, combine poverty with ferocious honesty. One of Nicky's sharpest memories is of a family holiday in the 1930s during the course of which his mother picks up a stray five-pound note. The discovery produces a terrible crisis of conscience ('this conflict between need and what was right and wrong'), sufficient to ruin their holiday even after the note has been handed in at the local police station. The elder Machins, alternatively, are poor, genteel, religious people, wary of their son's prosperity and the dubious associates it brings him. Mrs Haggerston is a little further down the social scale, hot-tempered – she will happily correct Arthur's obstreperousness with a hurled teapot – indifferent to the scandal that attaches to harbouring a male lodger, fearful of authority but at the same time keen to keep her son out of trouble for reasons which have as much to do with her own moral code as sheer prudence. The Seatons are much more rowdy and anarchic – draft-dodgers, grudge-bearers and score-settlers, eager to convert an imagined personal slight into an immediate collective grievance. Arthur's wounding of the mean-spirited and prying neighbour Mrs Bull with an air-rifle slug is simply seen as a good joke, paying an acknowledged irritant back with interest. Yet the Seatons are aware that lines have to be drawn. During the war they concealed relatives on the run from the military, but they would probably stop short of handling stolen property.

Buttressed by traditional notions of a broadly homogeneous working class, the reader examines the working-class fiction of the period expecting to discover class solidarity, and finds instead only the factors combining to weaken it. Even the Nottingham back streets inhabited by the Seatons harbour their own fractures and animosities. The fight between old man Seaton and a reluctant Mr Bull, which sparks off a mass free-for-all, also uncovers some telling social divisions. Another neighbour, Mrs Robins, faints and sends her husband indoors for whisky, 'a good excuse for him to stay out of the fight because he was a man who sent his sons to join the Scouts and always voted Liberal, a traitor to the solid bloc of anarchistic Labour in the street'. 'Anarchistic Labour' is a good enough phrase, but it is the anarchism rather than the support for the Labour party that seems to carry the most weight. The deliberate political note which is occasionally struck in Sillitoe's early writings invariably seems false. In the short stories collected in *The Loneliness of the Long-distance Runner*, for example, Sillitoe will occasionally make his characters sing anti-war songs or comment unfavourably on the monarchy, but the abiding impression is that of authorial tampering.

But there were much more significant factors operating against working-class cohesion. Chief among these were the demarcations of employment, in particular the divisions of 'skilled' and 'unskilled' labour, and the trades-union insistence on the preservation of 'differentials'. Nicky Chapman in *Common People* observes of the position held by an acquaintance of his in the factory that 'it was a skilled, aristocratic sort of job, very specialised and important'. As it happens the duties performed by Nicky's friend are not markedly different from those carried out by other workers, but they are invested with an aura of exclusiveness and mystery.

The exalted position of the superior operative, the 'craftsman', turns up repeatedly in fiction of this type. Bill Naughton's story 'A Skilled Man' (1959), for example, is built on the social and political divisions which such status was thought to produce. Edgar King's life and his social and political judgements derive entirely from the superior position he occupies at his workplace. He regards the requirement for skilled men to work extra hours on Saturday morning as an advantage – 'Folk never treat you with the same respect on a day off.' Considering the state of his marriage, he immediately remembers his mother's comments on the social background of his wife: ' "Never a skilled man in the family; nothing but labourers and blasted hod carriers. *Never rely on folks as don't do skilled work.*" ' Even in the pub, when a friend presses a pint on him, Edgar reflects: 'That's a sure sign of the unskilled worker ... he forces on you what he thinks you should have.' The most significant consequence of Edgar's status, though, comes when the talk turns to politics. His response to a disparaging remark about the government is that ' "the Tories aren't doing too bad" '.

And if the Tories weren't doing too bad, Labour, regrettably, weren't doing too well. To middle-class commentators the Labour party and the trades-union movement might have seemed a natural repository for working-class sympathies. The reality, as represented in the fiction of Sillitoe, Chaplin and Callow, is very different. The post-war Labour party, in particular, and the whole concept of municipal socialism is seen as little more than a racket. Arthur Seaton might complain about ' "these big fat Tory bastards in parliament" ' but he is equally hostile to ' "them Labour bleeders too" ' on the grounds that ' "they rob our wage packets every week with insurance and income tax and try to tell us its all for our own good" '.

Seaton's antipathy is merely selfish. A more wounding perspective on what the Labour party might be supposed to mean to the average working man comes in *The Day of the Sardine*, when Arthur Haggerston is finally forced to summon up family influence in his pursuit of a job. Arthur's celebrated Uncle George, to whom he applies, is amply characterised by his wife's admiring testimony: ' "He's worked his way up to the top of the tree ... charge o' the gang, big man in the Labour party, magistrate and once mayor." ' But Uncle George, with his memories of meeting Ernest Bevin, his stupendous ignorance and his immense conceit, is merely a fraud whose construction gang is busy swindling the municipality. The Labour party, consequently, appears as a vehicle for personal rather than collective advancement; the implication is that successful Labour politicians achieve their position by clambering upon the shoulders of their less fortunate fellow workers. A similar cynicism attends any discussion of trades-union activities. Arthur Seaton, for instance, is engaged in a conspiracy with his factory foreman to prevent the union representatives from finding out how fast he works and how much he earns; if his high wages were revealed it would probably cause trouble. Resentment at trades-union interference in the right of the piece-worker to make as much money as he can is balanced by a belief in the ultimate ineffectuality of organised labour. Colin in *Going to the Moon* takes part in a token one-day stoppage organised by shop stewards at his factory. Initially the idea appeals to him: 'A strike gave you an illusion of movement and power that was exciting.' Colin attends a mass meeting and is vaguely stirred by the proceedings, but the next day back at work he realises that 'nothing had changed. We were all stuck, we all had our different reasons, excuses for being caught by the short hairs.'

Socialism, then, is not something in which the average fictional working man takes any interest, unless it is to provide a target for his cynicism. Certainly it could not be described as a unifying force. The probability is that it never was. Political uncertainties have very little to do with one of the chief features of the working-class novel: the increasing detachment of most of the protagonists from their environment, and the fragmentation of the society of which they are part. Fictional depictions of the impending break-up of traditional working-class society can be glimpsed before Hoggart. On the rare occasions on which the gaze of a non-working-class writer strays downward, it is invariably caught by the evidence of cultural change. When Lumley in *Hurry On Down* (1953) visits the home of his working-class girlfriend Rosa he is disagreeably impressed by the contrast between Rosa's father and her brother, Stan. The former appears to Lumley to be a figure of 'genuine dignity'; the latter has merely a 'cheap sharpness'. Gradually Lumley comes to realise that Stan speaks a different language to his father, 'demotic English of the mid-twentieth century, rapid, slurred, essentially a city dialect, in origin essentially American'. As a judgement this could have come straight out of *The Uses of Literacy*, but its origins lie further back in Priestley and Orwell. The same point could be made of Mark Underwood, the middle-class student of David Lodge's *The Picturegoers* (1960), who feels that by lodging with the working-class Mallory family 'he had rediscovered the people'. However, the popular art he looks for to accompany this rediscovery is sadly lacking. Visiting a cinema he notes that the films are 'quite artificial and valueless'.

More than mannerisms acquired from Hollywood cinema, education can be seen as one of the singular forces affecting people's lives. Few of the protagonists of the fiction discussed here are unaffected by it, from Margaret Thorpe's brother in *Flight into Camden*, whose qualifications subtly detach him from his family, to Colin in *Going to the Moon*, whose interest in books is anxiously monitored by his parents. The prevailing attitude to education can perhaps be summarised as this: it may advance your prospects, but it will sever you from the class to which you belong. In general, enthusiasm over the likely material results of education is matched by wariness over the probable social outcome. ' "I suppose he gets his daft ideas out of a book. Never mind, you can't stop him reading. Education's a wonderful thing, get you a good job," ' the reaction of Colin's parents to their son's bookishness, is typical. Similarly in *The Day of the Sardine*, Flack, the elderly man with whom Arthur Haggerston works on the building site, urges him to 'Read books', 'Get learnin', 'Be a somebody'. Yet the injunction conceals a personal tragedy. Flack's nephew, whom he assisted financially during the young man's time at university, rewarded him only with contempt: ' "Well, he went and it was worse than goin' to the war. He came back a few times but it would have been better if he'd stayed away." ' The revelation has a particular significance to Arthur, as it transpires that Flack's nephew was a martinet schoolmaster against whom Arthur's class finally rebelled, and who eventually killed himself. The rewards of the scholarship boy, as John Kemp discovers to his cost in Philip Larkin's *Jill* (1946), are frequently not worth having. The tendency of education to split a family in two is an abiding theme of *Flight into Camden*. In the majority of the working-class novels of the period it has a dual purpose, both breaking down class structures and forming a fixed point between old and new orders. It is education, her status as a schoolmistress, which throws Margaret Thorpe into the orbit of her art-teacher lover. Similarly, it is education which gives her the articulacy and the confidence to argue her case with her distraught parents.

There are many such confrontations between older and younger generations. They are quite as likely to arise out of simple affluence. The principal complaint of Machin senior, aghast at Arthur's casual attitudes and moral disinterestedness, is the exalted but dubious company his son keeps. Arthur's defence is that ' "where there's money there's dirt" '. When his father suggests that ' "there's money and money" ', Arthur has no time for what he regards as moral superfluities. ' "Money's money to me. Nobody

can cut it up into good money and bad." ' But it is money that
has caused Arthur to forsake the moral standards of his family.
Like Seaton, he sees success in wholly material terms. Thus he
believes that his value to Mrs Hammond rests in his ability to
supply her with television sets, furnishings and knick-knacks. The
television, a subject which is largely outside Hoggart's frame of
reference, assumes a vast symbolic importance in post-war
working-class fiction: the sign of prosperity and a salve for turbulence. The Seatons stay glued to it throughout their leisure hours.
Seaton's sister Margaret considers a television to be a palliative
against the violence of her drunken husband. Edgar King has
purchased a set for his wife ' "after the Coronation put the idea
in your head" '. Seaton, alone among the army of eager watchers,
suspects a capitalist plot:

> 'they'd go barmy if they had them taken away ... Everybody'd
> go crackers. There'd be a revolution, I'm sure there would,
> they'd blow up the Council House and set fire to the Castle.'

Undoubtedly there were many other factors contributing to the
break-up of a settled way of life. Those writers who allowed
themselves to think about the consequences were uniformly
gloomy, adducing selfishness, a detachment from past values. The
cockney boy who works in the coffee bar frequented by Julia in
Doris Lessing's *Retreat to Innocence* (1956), carefully distancing
himself from bygone struggle, is perhaps typical:

> 'I've been raised on William Morris and Keir Hardie and all
> that lot and I wouldn't say a word against them – grand old
> boys they were. But I says to my dad, I says, what's in it for
> me?'

What indeed?
Very occasionally a writer will attempt to assess a character's
value in terms of his working-class affiliations. In *Flight into
Camden*, for example, David Storey suggests that the apparent
classlessness of Margaret's art-teacher lover is a kind of weakness.
Others see no value in class association unless it should be

threatened by the imagined social superiority of others – a reflection, perhaps, of a time-honoured question and answer formula from Wilfred Pickles's popular 1950s radio show: 'What do you dislike most?' 'Stuck-up fowk.' Philip Callow goes so far as to make an explicit comparison between the standards of his own youth and those of the generation which superseded it. Colin, supposedly writing *Going to the Moon* in the 1960s, frequently mentions a young man named Tommy with whom he has become friendly. Colin regards his new acquaintance with a sociologist's eye. He is attracted by Tommy's 'goon humour and his contempt for regulations and discipline', while acknowledging that the young man is a deracinated figure – 'like most of his generation he's already left traditional England behind'. Tommy lives a transient existence. 'He's temporary: job, flat, car, country, everything is for the time being.' Employment is a means to an end, 'with no pretence of worry or conscientiousness'; the reprimands issued by his superiors are intolerable. With deracination, predictably enough, comes confusion, a tremendous uncertainty over his place in society and relation to milieu. 'Nothing confuses him easier than class. He lives in a prefab and insults the tabloids . . .' To Colin, Tommy's distinguishing feature is his complete detachment from the old working-class standards of thriftiness and care, an absorption in an environment whose disadvantages were all too plain but redeemed themselves through familiarity. Colin notes:

If a thing's dilapidated his instinct is to chuck it in the dustbin . . . If I could take him back to my childhood in Ernaldhay Street, decent and respectable slum, I bet he'd turn up his nose.

The same point could be made of Arthur Seaton and Arthur Machin, Tommies in embryo, whose increasing affluence is distancing them from some of the consolations of poverty. Like the majority of working-class fictional characters of the period, they are on the move between an older, communal life and a newer individualism: transient, restless and dissatisfied. It would be an exaggeration to say that working-class novels of the 1950s simply illustrate the Hoggart thesis, for there are many ways in which they contradict it, but the connection between the two is very strong. Their message – that affluence or any form of social advancement is likely to have a destructive effect on fundamental patterns of ordinary life – is in any case identical to Hoggart's. Most conspicuous of all, perhaps, is their quietism. If one wanted an explanation of the failure to establish an effective working-class political movement in this country, it could be found in *Saturday Night and Sunday Morning*, both in Seaton's selfish anarchism and in the respectfully adhered to gradations of the world in which he operates. Oddly, for works so firmly rooted in the attitudes of a particular section of society, Sillitoe, Chaplin and Callow's novels are largely free of class antagonism. The deracination of the average working-class protagonist seldom led him to a direct political statement. As an examination of later, more conventional English fiction will show, this tended to be the prerogative of the radical middle classes. But then the class struggle in this country has nearly always been superintended by forces other than those it was immediately intended to benefit.

6

Some Liberal Dilemmas

Asking the question 'What is a liberal?' can still inspire a revealing parlour game. At the very least, a word which has at various times been associated with Voltaire, Gladstone, John F. Kennedy and Mrs Thatcher must have a certain elasticity of application. A century ago, of course, such an enquiry took on an immediate political importance: no doubt it occurred to the party managers of the 1905 Liberal landslide, a rainbow coalition of interest groups uneasily assembled beneath a single banner. But to separate a free-trader from an embryo Fabian, a die-hard imperialist from a dissenter – all significant lobbies represented in Campbell-Bannerman's administration – was to evade the broader question of definition.

Unlike Conservatism or English-style socialism, which might be better described as 'Labourism', liberalism has always carried with it large amounts of extra-political baggage – attitudes that were moral or even scientific and which, when added together, tended to place the collective label in doubt. Gissing, to take a far from representative figure from the late-Victorian twilight, would doubtless have described himself as a liberal, but it was a highly refined version of liberalism in which a belief in scientific progress – what Gissing would have called 'rationalism' – and a contempt for democracy uneasily contended. This confusion is typical. In fact, as John Gross suggests in *The Rise and Fall of the Man of Letters* (1969), in political, let alone moral, terms the word is what scientists would call a false isolate: there is no such thing as 'liberalism', only a series of liberalisms. Nevertheless, to a certain type of writer cautiously at large in the post-war world, 'liberalism' had a distinctive meaning, and the liberal tradition, however vaguely expressed, underpinned a whole view of communal and individual behaviour.

The 1950s were not a good time to be a liberal. Official liberalism was very nearly extinct. A decade of despotism had given way to an era of international power politics. The Liberal party, which had maintained a tenuous presence in the coalition governments of the 1930s and 1940s, emerged into the cold light of the 1945 House of Commons with a dozen MPs. Those of its members who migrated to the Labour benches discovered an inhospitable alliance dominated by trades-union corporatism. Suez; Europe; the colonial retreat: in a happier age these might have been classic liberal issues – as in a certain sense they were – but one had to look hard to find a whiff of Gladstonian principle in their resolution. There was also a sense that the intellectual heavy artillery had changed sides some time before: T. S. Eliot's notorious pre-war remark about a society 'worm-eaten by liberalism' was as much a betrayal as Kingsley Martin's refusal to allow readers of the *New Statesman* to face the facts about Spain.

The war, too, had emphasised the extent of the moral retreat. Caught between fascism and the democratic authoritarianism necessary to destroy it, pious assumptions about freedom of expression and a better world were allowed very little room for manoeuvre. As Orwell remarked, the choice seemed to be between bombing civilians and killing children with lumps of thermite, or becoming enslaved by people who were more prepared to do this than you yourself. These were harsh lessons for the average 1930s liberal, nurtured on a diet of international co-operation and spreading enlightenment – the League of Nations was a touchstone of inter-war liberal faith – to take to heart.

Much of the consequent disillusionment is reflected in the 1950s novels of C. P. Snow. The course of his hero Lewis Eliot's career – his date of birth is given as 1905 – demonstrates a drift from the optimism of a young man from a humble background on the edge of a world of almost limitless opportunity in the mid–1920s to the measured and occasionally cynical judgements of a middle-aged bureaucrat. *Homecoming* (1956) brings many of these sentiments together, notably in its account of the career of Eliot's friend

George Passant. An enthusiastic provincial solicitor in the late 1920s, Passant cultivates the creed of 'progress' a belief that with the aid of intelligence and hard work a poor boy can make his way upwards through a more mobile society in which class barriers are steadily breaking down. Sustained by these assumptions, Passant encourages his friends, Eliot among them, to learn and study and form a group of like-minded zealots to discuss 'freedom' and the prospect of a better world. Later we find him admitting to Eliot that in the 1951 General Election he has voted Conservative for the first time. Eliot, who retains his left-wing opinions, understands, adding that in the last thirty years on the whole things have 'gone worse than we could possibly have imagined'.

'Freedom'; 'the prospect of a better world' – these are abstracts of the kind gently mocked by Anthony Powell, but they point towards one crucial aspect of the liberal spirit, the utopian side that believes in the existence of 'men of goodwill' and a national interest that transcends narrow political expediency. The more concrete aspects of post-war literary liberalism were a matter of gesture – affectionate nods in the direction of the Spanish Civil War, pre–1939 pacifism. The definition of a 1950s liberal was harder to pin down. Professor Treece in Malcolm Bradbury's *Eating People is Wrong* (1959) espouses 'a firm assurance of the necessity for good taste, honest feeling, integrity of motive'. To which one might add words such as 'tolerance', 'charitableness' and 'generosity of spirit'.

If these attitudes have a literary model, they can perhaps be found in the figure of E. M. Forster – and indeed Forster is a significant presence in several novels written in or about the 1950s. When Louis Bates, Treece's difficult working-class student, writes a combative essay on the poverty of the post-war literary imagination, it contains an approving reference to 'our old figurehead'. Frederica, the undergraduate siren of A. S. Byatt's *Still Life* (1985), a novel which consciously explores some of the limits of liberalism, actually attends a Cambridge tea party at which Forster is present, a largely symbolic event as the novelist spends most of his time asleep. Elsewhere in the novel another student reverently quotes Forster's opinion that the only duty one can enjoin is tolerance. It is not quite accurate to call this a Bloomsbury attitude – Forster claimed not to have read G. E. Moore – and Forster's moral scrupulousness is a great deal less forced, less liable to founder on the rock of personal jealousies. It is significant that the chapter assigned to him in the final volume of *The Pelican Guide to English Literature*, published in the early 1960s, is entitled 'Mr Forster's Good Influence'. Its author, G. D. Klingopulos, has no difficulty in marking down Forster's appeal to the average liberal humanist: 'his attractive, though not easily imitable, intellectual shrewdness, delicacy and responsibility'. There had been a demonstration of what delicacy and responsibility might mean in practice, too, with the publication of the essay 'What I Believe' – a rallying point for many different sorts of people during the anxious and illiberal times of 1939–45.

The questions Forster asks are, as Klingopulos points out, the liberal questions that a free society must consider. How is one to remain true to a generous impulse in a world which imposes mere conformity? How can men and women achieve a good relationship with other men and women and avoid the dangers of selfishness and self-sufficiency? These were both questions which many postwar novelists wished to discuss, even if they – and their characters – occasionally suspected that this combination of moral principle and practical action was at best unfashionable and at worst anachronistic. Frederica, for example, has her doubts about the wisdom of meeting Forster. Above all, she feels that she and her friends 'were now living furiously in a world the novelist had said had changed beyond recognition and discrimination in his fiction. What could she have to say to him? Or he to her?'

Angus Wilson's story 'Such Darling Dodos' (1950) provides a detailed description of pre-war Fabian vigour now foundering in terminal post-war decay. Tony, an elderly Catholic dandy, is staying in north Oxford with his cousin Priscilla and her husband Robin, a dying Oxford don. The relationship between the two cousins is founded on mutual incomprehension, an uneasiness that surfaces when Priscilla brings her guest – a ghastly vista of cold cream and hair-net – his breakfast. 'Pathos always made her feel awkward, and at the moment she felt very keenly the pathos of this lonely, ageing, snobbish old man whom she tolerated through childhood ties.' But pathos, Wilson suggests, is a key liberal attitude, and a questionable one at that:

> Pathos was Priscilla's dominating sensation: it had led her into Swaraj and Public Assistance Committees, into Basque relief and child psychiatry clinics; at the moment it kept her on a Rent Restriction Tribunal; it fixed her emotionally as a child playing dolls' hospitals.

There follows a guided tour of the ambitions and attitudes of a more confident age. The sideboard is covered with mementos of a high-minded past: photographs of Robin as a conscientious objector farm labourer of 1916, Priscilla and himself attending Fabian summer schools in the 1930s. As the conversation continues, Tony becomes progressively more annoyed. In particular, he finds Priscilla's naïve sense of duty intolerable. When she observes wistfully that ' "there won't be so much time and I've been able to clear up so pitifully little of the mess" ', he retorts: ' "Oh, my dear, if you're going to constitute yourself charwoman to the world." ' Their quarrel, such as it is, is presented with a certain amount of even-handedness. Cataloguing his complaints against the type of socialist high-mindedness which his relatives represent, Tony is especially irritated by what he sees as officious interference, misdirected zeal. Robin, Priscilla and their kind are:

> too busy . . . covering reality over with reading and talking, too busy making things that were better not made and experimenting with things that should have been left alone, too busy urging rights and forgetting duties, a futile struggle to justify by works alone.

And yet Tony is honest enough to admit that in their company he feels a keen sense of his own limitations. Walking past their gate he is conscious of a 'curious, ridiculous sensation of having missed the essentials of life'.

But 'the essentials of life' are as indefinable as liberalism itself. Robin's self-confident *apologia pro vita sua* seems to lack something:

'We've made mistakes, but on the whole we've been on the right lines. Besides that fact, any feelings of fear or loneliness or doubt, even this beastly physical pain are irrelevant – squalid and unnecessary, but irrelevant.'

These are the words of a dying man, albeit an imaginary one, but all the same one rather wants to draw Robin's attention to some of the liberal mistakes of the previous twenty years – appeasement, for example, or some of the lies about Spain. In any case Robin's detachment from what is really going on in the world is made complete by the visit of Michael and Harriet Eccles. A young couple of scrupulous politeness but extravagantly right-wing views, church-goers and supporters of capital punishment, the Eccleses are opposed to nearly everything that Robin and Priscilla hold dear, from the United Front to the Hunger Marches. Later, as Tony accompanies Michael and Harriet through north Oxford, their criticism becomes a little less courteous. ' "I think it's rather pathetic," ' Harriet asserts, ' "and I suppose they *did* do good work in a way." ' Michael thinks that ' "so much of it was sentimentalism of a rather dangerous kind" '.

Though Tony has to acknowledge that the Eccleses' view of recent political history is absurdly oversimplified – at one point they seem eager to blame Robin and Priscilla for Munich – he is not disposed to correct them. In fact he is pleasantly surprised to find himself for once in sympathy with youthful opinion: 'he hadn't felt so modern since the first production of *L'après-midi*'. The story gains much of its tension from the feeling, reflected in exchanges of this sort, that the oppositions are not clear-cut and that authorial judgement is being withheld. It is not merely a conflict between Robin and Priscilla's high-mindedness and Tony's worldly cynicism, for Tony has the Catholic's highly developed sense of duty. Neither is it a conflict between matter-of-fact realism and idealistic smugness, for Tony's sense of diminishment in the presence of his relatives is openly acknowledged. Rather, it suggests that what was once an acceptable way of looking at the world is no longer adequate to deal with ever-altering circumstance.

There is a good deal more of this in the fiction of the immediately post-war period, much of it *en passant*. John Bowen's *Story-*

board (1960), for example, mocks a magazine called the *Radical*, loosely modelled on the *New Statesman*, whose 1930s liberalism is made to seem dated and hypocritical. More sustained criticism tends to surface in novels of the 1960s which look back, with a mixture of exasperation and affection, to a war-time upbringing among the radical middle classes.

In the 1960s the chief complaint concerns a paralysing tolerance which denies genuine importance to anything except the tolerance itself, even at the expense of the most vital demands of childhood. Thus both the sisters in A. S. Byatt's *The Game* (1968) nurture unhappy memories of their father's Quaker beliefs. Julia remembers him proclaiming pacifism but urging toleration of those who killed: exemplary liberal sentiments no doubt, but 'both the girls had intensely disliked the way in which the Friends familiarised the terrible and made it a comfortable possession', their habit of taming something that could not and should not be tamed. As a young woman Cassandra leaves the Society of Friends for exactly this reason, treating them to a distraught valedictory lecture:

> 'You always talk as though passive resistance will convert violence to love. But it can't, and it doesn't, and we ought to admit it, there *will always be* people who will slash open the other cheek when it is turned to them.'

To the sisters, their father's idealism is horribly suspect: after all, one wants to feel that one's parents stand for something other than the principle of *laissez-faire*. As it was, their childhood seemed compromised by sheer open-mindedness. Both the girls are at different times affronted by the fact 'that he could apparently feel so little involuntary emotion as to pursue this course successfully'. Cassandra reflects – a particularly damning thing for a child to say of a parent – that she was 'never *sure* of him'. Her conclusion is that 'out of this liberalism, extremism grows. What was in fact given to us was space to discover violence.'

This claim was to be made again, and with greater force. For the moment the charges levelled by writers such as Byatt and Margaret Drabble at the liberal ethic was that it betrayed a lack of understanding of human nature. Rosamund Stacey in *The Mill-stone* (1965), as exemplary a middle-class socialist as one could hope to find, is still irritated by the memory of her parents' high-mindedness, an attitude epitomised by their habit of 'letting the charlady sit down and dine with us, introducing her to visitors and that kind of nonsense'. The Staceys, their daughter concludes, were 'nice, kind and gentle'. However, 'people aren't nice and kind and gentle, they just aren't'. Eventually the charlady, who despises her employers, absconds with the silver cutlery. Significantly, Rosamund's complaint is at her parents' placid reaction: 'they weren't even shocked when she did it'.

The charges against liberalism can be easily summarised, perhaps a shade too easily: toleration often implies sheer spinelessness rather than emotional generosity; extending to people the limitless ability to choose can look dangerously like not caring about them; to commit oneself to 'freedom' and 'human understanding' is sometimes to betray one's lack of commitment. Above all there emerges a picture of the average liberal as a man or woman ham-strung by inanition, so dominated by principle as to be incapable of rational action.

Many of these issues are dramatised in Malcolm Bradbury's two early novels, *Eating People is Wrong* (1959) and *Stepping Westward* (1965). Comic, nurtured on a 1950s tradition of slapstick and literary in-joking, each operates beneath a veil of bantering conver-sation and stock situations whose effect is often to obscure the seriousness of the ulterior motive. Like much of Bradbury's fiction, these early novels might best be described as exposés of liberalism – thin scalpels of commonsense plunged into a soft underbelly of elevated feeling – but at the same time it is a rather rueful exposure: Bradbury, one feels, is a *Guardian* reader at heart, someone who wants desperately to believe in the brotherhood of man and the amelioration of the human lot, but who has come reluctantly to acknowledge the weight of the evidence stacked against him.

Despite the six-year gap between them, *Eating People is Wrong* and *Stepping Westward* are very similar books. Key passages echo and re-echo; old arguments are taken up and re-examined. There is also the question of milieu. Both novels, ominously perhaps, given the tide of later imitations, are set in universities. With hindsight one can only assume that this was deliberate, and not merely the consequence of Bradbury's concurrent career as a university lecturer. Post-Robbins Report academe, with its apparently limitless horizons, its commitment to tolerance and freedom of expression, must have seemed an obvious stage on which liberal principles could be put to the test. Liberalism in its watered-down post-war form might not mean anything to a rapacious politician, but surely it must mean something to an institution committed to disinterested enquiry, academic freedom, 'humanism' in its broadest sense?

Unfortunately there are few liberal certainties on display in *Eating People is Wrong*. Professor Treece, its central character, is a symbolic figure. As a young 1930s radical, comic misunderstanding prevented him from joining the Republicans in Spain; half-heartedness has dogged his subsequent career. A self-conscious and uneasy man, Treece is obsessed by questions of self-definition. What, he wonders on more than one occasion, does it mean to be a liberal in the 1950s? The era is permanently elusive, the political solution unsatisfactory. An early passage attempts to quantify Treece's *accidie*:

> The middle '50s kept dissolving curiously under his grasp. He was constantly in speculation as to what he might catch hold of. Thus his political affiliation was socialist, but the socialist party never seemed to be on about the right things nowadays and, further, it was curiously hard to determine what the right things were. The whole quality of injustice had changed now. Prime Ministers said 'You've never had it so good,' but intellectuals, surely, had never had it so bad.

It is a familiar lament. All the good, brave causes are dead. They died in Spain, at the Jarrow gate, on the Labour party conference platform when Lansbury went down before the re-armers. On several occasions in the novel Treece looks back wistfully to the 1930s, 'those busy days when to be a liberal was to be something and people other than liberals knew what liberals were'.

Treece, then, is a man out of time, a refugee from a more

purposeful age, fetched up on the scrap heap of a history whose controlling forces he cannot understand. His unease is compounded by a realisation that his belief in the essential goodness of humanity is unsupported by the facts. ' "I think of man as a noble creature who has only to extend himself to the full range of his powers to be civilised and good," ' he reflects at one point. But the great mass of humanity, he concedes, have signally failed to extend themselves in this way. In fact man's performance, by and large, 'has been intrinsically evil'. Treece excepts only the radical middle classes from these strictures: ' "practically everything that we value seems to me to have been won by their efforts" '. All this has cast severe doubt on the average liberal's sense of his identity, particularly in relation to the society of which he or she is a part. One might call oneself a humanist, 'but not one of those who supposes that man is good or progress attractive', and it is an odd sort of humanist, surely, who supposes that man is evil or that progress is unattractive? In these circumstances what are men of goodwill to do? Treece can only opt for an easy, disinterested fatalism:

'One has no firm affiliation, political, religious or moral, but lies outside of all. One sees new projects tried, new cases put, and reflects on them, distrusts them, is not surprised when they don't work, and is doubtful when they seem to. A tired sophistication runs up and down one's spine.'

A tired sophistication. A polite scepticism. These are the complaints of a man who has seen too much. They are also the complaints of a man who realises that in a highly developed society the role of the individual conscience and the scope for individual action will necessarily be limited. ' "What concerns me," ' Treece announces at one point, ' "is that the quality of life and standards people live by seem to me to be getting worse, and we're not doing anything about it." ' The implication is that we no longer possess the facility to bring about this type of moral change. Ominously, Treece's feelings towards other liberals of whose opinions he might be expected to approve are those of faint disgust: the Nicholsons, for example, a pair of free-thinking, high-minded socialists of the William Morris vintage who, invited to a party Treece attends, are pictured 'going about, trying to like everyone, as they always did, and ... finding it terribly hard'.

Whatever the strength of Treece's principles, his practice of them is fatally flawed. Most culpably of all, given his profession, he is deeply pessimistic about the whole value of higher education. The opening chapter of *Eating People is Wrong* finds him conducting the first tutorial of the academic year with three student freshmen, 'the usual unpromising examination material which three years of tuition and, more importantly, self-discipline, concentration, good influences, would bring to degree level'. But Treece has become disillusioned with his educative zeal. It is difficult, he feels, to engage in the issues he finds interesting students who don't buy books, who don't read the books they are invited to read, who have a scanty grasp of the contemporary or any other scene, who are unacquainted with the principles of logic and straight thinking. It seems obvious to Treece, even at this first meeting, that two of them at least are 'persons for whom statements about creativity meant nothing'. Even now, at the beginning of a three-year course, he can predict the books they will read, the essays they will write, and their eventual destiny: leaving university with a lower-second or a third-class degree, passing into teaching or business apparently untouched by whatever values Treece has attempted to impart to them.

Personal resonance, Treece feels, ought to play a part. Here, surely, is an environment where the individual conscience and the individual mind can wield an influence? Each year he plans to send out into the world 'a little group of discontented men who would share his own disgust, his own firm assurance in the necessity for good taste, honest feeling, integrity of motive'. But Treece knows that any attempt to set himself up as a surrogate G. E. Moore is doomed to failure:

Each year came to seem odious as he foresaw the profound weariness and depression of spirit that would overcome such people who, with too few vacancies in the faculties of universities, would find themselves teaching in grammar schools in Liverpool or working in the advertising departments of soap factories in Newcastle.

Doubtless Treece would admit that somebody has to perform these useful but unglamorous tasks – after all, not everyone can work as university dons – but Bradbury's point is an unavoidable one in any discussion of the value of a liberal education. Treece knows, as every junior lecturer knows, that the majority of undergraduates in the expanded post-war environment of higher education attend university not out of any love for their subject, but because a degree gets you a better job. His colleague Carfax puts it yet more bluntly: ' "A provincial university is just a modern version of the workhouse – we're trainers of the aspiring bourgeoisie." '

If Treece fails the test of belief in the virtue of an expanding educational system, he is yet more at fault in his treatment of a second liberal touchstone – the deserving minority. Treece's reaction to the West African student Eborebelosa might be described as the liberal death wish personified. Eborebelosa, who comes from a British colony, has been dispatched to England 'at the expense . . . of a terrorist society dedicated to driving out the British. He was to study English language, sociology, economics and chemistry, paying particular attention to the making of gunpowder.' Understandably this revelation places Treece in a 'cultural quandary'. He is quite prepared to help Eborebelosa become a terrorist 'if that really was his fulfilment, and people out there seriously felt they had to be terrorists'. Surely, though, Treece feels, 'reason would prevail' and the aspiring freedom fighters would end up working in a government building, 'creating rather than destroying'. To which one is entitled to ask: What if reason doesn't prevail? What if Eborebelosa blows up the government building with gelignite? But these are not questions which Treece ever cares to ask himself. That actions have consequences is a fact that his brand of personal scrupulousness conveniently ignores.

At least these consequences are hypothetical. Eborebelosa's ability to provoke dilemmas which require immediate practical solution is confirmed when he falls in love with Emma Peel, a graduate student who is also a friend of Treece's. Emma deflects this unwelcome suit by pretending to Eborebelosa that she and Treece are engaged. Her reasons for this deception are extraordinarily complex, her guilt overwhelming:

> she had never meant to lie, it wasn't as if it was an ordinary lie, which would have been bad enough: she was lying to a member of a race which had been lied to too much already.

If Eborebelosa finds out, Emma reasons, he will surely take it as an insult to his colour, although it was intended to spare him. In any case is it, for a liberal-minded person, fair even to spare him?

> Would one want to spare a white person in this way? If one told him what one would have told a white person – 'I don't love you' – might not this seem like an attack on his colour? And if he had been a white person, wouldn't one perhaps have married him?

As an example of misplaced guilt, of confusion between the personal and the general, of striving after moral invulnerability, this takes some beating. Treece, who has his own designs on Emma, is predictably non-committal, telling her that Eborebelosa 'deserves to be judged on his merits'. Emma, who at this point in the novel regards Treece with unfeigned admiration as a model of liberal tolerance, concurs.

But Treece, the remainder of the novel reveals, is a highly unsuitable confidant in the area of personal relationships. His own are irrevocably flawed, characterised less by maturity and emotional generosity than by a desire to have his moral cake and eat it too. His dealings with Louis Bates, a 'difficult' but enthusiastic working-class student, are fraught with unease and incomprehension. To Treece, Bates represents 'hard work, honesty, thrift, clean-living, self-restraint' – not all qualities with which Treece can sympathise: he finds in Bates's values a juxtaposition of 'taste and vulgarity', a problem exacerbated when Bates, like Eborebelosa, falls in love with Emma. At the same time Treece's desultory affairs, with Emma and his colleague Viola Masefield, come to nothing. Emma declines to marry him on the highly sensible grounds that: 'You never *do* anything."' It is left to Viola to provide what is perhaps the most penetrating survey of Treece's character. She defines him as:

'a sort of moral cheat... You do the proper moral thing, as it appears under the gaze of the *New Statesman* or whatever the proper moral agencies are these days. But after you've done that you've still left everything in the air. Your soul rests easy, but nothing is solved.'

Treece's gravest failing, as he himself comes belatedly to recognise, is that he doesn't stand for anything. His strongest wish is to evade definition. This lack of commitment is reflected in the scarcity of his possessions, for 'possessions are ties, and Treece wanted to be tied to nothing, because possessions define character and Treece did not want his defined'. Even the measuring of his ability to drive a motor-cycle is fraught with the danger of unwelcome revelation. ' "I'm an expert in English Literature and they're going to ask me questions about street signs... I shall *expose* myself, I know."' The novel ends with him lying in a hospital bed, having suffered a perforated ulcer – Bates, a failed suicide, is admitted during his stay – gloomily reflecting that 'he had not learned very much. His passage had left nothing. He had never really come to grips with the world, after all, and now it was getting rather late.' What, Treece wonders, is the poor little humanist to do? 'The world was fragmented and there was no utopia in sight, and as a liberal he was a symptom of the fragmentation he abhorred.' And also, the implication is, rather a dangerous person to have about, practising all sorts of moral equivocations and fomenting all sorts of trouble merely through a desire to preserve his moral integrity.

Eating People is Wrong is slightly one-dimensional because Treece's liberalism goes unopposed. It is merely *there*: flawed, fractured and endlessly compromised, without meaning, in fact, except to a few like-minded colleagues. *Stepping Westward* sharpens the dilemma by contrasting a weary English liberalism with a foreign version, whose advocates have a much clearer idea of what it might be thought to represent. Bradbury's hero, James Walker, is a novelist of the Angry Young Man/provincial category rather than a don; here the academic background is provided by the American university at which he is appointed to a creative writing fellowship. Like its predecessor the novel is built upon a framework of literary references and allusions, the most notable drawn from Henry James, whose stories of American innocence meeting European sophistication Walker might be said to re-enact in reverse. Certainly the cultural context is one of which his hosts are keenly aware. Walker's appointment is engineered by a liberal academic named Bernard Froelich, who sees Walker as a potential ally and, it seems reasonable to assume, someone who can assist his career. From the outset, however, Froelich's view of Walker can be seen to be based on a number of highly questionable assumptions. A devout democrat, 'charmed by the English class system', Froelich senses in his new colleague 'a man who was in much the same position – a man poised between an old order and a new one, looking forward, looking back, hung between revolution and restoration'. Even more ominously, perhaps, Froelich regards Walker's novels as 'so splendidly typical, so socially representative, so aptly full of the liberal dilemma, loss of self and us versus them'.

But Walker, first seen receiving the invitation at his gloomy Midlands domicile, subsequently pictured taking diffident leave of his cheerful, matter-of-fact wife, is built on a less heroic scale. His liberalism, like Treece's, is a narrow middle-class radicalism, resting on what have since become stereotyped affiliations: on his departure, for example, his wife presents him with a copy of the morning's *Guardian*, remarking playfully: ' "You mustn't forget to take your values with you." ' Later Walker will reflect gratefully on the *Guardian*'s 'decent, modest radicalism', imagining it to mirror his own beliefs:

> His unassuming faith in the gradual betterment of the world was supported here; when experience seemed sombre, and the bland egalitarianism of the new Britain began to jar, he could turn here to find that it was, after all, for the best.

Bradbury's tone, it should be said, is relentlessly tongue-in-cheek. Just as he mocks Froelich's belief that the sociological basis of post-war English writing is such as to render any one of its practitioners an archetype, so he winks at Walker's assumption of egalitarianism: one of *Stepping Westward*'s abiding targets is the thought that society and the literature that reflects it can be reduced to such casual generalisations. But however imperceptive he may be, Walker's pessimism is genuine enough. Like Treece, again, he believes that he lives 'in the midst of a vast degeneration, a major abnegation of any regard for the quality of human life'. To Walker all the social forces which have hitherto kept intellectual, moral and spiritual aspirations alive seem inexplicably to have lapsed. He welcomes America, consequently, as a chance to escape 'the bland, uncreative British liberalism that gave him his perspective on life'.

In seeking to escape bland, uncreative British liberalism, Walker is also seeking to escape something a great deal more resistant to change. Like Treece, his life is flawed by his inability to take a decisive step, and by the weariness of spirit that is the result of this inanition. An early example of this continual equivocation comes on board ship. Here Walker becomes enamoured of a glamorous American girl, but is simultaneously ensnared by a dull and timid Englishwoman. Having failed to seduce the Englishwoman Walker, in a passage oddly reminiscent of Angus Wilson, is reproached for his excessive susceptibility to pathos. ' "You see, Mr Walker," ' Miss Marrow tells him, ' "you are a liberal. You are tempted by pathos. I think a really free man would have followed the path of Miss Snowflake." ' Walker, it scarcely need be said, is not a free man. He is tied to a consciousness whose single motivating force seems to be his own self-esteem, and whose exercise results in a feeling of profound lassitude. This weariness is reflected in his published work. As Froelich's wife, who has done her homework, observes: ' "Your book gave me the feeling that you felt a bit exhausted, just living." '

Walker's arrival at Party, situated 'in the American heartland near the point where the various wests collide', and his initial attempts to integrate himself into campus life, provoke a number of stock responses on either side. With its jokes about the peculiarities of American diction and its complaints about the degree of licence extended to American children, the novel can be seen as a less extreme version of Kingsley Amis's *One Fat Englishman* (1963). But the same dilemmas that make Professor Treece's life such a tightrope-walk of indecision are not slow in surfacing. The American university system, in particular, is seen to proceed along the same lines as its English equivalent – grooming the academically third-rate for employment – but labouring under even greater limitations. Revealing the existence of an undergraduate course called 'Reading, Writing, Speaking and Listening', for example, Walker's faculty head explains that ' "some of these kids, I mean they're all good kids, but they've not had the schoolin'. Some of 'em can hardly write their names in the dust with a stick." ' The liberal dream of unlimited educational access, personal fulfilment, a trajectory of academic advancement, sickens and dies.

Culture clash, it transpires, means much more than adenoidal accents, 'students' who are barely capable of writing their names and ill-bred children. Without having any clear idea of the likely consequences of his actions, Walker declines to swear the Oath of Loyalty required of every American university teacher. As the implications of this display of principle gather in the background, Walker feels understandably nervous:

> here was a political matter, a public matter, and he felt he was being invited to do something rather improper, to perform an indecent exposure of his moral core on the platform and the stage, and expose it, too, in a world of political nuances he didn't understand.

In fact Walker's explanation of his refusal is simple – he feels that as a British citizen it would be wrong to swear allegiance to the flag of another country. But this will scarcely do for Froelich and the faculty radicals, all of whom see him as liberal crusader, a man from the old world come to redress the ethical balance of the new:

> '*Because* you're from outside [Froelich explains], *because* there's no cause or flag you've got to wave except a simple matter of principle that has to do with the one thing you are, which is that you're English . . . you're the man, the fingerpoint, James.'

Stiffened by some reminiscences of the McCarthy era, Walker resolves to fight on, for all that the consequences of this moral exposure, this act of self-definition, continue to disturb him. ' "All I want on my headstone are just three words: 'He eschewed definition'," ' he tells Froelich. ' "I suppose that's what's called liberalism in England," ' Froelich replies.

The conflict between Walker's diffident, uncommitted liberalism and Froelich's blunt belief that values of this kind have to be fought for is sharpened by the intervention of a third academic, Dr Joachim. Joachim, a refugee from totalitarianism, thinks that freedom needs to be vigorously defended, and that Walker's refusal to swear the oath is merely self-indulgent posturing. At intervals throughout the novel he emerges to pour scorn on many of the most cherished liberal notions, in particular the idea that individuals are fashioned by their environment. ' "Of course character is not a fashionable concept," ' he tells Walker.

'Now we think we act because our family situation was so, because our historical situation is so, because we are sailing with the tide of history, because it has abandoned us as reactionary deviants. Today all our activities are really performed by our grandfathers; we take no responsibility; like the owners of umbrella stands in hotels.'

Though framed by an extreme conservative, these remarks are enough to undermine Walker's position. After all, what does liberalism represent if not personal responsibility? Would not all liberals agree that we are, to a greater or lesser extent, responsible for our actions? That it is the duty of every civilised person to reach decisions based on a core of moral integrity and stick by them? Matched against these daunting imperatives, Walker, with his engrained reluctance to commit himself, looks pitifully inadequate.

Like *Lucky Jim* (1954), a novel to which it makes several passing references, *Stepping Westward* reaches its climax at a public lecture. Here, before an audience of local dignitaries, Walker is billed to expatiate on 'The Writer's Dilemma'. He chooses to make his speech a defence of his lack of commitment: his loyalty, he informs the pride of Party, is to being a writer, and this means not being limited. If the audience thinks highly enough of Walker to ask him there, then they should not attempt to limit him by, for example, making him sign the loyalty oath. It is a fatal remark. As the flashbulbs pop and the Mayor sweeps noisily from his seat, Walker presses on. The writer's dilemma, he continues, *is* the liberal dilemma. For a long time literature has demanded that writers be concerned with 'matters of conduct and good living'. If he, Walker, has a dilemma it is not meeting up to the ethical demands of the profession, because the writer is more confused about good living than ever. ' "We know too much," ' he concludes. ' "We know the falsity that lies behind our profession of honesty, the vanity that lies behind our moral stance." '

The reactions to this exposure of unbelief neatly define the differences between Walker and his hosts, even those disposed to sympathise with his aims. Froelich, listening in the audience, realises that Walker's 'very English brand of liberalism' is no more than 'a cultural artefact', whose most committed assumption seems to be that one shouldn't do anything to anybody 'because people, and the world, like to be the way they are'. His own liberalism is more vigorous, a militancy imposed by the national situation: 'the English had not had to fight for it for a very long time, and they didn't recognise, even now, that the odds were against them, that every freedom, any freedom, had to be won by political energy'. Walker, alternatively, steps down from the podium feeling 'a gay good glow'. Briefly the flabbiness of the present is cancelled out and he is back, like Treece, in his student days, 'when causes were just and righteousness was assumed'. Predictably Walker's subsequent elevation into a symbol of dissent, and the transformation of his speech into a *cause célèbre*, is more than he can stand. In company with Miss Snowflake, who is making a providential visit to the area, he flees the campus, eventually penning a letter of resignation which acknowledges Froelich's role as *agent provocateur*. Oddly, the strongest condemnation comes not from Walker's faculty head or the university's many conservatives, but from Jabolonski, the most cretinous member of his creative writing class. Praising John Stuart Mill on the advantages of human dissatisfaction, Walker is rebuffed by Jabolonski's halting equation of liberalism with arrogance and intellectual patronage:

'I didn't come to university to improve my *mind*, Mr Walker. I came here to, duh, train me for a job. That's what you guys don't realise. You're always wantin' to change my values. You want us to think like you do, irony and all that crap, and what happens? You just get yourself into trouble is what happens.'

Jabolonski's grievance is genuine enough: Walker, for all his tolerance and good intentions, suddenly looks like a cultural snob.

Stepping Westward ends predictably. Despite a brief, picaresque idyll with Miss Snowflake, Walker returns to New York, the boat home and, the implication is, a resumption of the bland equivocations of his former existence. An epilogue pictures Froelich expertly manipulating the meeting convened to appoint Walker's successor to his own advantage (the post is cancelled and replaced by a literary magazine), though, to do him justice, Froelich feels a genuine personal regret at Walker's departure. The broader implications remain, in particular the thought that occurs to Walker in the midst of his paean to the writer's lack of commitment. Here he realises that the arguments against what he has been saying are those of Dr Joachim: 'that the specialty of liberalism is the betrayal of the society in which liberalism is permitted to exist'. Walker's equivocations and his impregnable conscience are no more than a moral smokescreen obscuring not only his own uncertainty but a much more dangerous and insidious threat to liberal principle.

Eating People is Wrong and *Stepping Westward* are comic novels, in which the paraphernalia of the form frequently deflects attention from the serious point. Each locates and analyses a characteristic post-war mood, that of the disillusioned middle-class radical who fears that the struggles of the 1930s – and their partial fulfilment in the Second World War – may have accomplished far less than they first imagined, that the exercise of scrupulousness, that fundamental liberal nostrum, was no longer possible in a world run behind closed doors by unaccountable politicians, where a mass society is frustrating the role of individual integrity. Both novels are sharply prefigurative. If the left-wing politics of the 1960s and beyond had a distinguishing feature it was their habit of using the banner of liberalism to achieve highly illiberal ends, and in this they were assisted by a great deal of liberal neutrality. It was tolerance of extremism, after all, that ruined the Labour party as an effective political force in the 1980s. Later, in *The History Man* (1975), Bradbury would create a character with the ability to exploit the moral flabbiness that typifies the clumsy interventions of his predecessors into areas of public and private morality. For the moment Treece and Walker are powerful, if essentially powerless, symbols of a cultural tradition betrayed not only by their own compromised and almost frivolous integrity but by the historical process itself.

7

Scenes from the Class War

The novelist, writing of his dreary egalitarian never-never land, has become a bore. When we read novels, we want the hero to triumph and the villain to be damned, but in the horizontal society of contemporary fiction there can be neither triumph nor damnation.

Simon Raven, 'Class and the Contemporary Novel' (1967)

By the early 1960s 'class' occupied a peculiar position in British society. Officially its days were numbered, and an assortment of social taxonomists of both Right and Left stood by to witness its disappearance. In particular its demise was thought to be reflected in the collapse of Conservative rule. The stagnation which enveloped the last years of the Macmillan government, and the accompanying stink of the 1963 Profumo scandal, was perhaps too easily interpreted as a symbol of aristocratic Tory decadence. Certainly the elevation of Sir Alec Douglas-Home, minus his peerage, to the Tory leadership after Macmillan's resignation later that year, in preference to less socially exalted candidates such as Butler and Maudling, and the manner of his appointment – achieved by a 'magic circle' of grandees (the phrase was Iain Macleod's) – were seen as an illustration of the government's detachment from the aspirations of ordinary people, and indeed from the democratic process itself.

Whatever their basis in truth, these imputations stuck. In the dispute between the party leaders that characterised the 1964 General Election – the first to be fought in the confrontational style of American presidential campaigns – Harold Wilson seemed a people's tribune when compared to the luckless 14th Earl. In fact

Wilson's credentials were those of the clever don, the consummate party politician and the canny opportunist; television preferred to emphasise his homely qualities – the pipe, the support for Huddersfield Town, the unassuming wife. An early exponent of the media opportunity, Wilson duetted with Violet Carson (*Coronation Street*'s Ena Sharples) at a television awards dinner and was photographed meeting the Beatles. Sir Alec, who was clearly not up to this fighting weight and whose badly managed public performances tended to end in vociferous heckling, faded away towards what was in the end a surprisingly narrow defeat.

The election of 1964 was not 1945 mark two – not even the most bright-eyed Wilson apologist could accept that. Nevertheless, it had a definite symbolic importance. The majority of the first Wilson cabinet had been backbenchers during the Attlee administration and venerated its traditions. Clause IV socialism with its commitment to nationalising the means of production, defended against Gaitskell's attack by an alliance of trades-union barons and constituency parties, survived. 'Classlessness', consequently, featured strongly in the Labour government's early public statements. George Brown, for example, introducing a Declaration of Intent signed by employers and union representatives for a voluntary accord on prices, productivity and income in 1965, went so far as to proclaim that: 'Here on one sheet of paper are stated the aims of a modern society which has put the class war behind it.'

From another angle, the angle of the working class, or at any rate its fictional representatives, the view was less optimistic. I read the other day an article about class going,' observes Frederick Clegg in John Fowles's *The Collector* (1963). 'I could tell them things about that.' George Brown might talk about a society which had put the class war behind it. In fact the attempted alleviation of social inequality was a feature of the political landscape of the mid–1960s; the faint scent of egalitarianism hung in the air. Crosland's assault on the grammar schools had begun by 1965. An advantage of the wave of post-Robbins Report new universities was their apparent susceptibility to admissions from the working class. Wilson was the most cautious of operators, obsessed with middle-class popularity and the judgement of the press; the 'socialism' professed by most of his ministers might have been pale pink in tone, but even so redistribution of wealth remained a manifesto commitment.

As it turned out, the results of this circumspect social tinkering were almost negligible. Once the grammar schools had been denied them, middle-class children (who had always comprised most of the grammar schools' population) flocked to the private sector. The universities, whether at Oxford, Keele or East Anglia, maintained their middle-class bias. Writing over a decade later, A. H. Halsey found that class-based inequality had persisted throughout the 1960s and 1970s. The top half of the population now owned three-quarters of the personal income, the bottom half, a quarter. Personal wealth, too, despite some equalisation between the top and the very top, was now concentrated to an unprecedented degree, with three-quarters of all personal wealth owned by 20 per cent of the population. Hindsight makes the beginning of the Wilson era, with its proud talk about the white heat of technological revolution, look tame. At the time there was an ominous feeling, especially in certain quarters of the City, that Labour were serious. (Desmond Briggs's *The Partners* (1982), one of the few novels to give an account of the period surrounding the 1964 General Election, paints a convincing picture of the uncertainties whipped up by the prospect of a Labour victory.)

Class, of course, is not only to do with wealth: it is equally concerned with ability and status, externals such as dress and accent, indefinable half-tones of mannerism and nuance. If class was disappearing – and most people assumed that it was – then the implications for the novel lay here, in the field of vanishing social differentiation. This, at any rate, was the opinion of Evelyn Waugh. The elaborate stratifications of the British class system were, he suggested, 'essential to the national character'. Their disappearance would have a necessarily profound effect on the national artistic life. Gazing back from the vantage point of 1960 at a roseate and class-bound past, Waugh praised the advantages of different vocabularies and intonations of speech, and different styles of dress. Now all those things 'that gave salt to English life and were the raw materials of the Arts are being dissolved'.

Looking back at the Victorian novel, let alone the earlier fiction of Fielding and Smollett, one can accept Waugh's point. Sam Weller's charm, after all, is his accent. Much of the humour of the early Dickens is class-based, the footmen's 'swarry' in *The Pickwick Papers*, for example, where servant-hall aping of genteel life is held up to mockery. Later a more serious note prevails. *Dombey and Son* is a progress report on the new Victorian manufacturing and commercial class, Mr Dombey's success being symbolised by his marriage to the quasi-aristocratic Edith. Thackeray, too, is greatly interested in the social pretensions of people who are attempting to transfer from one class to another. 'A Little Dinner at Timmins's', one of the finest of his short pieces, is the story of an easy-going barrister with an ambitious wife who is persuaded into giving a dinner party beyond his means. The event is a disaster: ultimately the Timminses find that they have alienated most of their genuine friends (whom social snobbery prohibited them from inviting) and nearly ruined themselves in the process. Thackeray's touch is relatively genial, but the class aspects of the Victorian novel could spill over into outright antagonism. In Gissing's *Born in Exile*, Godwin Peak discovers that his plebeian uncle plans to open a tea shop outside the college where Godwin is a student. Peak decides to leave the college immediately, throwing over a promising academic career, as he knows he will be unable to bear the social shame. This sort of dilemma has little meaning in the post-war novel, where a democratising spirit can be seen intermittently at work. Dropped aitches might still be funny, in a certain type of novel aimed at a certain type of reader, but only incidentally so, and in general humour based on departures from an accepted norm of polite speech is on the way out from the 1940s onwards. Significantly, in the post-war novel mockery is much more likely to be applied to the cut-glass accent, a marked contrast to the Victorian era, where every *jeune premier*, even Pip in *Great Expectations*, raised in the working-class Gargery household, speaks the equivalent of BBC English.

The novel of the late 1940s and early 1950s, while conscious of class differences and distinctions, was not disposed to examine them in detail or to use their juxtapositions as a basis for situational development. The reluctance of writers such as Amis, Wain and Waterhouse to use class in an antagonistic way is well documented. Even obvious contrasts between livelihood and aspiration are examined in a spirit of neutrality. The account of Charles Lumley's visit to the home of his working-class girlfriend in John Wain's *Hurry On Down* (1953) has all the benignity of an anthropologist's survey. At the same time few novels of the period fail to yield up some awareness of social distinctions, background and status. John Kemp in Philip Larkin's *Jill* (1946) instinctively notices the clothes worn by every other young man in Oxford and is able to tell, in his mother's terms, whether the young man is like himself or not. Margaret Thorpe in David Storey's *Flight into Camden* (1960) cannot look at a group of men without trying to establish who is a workman and who is not.

Similarly, the attitudes of individual characters have a habit of radically altering themselves as a consequence of some class-based perception. Jane Graham, the pregnant middle-class heroine of Lynne Reid Banks's *The L-Shaped Room* (1960), falls into conversation with a shopkeeper whose windows advertise the room she has just taken. His hostility turns to sympathy when he realises that she is living in the room, a bed-sit in a working-class district of Fulham. ' "Bloody Commies . . . Why couldn't they leave the middle classes alone?" ' Appropriately enough, the man then apologises for his bad language. This is an inverted class distinction. Much more typical are middle-class attempts to use class to their own advantage. Even the most scrupulous protagonists in the fiction of the late 1950s and early 1960s have a tendency to play the class card whenever the situation demands it. A good example occurs in Andrea Newman's *The Cage* (1965), in which a bright middle-class girl, having been made pregnant by a young man from a slightly lower social stratum, throws over the chance of a university career. Class, which has so far been conspicuously absent in discussions of their relationship, finally rears its head at the wedding in the narrator's description of Malcolm's mother's 'so carefully chosen navy suit that she called a costume, with white shoes and gloves and a plastic handbag and a pink straw hat with an artificial rose on her head'. Val's mother, in contrast, 'had looked so unquestionably right'. In other words, some people know how to dress and others do not. This is an elemental legend. Similar distinctions, for example, attend the wedding scene in Wells's *The History of Mr Polly* (1910).

Few novelists, by this time, were following Evelyn Waugh's prescription for novels of English social life. The handful of books taking the Waugh line tend to be set in slightly archaic institutions, whose protocol provides the framework for an examination of class differences, for example the army. Waugh's army novels rarely stray outside a select circle of upper-class acquaintances; the occasions on which Guy Crouchback comes face to face with anyone below NCO rank can be counted on the fingers of one hand. Much more imaginative in their juxtapositions of the officers' mess and the NAAFI bar are Simon Raven's novels of army life, *The Feathers of Death* (1959) and *The Sabre Squadron* (1966). Raven's attitude to the army may be compared with Waugh's mixture of gentle mockery and deep affection suffused with apparently anachronistic notions of 'honour'.

Both the novels in question are built on assumptions of patrician invincibility, and a series of situations in which aristocratic officers and their willing troops ally themselves against an interfering and puritanical middle class. Thus *The Feathers of Death*, whose action takes place during an episode of colonial insurgency, describes the semi-homosexual relationship between an upper-class officer and his working-class batman. *The Sabre Squadron*, a somewhat jollier affair set in occupied Germany in 1952, draws much of its bite from the rivalry between two socially distinct English regiments, on the one hand 'Earl Hamilton's Light Dragoons', an inglorious collection of upper-class half-wits (' "Who's got a map thing? . . . Ta. I can never remember: is it *up* first or across?" ') sustained by competent and indulgent NCOs, on the other a group of furiously enthusiastic middle-class Fusiliers. Inevitably, patrician charm demolishes every obstacle placed in its path, 'other ranks' cheerfully connive in what is little more than an upper-class racket, and the superiority of aristocratic civility over bourgeois punctiliousness is confirmed by the station's less than aristocratic medical officer:

'When these cavalry chaps got here they just about saved my life. Do you know, the Fusiliers were too snooty to talk to me. Me and my Liverpool accent. Then along came the Dragoons,

who were far too grand to talk to the Fusiliers but seemed to
have all the time in the world for me.'

In Raven's elegant and extensive vocabulary there is no more
wounding adjective than 'middle-class'.

Such alliances, and the antagonisms that fuelled them, were in
any case exceptional, quite detached from the mainstream of writing about class. This, however, was far from static. With a few
blatant exceptions, the class distinctions of the 1950s had not been
expressed in combative terms. The tendency of the early 1960s
novel was much more aggressive; the emergence of a type of left-
wing fiction hostile to privilege, whether conferred by inherited
wealth, status or ability, dates from and derives much of its stimulus from the end of the Macmillan era.

One feature of the period was the attack on upper-class life by
the upper-class renegade. Robin Douglas-Home – a name of some
significance – provides a crude but effective example of this tendency in *Hot for Certainties* (1964), an account of an upper-class
boy's increasing disillusion with the racket of double standards
and moral evasions that pursues him relentlessly through home,
school and military service. David Melrose, Douglas-Home's hero,
is the son of wealthy divorced parents. As a consequence he spends
much of his time at the home of his grandparents, where an
atmosphere of pre-war upper-class comfort still prevails (dressing
for dinner, servants). Sent to 'Glazebrook', a public school which
seems to be modelled on Eton, Melrose discovers an old-fashioned
ethos – 'Play up the school and all that' – which manifests itself
in an indulgent attitude towards the stupid but highly born. Its
chief beneficiary is an oaf named Lord Charles Hemsley, who is
enabled to pass his school certificate examination when the invigi-
lator – the school cricket coach – allows him to cheat. In his
capacity as Hemsley's fag, Melrose is involved in a cover-up when
a servant girl who claims that Hemsley is the father of her unborn
child commits suicide. His subsequent progress through school
and the army reveals that everything is fixed in the interests of the
well-born and the well-connected. At his interview for a National
Service commission in 'The Windsor Guards', he is asked if he
knows Hemsley who, it transpires, has recently been awarded the

Sword of Honour at Sandhurst and is considered a 'very promising officer'. No aspect of Melrose's tight-knit world is free from the taint of corruption. His father's new young wife makes a clumsy attempt to seduce him. The unappetising 'county' girl who is at one stage the unpromising object of his faltering advances returns from Italy in a yet more disagreeable guise, that of a pouting sexpot. The catalogue of deceit and betrayal reaches its climax when David's mother announces her remarriage to a government minister. On the night before the wedding Melrose's girlfriend decamps with Hemsley. Found drunk and wandering in the Mall, Melrose is apprehended by a sympathetic policeman who, having established his identity declines to arrest him in token of ' "the festive nature of the evening" '.

Hot for Certainties differs from the anti-establishment novels of the late 1950s in its scope. Rather than focusing on a single, flawed institution – Eton, the army – it takes in a whole society, each aspect of which is damned for its easy venality. A more extreme case can be found in Derek Raymond's *The Crust on its Uppers* (1962), an account of an upper-class youth who drifts into a restless sub-world of metropolitan crime. Raymond's hero is consciously motivated by an urge to betray his class. Expelled from 'the most super public school in the country at the age of sixteen', thrown out of his tutorial college having contracted a venereal disease, unreformed by National Service, his overriding aim is 'to chip my way out of that background which held me like a flea in a block of ice'. Crime, a life of car scams, crooked gambling parties and the laundering of counterfeit money (the latter sponsored by the Eastern bloc) – is 'the only chisel I could find'. Raymond's protagonist merely associates with other criminals. In contrast, one of the chief interests of Douglas-Home's novel is its hero's attempts (occasionally forced upon him) to 'connect'. The pregnant servant girl who asks him to convey a letter to Hemsley makes a successful appeal to his better instincts. Having laid the whole story before his housemaster after her death, Melrose is genuinely shocked by the man's refusal to investigate. Later he conducts an intermittent relationship with a girl named Jean, one of his grandparents' servants, which ends when she becomes engaged to her working-class boyfriend. In each case

Melrose is surprised and intrigued by his contact with a stratum of people whose outlook is substantially different from his own. But there is no future in his relationship with Jean, and her return to what a novelist of an earlier generation would have called 'her own people' is inevitable.

By the mid–1960s, consequently, class had once again become a definite concern of the English novel. In a provocative essay published in 1967, Simon Raven attempted to catalogue prevailing attitudes. Raven's division is threefold: first the 'Old Right' – writers such as Waugh and Powell – who accept all class distinctions, tempering upper-class ease with the obligations of 'duty' while remaining unenthusiastic about money-grubbing; second a meritocratic 'New Establishment' composed of writers such as Amis, Wain and John Braine who, while rejecting traditional divisions of rank and resenting the merely wealthy, are definitely in favour of privilege and rewards conferred by professional merit; and third a group of writers to whom prestige and status won by ability are almost as suspect as those won by birth and wealth. This is a crude summary of what are frequently quite complex positions, and it is impossible to ignore Raven's role as a gadfly of the Right, but his point about the anti-meritocratic spirit of certain leftish-leaning novelists is a valid one. In the novels of Angus Wilson, for example, it is occasionally suggested that intelligence and achievement do not entitle those fortunate enough to possess them to assume a personal superiority; such advantages merely illustrate differences of aptitude. Margaret Drabble's early fiction frequently conveys the message that professional success is the result of a privileged education, which is itself the result of a privileged upbringing. Thus Rosamund Stacey in *The Millstone* (1965), conscious that she owes her professional status to her dexterity with Elizabethan sonnet sequences, is troubled by what seems an arbitrary bestowal of intellectual gifts calculated to exclude the less fortunate.

An immediate consequence of these attitudes was the emergence of some novels of genuine class antagonism. John Fowles's *The Collector* is a fine example of this type of book, the thoroughly nasty story of a depraved town hall clerk who wins a fortune on the pools, buys a house in the country and imprisons a young girl in it to observe at his leisure. Fredrick Clegg is a man of accumulated resentments, each turn of his reminiscent mind guaranteed to uncover some class-based slight. The memory of the post-pools win reception infuriates him:

> the way people looked at us and the way the slimy foreign waiters and everybody treated us and how everything in the room seemed to look down on us because we weren't brought up their way.

London, in particular, is a repository for class distinction. 'If you ask me London's all arranged for the people who can act like public schoolboys, and you don't get anywhere if you don't have the manner born and the right la-di-da voice.' Men who conform to the public schoolboy type are one of Clegg's lasting obsessions. He despises the estate agent who sells him his country hideaway, describing him as:

> my age, but the public schoolboy type, full of silly remarks that were meant to be funny, as if it were below him to say anything and there was some difference between selling houses and something in a shop.

Clegg's attitude to Miranda, the girl he kidnaps, abuses and eventually allows to die, is a curious mixture of deference and contempt. His reasons for selecting her are straightforward: as well as being pretty she belongs to a social category higher than his own. Trying to describe her in the terms he uses to classify his butterfly collection, he comes up with words such as 'elusive, sporadic and very refined'. Miranda is sexually enticing (Clegg, predictably enough, is a sexual 'loner' who derives most of his gratification from pornography) but the concept of 'respect' is swiftly introduced. 'She was not like some woman you don't respect so you don't care what you do, you respected her and you had to be careful.' A bit of class, in other words. At the same time Clegg resents her manner, her voice, her poise and her education. 'She often went on about how she hated class distinctions,' Clegg reflects bitterly, 'but she never took me in. It's the way people speak that gives them away, not what they say . . .' At one point in their discussions Miranda tells him to 'stop thinking about class'. This, Clegg decides is 'like a rich man telling a poor man to stop thinking about money'. Looking back on the edgy relationship between gaoler and prisoner, Clegg concludes: 'there was always class between us'. After her death from pneumonia – Clegg cannot bring himself to summon a doctor – he turns his gaze to a humbler victim, a local shop assistant. Miranda was a mistake from the outset, he decides. 'I ought to have got someone who would respect me more. Someone ordinary I could teach.'

Even now, thirty years after its first publication, *The Collector* seems a rather disgusting book, not merely because of its central situation – the imprisonment and abuse of a defenceless woman – but because of the easy nature of the connection between environment and human wickedness. For it is class, Fowles seems to be saying, that is at the root of Clegg's warped mental outlook. Class has given him his grinding resentment, class has given him his false values (there are some women whom one has to 'respect', but the others, presumably, you can do what you like with). Fowles emphasises this message not by making Clegg an authentic class warrior, someone who is above social distinctions, but by suggesting that his dissatisfaction stems from his inability to secure a better place for himself on the ladder. In reality Clegg is in favour of class distinctions – after all, what he looks for in the 'ordinary' shop girl is 'respect', that is, confirmation of his own superiority. This, Fowles implies, is the extent of his corruption at the hands of a system that has been forced upon him and which he only imperfectly understands.

The Collector obliquely raises another question. Clegg is a monster. But what about the other, non-monstrous Cleggs, their aspirations and the wholly legitimate expression of their tastes? Early 1960s grappling with the implications of a mass culture produced some strange spectacles. Simon Raven mockingly claimed to have located a general agreement between writers of all political persuasions:

The general increase in education and literacy has led to the wider expression, by and for the population at large, of its moral, intellectual and artistic preferences. The *vox populi* has been heard, at last, crying out for what it wants, and ... what it wants has been found truly appalling by every serious novelist, whether right or left, who currently puts pen to paper.

This is not completely true, but it is true enough. The government minister in Raven's own *Friends in Low Places* (1965) might declare the scope of popular desires to be ' "cars, cookers and fancy cans, and up yours I'm laughing" ', but there exists simultaneously a large number of left-leaning characters in early 1960s fiction whose professed egalitarianism cannot survive exposure to 'ordinary people'. Thus we find Rosamund Stacey in *The Millstone*, outwardly so sympathetic to the interests of the man in the street, happily patronising her fellow hospital patients and their talk about washing machines. Miranda in *The Collector* is an even more important witness, a left-wing student with impeccable views about the Bomb and the class system who ought, the fact of her imprisonment notwithstanding, to take a sympathetic line on the Cleggs of this world. In fact Miranda's understandable loathing of Clegg is mixed with some wider social prejudices which are quite as engrained as those expressed by Clegg himself.

The most striking charge which Miranda levels against Clegg and people like him is spiritual deadness. At one point she tries to visualise the aunt who brought Clegg up:

A thin woman with a white face and a nasty mouth and mean grey eyes and cloudy beige tea-cosy hats and a thing about dust and dirt. Dust and dirt being everything outside her foul little back-street world.

In the use of hats as a focus for moral disapproval we are back at the level of *Lucky Jim* (1954). Quite as pronounced, though, are Miranda's complaints about Clegg's aesthetic sense. In her judgement he has ruined the house by redecorating it in '*the* most excruciating women's magazine good taste'. Later the reader is informed that he or she 'wouldn't believe' Miranda if she described the 'awfulness of the pictures'. Predictably, these failings are compounded by a political divide. Miranda is a Labour-voting CND supporter, Clegg a working-class Conservative. Their rudimentary political discussions provoke in Miranda an intransigent élitism. 'I'm so superior to him,' she observes at one point. 'I know that sounds wickedly conceited. But I *am*.' Superior, that is, in terms of the gallery-visiting, issue-chewing world which Miranda inhabits. Clegg, although a psychopath, is not unskilled: he is something of a carpenter and takes and develops his own photographs. An assumption of superiority inevitably leads to patronage. ' "I don't bore you," ' Miranda explains to her captor. ' "I try to teach you." ' Later, in a development of the novel's roots in *The Tempest*, Miranda marks Clegg down as a representation of 'the Calibans of this world'. The Calibans can be defined as the newly affluent but spiritually impoverished. 'I hate all the ordinary dull little people who aren't ashamed of being dull and little,' Miranda proclaims. 'I hate ... the New People, the new-class people with their cars and their money and their stupid vulgarities and their stupid crawling imitations of the bourgeoisie.' No contributor to the arts pages of Kingsley Martin's *New Statesman* could have put it better. Miranda's explanation of Clegg's descent into crime is perhaps the most reactionary of all: 'The only thing that kept him decent was being poor.' In other words, money corrupts, but only the people who are not used to it.

The Right/Left debate about popular culture is a very ancient one, generally conducted with considerable disingenuousness on either side. On the one hand the Right will argue that expressions of popular preference will almost automatically incline to the worthless and vulgar, while ignoring the fact that the economic system which sustains it depends on the mass sale of the worthless and vulgar. The well-to-do suburbanite may look down his nose at the McDonald's restaurant, but he would probably not want the company to go out of business. No twentieth-century economic system could survive for very long without appeasing the mob. On the other hand the Left will argue that the vulgarity of popular aspirations is rarely the people's fault – television and the newspapers hoodwinked them into buying the VCR – while ignoring the rapt enthusiasm of large sections of society for the items they are being seduced into buying and, presumably, the existence of free will. In recent years the debate has grown markedly more complex, with the rise of right-wing populism and the disappearance of anything that might be described as genuine left-wing popular culture. The suggestion that a particular soap-opera is fit only for the half-witted is more likely to appear in the *Guardian* than the *Daily Mail*. But then, English socialist culture in this century has nearly always been depressingly middle-class in tone.

Generally speaking, the novels of the late 1950s and early 1960s tend to avoid any deeper investigation of these issues. The forces at work to shape popular attitudes and aspirations – advertising and popular newspapers, for example – went almost ignored. While there are some revealing exposés of advertising, notably Roger Longrigg's *A High-pitched Buzz* (1956) and John Bowen's *The Centre of the Green* (1959), they tend to focus on obvious fatuities rather than the more sinister implications. A. J. Cronin's novel about a provincial newspaper, *The Northern Light* (1958), is simply a black-and-white conflict between 'decency' and the salacity of the yellow press. In general left-wing writers were content to erect their standards on the rock of classlessness and populism, only retreating in the face of an unignorable onslaught on some deeply cherished belief.

The confusions and limitations of the average left-wing attitude towards class, wealth, status and the rewards of ability are flagrantly displayed in *The Millstone*. Outwardly Drabble's novel seems to confront one of the era's more contentious 'issues' – the unmarried mother. But it is less an examination of birth out of wedlock than a repository for social attitudes, in this case the attitudes of the educated, conscientious, left-wing bourgeoisie. Rosamund Stacey comes from an impeccable parlour socialist background (her home life is discussed in Chapter 6), which has impressed upon her the importance of *laissez-faire*, tolerance and a dozen other exemplary sentiments. Her adult existence, consequently, is founded on guilt. A queer reminiscence of her childhood makes this point with some force. Loitering in a public park, Rosamund and her sister Beatrice fall in with two working-class boys. The extent of the social gulf between them is soon established. The boys are allowed to eat the bread that was intended for the ducks. Greatly to Rosamund's surprise, they appear to bear no resentment over this inequality: 'we knew where we stood with these boys, and we were full of fright. But the boys did not mind; they had enjoyed the afternoon, they were interested, impressed.' Rosamund decides that the pair fall into Shaw's category of the deserving, as opposed to the undeserving, poor. 'But Beatrice and I knew that for our part, we were undeserving; we had not deserved their kind interest, but their contempt.'

Of course, it is a habit of the working classes to defy middle-class assumptions of their behaviour. Rosamund's later life is conditioned by these attitudes. She chooses teaching as a profession 'because of my social conscience'. Her personal life is governed by a scrupulous attention to people's feelings and an unwillingness to offend. For all that, Rosamund's is an odd form of scrupulousness. Most obviously, it is compromised by an engrained habit of passing social and moral judgements on people with whose political opinions she happens to disagree. Her boyfriend Roger, for example, is written off with maximum snootiness as 'a wealthy, well-descended Tory accountant person' (somehow it is that final 'person' that establishes the awesome level of contempt). Then there is her unfortunate brother, married to a 'ghastly girl' whose father was a colonel, who now resides in Dorking in a sort of sink of middle-class infamy and spends his time 'having absolutely worthless people to dinner'. Scrupulousness, in fact, seems set to exclude Rosamund from much of society rather than to admit her to it. Adult life, let alone the brief encounters of her childhood, provides an insight into some very real social demarcations that no amount of tolerance or good nature seems able to push aside. There is a revealing incident in which Rosamund, visiting her sister's home, witnesses Beatrice forbidding her children to play with a working-class girl named Sandra. Rosamund tells Beatrice that ' "it ought to be against your principles. I'm sure upper-class children are just as silly and vulgar and horrid, aren't they?" ' Beatrice thinks they probably are, ' "but in a way I can deal with . . . I can't do anything with that child but shout at her . . . I really don't see what else I could do." ' Rosamund doesn't see what else she could have done either, though she does think that if placed in the same situation she herself 'might have tried to stick it out'. Subsequently she broods over the 'square and yelling'

Sandra, and thinks 'what a pity it was that resentments should breed so near the cradle, that people should so have had it from birth'.

But Rosamund's own attempts to 'connect', as Forster might have put it, are sadly defeated, and by the upbringing that has allowed her to recognise and disapprove of social inequalities in the first place. Set down in the ante-natal clinic with a group of predominantly working-class mothers-to-be, she realises that she feels 'nothing in common with these people, that I disliked the look of them, that I felt a stranger and a foreigner there'. Simultaneously she acknowledges that she is 'one of them ... I was trapped in a human limit for the first time in my life, and I was going to have to learn how to live inside it.' Previously Rosamund has seemed unaware of the ironies of her position. Despite her belief that ability, on which worldly success depends, is arbitrary and therefore unfair, she is a howling intellectual snob who, for example, despises Roger because he is 'clearly set for a career that would be advanced more by personality than ability'. However, the supreme irony of her pregnancy is plainly apparent to her: her ability to give birth unmarried and alone is solely dependent on her social status. Rosamund is quick to acknowledge that 'if I had not been who I am ... I would probably never have done it'. She can only assume that she 'got away with it' because the ambulance came to collect her from a good address 'and not from a bedsitter or from a basement in ever-weeping Paddington'. Rosamund survives the potential embarrassment and humiliations of single parenthood merely by virtue of her social position. She has exploited the fabric of a society which she has always distrusted: 'by pretending to be above its structures, I was merely turning its anomalies to my own use'. Middle-class privilege, however much individual members of the middle classes might resent it, is ineradicable.

The Millstone is a significant work – not perhaps in its discussion of the 'issue' of illegitimacy, which other writers were to examine with much greater attack, but in its foreshadowing of later fictional preoccupations. Rosamund Stacey, or persons like her, is a familiar figure in the fiction of the late 1960s and early 1970s, seen at bourgeois dinner tables discussing the dilemma of comprehensive education (however strong one's support of the principle, should this extend to sending one's child to an obviously inferior school?) and, a little later, the drawbacks of practical socialism (the rights of organised labour are inalienable, but what if its actions hurt those sections of society least able to defend themselves?).

This is not to dispute the fact that comprehensive education and trades-union excesses are fit subjects for debate – and no doubt many a middle-class drawing room did resound to such conversations – but merely to speculate on the implications for fiction itself. For in creating personifications of the middle-class liberal conscience such as Rosamund Stacey, or indeed working-class 'victims' such as Clegg, novelists like Drabble and Fowles set the question of reader response to imaginary characters in sharp relief. They do this by denying the reader his or her traditional satisfaction of judgement. For example, in reading *The Collector* one wants to dislike Clegg, 'the villain', violently, and yet Fowles is constantly redressing the balance in his favour, labouring the point that he is the victim of his environment. Similarly, one wants to admire Rosamund Stacey in her struggle for independence and self-fulfilment, but her dreariness as a person makes this very difficult. Her friend the novelist Joe Hurt may be boorish and chauvinist, but he has twice her vitality. By taking free will away from character and stressing the effects of environment, left-wing novelists merely made their creations tedious and predictable.

If everything can be reduced to a question of upbringing, then the traditional situation of the novel – an individual intelligence in conflict with circumstance – no longer applies. David Copperfield versus Uriah Heep might have been an unequal struggle – for Heep, patently, will never match his opponent's moral probity – and a modern novelist would undoubtedly pronounce on Heep's Jewish pride and underprivileged background, but somehow he is preferable to nasty, resentful Clegg, just as a guileless Victorian heroine is preferable to Rosamund Stacey. This is not to blame writers such as Fowles and Drabble for wanting to inject an all too rare leftist viewpoint into the novel, merely to say that their fiction seems the poorer for it, their characters rather too conspicuously in thrall to the environment that created them. From the reader's point of view, this has precisely the reverse effect of what was intended. Invited to understand, if not to sympathise with, Clegg's behaviour we end up hating him even more. We would prefer to think him evil rather than the victim of social circumstance, and we would prefer to see him as an individual rather than a social phenomenon. As it is, Fowles's refusal to devictimise him robs him of an essential fictional characteristic – a life of one's own.

8

The Search for Value

With the death of James the religious sense was lost to the English novel, and with the religious sense went the sense of the importance of the human act. It was as if the world of fiction had lost a dimension: the characters of such distinguished writers as Mrs Virginia Woolf and Mr E. M. Forster wandered like cardboard symbols through a world that was paper-thin.

Graham Greene, *François Mauriac* (1961)

Character, according to Professor Joachim in Malcolm Bradbury's *Stepping Westward* (1965), is an out-dated concept. By 'character', of course, Joachim means people's sense of their inner selves. The post-war era revealed people's sense of their external selves to be equally flimsy. By the end of the 1950s, if not before, some salient changes had begun to affect the people in what was beginning to be known as the 'serious novel'. The old upper-class hero, the slightly louche young man with his *ennui* and his sexual difficulties, seemed ripe for superannuation. In his place came an equally louche young man, his sexual difficulties no less intense but exclusively heterosexual, yet pitched slightly lower down the social scale. Preoccupations, too, had begun to alter. Waugh and Powell's diffident heroes might seem ineffectual, but at least they were confident of their position in the society of which they were a part. Amis, Wain and Waterhouse's young man is concerned, perhaps unreasonably so, with status, social uncertainty, his ability to fend for himself in a world to which he has rather surprisingly been allowed an admission ticket.

There were other factors which the character of the 1950s had typically to consider: his or her relation to a class system which had proved to be surprisingly resistant; the decline of an old-fashioned liberalism that, twenty years before, had supplied an absolute creed for civilised behaviour. Yet the greatest change lay in the diminution of their private selves, the realisation that somewhere along the line a human dimension had been lost. Dixon and Co. may have vigour and adaptability, but they are generally helpless in the face of events, victims of circumstance, people to whom things happen. They inhabit a world of unappeasable contingency, whose effect is to reduce them to the status of minor actors, frail, insubstantial creations liable to be swept away at any moment by a complex, unpredictable tide. It is not that Jim Dixon has no metaphysical life, it is not even that he lives in a world without God, but that he inhabits an environment in which the moral sense, ultimately derived from God, is conspicuous only by its frailty. It is instructive to compare Amis's position with that of a novelist like Trollope. For all his propensity to write about clergymen, Trollope is not outwardly a 'religious' novelist, but God and Christian morality are there with the roast beef, the fire-irons and government stock at 4 per cent interest to impart the feeling of solidity, the delight in being able to watch people behaving 'in character', that is the touchstone of the mid-Victorian novel.

God, of course, had been on the way out throughout the nineteenth century: novels about religious doubt were a staple of the Victorian best-seller lists. Thackeray had linked virtue to environment rather than divine inspiration, and there is a slightly wistful moment in *Vanity Fair* where Becky Sharp suggests that £5,000 a year would have made her a good woman. Doubtless the roots go deeper than this: A. S. Byatt, for example, considers *Paradise Regained* to be the last believed Christian narrative in the language. The consequences of this displacement reverberate around the corridors of Victorian intellectual life. George Eliot's conviction that though belief might disappear a secular morality incorporating its chief components would remain was one of the shibboleths of contemporary rationalism. Numbers of late Victorian novels suggest that the Eliot view was a powerful motivating force. In Gissing's *Born in Exile* (1892), which matches unbelief against older orthodoxies, joint moral seriousness is sharply apparent. The result is a dramatisation of a uniquely painful dilemma, conducted with maximal scrupulousness on both sides.

Peak, an ambitious and intellectually superior young man of humble origins, wishes to marry a genteel woman. He selects as his target Sidwell Warricombe, the sister of one of his old college friends. Unbeknown to the devout Sidwell, Peak, a follower of Lyell and Darwin, is the author of a ferocious and controversial article in a rationalist journal, pouring scorn on attempts to reconcile science and religion. To assist his marital ambitions, Peak lets it be known that he has decided to study for the Church. In the guise of a theology student he befriends Sidwell's father, an amateur geologist much troubled by the evidence of the stones, and in a series of discussions succeeds in simultaneously propping up the older man's faith and intellectually perjuring himself. However, Peak's cover is blown when Sidwell's brother Buckland, long suspicious of the sudden interest in theology, makes enquiries which enable him to expose the suitor to the family as an impostor. There is a final confrontation in which Peak and Sidwell argue their respective positions and then decide to part. To the modern reader their dilemma will seem almost ridiculous – they love each other, so why not marry? Yet the fervour of their beliefs makes this impossible. Sidwell continues with her modest, provincial life. Peak retires abroad to his lonely exile's death.

Though *Born in Exile* is enacted in an atmosphere of intellectual ferment, prompting the sense one frequently gets in the Victorian novel of the ground visibly shifting beneath the characters' feet, it is still a novel about certainty – not, perhaps, the certainty of belief, but the certainty of one's own moral position. Despite his initial deception, Peak's arguments with Sidwell are characterised by absolute scrupulousness. He cannot compromise or feign a retreat: to do so would be to commit intellectual suicide and thereby lose his self-respect. For her part, Sidwell cannot abandon her principles for love. Each somehow rises above the world around them, to the extent that they are the principal characters who reside in it. By the novel's end all that matters is that Peak and Sidwell shall have their final conversation and either agree or disagree. Turn to post-war fiction and the landscape, despite a pervasive sense of material well-being, is markedly less solid. Belief, whether in religious or secular principles, has been weakened by a keen sense of uncertainty. Maurice Fisher, the clergyman in Pamela Hansford Johnson's *The Humbler Creation* (1959), provides a shrewd summary of the mental atmosphere of the time. Reflecting on the futility of attempting to proselytise his cause, he decides that he has never been less sure of the value of the mission field: 'Today, in a world alternately crawling with fright and making Zulu noises, it seemed more vain than ever.'

Novels of the 1950s and early 1960s which penetrate beyond the social mainstream are often about disintegration, 'civilised' values put to the test and found wanting (Golding), man confronted with unappeasable dark forces. Alternatively, they show man no longer in control of his environment, psychologically or genetically detached from normality (John Wyndham's *The Midwych Cuckoos* and *Chocky*), or caught up in eco-destruction (John Christopher's *The Death of Grass* and *The World in Winter*). These cautionary tales depict ordinary people set down and forced to operate in a world where civilised values can no longer be enforced, with predictable results. At the same time the frailty of these values, even within a conventional domestic environment, is frequently held up for scrutiny. There is, for example, a widespread feeling that twentieth-century power politics, warfare and its attendant horrors have bludgeoned people into a state of insensibility, thereby limiting their ability to make moral choices. An odd passage in *The Humbler Creation* emphasises this point. Fisher, the clergyman, is watching the members of the church youth club giggling over a private joke (in fact the relationship which he is pursuing with a fellow-parishioner, although Fisher does not know this):

Some of them were innocent, some good, some generous. Some would make successes of their lives: but they were all potential witnesses, titillated and charmed; at a ceremony of torture. In Nuremberg, twenty years ago, they would have stood by grinning while Jews scrubbed the pavements with acid-soaked rags, while the guards swamped their buckets over the fur coats the women had not been allowed to remove. They would have laughed, not because they were essentially cruel, but because they could not feel at all for others, could barely feel for themselves.

That modern life has the capacity to dehumanise is a commonplace of twentieth-century fiction. It is rather shocking, all the same, to see the tendency at work in a Kensington church youth club. In this atmosphere, humanity's confidence in its own judgement, whether or not that judgement was spiritually sanctioned, seemed gravely compromised. Dixon, Lumley, Lampton, Seaton are not anti-heroes in the strict sense, but it would be difficult to argue that their lives are conducted on anything but the most rudimentary pattern. Whatever their private doubts, history is turning them into moral relativists. As Bates, the anguished proletarian scholar of Bradbury's *Eating People is Wrong* (1959), puts it:

'These are the 'fifties, not the 'twenties. We're even sophisticated about being sophisticated: we can't believe that *anyone's* right; their rectitude turns to ashes in our hands.'

One consequence of this uncertainty was a profound unease over the concept of finite 'truth'. This anxiety surfaces in several major novels of the period. Angus Wilson's *Anglo-Saxon Attitudes* (1956), for instance, which centres on the excavation of a seventh-century bishop's tomb, can be read as a deliberate satire on the human pursuit of truth. The various misguided forms which this quest assumes have been enumerated by James Gindin. Foolish scholars assemble to promote the 'interchange of ideas', only to relapse into gossip. A publicist such as John Middleton wishes to expose government misdeeds, but succeeds only in having a competent civil servant sacked and making an incompetent, though amiable, market gardener miserable. John's wife Inge is a well-intentioned fantasist who busily transforms all her experience into sentimental fairy-tales while refusing to acknowledge anything unpleasant, even the homosexual, invited into their home by John, who steals her jewellery. All, in Gindin's words, are 'ludicrous, malicious or inadequate'. Only Gerald Middleton, the archaeologist present at the first opening of the tomb many years before, can reveal the 'truth', and this – the insertion of a bogus artefact – is by no means as portentous as his onlookers would like.

Other 1950s novelists exhibit a deep reluctance to pursue this kind of exactitude. The Magus-figures of Iris Murdoch's early novels reach out to embrace the palpable and the finite, but as soon as any sort of absolute drifts into view they are immediately hustled away and ridiculed. In an increasingly secular age, what was to be believed and what was not? Garnett Bowen's lament in Kingsley Amis's *I Like It Here* (1958) is characteristic. Visiting Fielding's tomb at Lisbon, he reflects how enviable an experience it would be to inhabit the world of his novels 'where duty was plain, evil arose out of malevolence, and a stray wayfarer could be invited indoors without hesitation and without fear'. These certainties were denied to protagonists of the post-war novel. Much more typical is the question put by Professor Treece to Emma Peel: ' "Do you believe?" . . . "No," ' Emma replies. ' "I just do things." '

Action, then, was contingent, not premeditated. Yet the question: how are we to behave? – or, as Strickland in Piers Paul Read's *A Married Man* (1980) puts it, 'What are we to do with ourselves?' – still exercised a necessarily potent spell. This was an enquiry that had implications for the form as well as the moral content of fiction. In 'Against Dryness', an influential essay published in 1961, Iris Murdoch provided both a text about morality in a post-Christian world and what A. S. Byatt has called 'a text about the appropriate fictive form with which to explain that world in its complexity and depth'. Ultimately Murdoch defends, on moral grounds, the Tolstoyan 'old-fashioned naturalistic idea of character', while admitting that we cannot now merely mimic Victorian realism. But the 'complexity and depth' which Byatt acknowledges is surely the problem. We live in a highly sophisticated, technological world governed by huge, distantly glimpsed and apparently impersonal forces, in which communications as much as morals have tended to invalidate the traditional novel of character. The whole plot of a novel like Trollope's *The Last Chronicle of Barset*, which hinges on the absence overseas of a crucial witness, could not take place in a world with telephones. Moreover, in a world about which we know so little, in which government – to take an obvious case – seems concerned with concealment rather than revelation, our own ability to act in a moral way is substantially diminished. The great Victorian fictional beings seem to bestride their world; its concerns are theirs; they invariably dominate it. We – and the people novelists among us create – do not have this luxury. For this reason 'character' seems remote and occasionally almost useless in the modern environment. Put Godwin Peak down in one of Martin Amis's urban nightmares and he would merely be engulfed. The morally scrupulous would meet the narrowly contingent, and with predictable, gloomy results.

At any time since the Second World War there has been a substantial body of novelists working to confound this thesis, ranging from specifically Christian writers to those concerned to justify a secular ethic. Even here, though, decay, the signs of retreat from an authentic moral position or area of moral debate, is at hand. The 'Catholic novel', in particular, remains a significant literary genre, but it is arguable that the majority of Catholic novels have less to do with the working-out of divine providence than with what might be called the glamour of religious belief or its technical appurtenances. The Catholicism of Graham Greene and Evelyn Waugh, to take an obvious example, can often seem simply exclusive – an exclusivity that carries a nasty sting in the tail. John Carey has drawn attention to the implication, contained in *The Heart of the Matter* (1948), that it is better to be an erring Catholic than a virtuous pagan. As Carey acknowledges, this charge first surfaced in Orwell's contemporary review of the novel, in which he objected to:

> the fairly sinister suggestion that ordinary human decency is of no value... In addition it is impossible not to feel a sort of snobbishness in Mr Greene's attitude ... He appears to share the idea, which has been floating around ever since Baudelaire, that there is something rather *distingué* in being damned. Hell is a sort of high-class nightclub, entry to which is reserved for Catholics only.

There is a kind of epic presumption in insisting that secular virtue is meaningless. The implications of this position are terrifying, for as Catholics will presumably remain a relatively small part of society – very few Catholic writers are particularly animated by the idea of mass conversion – the great majority of the population is effectively damned.

Waugh follows a slightly different track, although his final position is broadly similar. The religious sense in his fiction tends to be hopelessly mixed up with, and undetachable from, the whole parade of Brideshead-type snobbery. To Guy Crouchback, it seems fair to say, Catholicism is not much more than the spiritual equivalent of White's Club. To do Waugh justice, he does try to stress the ennobling effects of Catholicism, notably in his portrait of old Mr Crouchback, but it is also true to say that here his touch deserts him: Mr Crouchback, with his covert charity and his immense courtesy, is just a little too good to be true. For all Waugh's undoubted piety, his concern to show God tangibly at work in the lives of men, it is difficult to dismiss Rebecca West's charge that both he and Greene 'created an intellectual climate in which there is a crackbrained confusion between the moral and the aesthetic'. How you behave somehow seems of less importance than wearing the correct spiritual old boy's blazer. Thus Hooper in *Brideshead Revisited* (1945) is treated with unfeigned contempt, but Hooper is not a bad man, simply foolish and ineffectual. His conspicuous failing is to be middle-class and to have no knowledge of the Brideshead mystique. A lack of *style* damns Hooper, not the want of a moral sense, but for Waugh the two are indissoluble.

It can be said in Waugh's defence that he does at least raise Catholicism to the status of a subject for intellectual debate, or at least, in the final confrontations between Charles and Julia, try to show why Catholicism matters. He is also consistent in his attempts to show divine purpose working itself out, even if the results (for instance the death of Lord Marchmain) can seem excessively stagey. Much more typical of the post-war Catholic novelist is a habit of using the appurtenances or dogmas of the Church for technical purposes. David Lodge's *The British Museum is Falling Down* (1965), which concerns the efforts of a young Catholic couple to avoid adding to their already substantial family, is a good example of this type of book.

An exception to this rule exists in Lodge's excellent first novel,

The Picturegoers (1960), in which some authentic dilemmas of the faith are given greater immediacy by the underlying sexual content. Mark Underwood, a cynical undergraduate, comes to lodge with the working-class and devoutly Catholic Mallory family in the tatty London suburb of 'Brickley'. His eye quickly falls on Clare, the elder daughter, who has recently emerged from an unsuccessful novitiate. They become friends, although Mark's attempted fumblings are sternly repulsed. Subsequently Mark, who was brought up a Catholic, finds his faith renewed. He attends Mass and worries about transubstantiation. For her part Clare is oddly bored by his efforts to discuss these issues. It seems incredible to her that Mark – 'cynical, idle, sophisticated Mark' – has actually joined a file of Catholic students who, during Holy Week, carry a heavy wooden cross through the streets and along the open roads to the shrine of Our Lady at Walsingham. A final irony comes on the occasion when an emboldened Clare presses Mark to greater intimacy and is herself sharply rebuffed. Their relationship ends when Clare's mother finds some of Mark's pornographic (and wholly fantastic) scribblings on the subject of her daughter, and he is compelled to leave.

As it stands *The Picturegoers* is a clever inversion of the Catholic novel's traditional prohibitive motif, its redemptive aspects made keener by the sexual undertow. It is a measure of Lodge's achievement that Mark's conversion, to the point where he proposes to offer himself as a candidate for the priesthood, seems generally plausible. Other Catholic novelists concerned to stress the redemptive nature of their faith are sometimes less convincing. Piers Paul Read's characters, for example, have a tendency to get converted to Catholicism almost at the drop of a hat. *The Upstart* (1973), one of Read's best novels, is a fine, grim little tale of the revenge exacted by a middle-class clergyman's son on a local artistocratic family by whom he considers himself to have been patronised in adolescence. It is a comprehensive attack – one daughter humiliated, another impregnated under-age, Mark, the son, ruined – and yet the dénouement comes merely with nasty, unprincipled Hilary Fletcher's decision to stroll into a confessional, leaving the novel's architecture in fragments and the reader wondering how someone as loathsome as Fletcher could behave so implausibly. This is Read's point, of course, that the working-out of divine providence can effect precisely this sort of change, but within the context of an otherwise realistic novel the solution looks forced and somehow arbitrary.

Spiritual epiphanies are not always so casually presented. In the 1950s and 1960s, as A. S. Byatt observes, novels dealt with the numinous in an almost hectically ordered way. Murdoch and Golding, in particular, described a spirituality insecurely and ambivalently attached to any essential beliefs and symbols, and possibly for that reason tended to be more interested in the apocalyptic vision of disintegration and darkness than in the rarer moments of beatitude. However strong the intensity of Golding's vision, it was, one might say, a spirituality remote from ordinary life. Predictably an examination of 'faith' at the drawing-room level is very difficult to find in books not consciously aimed at the propagandist market. In some ways this is a queer discrepancy, as the late 1940s and early 1950s were a time of significant religious revival. However, this new post-war focus on spiritual renewal found little reflection in the literary fiction of the time. The preferred medium tended to be allegory, of the sort practised by Charles Williams, C. S. Lewis and J. R. R. Tolkien (although Tolkien always denied that *The Lord of the Rings* (1954–5) possessed an allegorical content, internal evidence suggests otherwise).

An echo of the religious ferment of the time can be found in Wain's *A Travelling Woman* (1959), in the figure of Edward Cowley, some years previously the author of an enormous bestseller entitled 'The Discovery of Faith' but now wracked by spiritual uncertainty. At least Cowley is a compelling and vital figure compared to the moral invertebrates who surround him. Generally speaking the religious make a poor showing in the post-war English novel. The clergyman, in particular, tends to be a figure of fun, either remote and austere (*The Upstart*), decent but anachronistic (John Fowles's *Daniel Martin* (1977)), a puzzled man vainly trying to come to terms with an inhospitable modern world (J. L. Carr's *A Day in Summer* (1964), Auberon Waugh's *Consider the Lilies* (1968)), or a slightly sinister opportunist exploiting his position for personal gain (Gideon Farrar in Byatt's *Still Life* (1985)). All, however depressed, ineffectual or bewildered, are unhappily conscious of the Church's changing role. Maurice Fisher in *The Humbler Creation*, whose duties include the escort of delinquent teenagers back to the police station from which they have absconded, is conscious that his responsibilities are increasingly secular rather than spiritual. ' "I'm a glorified social worker," ' admits Daniel Orton in *Still Life*, ' "only I don't do it for society, which I'm not that bothered about as an entity." ' Other professional people look on ruefully, aware that they are the victims of displaced religious sensibility. Lorna, the doctor in Francis King's *The Needle* (1975), makes a typical complaint:

> 'Things happen to my patients. I don't mean only things like birth and death and illnesses, but also all those emotional and spiritual crises that would once have been confided to the parish priest.'

The Church, then, seemed a spent force when it came to the eternal questions. Yet the battle to preserve Christian moral precepts in the absence of spiritual authentication continues. Byatt is one of a number of novelists to hark back to George Eliot's prescription. In fact Daniel and Stephanie's inability jointly to adopt the Eliot line invests one of their many pre-marital arguments. For Daniel, an instinctive rather than theoretical Christian, Stephanie's obvious virtues are Christian virtues:

> her scrupulousness, her gentleness, part of what he valued in Christ, and were derived from Christ, and that was that. You could have good Christians who thought they weren't, and into that category she indisputably and tiresomely fell.

Stephanie, however, is conscious only of the disabling historical distance. ' "In the nineteenth century, I would, I would have made a good vicar's wife. In the twentieth, it's not morally possible." '

What was then morally possible in a post-war world whose recent turbulence had called into question not only the existence of God but the existence – let alone the successful enforcement – of any kind of ethical standards? Examining the list of 1950s writers whose work was supposed at the time to have some conspicuous moral dimension, one is liable to become extremely confused. Kingsley Amis, for example, is often labelled a 'moralist' – and there is a critical work by John McDermott starkly entitled *Kingsley Amis: An English Moralist* (1989). On the strength of his early novels, at least, this is a rather doubtful presumption. A great deal of 'integrity' and 'decency' might have been claimed for Jim Dixon on his first appearance in the stamping grounds of literary London, but his behaviour and the standards which he sets himself are notoriously erratic. Loathing, whether of oneself or other people, is not morality. What Jim wants is what he can get – the nicest girl, the best job – and no creed sustains him in this pursuit except opportunism. *Lucky Jim*'s ending, too, is unsatisfactory: merely a waving of the authorial wand to give Jim what he desires, and nothing to do with the moral issues of selfishness and responsibility raised by the main body of the text. *That Uncertain Feeling* (1955), Amis's second novel, is similarly non-committal. Certainly there are animating questions: two of them might be 'What happens if you betray your wife's trust?' and 'Of what value is a job gained through your mistress's influence?' John Lewis, however, is badly equipped to answer or even understand these questions as he is unable to understand his wife's feelings, notably when he resolves to give up the job won by his adulterous liaison with Elizabeth Griffiths. As he has already ruined their marriage, this can never be anything other than a token gesture. As Gindin remarks, Lewis 'can neither understand or follow a moral line of conduct, nor live with the consequences of his own immorality'. This tendency recurs in Amis's later novels. With their gallows humour and their grim jokes about extinction they are the work not of a moralist but of a writer obsessed by the imminence of death and the absurdity of lives that are merely a preparation for it.

Among Amis's immediate contemporaries, a more deserving candidate for the title of 'English moralist' is John Wain. By the standards of the Victorian age Lumley, the hero of *Hurry On Down* (1953), seems an unlikely moral exemplar: after all, he merely drifts from one unpromising occupation to another. But Lumley has principles, even if they are couched in the vague terms of preserving his integrity and avoiding what he imagines to be the racket of middle-class professional life. Matched against these yardsticks, his eventual ascent to the status of a radio gag-writer is evidence of failure. Another point of view insists that Lumley's progress is a reward for good behaviour. Unlike Dixon he has gained the job (and won the girl) through the exercise of his talents and his adaptability to prevailing circumstance. Whatever else can be said about it, Lumley's success is not arbitrary. The maxim which Wain seems to be advancing is 'Compromise, but retain your principles' or – bluntly – 'Surrender, but don't give yourself away'. Later novels sharpen this focus, if only by suggesting that some ways of life and some environments are 'better' than others.

In *The Contenders* (1955) and *A Travelling Woman* Wain seems content that his characters should throw over a false metropolitan veneer in favour of a quieter but more honest provincial life. In the former the worth of the journalist, Shaw, stems from the fact that he has never really left the Midlands town in which he grew up. Links, the neurotic provincial solicitor in *A Travelling Woman*, only seems to 'behave well' when he leaves the furtive round of London adulteries and returns to his wife and his office. This is a moral lesson, if you like, but it is still vaguely unsatisfactory. Rather than itching to make moral choices based on the rational exercise of his intellect, Links is a tired, feeble creature, easily ground down by circumstance and content to grasp the easy option. In his defence, 'heroism' in the old sense of the word is not a conspicuous feature of the contemporary novel.

If nothing else, the early novels of Amis and Wain show the enormous difficulty that post-war novelists have in writing about 'moral issues' in an aesthetically satisfying way. The reader would like Links to be more in control of his life, to take greater responsibility for his destiny. But for Wain to convert him into a beacon of moral scrupulousness would be to ruin his position as an average *homme moyen sensuel*. Writing moral fiction in an absence of virtue was, as later novelists were to discover, an increasingly problematic activity. That moral dilemmas could still be combined with aesthetic satisfaction is demonstrated by a novel like Pamela Hansford Johnson's *The Humbler Creation*, which might be described as a study in character and moral responsibility. Significantly, to bring off these effects Hansford Johnson has to concentrate on a small, tight-knit community in which 'belief' can be taken for granted. Maurice Fisher, the middle-aged rector of a decayed Kensington parish, inhabits a cramped vicarage with his vain, idle wife and three generations of her family. Disillusioned with his marriage, the trivial concerns of parish administration and what he regards as the Church's inability to perform any useful function, he seeks solace in the friendship of a widow named Alice Imber. Meanwhile his sister-in-law Kate has begun an affair with a raffish journalist.

Both these developments are monitored with a good deal of prurience by the Church congregation. However, what follows is not merely an exercise in suspect moral outrage. *The Humbler Creation*'s distinction lies in the way in which each of its characters is shown to live his or her life according to carefully thought out moral precepts. These are brought dramatically into play to consider the novel's two chief issues – Maurice's liaison with Mrs Imber and Kate's intention to commit perjury in a court case as a means of defending her lover, Westlake, who has crashed a car while drunk. The effort involved in balancing friendship with principles can sometimes lead to an uncomfortably abrasive note. Plym, the church organist, himself a passenger in Westlake's car at the time of the accident, loses his temper with Kate:

'I've had to put up with my life. I've had to stick it out for years. Why should I encourage you to make the sort of filthy mess I have always restrained myself from making?'

This is less censorious than it sounds. Plym, who regards Kate's relationship with Westlake as dangerously imprudent, cannot imagine why she should wish to make a bad situation worse by telling a lie, shielding Westlake by pretending to have been at the wheel of the car herself.

Throughout these debates, Hansford Johnson's most important distinction is between those who think carefully about the consequences of their actions and those who do not. Westlake, for example, is unable to comprehend the fact that to Kate's acquaintance the idea of telling a lie under oath is morally repugnant (' "What is all this raving on and on about a tin-pot matter like this?" '). In the matter of the vicar's supposed adultery, Kitson, the churchwarden, decides to refer the matter to higher clerical authority, ' "because nothing else except the Church has got any rules for promoting decent social behaviour" '. Consequently, it behoves the Church to make sure that these rules are enforced. Kitson's action infuriates David Beattie, the curate, as it seems to imply that morality is ' "just a discipline to keep the natives in their place" '. But according to his lights Kitson is an honest man. He regards the Church as a moral beacon above a sea of darkness and cannot tolerate any assault on its integrity. Eventually Maurice gives up Alice – it is a measure of the time that they do not sleep together – and a number of judgements fall into place: Maurice's decency, his wife's falseness, Beattie's naivety redeemed by good intentions. The result is all the more satisfying in that one can see character at work, moving into a confrontation with a particular dilemma and emerging on the other side either renewed or subtly redefined.

Inevitably, to a modern eye *The Humbler Creation* seems an old-fashioned novel; the rigour of its principles belongs to another age. It is worth noting, however, that these principles do not go unchallenged. Already the idea of responsibility for one's actions is coming under attack, most obviously in the case of Derek Fraser, son of the church cleaner, a teenager who is taken into care after sexually assaulting a younger child. Derek plays two roles in the novel. On the one hand he provides a traditional excuse for denying the existence of God (' "if there had been a God he wouldn't have made Derek like he is," ' Mrs Fraser tells Maurice). On the other he himself is anxious to deny that he is morally responsible for his actions – ' "It's not my fault, see? It means I've got something wrong. So they ought to get me right" ' – a removal of blame which at the same time contrives to suggest that Derek's habit of interfering with little girls is somehow 'their' fault because 'they' have failed to correct it.

In the 1960s this attitude became much more common in the novel. The protagonists in fiction by John Fowles and Margaret Drabble tend to operate by instinct, to act first and consider the consequences of their actions afterwards. The character who, to take an obvious example, commits some sexual indiscretion whose result only becomes apparent in the grim light of dawn is a commonplace of 1960s fiction. Fowles, on the strength of novels such as *The Collector* (1963), *The Magus* (1966) and *The French Lieutenant's Woman* (1969), is virtually a moral relativist. Not only does *The Collector* make a scapegoat out of Clegg's social background, it also suggests that the moral difference between Clegg and his captor is simply the result of upbringing. It is back to Thackeray and Becky Sharp's contention that she could have been a virtuous woman on £5,000 a year. *The Magus* (which, interestingly, Fowles wanted at first to call *The God-Game*), with its mages, illusions and elaborate double-crosses, is merely a hymn to contingency. Even *The French Lieutenant's Woman*, the 'freedom' of whose alternative endings attracted much contemporary applause, is ultimately sterile, each conclusion pre-programmed by the author, and consequently fixed.

But this kind of moral relativism is pervasive. The academic romp, which began to be fashionable at about this time, the campus frolic of sexual and scholastic indignity, is a good example of the disregard for absolute standards. The globe-trotting professors in David Lodge's fiction, for instance, are seldom motivated by a desire to locate the 'truth' about a particular author or a particular text. On the contrary, their actions are prompted by professional envy; their ambition is less to enjoy the exercise of their talents than to secure publication in a prestige journal or a keynote speech at the conference of the Modern Languages Association. In the same way their approach to literature relies not on honest evaluation but on whatever is the most modish critical technique.

In the 1960s, too, one had the odd spectacle of relativism being abetted by form. This, after all, was the great age of the experimental text: spare, random, confused, contingent, in which character has only a marginal relevance. The protagonists of experimental fiction have little moral life. Their lives are governed by chance; their role is merely to be battered by events, to wander around in a fog of paranoid uncertainty. Like the terrified subterranean in Kafka's 'The Burrow' (1931), they have no control over their destiny and no real inkling as to its probable shape. In this atmosphere the concept of 'judgement' could seem simply arbitrary. The judgements in *Lucky Jim* (1954), for instance, of which there are a great many – judgements made by Dixon on other people's characters, appearance, dress or opinions – are based on personal or aesthetic prejudice. In this they do no more than ape the Brideshead atmosphere against which, ironically enough, Amis was reacting. Frederica in *Still Life* makes a deliberate connection between the moral precepts of *Brideshead Revisited* and *Lucky Jim*. As she points out, Hooper in the former is nastily mocked for his accent, his hair and his ignorance of the Brideshead world. But it seems just as culpable to her that Dixon should mock Bertrand Welch for wearing a beret, liking art and enjoying foreign travel. Jim's confidence in his ability to distinguish a nice skirt from a nasty skirt, and his conviction that nice girls wear nice skirts and nasty girls nasty ones, seems to her truly terrible – a reduction of serious moral issues to the tawdry level of style.

Despite these confusions, it is impossible to deny many 1960s novels a conscious ethic or a definite moral atmosphere. At their best they profess a sort of vague liberal humanism of the type evident in Margaret Drabble's fiction. A book like *The Millstone* (1965) is characterised by an endless tolerance and a deep reluctance to judge – unless, as already noted, one happens to be a 'well-descended Tory accountant person'. Rosamund Stacey might disapprove of the actions of a friend or relative, but although she might make (at least mentally) some mildly censorious comment, she would probably stop short of taking positive action to prevent them. Fowles's *Daniel Martin* is a revealing book in this context. Intended in the author's words as 'a defence of humanism', it is the *apologia pro vita sua* of a successful playwright turned film scriptwriter whose life, so far as we can judge, has been a series of betrayals – a betrayal of his clerical father and rural upbringing, of his talent (he throws over the English stage for Hollywood), his wife and two of his oldest friends. The novel begins with a visit paid by Daniel to Anthony, an Oxford philosophy don and devout Catholic now dying of cancer, and his wife Jane, to whose sister Daniel was once married. The visit is a source of some trepidation as, at an early stage in his career, Daniel wrote a crude and satirical play burlesquing these relationships. Though the visit goes well, Anthony commits suicide shortly afterwards. Subsequently Daniel retraces his steps, goes back to his former existences, considers past relationships, the great web and weave of his life over three decades, but all that seems to remain is a sort of complacent hindsight, self-knowledge perhaps, but of an oddly preening sort. 'Humanism', as represented in *Daniel Martin*, might be defined as never having to say you're sorry. Moreover, such wisdom as one acquires after the event is invariably compromised by the individual's inability to make use of it as a guide to future behaviour.

Needless to say, 'liberal humanism', the characteristic 1960s insistence on 'liberty' and 'freedom', even if that meant only the liberty to exploit and the freedom to be exploited, did not escape contemporary censure. A considered attack on 'liberal humanism' comes, for instance, in A. S. Byatt's *The Game* (1968). Set in 1963, the novel examines the question of the artist's moral responsibility for his art while at the same time opposing an allegedly pragmatic humanism with the apparent certainties of religious belief. Byatt's most significant opposition is the relationship between two sisters: Cassandra, a highly strung Oxford don, and Julia, a modish novelist married to a Quaker activist. The two are linked less by present circumstance than by shared memories of their North of England Quaker upbringing, the peculiar, massively schematised 'game' of the title which they played as children, and a naturalist named Simon Moffat, now a presenter of television documentaries about the Amazonian jungle, with whom they were both involved. These memories are rekindled by a joint visit to the family home at Durham, on the death of their mother, and Moffat's return to England.

The Game is much more than the juxtaposition of personalities. It is also a novel about two different ways of looking at the world and devising a framework for acceptable behaviour: on the one side Julia's facile glibness, her receptivity to almost any suggestion, a consciousness of personal rectitude mixed with a tremendous ethical uncertainty that causes her to submit 'unquestioningly to the beauty of a situation'; on the other Cassandra's dour Anglicanism, built on a rigid platform of 'order' and, in the last resort, not much more than a sort of overdressed medievalism. Throughout this exploration of two distinctive and opposed personalities, Byatt is concerned to stress the inadequacies of their contending positions. Her account of Cassandra's figurative Christianity, in particular, is worth quoting at length:

> The complexities of existence were the interrelation of roots and roses, strange heads and fruits, in a walled garden, outside which the sea rose in formally dangerous peaks. She had elaborated, and believed, a network of symbols which made the outer world into a dazzling but comprehensible constellation of physical facts whose spiritual interrelation could be grasped and woven by the untiring intellect: suns, moons, stars, roses, cups, lances, lions and serpents: all had their place and also their meaning. This network was overlaid by another network, interweaving other roots, footnotes, cross-references, bibliographical data, paleographical quirks. Somewhere, under the network, the truth shone; Cassandra had come, like many others, looking for final Authority, logically to see it in the Church. This was a symbol, and also real; it was a guarantee. A passion for symbolism is in some cases an automatic precursor of a passion for theology. Cassandra had embraced both.

The numinous, and the moral, exists for Cassandra, then, at the level of a medieval wall painting, or in the traceries one finds drawn by monks on the flyleaves of Dark Ages chapbooks: a dense, figurative landscape pregnant with hidden meaning. At the same time it is clear that Cassandra has great difficulty in applying these precepts to the ordinary field of human contact. She remains aloof, austere and forbidding. Yet somehow this seems preferable to Julia's fatal susceptibility. At one point Julia begins an affair with a shallow, sophisticated television producer who, knowing something of her circumstances, remarks:

> 'you do let things get you down, don't you? And make an awful fuss about personal relationships which it's much better to take with a bit of gay abandon as they come . . . Try a bit of deliberate and *conscious* selfishness. You're an artist after all and artists have got to be detached and ruthless and better if they admit it sincerely.'

We know enough of Byatt's standpoint by this time to infer that this is precisely what the artist should not be, but to Julia it seems a welcome dispensation.

The notion that artists are somehow 'different' from ordinary people is, of course, a form of totalitarianism. As it proceeds, *The Game* is increasingly taken up with contending extremes. There is Cassandra's personal rigidity. On a basic, spiritual level there is the decision of Thor, Julia's husband, to follow Gospel teachings literally and fill the flat with the homeless at the expense of their family life, and attempt missionary work in Africa. Above all, there is Julia's extreme tolerance, fatal in that it extends to herself and includes the assumption that nothing she does can hurt any other person. This attitude is made worse by Julia's inability to comprehend the structure of other people's lives. Spiritual pre-occupations, to take a very obvious example, are beyond her. Hearing Cassandra and her parish priest discussing clerical vestments at an Oxford dinner table, she can only regard the conversation as 'low comedy'. Ultimately Julia writes a novel thinly dramatising herself, Cassandra and Moffat (whose enigmatic reappearance has been the catalyst for all this activity) and the Game, whereupon Cassandra kills herself. The 'fault', if there is one, lies with Julia: it is noticeable that Byatt, normally the least censorious of writers, reserves her sharpest barbs for the surviving sister. Yet the wider environment seems equally to blame. No finite beliefs or behavioural certainties unite Julia, Thor, Cassandra and their minor attendants. Their tragedy, in a world of collapsing ethics, is that they do not know how to behave. Moral responsibility might have saved them – literally so, in Cassandra's case, as her preparations for suicide, papering up the windows prior to turning on the gas, are observed by a colleague who declines to intervene. Yet the strongest admonition remains the remark made by Cassandra to Julia: ' "I think perhaps we should make a real moral effort to forgo one's need for a sense of glory" ' – words that could profitably have been said to the rather similar figure of Daniel Martin.

Of all the roles which the writer may choose to adopt in the last decade of the twentieth century – savant, philosopher, clown – the most elusive guise is that of 'moralist'. Whether he or she likes it or not, the writer who chooses to introduce a pressing moral element into fiction, even the impresario of a gentle comedy of manners, does so in the knowledge that they will run up against some almost insuperable problems. Chief among these is the knowledge that we inhabit a society in which traditional Christian morality has become steadily eroded without anything tangible taking its place.

Aside from the old 1960s street signs of 'freedom' and 'liberty' it is difficult to know of what precisely 'liberal humanism' consists. It is a commonplace to say that 'freedom' as defined by a reader of the *Daily Telegraph* means something very different to the view of a works committee anxious to enforce the closed shop, and doubtless such confusions are sometimes worth preserving: a society run on lines advocated by the *Daily Telegraph* would, one feels, be a very queer place indeed. This is a novelist's quandary as much as a politician's. The contemporary writer, even one whose contact with the outside world is limited to sporadic glances at a newspaper, will be aware that the pace of social and technological change has been sufficient to set traditional values in flux. At the very least he will know that the world of his adulthood is fantastically removed from the world of his childhood, and that there exist whole communities of people to whom the words 'moral responsibility' mean very little. The genderless narrator of Jeanette Winterson's novel *Written on the Body* (1992) attempts to put a mitigating gloss on romantic agonising by wondering why he or she has been 'allowed to grow up without the necessary apparatus to make sound ethical decisions'. Why indeed? The current Secretary of State for Education would invoke an absence of divinely inspired imperatives; his opponents would point to a morally stunted economic liberalism, but whatever the answer the novelist searching for shared values and bewildered (or, less frequently, inspired) by his inability to find them, is likely to be aware of effect rather than cause. Listen to a Tory politician of the 1990s and you could think that all English people believe in marriage, the nuclear family, hard work, 'community', parental authority and unlocked doors. The reality, as even the most generalised statistics demonstrate, is sharply different.

This kind of confusion affects the novel as much as any other social product. It is, for example, practically impossible to function as a satirist at the present time. Satire flourishes in a morally stable society, or one which is only just beginning to break down, at any rate an environment where wickedness or 'folly' is acknowledged for what it is and can be made to seem ridiculous through contrasts with accepted norms. From the point of view of the English novel 'satire' was in its death-throes nearly sixty years ago. It is customary to mark Evelyn Waugh down as a satirist on the strength of his Bright Young Thing novels, but his complex relation to the social groupings he was writing about – fascination mixed with disgust – robs him of the necessary detachment. But perhaps the greatest change has to do with the protagonists of the novel. The novel without a hero is, of course, a staple of fiction (Thackeray uses the words as the sub-title of *Vanity Fair*), but over the last quarter-century the anti-hero has become markedly more anti-heroic. The 1970s and 1980s brought characters who were rapists, violent criminals, child-abusers, moral invertebrates. To complicate matters, they were often *comic* rapists, violent criminals, child-abusers or moral invertebrates. Meanwhile, the fictional portrayal of 'virtue' found itself fighting a savage rearguard action. The 'good man' of Trollope's novels, whose principles never decline into priggishness and who can be calculated to behave in a consistently scrupulous way, still exists in English fiction, but he is becoming increasingly rare.

Some of the difficulties involved in writing 'moral fiction' in a moral vacuum can be seen in the work of Martin Amis, a writer who is held up to public inspection as a 'moralist' on a fairly regular basis. Amis's chief characteristic is an intense and fascinated disgust, in which the exposure of his characters' appalling behaviour is invariably followed by retribution and, occasionally, outright obliteration. Thus the inhabitants of Appleseed Rectory in *Dead Babies* (1975) are destroyed by the man they had assumed to be the impresario of their decadence; John Self reaches the end of *Money* (1984) to find that he has been the victim of a nightmarish exercise in score-settling; Keith Talent's destiny in *London Fields* (1989) is to have his ambitions snuffed out by a superior intelligence which has planned his downfall all along. But disgust is not necessarily a moral statement. Certainly, Amis's fiction is built on the assumption of impending social and ethical collapse. The world of *London Fields* may be a claustrophobic urban battleground, but one could glimpse this tendency as far back as *Success* (1978): ' "We *are* getting nastier," ' muses yobbish Terry Service.

> 'We don't put up with things. We do what we want now. I wouldn't go out late too often, if I were you. There are plenty of people here who would be quite happy to do you harm.'

The truly terrifying thing about this is its laconicism, its underlying chirpiness. Terry, who is on the way up, rather likes the way the world is changing, and applauds his own transformation from oppressed to oppressor. In contrast, his foster-brother Greg's lament – ' "everyone *is* getting nastier; everyone is drunk; everyone is desperate" ' – simply expresses the terror of the socially defeated. There are sharply defined oppositions in Amis, but they are rarely the oppositions of 'good' and 'bad'.

This tendency is markedly apparent in *Dead Babies*, which at first glance looks like a straightforward moral fable. Set in a ghastly near-future, it concerns a debauched weekend enjoyed in the confines of a country rectory by a group of hedonistic young people. During the course of the weekend they are joined by three Americans whose depravity is, if anything, on an even higher level. Simultaneously, their lives are being disrupted and threatened by a mysterious intruder known only as 'Johnny'. The conflicting views of Quentin Villiers, the owner of the rectory, and Marvin Buzzard, spokesman for the Americans, form the novel's chief contrast. Buzzard's opinions are a parody of the extremes of the US counter-culture. Sex, he maintains, is ' "just something your body does" '. The current preoccupation with sexual activity is the consequence of ' "a million years of denying your needs" '. Perversion is ' "justified – no, *demanded* – by an environment that is now totally man-made, totally without a biology" '. Additionally, Buzzard is the author of a book entitled *The Mind Lab*, whose premise is that the human brain is now entirely subservient to external control. As he puts it:

'*Fuck* all this dead babies about love, understanding compassion. Use drugs to . . . cushion the consciousness, guide it, protect it, stimulate it.'

Quentin courteously dissents from all this malign hedonism. He defends his marriage, contrasts Buzzard's apocalyptic anarchism with the advantages of feudalism (on the grounds of mutual obligation), even restrains his companions in some of their wilder excesses. In the guise of 'Johnny', however, it is Quentin who brings about the novel's dreadful dénouement. But to get rid of undesirable characters is not to settle a moral argument. Quentin defeats Buzzard merely by extinguishing him. His superiority lies simply in his cunning: the final impression is of an environment so warped that individual character has largely ceased to matter.

The same point could be made, in a slightly different way, of *Success*, Amis's third novel, set in the sharply observed London of the 1970s. The reader's suspicions over the author's intent are immediately aroused by the symmetry of the design. Gregory Service, an apparently wealthy socialite who works in an art gallery, shares a flat with his foster-brother Terence, a yob in the grand Amis manner, who works as a telephone salesman. Greg is distinguished by a smug patrician superiority ('Can't they see that I am here to be tasted, to be mulled over, to be adored?'), Terry by rank proletarian greed ('I want all that and I want all that, and I want all *that* and I want all *that*'). Subsequently their careers invert, to the point where Terry succeeds in acquiring both Gregory's job and his incestuous relationship with his sister Ursula. Gregory becomes a gibbering neurotic; much of his earlier bragging is revealed as self-delusion. As one might expect, however, Terry's 'success' is scarcely worth having. Though he succeeds in sleeping with Jan, a woman Greg has earlier contrived to detach from his grasp, the act falls short of his expectations. At the same time money and newly acquired status make him an even worse person than before, for example in his gratuitous assault on a down-and-out to whom he has previously been content to talk. The landscape described in *Success*, consequently, and the ambitions that float above it, is entirely ignoble, the social theme of a supercilious paternalism overthrown by a yob culture set in sharp relief by the moral void.

If *Success* has a 'moral' it is that triumph debases you even more than failure. *London Fields* discloses a more subtle yet equally depressing purpose, much of it detectable in the gargantuan figure of Keith Talent. A sublime barbarian – criminal, womaniser, cheat – Talent was, as the author admitted at the time, an attempt to create the 'very worst' character. But the horrifying thing about Keith is not his excesses, but the fact that his is an existence not without its standards, its checks and admonitions – a sort of warped and repellent sub-moral life pieced together out of television, tabloid newspapers and the spurious concept of 'respect'. Thus he is joined in an attack on a girl who has given him a venereal disease by the girl's brother, male solidarity outweighing family loyalty. He beats up an unfortunate who makes the mistake of tampering with his darts to the unspoken approval of the pub onlookers. He accepts the fact that failure to satisfy the loan sharks to whom he is indebted will result in grave personal injury. In each of these instances we can see a parodic moral code being infringed. But at the same time Amis is playing an insidious game of cat-and-mouse with his creation, allowing him the glimpse of a shred of integrity, the ability to make a moral choice, and then removing it. There is, for instance, the scene in which he dismisses Nicola Six, the latter masquerading as a social worker, from his flat. To reassure his wife he tells her: ' "They can't touch you girl. You are who you are." ' This causes Kath to turn slowly towards him 'as if he were a wonderful doctor, as if he were a wonderful priest'. But the words are not Keith's. They come – at least this is the implication – from the tabloids and the soaps; they are what Keith, whose whole life is mediated in this way, considers to be an appropriate response to the situation. Keith's one admission of moral nullity has a similarly faked quality. ' "I'm a piece of shit," ' he murmurs, during an unsuccessful and violent burglary. Again, this is mimicry, not revelation.

Keith may be there to make a moral point – that environment has disqualified certain people from the right to live a moral life – but he is not an actor in a moral drama. He has no life of his own, and is the subject of endless manipulation by his creator. In the end, hoodwinked and cast aside by Nicola, he is merely snuffed out. But there is another way in which Amis confuses the moral issue. This is his habit of allowing the joke to take precedence over sympathy or condemnation. A good example of the former comes in the scene where Trish Shirt, Keith's least favourite and most decrepit girlfriend, arrives at the pub in which Keith is competing in the semi-final of the darts competition whose progress the novel monitors. Trish complains of Keith's treatment of her with these words: ' "Keep myself got up like a titmag. In my owce. Case he wants to come round and lam the yell out of me. In me oh *nous*." ' This has the effect of making the reader laugh at Trish before sympathising with her. A good example of the latter comes in the scene where Keith becomes righteously annoyed at his near-comatose wife's attempt to hand him their baby daughter while he is eating his dinner. It is an exceptionally funny passage, but it does not allow us to repose very much confidence in Amis the moralist. If there is a consolation it lies in the fact that these are not real people – certainly not in the sense achieved by Pamela Hansford Johnson's characters. Amis's people cannot better themselves. They cannot even make choices. They can only be extinguished. But this is as much a consequence of environment as of writerly intention.

The protagonists of the immediately post-war novel might have been distinguished by their inability to live moral lives, by their continual recourse to stylistic preference in any matter of judgement. Their late 1980s successors have even less ability to make moral choices, and consequently even less sense of possessing lives of their own. In any fictional battle involving moral relativism, unfortunately, the only victor is the author.

9

Harold's Years

All over the country people blamed other people for all the things that were going wrong – the trades unions, the present government, the miners, the car workers, the seamen, the Arabs, the Irish, their own husbands, their own idle good-for-nothing offspring, comprehensive education. Nobody knew whose fault it really was, but most people managed to complain fairly forcefully about somebody: only a few were stunned into honourable silence.

Margaret Drabble, *The Ice Age* (1977)

Despite a three and a half year interregnum and a postscript of similar length conducted by a trusted lieutenant, the period 1964–79 will always be associated with the puzzling figure of Harold Wilson. Over a decade and a half since he removed himself from office, Wilson exhibits a mass of contradictions: the Bevanite who became a byword for establishment quietism; the populist communicator who retreated into Sphinx-like introspection; the technologist who never delivered; the democrat who effectively destroyed the concept of cabinet government. Though there have been several recent attempts to rehabilitate him, for example the biography by Ben Pimlott and a number of articles by the Oxford historian Ross McKibbin which appeared around the time of the 1992 General Election, he remains the least regarded senior politician of the post-war era.

What can be salvaged from the wreck of this once mighty reputation? Wilson, after all, won four elections, a record superior to Mrs Thatcher's. It can be said of him, at the very least, that it was not entirely his fault. It was his misfortune to preside over national government during a period when the country's post-war inability to find itself seemed to have become sharply apparent. Similarly, it was his misfortune – a lasting, personal misfortune – to constitute the bridge between a socialist political party and a democratic government in a weak economy. Both these positions were eventually to prove untenable, but not before a great deal of pragmatic activity had temporarily concealed their frailty. Yet his legacy remains. Wilson was not responsible for the fundamental economic problems that beset the United Kingdom in the 1970s, but by short-term opportunism he exacerbated them. He did not 'cause' monetarism, but the conditions for the 1976 IMF crisis and monetarism's imposition were in place at his departure. He did not bring about the split in the Labour party, but his management of the contending factions increasingly took the form of a holding operation against the inevitable. The impossibility of his task has perhaps not been fully appreciated, either by historians or novelists.

The uncertainties of Wilson's position were not slow to declare themselves during the tenure of the 1964–70 Labour government. Despite the achievements of the Jenkins Chancellorship, these were largely economic. Wilson had won the 1964 election promising to reforge British industry by means of technological expertise, but the economic history of the next six years was a catalogue of decline, false dawns and blighted hopes. In the 1960s, far more so than in the previous decade, Britain paid the price for not having won the war. A traditional reluctance to invest or to replace archaic industrial equipment was reinforced by an hostility to change from management and workforce alike. The failure of 'In Place of Strife', the 1968 Industrial Relations initiative, brought down by an alliance of trades unionists and Labour MPs, foreshadowed the unrest of the 1970s. Meanwhile there was pressure on sterling, devaluation and the resignation of a chancellor. 'The pound in your pocket' joined 'the white heat of the technological revolution' as a phrase that was to haunt Wilson's later years.

At the same time Britain was becoming endangered, both internally and externally, by confusion over its international role. Wilson began by regarding his relationship with the United States as crucial, but with President Johnson's support for sterling dependent on Britain not devaluing or acting east of Suez without consultation, it was tempting to ask how much this bargain was worth. The American alliance, the vestiges of a fading Empire, the famous xenophobia – none of these seemed of much account when set against the concerns of an energetic new world that was beginning to take shape on the other side of the Channel. Significantly, French objections to British entry into the European Economic Community were directed at US defence links, favourable Commonwealth food contracts and a reluctance to commit to monetary union. Increasingly Britain could please neither its old war allies nor its prospective trading partners, a crisis in confidence that was to have profound economic consequences. The 1976 IMF crisis, for instance, is thought to have been worsened by the hostility of US bankers on the IMF board.

In the 1960s uncertainty; in the 1970s, palpably, crisis. The first Wilson government bequeathed a legacy of high public expenditure, state intervention of varying degrees of usefulness, wage inflation untrammelled by bargaining procedures. Oddly it was not a course that Heath's Conservative administration of 1970 – returned on a late swing, against public expectation – seemed disposed to alter, certainly not in the field of intervention. The ministers who assembled at the Department of Trade and Industry under the supervision of John Davies, himself a former industrialist, imagined that they would be allowed to leave industry to market forces. As the ailing Rolls-Royce became the first of half a dozen lame ducks to be helped on its way to oblivion with large amounts of public money, it became clear that Heath's manifesto commitment to economic 'freedom' was highly equivocal. Government intervention in the field of wage bargaining fared little better. The miners forced an humiliating climbdown as early as 1972. In the 1973–4 crisis of power cuts and reduced working weeks, the scent of anarchy was added to simple intransigence. 'I want to see the end of your government,' McGahey, one of the miners' leaders, is supposed to have told Heath during the course of the final, fruitless negotiations at Downing Street. McGahey's words were his own – they were certainly not the views of Gormley, the bluff and pragmatic miners' leader – but their substance echoed down through the 1970s. Wilson, who returned precariously to power after an inconclusive general election, found the predicaments of the 1960s greatly magnified.

By July 1975 the unemployment figures were the worst since the Second World War. Public expenditure had reached 45 per cent of national income. It was not merely a renaissant Tory opposition but senior Labour figures such as Jenkins and Crosland who wondered whether such a figure was compatible with the aims of a free society. Such dilemmas were, in any case, of little interest to their leader. Wilson, by now a remote and insubstantial figure in the eyes of the parliamentary party, resigned on his 60th birthday in March 1976, leaving Callaghan to preside over the slow decline to the 1979 'Winter of Discontent' when pay restraint collapsed, the dead lay unburied and, in the words of one Labour cabinet minister:

> We were engaging in what I called occupational tribal warfare, as though every separate group in the country had no feeling and no sense of being part of a community, but was simply out to get for itself what it could.

Peter Shore's words, spoken several years into the 1980s, would have seemed ominously pertinent to the novelist of the 1970s. The novels of Margaret Drabble and Piers Paul Read, for example, are full of frightened middle-class people wondering what has happened to the certainties of their youth; this isolation was magnified by an awareness of the powerful vested interests manoeuvring beyond the gates. But while novelists recognised and occasionally engaged with the political and economic disturbances, the majority of their concern was expended on the prevailing social crisis. With hindsight it is easy to see the 1960s as a series of buzz-words: 'Permissiveness'; 'Freedom'; declining standards; collectivism; social reform; the crisis in authority. Undoubtedly each of these has its place in any discussion of 1960s culture, but to present the decade as an unheralded social cataclysm is to ignore some very obvious continuities. It ignores, too, the fact that most 1960s *causes célèbres*, from flower power to student demos, were perpetrated by small groups of people attended by maximum publicity. Television did not create the 1960s, but it fashioned public awareness of the decade, and very much to its own agenda. Born in 1960, I have two overriding memories of the subsequent ten years – England winning the 1966 World Cup and the 1969 moon landing. Each takes on its recognisable shape, assumes its own private focus, by way of television. Meanwhile, of course, great stretches of ordinary life continued unhindered and without reference to the preoccupations of the media.

The novelists of the 1970s and early 1980s who wrote about the 1960s did so, on the whole, with very great hostility. The anti–1960s novel is a definable literary genre from about 1968, the year in which Kingsley Amis published *I Want It Now*. As a medium it is relatively elastic. *The History Man* (1975) is an anti–1960s novel, as is Piers Paul Read's *The Professor's Daughter* (1971), although the former is set in 1972 and the latter takes place in America. Each novel occupies itself exclusively with the attitudes which the 1960s were popularly supposed to have spawned – an extreme and ultimately violent liberalism whose consequences are in the Bradbury novel more or less comic and in the Read novel definitely tragic.

Typically the focus of such exposés is social, although *The Professor's Daughter*, concerned with senatorial influence and the translation of governmental theory into practice, has an obvious political dimension. Despite overwhelming evidence that the national political fabric was tearing at the edges, few novelists felt that they possessed the purely technical equipment to deal with the complexities of government. An exception can be made of Max Egremont's *The Ladies' Man* (1983), which provides a revealing fable of post-war political life. John Price, its protagonist, is an ageing, bankrupted, ex-Tory minister, compelled by scandal to leave the government before a general election at which it is defeated (an obvious parallel is with the events leading up to the 1964 election, but Egremont is evasive about dates). At university, Price was the friend of 'Peters', then a scholarship boy from a poor home, now a charismatic left-wing Labour politician. The novel is set in motion by Price's discovery that his erstwhile friend was implicated in his fall. Throughout, Egremont's chief contention seems to be that each side of the political divide is unfit to govern the country, hamstrung either by shallowness, obsolete ideas or sheer venality. Peters's apparent probity is worth little in the light of his involvement with Price's demise. Price himself stands convicted of a tendency to value 'style' over substance. But the models, too, are flawed. There is a telling portrait of 'Brodie', Price's former mentor and a failed candidate for the Tory leadership, who now occupies his old age by peddling a whimsical, televised version of a bygone England and producing volumes of essays and speeches with titles such as *No New Utopia* and *A Wrong Future*. Tory paternalism, Egremont constantly implies, is dead, and Brodie no more than a relic of what was in any case a manufactured view of the past. Watching one of Brodie's television performances, Price's mistress makes a criticism that could be levelled at many a post-war politician of both Left and Right:

'I hate that man . . . To me he represents all that was rotten. He appealed to the worst in people, to the dead rather than the living. The complacency. The deadness.'

Tory paternalism might have clothed itself in a specious nostalgia. Radicalism seemed similarly fraudulent. In the aftermath of what one supposes to be the 1964 General Election, Price visits his club to witness the passing of the government of which he had been a member. Here, reassuringly, nothing has changed. 'The election to power of what was described as a radical party, the new emphasis on scientific and technical merit, the public castigation of England's old order and government' – all these, Price reflects, must have been recorded on the ticker-tape machine next to the hall porter's office, 'yet still the club's apparently immutable routine continued amid members' ritual prognostications of national doom and personal bankruptcy'.

Such complacency was not universal; the prospect of a Labour government was regarded with horror in some quarters. But it quickly became clear that, from the point of view of the body politic, King Log had replaced King Stork. Wilson donned his white tie and addressed the Lord Mayor's Banquet; the bill to nationalise the steel industry was obstructed by some of his own backbenchers. In any case the objections of industry to government policy paled in comparison to the obstruction offered by supposed allies in the trades-union movement.

Power, it seemed increasingly clear, was no longer the government's or the Prime Minister's to exercise. America had to be consulted. Our potential European partners could not be ignored. Doubtless there has seldom been a national government whose activities were not constrained in some way by external factors. Wilson, more so even than Eden or Macmillan, seemed the victim of extra-governmental pressure, whether it was the nudging of the banks or the beady eye of President Johnson. William Clark's novels *Number 10* (1967) and *Special Relationship* (1969), the work of a political insider who had served as Eden's press officer at the time of Suez, are concerned with what Christopher Harvie has called, 'the migration of power, both within the British political establishment and beyond'. More general was a widespread assumption of the futility of disinterested political action – if any political action can be said to be disinterested – a conviction that politics had somehow 'gone wrong', were beyond the ability of honest individuals to amend. ' "Politics were fair in the '50s," ' says a regretful sociology don in *The History Man*. In the 1960s and 1970s they seemed unfair, deliberately weighted on the side of self-interest and collusion.

This feeling underlies what is perhaps the most considerable political novel of the period, Piers Paul Read's *A Married Man* (1980), set in the strike-bound winter of 1973–4. John Strickland, a successful barrister of relatively humble origins who has married into a grand recusant family and thereby acquired a circle of upper-class friends, undergoes a mid-life crisis when a chance encounter with a volume of Tolstoy leads him to ask the question: ' "What are we to do with ourselves?" ' This translates into a personal dilemma: how he is to help the predominantly disadvantaged members of the society of which he is a part? Strickland, a fine example of the Read 'good man' determined to make a contribution, resolves to become a Labour MP. His mission to do good is fraught with difficulty. On the one hand he has to negotiate a path through the embattled factions of his chosen constituency party, where his accent and his background make him a natural object of suspicion. On the other, he has to contend with what seems to him an appalling polarisation of society, represented equally by elements of the political party he is commissioned to represent and by his banker acquaintances, disgusted by the supposed intransigence of organised labour, who are motivated by their own sectional concerns. The 'national interest', consequently, is an absurd chimera, invoked occasionally by politicians but with no real meaning. Matched against these powerful sectional interests, Strickland's decency is of little account. The legal system, in which he is professionally engaged, seems to him a racket operated for the benefit of the ruling class. Yet he is simultaneously aware that many of the arguments he puts forward in favour of striking trades unionists are no more than a justification of selfishness. The awareness of his inability to act in this tough new world is compounded by personal betrayals: that of his wife, who commits adultery with a mutual friend; and his mistress (Strickland's own moral position is not beyond reproach) who contrives to have her murdered. The novel's conclusion, in which Strickland throws over his political ambitions and settles for a sort of quietism – ' "we have to take what we can get and make the most of it" ' he tells his former father-in-law – implicitly condemns a society which refuses to allow the honest and conscientious individual to operate within it.

Though it is concerned with the minutiae of contemporary social and political circumstance, *A Married Man* constantly glances backwards, back to bygone Labour party history and past economic mismanagement. Many of its themes – decline, national malaise, sectionalism, the abrogation of moral responsibility – can be found in Ferdinand Mount's *The Clique* (1978), subtitled 'A novel of the '60s'. Here the confusion and complexities of national life are reflected in the experience of Gunn Goater, a Fleet Street reporter – ' "There's a social revolution going on out there and we need chaps like you to project it" ' – and his simultaneous involvement with rackety Brondesbury bohemia and a husband and wife team who run a down-and-out hostel near the Embankment.

Appropriately enough, for a study of national decline, *The Clique* begins in 1965 with the final illness of the 'Last Great

Englishman', an event covered by Gunn and his colleagues. The symbolic properties of Churchill's death are self-evident. To them can be added an awareness that their potency has somehow been compromised by external factors. 'It was the end of an era all right,' Gunn reflects:

> There was a feeling abroad that this must be it at last, which concealed a further feeling, not to be openly voiced naturally, that it was about time. An unpleasantly jocular assessment of the ambience? Nations exhausted by their history lack the resources for public tragedy. Situation comedy is their only authentic genre.

Churchill dies, consequently, in an atmosphere of near farce, journalists congregating on his doorstep, cameras monitoring each lighted window from the vantage point of adjoining houses. A similar air attends his funeral. Watching from the Embankment as the barge carrying the former Prime Minister's coffin moves up-river towards Westminster, Gunn reflects that this is a 'factitious' event. 'All over England middle-aged men were dressing up.' In an exhausted, changing world there seems no appropriate response to what is essentially a throwback to a bygone age. The Memorial contrived by Gunn's bizarre friend Antic, a collection of Churchilliana including Toby jugs, table mats, ashtrays and fire screens, seems more in keeping with the spirit of the times.

Zeitgeist is an elusive quarry in the best of circumstances. Mount's England is a drab, twilit landscape inhabited by faded, bustling creatures, their lives made onerous by the acknowledgement of radically lowered morale. History sharpens this sense of receding glory. There is a symbolic scene in which Gunn, wandering through the down-at-heel East End terraces, notices that each street name – Tel-El-Kebir, Balmoral, Inkerman – awakens some imperial memory. Very few of the characteristic Aunt Sallys of the anti–1906s novelist escape Mount's attention, from the excesses of 'Swinging London' to the foolishness of 'alternative' communities. Dick, the ex-priest, and Margaret in their dossers' hostel propound a complacent but fashionable relativism: ' "We don't want to imply any moral blame: their plight is an indictment of society as a whole, if it is anything." ' Elsewhere, Gunn's attendance at an 'artistic happening' in which the performers mingle with the audience, thereby expressing the 'spontaneity of the artist', is used to deflate the Warhol/Greenwich Village attitude to art, an approach whose essential fraudulence is never in doubt.

Mount's targets are often predictable and his treatment of them is frequently crude, but at its best *The Clique* conveys an air of poignance rather than exasperation. This feeling is emphasised by the novel's conclusion. After various journalistic adventures and an interlude in America, Gunn returns to provincial England and Margaret (Dick having died of cancer) to report on cricket matches. His chief desire is to cast off sophistication. 'He wanted to be with people who if they changed their minds at all changed them clumsily and with pain, not rapidly and gracefully like a skater coming out of a jump-turn.' In ancient cricket pavilions, watching the relentless summer rain, Gunn comes to cherish the advantages of an untidy life.

Such serenity is comparatively rare. Gunn is sympathetically presented, a character sucked into an environment of which he would rather not be a part. The chief feature of the anti–1960s novel, however, is the dreadful people who wander about in it, their inadequacies mercilessly anatomised and caricatured: Julia in A. S. Byatt's *The Game* (1968), who cannot understand that her actions are likely to have consequences for other people; Kingsley Amis's cynical and opportunistic TV presenter Appleyard ('He passed for political, and left political, because politics, and left politics, were the trend and therefore the route of advancement'); Gareth in Melvyn Bragg's *Autumn Manoeuvres* (1978), a vicious, stupid radio man whose clarion cry is 'we are all free – that is the message'. In fact, as Bragg unerringly demonstrates, Gareth's life, with its dubious imperatives and its truckloads of obsolete 1960s baggage, is terribly constrained. Perhaps the most extreme contempt is that extended to the American visitors to Appleseed rectory in Martin Amis's *Dead Babies* (1975). Buzzard, Skip and Roxeanne represent West Coast humanism, the whole hippy package of self-gratification and sexual availability, pushed to its logical extreme. To Buzzard, whose speech is uncannily reminiscent of drugs gurus such as Timothy Leary or the more radical American student leaders, existence is no more than hedonistic functionalism. He despises Quentin's claim that he and his wife married ' "to keep sex emotional" '.

Gurus, cults, chatter about 'freedom', personal relationships presented as a collective Holy Grail: the ability of this 1960s paraphernalia to impinge on the processes of ordinary life is apparent even in a novel such as Anthony Powell's *Hearing Secret Harmonies* (1975), the concluding instalment to *A Dance to the Music of Time*, large parts of which are taken up by doings of Scorpio Murtlock's 'Harmony' cult and Widmerpool's ultimately fatal embroilment in its rituals. At the time several critics expressed reservations about this final volume, adducing as a reason for their dissatisfaction the unlikelihood of Widmerpool's involvement in such a bizarre and sinister organization. In fact Powell's treatment of Widmerpool's decline demonstrates his grasp of contemporary events rather than a remoteness from them. The Labour peer who is appointed chancellor of a new university, who hankers after the company of 'young people', who begs interlocutors to call him 'Ken' and finally perishes during the course of a ritual run has no exact parallel, but his authenticity is not in doubt. In any case one of Powell's recurring themes is the exercise of power – very much a 1960s subject.

In their way Murtlock and Widmerpool are as recognisably 1960s people as more obvious exemplars such as the Kirks in Bradbury's *The History Man*. The difference is that of emphasis. In creating Howard Kirk and his wife Barbara, Bradbury lingers over nearly every significant aspect of 1960s radicalism, as conceived by its opponents, from bandwagon-jumping to moral dishonesty. As a piece of social analysis it is remarkably acute. In an echo of Richard Hoggart, the Kirks' ascent from relatively modest backgrounds comes by way of enhanced educational opportunity. Both have had their sights lifted by a grammar school and university education, yet they extend towards that education the attitudes of their parents: 'it was an instrument, a virtuous one, for getting on, doing well, becoming even more respectable'. Their *annus mirabilis*, the year that transforms them and launches them on their incorrigible path, is 1963: 'Historical circumstances were changing, the whole world was in transformation, undergoing a revolution of rising expectations.' Profumo, the Beatles, the advent of Harold Wilson – all combine to make Howard the man he is. Unhappily, historical circumstances cannot change him into a decent human being. The contradictions of the Kirks' existence, their adoption of a series of modish attitudes which their inner natures cannot sustain, are conspicuous to everyone but themselves. The Kirks continue to aspire in a world where conventional aspirations are held in contempt. They have an 'open marriage', which is characterised by subterfuge and concealment. Howard writes a book gleefully celebrating the death of privacy, and is outraged when his own privacy is violated by a student. His personal and professional life is typified by a duplicity made all the more culpable by its veneer of moral rectitude. ' "You have an elegant conscience when it suits you," ' a colleague tells him, which is perhaps the most damning judgement in the book.

Character, naturally enough, is closely linked to environment. Significantly, many of these 1960s monsters have some connection with the world of the arts or media, work as television presenters, say, or appear on chat-shows (Howard Kirk is a pioneering example of the TV don). Without exception this world is seen to be corrosive, debasing and morally flawed. Television, in particular, at once a manifestation of and an influence on contemporary social development, attracts an unprecedented degree of hostility. At its most basic level, television is assumed to be trivial and intrusive. Jenkins, for example, in *Hearing Secret Harmonies*, dislikes what he regards as impertinent enquiries into the private life of the novelist St John Clarke.

A. S. Byatt, whose *The Game* is perhaps the earliest examination of a burgeoning media culture, appears to write off the entire phenomenon as a patronising confidence trick. Even shallow and biddable Julia has her doubts as to the medium's value. She considers television 'a new world to be entered'. Yet watching it seriously for the first time, in preparation for her own appearance on an arts programme, she is disappointed. She intends to 'respect' television, but 'here was this girl addressing her millions of audience with a prepared, gentle condescension – as though they were all very slightly mentally defective'. 'The Lively Arts', on which Julia appears along with Simon Moffat and various other minor celebrities, is a disaster of egotism and stupidity. Julia is amazed, less by its ineptitude than by the fact that it is taken seriously by the producers, 'since this accorded so badly with the rest of their personalities'. Those professionally involved in the production and presentation of programmes are notably glib and insincere. Ronnie Appleyard, for example, who conducts a talk-show entitled 'Insight', cares nothing for the subjects in which he is compelled to feign an interest: his role in browbeating politicians and being rude to people is played out merely for the entertainment value it provides.

Invariably fictional discussion of television returns to its intrusive side, its capacity to bamboozle and mislead a largely passive audience. There is a terrific moment in J. L. Carr's *How Steeple Sinderby Wanderers Won the FA Cup* (1975), the story of a village footballing side's miraculous progress to Wembley, in which the local magnate, Mr Fangfoss, infuriated by questions about his private life, turns the tables on his interviewer:

> You do, yes you really do believe that folks so yearn to be shown on TV that they'll strip down to the last clout. Well, I'm not some show-biz baboon or politician who will grin through your slimy gibes just so you let him push his grapefruit face into people's hearths and home.'

As a result of this performance Mr Fangfoss receives eleven sacks of adulatory letters. At the same time knockabout comedy at television's expense co-exists with hints of a more malign influence. Simon Raven's *The Judas Boy* (1968) suggests that the BBC, here depicted as a vast and rather sinister bureaucracy, is actively opposed to the exposure of historical truths should they conflict with the Corporation's own progressive political standpoint. Fielding Gray, invited by his friend Tom Llewellyn to contribute to a programme about the struggle for Cypriot independence, in which Gray as a serving soldier lost an eye, is confounded by all manner of official obstructiveness.

If television was thought to be at once trivialising, corrosive and sinister, contemporary attitudes to 'art', or what novelists presumed to be contemporary attitudes to art, formed an equally beguiling target. Warhol's soup tins, 'free expression', unrhymed poetry, the more generalised notion that some form of artistic achievement is attainable by every human being – each of these cultural manifestations seemed fair game to the anti–1960s writer. Penelope Lively's *Next to Nature, Art* (1982), very much an anti–1960s novel for all its mid–1970s setting, is an acidulous attack on a bogus artistic community. 'Framleigh', run by an unsuccessful painter named Toby Standish and his wife Paula (who has pretensions to being a sculptress), is an old Warwickshire estate recently transformed into a cultural centre. The ordinary people who sign up for its courses – housewives, dentists' receptionists and the like – are naively impressed by the meagre display of artistic expertise that awaits them, and quite prepared to swallow the benefit of clergy line adhered to by most of the centre's staff. ' "I mean, you'd kind of know, looking at her, that she was somebody interesting," ' one woman remarks of Paula. ' "That's true of all of them." ' Even Bob the libidinous potter is 'different' in the eyes of a girl who is momentarily attracted to him: 'he is an artist'. In reality, nearly all the Framleigh tutors are complete frauds, both personally and professionally, none more so than Toby, who is plotting to sell the estate to a merchant bank. Alternatively, this may be a sign of integrity: Toby has already announced publicly that ' "the artist's responsibility . . . is to himself" '. As might be expected, Lively extracts the maximum amount of fun out of the kaleidoscopic range of artistic pretensions on display – the dreadful stream-of-consciousness monologues produced by Greg, the narcissistic American poet, Paula's chicken-wire sculptures – but the implications run deeper. For by allowing themselves to be temporarily seduced by the Framleigh atmosphere, by incubating mad schemes to throw over their jobs and embrace the artistic life and by assuming that the status of 'artist' entitles you to do what you like, several of the guests go some way towards wrecking their comfortable and settled existences. It is left to Mary, the humble dentist's receptionist, to make the obvious but unavoidable point:

There is a sense in which you could expect a real artist to behave better than other people rather than the same or worse . . . But just like creative people are expected to look different – though nowadays everyone looks like that, what with long hair for men and long dresses for women – so they are expected to behave like creative people too. It's as though people couldn't be sure they were artistic otherwise.

The unease which the majority of novelists felt about the 1960s filters through into their treatment of its artistic life. Yet the strongest condemnation was reserved for developments in education. The 1960s were the years of student unrest (restrained in comparison with events in America and Europe), which finds a predictable echo in novels of the period – *Hearing Secret Harmonies*, Raven's *Places Where They Sing* (1970) – but they were also the setting for a prolonged and acrimonious debate about standards. While this extended across the whole educational process, its force was most conspicuously felt in the universities. The extension of the university system, proposed by the Butler Education Act of 1944, confirmed by the Robbins Report of 1963, underlay post-war educational policy. An acknowledgement of enhanced opportunities contended with an awareness of their probable consequences. 'More will mean worse,' Kingsley Amis had predicted – the origins of this statement lie way back in a remark thrown out by Jim Dixon. Several decades on, this seems uncontentious. The more people you admit into higher education, the less able the majority of them will be to cope with its present demands. Consequently, if that majority is to leave university with any sort of qualification, then standards are going to have to be lowered to accommodate them. The choice, starkly put, is between maintaining standards and conciliating the student population. However, such views were regarded as practically fascist in left-wing circles at the time. Simultaneously, attempts were under way to change the character of secondary education. Crosland, when Secretary of State for Education, had announced that he would destroy the grammar schools and abolish the principle of selection at 11. Crosland's private remarks on the subject suggest that he viewed it very much in the light of a personal crusade.

Such a view was naturally anathema to the Right, which tended to see the government's entire education policy as a destructive conspiracy. A feature of the late 1960s was the circulation of 'Black

Paper' polemics with titles such as 'The Comprehensive Disaster', in which advocates of selection such as Burt and Eysenck mingled with writers of the Amis type, who lampooned prevailing fashions in higher education. But it is significant that much of the criticism of government policy at secondary level comes from, or is attributed to, the old Left. By adopting fashionable, non-selective methods of education and abandoning traditional teaching styles, progressive Labour-controlled education authorities were felt to have betrayed their original supporters and to have created an educational system geared to the interests of the radical middle classes.

This theme emerges very strongly from *A Married Man*, notably in a conversation between Strickland and his brother-in-law Graham, a bedenimed, Liverpool-accented school teacher. 'He saw the denims and the Liverpool accent as advanced professional qualifications.' With 'matching attitudes in education (anti-streaming and so on)', he has managed in his late 30s to become the headmaster of a comprehensive school. Strickland's old-fashioned Labour views and his belief in equality of opportunity seem archaic when set against the opinions of this modish ideologue. After Graham has acknowledged the degree of political motivation which informs his professional career, Strickland asks if he would encourage his pupils to vote for him. ' "If they voted for you I'd feel I'd failed," ' Graham replies seriously. To Strickland his sister and brother-in-law exemplify a new bourgeoisie which has appropriated and exploited the Welfare State. They pay no school fees but scheme to get their children into 'good' comprehensives, 'while the children of the working classes were relegated as before to the second-class schools'.

A similar complaint, this time produced at ground level, surfaces in David Storey's *Present-Times* (1984). Here Attercliffe, a Northern journalist and former professional Rugby League player – the resemblances to Storey's own career are strong – attends a PTA meeting at his daughter's state school. None of his anxieties over the ruination of her prospects by fashionable educational theories are calmed by hostile and evasive teaching staff, an emollient headmaster or a tribe of progressively minded parents.

The sharpest battles of all were being fought out on the university campus. Even at their most comic, they tend to have a sinister side. Widmerpool's installation as chancellor of a new university, disrupted by paint-throwing undergraduates, is simple farce and the excuse for Widmerpool to make a foolish speech to the television cameras, but it inaugurates an obsession with 'youth' that will eventually lead to his death. Raven's *Places Where They Sing* (student unrest at 'Lancaster College, Cambridge') has its share of high comedy, but it ends in violent death. Raven, an unreconstituted pillar of the Right, sees nothing but bloodymindedness in undergraduate demands for better treatment. The motivation is neither the sense of a just cause nor a legitimate grievance, but the malevolent resentment of privilege. Balliston, the student revolutionary, is portrayed as a well-meaning but arrogant fool, exploited and ultimately cast aside by superiors who do not possess his integrity: it is Hetty, Balliston's girlfriend, who dies in the final assault on the college chapel.

Raven writes as a waspish outsider. The most profound indictment of a particular type of mind avidly at work in the higher educational system comes from an insider, a Professor of English and American Studies at a new university who had presumably witnessed something like it at first hand. *The History Man*'s overriding theme is the ability of extreme liberalism to degenerate into totalitarianism, the fault lying, unhappily enough, with other liberals who have permitted the degeneration by the over-scrupulous exercise of principle. Kirk's provocative mean-mindedness pervades the book. It is evident in his harrying of Carmody, a painfully conventional undergraduate who dares to interpret sociology from a Conservative point of view, in his cultivation of the rumour that a distinguished but controversial geneticist has been invited to speak at the university, in his marking of the essays of female students on the criterion of sexual availability. But perhaps the nastiest moment comes in a meeting of the sociology department convened to discuss Professor Mangel's invitation (an equally provocative Right has been at work, as Kirk foresaw). Here a sympathetic colleague bases his opposition to Mangel on the principle that genetics is not an 'innocuous science', that it harbours deep social implications, and that those involved with it have a duty to protect their results from 'racialist overtones', even if that means falsifying data. Similar debates, notably those concerned with the relationship between environment, race and IQ, continue to disrupt American campuses. The novel's core can perhaps be located in a conversation between Kirk and his professor over the former's determination to have the unfortunate Carmody expelled. ' "There are two sides to every question," ' Professor Marvin ventures. Kirk demurs. ' "You'll just sink into your Liberal mess if you accept that." ' The link between *The History Man* and Bradbury's first two novels is deliberate. But whereas *Eating People is Wrong* (1959) and *Stepping Westward* (1965) examine the early symptoms of an illness, the third novel diagnoses a full-blown disease, abetted, the implication is clear, by the prevailing social and political environment.

Fictional judgements on the 1960s made from the vantage point of the 1970s and the early 1980s were rarely circumspect. Given this preoccupation with what was contemporary, and the assumption of its absolute novelty, it is instructive to examine the spectacle of Anthony Powell finishing a sequence whose roots go back to the early 1920s with a novel set in the period 1968–70. Powell's eye is attracted by contemporary detail – Widmerpool's absurdities, a dinner at which his neighbour wheels out fashionable talking-points ('The Permissive Society', 'Vietnam', 'Enoch') with the air of one engaged in a burdensome ritual. Elsewhere, though, Powell is concerned to emphasise continuities, the sense of older patterns reasserting themselves. This is not only achieved through the habitual Powell stratagem of unexpectedly reintroducing characters from earlier novels (for example Bithel, whose privilege it is to regale Jenkins with an account of Widmerpool's death); the historical links seem a great deal older. Invited to a Royal Academy dinner, Jenkins notes that the unconventional dress affected by many of the guests is reminiscent of the Romantic era. Even Murtlock's grotesque cult is thought by Professor Gwinnett to be a Gothic throwback.

This broader perspective is comparatively rare. Much fiction of the period was more concerned with short-term point-scoring. In Kingsley Amis's *The Alteration* (1976), a fantasy of a Europe which has never known the Reformation and an England which still labours beneath the Inquisition's thrall, the sinister officers of the organisation's secular arm are given the names 'Foot' and 'Redgrave' – two popular, or at least well-publicised, left-wing ideologues of the day. Increasingly, however, the perspective was serious rather than comic or serio-comic. The mid–1970s, with their rising wage and price inflation and social insecurity, hurt the middle classes badly. Even the certainties of bourgeois comfort seemed suddenly to be imperilled. Margaret Drabble's *The Ice Age*, the title a none too subtle comment on a national predicament, made the point that the headline's phrases of freeze and shutdown were now a universal reality: 'Millions who had groaned over them in steadily increasing prosperity were now obliged to think again.'

In the search for scapegoats the Labour party and the trades unions ranked very high. There were few leftist defences of the rights of organised labour. In Barry Hines's *Looks and Smiles* (1981) a young unemployed man reflects bitterly that the blame for a mass of redundancies at a large engineering firm will be attributed to the unions:

According to the papers the unions were responsible for all the economic ills of the country. They were too greedy (i.e. tried to keep up with rising prices), too strong (i.e. organised), always on strike (i.e. only as a last resort).

Similarly, John Harvey's *The Plate Shop* (1978), an account of shop-floor life reminiscent of Sillitoe's *Saturday Night and Sunday Morning* (1958), suggests that the pressures on working people were quite as considerable as those experienced by the beleaguered middle classes. But these voices were insufficient to shut out the rising note of bourgeois hysteria. Julian Fane's *Revolution Island* (1980) is a typical minor work of the period. Evidently written during the strikebound winter of 1978–9, it envisages a near-future of unbridled anarchy: 'In 1982 our last Conservative government was deposed by the Trade Unions, over whom it had again attempted to assert its democratic authority.' Fane's prognosis is wildly over-done, and subsequent events rendered the novel obsolete by the time of its publication, but as an expression of middle-class anxieties it is an authentic reflection of the views of contemporary right-wing lobbyists. Robert Moss's *The Collapse of Democracy* (1975), for example, published to coincide with the launch of the National Association for Freedom, an influential right-wing ginger group, begins with a fictitious letter from the London of 1985, now in a state of 'proto-communism'.

In fact Fane had already provided a more subtle set of dispatches from the middle-class front line in the short story collection *Happy Endings* (1979). Here the predicaments of Fane's embattled 1970s gentlefolk are that much more convincing in that they have clearly been going on for some time, in many cases since the war, a long-term decline barbed by diminishing capital and the consciousness of having lost out to an unscrupulous newer generation in the struggle for prestige and advantage. Occasionally the tone descends into sheer rancour. 'Notes for a Ghost', for instance, the instructions given to the ghost-writer of a Labour peer's autobiography, is a crude recital of betrayed ideals and blatant hypocrisies. Elsewhere Fane is capable of striking a more delicate note. In 'Minnie Rykehurst' a silly but decent woman, fallen on hard times and involved with a circle of people she despises, finds a crumb of comfort in memories of her remote, unfallen girlhood. Minnie and her fellow protagonists aspire to a type of redemptive doggedness. Thus Edward Repton in 'The Life-line' expends his energies in trying to solve the problem of his impoverished, genteel and largely ungrateful family. Ella Martin in 'The Old Hard Story', a plain girl compelled to spend her best years looking after her bedridden mother and an aged family retainer, survives to stage-manage a family reunion and make a successful middle-aged marriage. Fortitude, Fane implies, is all. Ella, for instance, tells well-wishers that 'she could not get over her good luck. She was certainly not complacent. Yet she was inclined to believe that she had earned her luck by having learned to live without it.'

The late 1970s crystal ball-gazing of writers of Fane's persuasion might have been risibly inaccurate; more considered speculations from the moderate Left had a similar habit of missing their target. An impressive final snapshot of the Wilson years, or rather their aftermath, is provided by Melvyn Bragg's *Autumn Manoeuvres*, one of the few substantial political novels of a period when it had already come to seem doubtful whether political novels could continue to be written. Set during the general election of 1978 that never happened, and whose postponement Callaghan was eternally to regret, the novel largely ignores the wider arena of national politics in favour of a minute absorption in a single constituency, located in the fading industrial belt of western Cumbria. Despite this exclusive focus, Jimmy Johnston, the incumbent Labour MP, is deeply conscious of his party's national responsibilities, and the long-term failure to uphold them. In an early moment of reflection Jimmy tries to quantify what he regards as the precipitous decline of a once-great movement, how 'euphoria had gradually slithered into desolation'. The splits between Right and Left are, he feels, a waste of energy that could have been put to better use in improving people's lives. The judgements of his colleagues over a quarter-century's worth of 'issues', from Suez to disarmament, are either glib or opportunistic. A new generation of anarchistic radicals, represented by his son Gareth, regard him as an obsolete and obstructive creature of the establishment. Above all, there is a sense that Westminster politics, the fudges and cynicism of the debating chamber, have lost whatever relevance they might once have possessed. There is a queer scene in which Jimmy writes his personal manifesto, conscious all the time that the majority of its contents are irrelevant to the needs of his constituents. Walking around the main town in his constituency, where the old staples of steel and coal have faded away, to be replaced by a precarious light industry, Jimmy can only sorrow over 'three generations of disappointed expectations'.

The novel ends with both Jimmy and the Callaghan government winning a small majority. Life, unhappily, was to confound art. Neither Fane's socialist state nor Bragg's vision of a renascent Labour gradualism bore the slightest resemblance to the political events of the next decade. Read fifteen years after its first appearance, *Autumn Manoeuvres* seems an old-fashioned book, not merely in its espousal of a political standpoint that many people assumed to be an historical curiosity, but in its assumptions. To Bragg, it seems fair to say, power is a simple business, the will of the people translated into policy, which it is the responsibility of government to implement. The ineptitudes and concealments of the Wilson administration perhaps encouraged such a view. The experience of the Thatcher years was to call it sharply into question. The 'political' fiction of the 1980s, and the characters who populated it, were of a correspondingly different order.

Sex and Sensibility

A. Alvarez's novel *Day of Atonement* (1991) is one of those curious books which, though unexceptional in themselves, manage to frame some wider point about the workings of fiction in immediate relief. The framing is perhaps all the more significant in that the author seems largely unaware of it: the general effect, consequently, resembles one of the bristling passages in Lawrence where, amid the detonation of all manner of erotic charges, all that seems to emerge is a profound sense of the writer's own homosexuality. At least Alvarez's trick is not that of sexual disguise. It consists, rather, in establishing a mechanism which is in the last resort inadequate for propelling the story forward. An experiment with genre written with sufficient *élan* to neutralise many of the drawbacks of genre convention, *Day of Atonement* concerns the struggles of a Jewish photographer and his wife who are brought unexpectedly into the orbit of a lurid gangster named Ray Fernandez. Though the novel explores a number of themes, notably Jewishness and Jewish guilt, its pivot is an ancient hostages to fortune device: the thraldom in which Fernandez, who wants to recover money owed by him by a dead mutual friend, holds the principal characters. Alvarez's twist to this stock situation is to give it a sexual element – to have his characters quite literally sleep with the enemy. Thus Judy has an affair with Fernandez, while Joe almost absentmindedly succumbs to the gangster's glamorous personal assistant. It is here in its easy solutions, its moral dilemmas which are scarcely moral dilemmas, that the novel conveys its chief message: that sex as dealt with by the contemporary novelist is no longer a fit subject for the contemporary novelist.

This might seem an alarming claim to make. After all, sex is a staple commodity on the modern literary *bourse*, and it is a fact that most commercial novels are erected, if that is not too emotive a word, upon a groundplan of colossal orgasms. Perhaps the greatest outward change which has come over the English novel since 1945 is the degree of sexual frankness allowed to the writer by publisher, audience and censor alike. Forty years ago Joe Lunn in William Cooper's *Scenes from Provincial Life* (1950) might sleep with his girlfriend Myrtle, but the proceedings have an almost unbelievable decorousness in comparison to what came later. Yet the difference between a contemporary Don Juan and Jim Dixon trying tentatively to place a hand inside his girlfriend's dressing gown is a difference in degree, not in kind. From an historical point of view sex, or rather bourgeois sexual morality, is one of the great themes of the English novel, in a line of descent that goes back to Richardson and Sterne. *Vanity Fair, David Copperfield* and *New Grub Street* are all novels about sex, even if the sex usually comes disguised as something else – snobbery or money, for example. A hundred years before, these preoccupations were even more obvious. Examine nearly any novel of the mid-eighteenth century and you are immediately plunged into a tremendous sub-world of rapes and adulteries, sexual adventurers and predatory old maids, where every man's aim is seduction and every woman's, if not the preservation of her honour, then the maximum reward from its surrender.

Compared to what came later, the conventions of eighteenth-century fiction allowed a relatively frank treatment of sex. Roderick Random, the hero of Smollett's eponymous novel of 1749, is perhaps the first character in British fiction to catch a venereal disease ('She gave me to understand that she was a woman of the town by profession, that in the course of her adventures, she found herself dangerously infected with a distemper to which all persons of her class are particularly subject...'). Defoe's *Moll Flanders* is simply a harlot's confession. To focus on these highlights ignores the much wider preoccupation with sex that invests the novels of the Smollett-Fielding-Richardson type, a fascination embodied in the accounts of elderly ladies who retain their urine for days on end, the better to extinguish fires, or the stock scenes in which breechless postilions inadvertently display their hind-quarters to shocked gentlewomen.

At the same time this general catalogue of licentiousness, the prostitutes' earnings and old women's favours by which Smollett's heroes cheerfully support themselves, exists within a clearly defined ethical framework. The object of the sexual game is marriage – marriage with money, perhaps, but marriage all the same. Roderick's lack of scruple, consequently, is temporary. His status as an adventurer is forced on him by circumstances. Once he has sown his wild oats and evaded the attentions of the elderly Miss Gripewell, Roderick wants nothing better than to settle down with his beloved Narcissa, a comfortable private income and connubial bliss. The roots of the sprawling early Victorian novel, with its final chapter panorama of crowded nurseries and idle domesticity, are fixed squarely in this bourgeois fantasy land. It is this that gives Smollett's fiction its slightly schizophrenic feel, the genuine horrors of military service (Smollett served as a naval surgeon on the ill-fated Cartagena expedition) and life at street-level in the 1740s co-existing with roseate exercises in wish-fulfilment.

The sexual concerns of a writer like Smollett survived even the onslaught of early Victorian censorship, observable from about the mid–1840s. Smollett himself survives among the young David Copperfield's reading material, and in the scene in *Middlemarch* where old Mr Brooke advises Dorothea that her status as a married woman will permit her to read *Humphry Clinker*. The effect of the shifting moral climate on the amount of elbow-room that writers allowed themselves can be seen in a comparison of *The Pickwick Papers* with the novels of Dickens's maturity. *Pickwick*, with its jokes about men being accommodated by accident in ladies' bedrooms, many of them derived from Smollett and Fielding, seemed vulgar to many an *echt*-Victorian. The complaint about Dickens's 'vulgarity' survives as late as the drawing-room conversations of Maugham's *Of Human Bondage* (1915). Thackeray's relation to the new moral ukases is even more uneasy. There is a surprising frankness about some of his early sketches, with their matter-of-fact descriptions of fast women and loose living: a magazine piece like 'Captain Rook and Mr Pigeon', which describes the fleecing of silly young men by professional gambling sharks, has a curiously outdated Regency air. But the later Thackeray was studiously respectable. As editor of the *Cornhill* magazine he was to decline a fairly innocuous Trollope serial on the grounds that it might offend his family readership.

No doubt Thackeray found the buttoning-up process demanded by the Mrs Grundys of the mid–1840s perennially irksome. Despite their strenuous pursuit of respectability, his novels have a habit of supplying odd, incidental details of the vast world that existed outside the palisades of Victorian probity. In *Vanity Fair*, for example, he will happily describe a minor character as the sort of man 'whom men introduced to their mistresses rather than their wives'. This seems daring for the time, not only in its use of the word 'mistress', which contemporaries like Dickens tended to avoid, but in its suggestion that the keeping of mistresses was widespread. Thackeray's claim in the introduction to *Pendennis* that 'a little more frankness than is customary has been attempted in this story' seems absurd by modern standards, and the book itself no more than a list of concealments, but in the persons of Major Pendennis and his circle he manages to provide a shrewd account of the old Regency world of ageing bucks in stays, Miss Decamp's dance: the glimpse of a less corseted existence. At the same time Thackeray's absorbing interest in sex and sexual attraction is never quite snuffed out. One of his great strengths as a novelist is his ability to convey sexual feeling obliquely. Often this is achieved through the medium of food. John Carey has suggested that Thackeray demonstrates 'the enticing delicacy of women through the food they eat'. When Becky Sharp sets up as a hostess and inveigles Lord Steyne into her drawing room, her awakening of his desire is made manifest through her skill at provisioning a table. In the same way the debauched atmosphere of Lord Steyne's house in New Gaunt Street is hinted at by the revelation that in the little private kitchen 'every saucepan was silver and all the spits were gold'. The link between food and sex reaches its height in *Pendennis* when Mirobilant, the French chef employed by the Amory family, falls in love with Blanche, the daughter of the house. Despite Mirobilant's immense personal prestige, the distance between the drawing-room and the servants' hall is still sufficient to prevent him from declaring his hand. Thus he attempts to express his feelings through the delicacy of the dishes he prepares:

'Her lovely name is Blanche. The veil of the maiden is white; the wreath of roses which she wears is white. I determined that my dinner should be as spotless as the snow.'

Each course in Mirobilant's extensive menu consequently makes some reference to Blanche's virginity – delicate *plats*, pudding *à la Reine Elizabeth* (' "a maiden princess" '), a jelly of marasquin, ' "bland, insinuating, intoxicating as the glance of beauty" '. There is something slightly sinister about Mirobilant's reflections, something gloating and inhuman, but they suggest very well both the depths of his obsession and Blanche's combination of childishness and intangibility.

Despite the prohibitions that encouraged these concealments, the very strong feeling one gets whenever sex rears its head in a mid-Victorian novel that the whole business is being transacted in a sort of outlandish code, the novel still manages to fulfil the function of a piece of moral litmus paper. For all its evasions and false pieties, *Pendennis* is a good example of the way in which a book can pinpoint contending sets of moral attitudes, notably in the scene where Arthur's relatives, visiting him after a near-fatal illness and encountering a shamefaced serving maid, automatically assume that he has slept with the girl. It is a measure of the time that Arthur's supposed 'sin' is never stated in so many words (in fact he has managed to resist temptation), but Thackeray characteristically uses the episode to contrast the moral standpoints of the onlookers. Young men, thinks Major Pendennis the superannuated Regency rake, will be young men. Mrs Pendennis is deeply shocked, a division that exposes the gap between the relaxed attitudes of the pre-Victorian age and the middle-class puritanism that was beginning to supplant them. For Thackeray, the official Thackeray who lectured to fashionable salons and who was not above toadying to the nobility, the object remained wedlock.

Trollope, writing slightly later, provides an even better example of a writer for whom a fairly strict though biased moral code (female virginity before marriage mandatory, a certain amount of youthful male folly generally forgivable) allows a wide range of psychological treatments. Trollope's key sexual themes – increasingly the two key themes of the Victorian novel – are adultery, whether real or imagined (the plot of *He Knew he was Right* rests merely on a deranged husband's suspicion), and courtship. But Trollope is also capable of conveying extreme sexual desire merely through dialogue and terse, exact description. In *Phineas Finn*, for example, Lord Chiltern proposes marriage to Violet Effingham:

> 'How is it then? Violet, speak to me honestly. Will you be my wife?' She did not answer him, and he stood for a moment looking at her. Then he rushed at her, and, seizing her in his arms, kissed her all over – her forehead, her lips, her cheeks, then both her hands, and then her lips again. 'By G–, she is my own!' he said.

The animal imagery ('he rushed at her' suggests that Lord Chiltern resembles an enraged bull), the actual brutality and literalistic description combine to produce an atmosphere of violent sexuality, leading to the assumption that Lord Chiltern is almost uncontrollable in his passions (though the couple eventually marry, Violet frequently confesses that she is 'frightened' of her future husband). The reader might never see Lord Chiltern outside a drawing-room or a hunting field, but his virility is not in doubt.

Trollope was perhaps the last of the great nineteenth-century novelists for whom the old moral certainties still held, and, like Thackeray, able to write convincingly about sexual topics without describing the sexual act. What is it, for example, that gives Becky Sharp her charm? For Thackeray scarcely describes her – a few references to her green eyes, her 'famous frontal development', bare arms emerging from her gown when she plays Clytemnestra in the charades at Gaunt House, the enticing disarray of the foreign boarding house bedroom in which she receives Jos Sedley. It is all done by hints and allusions, a code of occlusion which demands the reader's participation and has the effect of increasing, rather than diminishing, Becky's appeal. Reticence of this type, however, was in decline: by the 1880s, as Peter Keating has shown in his brilliant account of early English modernism, the forces of fictional respectability were in sharp retreat. John Gross supplies an amusing portrait of Leslie Stephen sitting in his office at the *Cornhill* gloomily annotating Hardy's manuscripts ('Delete "amorous", substitute "sentimental" '), but the stranglehold of the circulating libraries had relaxed to the point where Mudie's shelves accommodated open attacks on the sanctity of the marriage vow. The 'New Woman', sexually inquisitive and, more important, unchaperoned, makes her appearance in fiction from about the 1880s (rechristened 'the bachelor girl', she was still going strong in the novels of the inter-war years), closely followed by the keen-eyed lovers of the 'Hill Top' novel, so called because of its characteristic *al fresco* dalliance. Grant Allen's *The Woman Who Did* (1895) effectively parodied a legion of fictional heroines who, their copy of Ibsen in one hand and their volume of *Fabian Essays* in the other, sallied forth in search of physical enlightenment.

Nadine (1882) by Mrs Campbell Praed might be taken as an example of late Victorian raciness. George Moore made it the subject of a bitter polemic on the double standards of Mudie's censors, which excluded his own novels of scrupulous realism from the gaze of library subscribers while tolerating many a more lurid and sensational work. The discreet accounts of sexual congress which occupy a small part of Moore's *A Mummer's Wife* (1884) seem innocuous when set against this catalogue of adultery, promiscuity and blackmail, itself painfully innocuous by modern standards, but it was Moore who was judged by the circulating libraries to have written 'an immoral publication'. Mrs Campbell Praed and Ouida (another enduring source of scandal to prudish Victorian readers) remained on the shelves.

Two persistent themes dominate the fiction of the first part of the twentieth century: the struggle to get the married woman to throw over her husband, and the struggle to get the unmarried girl into bed. The history of the English novel until the 1950s and beyond, it is fair to say, is the history of pre-marital and extra-marital sex, however coyly outlined or euphemistically framed. Form, however, lagged some way behind content. The move towards freedom of expression in the treatment of sexual subjects was a long drawn out war of attrition. The Lady Chatterley trial is usually supposed to have promoted the cause of frankness, yet for many years before this any serious novelist with a modicum of ingenuity could generally find ways of getting round censorship. William Cooper's *Scenes from Provincial Life*, whose account of the uninhibited relationship enjoyed by Joe Lunn and his girlfriend Myrtle caused something of a stir in 1950, even contrives, by way of allusions that can be understood by any alert reader, to describe an erection:

> She was smiling at me. I went over and stood beside her. She looked appealing; resting on one elbow with her dark hair sweeping over her smooth naked shoulder. I looked down on the top of her head.
> Suddenly she blew.
> 'Wonderful Albert,' she said.
> I may say that my name is not Albert. It is Joe. Joe Lunn.

Albert, of course, is the Albert Memorial. Simon Raven was another pre-Chatterley author who delighted in conveying all manner of naughtinesses without descending to descriptions of sexual organs. Thus in *Brother Cain* (1959) Jacinth Crewe takes part in aquatic high-jinks with the sexually disturbed Eurydice (' "Eurydice will take care of Jacinth. Eurydice will give him a bath and make him a nice clean boy" '). In *Close of Play* (1962) this technique reaches its apogee. Hugo Warren, another of Raven's appalling young men, encounters the altogether esculent Jennifer Stevens at a Cambridge party. It is love, or rather lust, at first sight, and the pair immediately depart:

> When they got outside, they walked over a bridge and sat down on a bank. Without having been invited, Miss Stevens put her hand inside Hugo's trousers. Since no girl had ever done this to him before, Hugo began to pant with pleasure.
> 'Go on,' she said, 'you do it to me too.' She guided his hand. 'There,' she said, 'like that.'
> They played this nice new game with great enjoyment, but in the nature of things it could not last very long.

'Well,' said Miss Stevens, standing up and getting to work with her hanky, 'that was delicious.'

As a description of a casual sexual encounter, this comes very close to the ridiculous. But the passage is given a slightly disturbing edge by Raven's hint that the act is really being carried out by two children. Juvenile imagery ('They played this nice new game with great enjoyment'), the use of nursery words like 'hanky', the nod towards 'manners' (Jennifer puts her hand inside Hugo's trousers 'without having been invited') combine to suggest an unreal, fairy-tale scene in which, to use the words of a character in a later Raven novel, 'the babes in the wood came on and started having a poke'.

The 1950s was the last great age of the male courtship novel. There were several reasons for this. The fictional heroes of the 1950s and their creators were predominantly heterosexual, interested in women in a way in which some of their 1930s predecessors were not. Moreover, women were an important part of the aspiration process which underlies so many novels of the period. This is not merely a result of their sexual attractiveness. Several 1950s heroines, or at any rate several of those devised by male authors, have the additional advantage of being connected to money. Christine in *Lucky Jim* (1954) is the niece of Gore-Urquhart, a wealthy cultural philanthropist. Joe Lampton's girl-friend in *Room at the Top* (1957) has a wealthy father. These connections are rarely spelled out, but they cannot be ignored. Christine, for example, captivates Dixon by her good looks, but the reader nurtures a suspicion that much of her poise, and Dixon's appreciation of it, is brought about by financial security. At the end of the novel Dixon hits the jackpot by acquiring the best job (a post as Gore-Urquhart's secretary) and the best girl (Gore-Urquhart's niece) – a very eighteenth-century solution, as Amis, with his love of Fielding, no doubt intended it to be.

Amid the relentless sexual pursuits enacted by Dixon, Lumley, Billy Fisher and others, it is worth pausing to ask what is the attitude of the average 1950s protagonist to his brightly plumaged quarry. Almost without exception the feeling is one of contempt, mixed with gentle – and not so gentle – patronage. Curiously, this attitude extends even to the 'progressive' novelists of the period. In describing the female characters of *Daylight on Saturday* (1943), Priestley alternates between derision ('a comfortable little woman with no brains at all') and lofty condescension ('the alien but wonderful presence of Woman herself, the unfathomable feminine idea'), a view neatly summarised by Alan Munton as 'a clutter of understanding, idealisation and contempt for women'. Elsewhere, the misogyny of the average 1950s hero takes many forms. Most common of all is the imputation of stupidity. ' "What do you mean? You are silly," ' a girl informs Henry Fenwick, the narrator of Roger Longrigg's *A High-pitched Buzz* (1956). 'I daresay I was,' Fenwick reflects, 'but not half so silly as she.' When Bumbo Bailey in Andrew Sinclair's *The Breaking of Bumbo* (1959) cracks a joke, his girlfriend is said to laugh 'dutifully, as though she understood'. At the same time the average 1950s man is keen to judge the women with whom he is involved by absurd and arbitrary criteria. Dixon's contempt for Margaret's outmoded dresses and unskilful use of cosmetics is well-known, but it is shared by any number of his sharp, satirical contemporaries. Fenwick describes a girl who works in his advertising agency's design studio as:

> a very dreadful sight . . . a style of dress in which Bohemianism and the terrible orthodoxy of her background strove in sad and inconclusive conflict, like two very weak old ladies hitting at each other with broken parasols.

Billy Fisher's attitude to his girlfriend is even more ludicrous: 'I disliked her for her impeccable shorthand, her senseless, sensible shoes, and her handbag crammed with oranges.'

Stupidity and bad dress sense were only an entrée to the male view of women. The protagonists of the 1950s undoubtedly wanted to go to bed with their girlfriends, but what did they think of them as people? The predominant attitude is one of edgy contempt. Joe Lunn, whose chief interests are writing and making love with Myrtle, is in no doubt as to their relative importance. As for Myrtle's lack of enthusiasm for his novels, 'I would gladly have thrashed her for it.' Billy Fisher despises each of the girls to whom he is simultaneously engaged, one, whom he refers to as 'the witch', for being 'large, clean and wholesome' (i.e. sexually unavailable), the other for her vacancy: 'Everybody I knew spoke in clichés, but Rita spoke as though she got her words out of a slot-machine, whose sentences were neatly packed in a disposable tinfoil wrapper.' An important aspect of this contempt is the constant filing away of female characters into pejorative categories. Either girls are frigid, damned instantly for their sexual timidity, stigmatised as husband-hunters (Joe Lunn's determination to have his cake and eat it too in this respect is notably disgusting), or written off as harlots. The assumption that there are some girls to whom one can behave as one likes and who deserve no better than they get is very common. Fenwick in *A High-pitched Buzz* buys off – literally – a girl at work with whom he has had a fling. 'She's pure tart, I think. What I'm wondering is, would gold keep her quiet?' It would (' "Well, I must say, that's generous" '), and Fenwick's assumptions about women, or a certain class of women, are confirmed. Significantly, Fenwick treats his nice upper-class girlfriend with rather more respect.

In its categorisation of women along class lines, *A High-pitched Buzz* is Trollope brought up to date. Like Charley Tudor in *The Three Clerks* (1858), who is allowed to trifle with the affections of a bar-maid before setting his sights on pure Katie Woodward, Fenwick can muddy his fingers before setting off in pursuit of something more *soignée*. Paradoxically, though, no woman can quite escape the suggestion of lubricity, if only of the mental kind. Thus the narrator of David Lodge's *Ginger, You're Barmy* (1962) reflects that 'women look maddeningly desirable in army camps. Perhaps that is why they choose to work in such places: it must be exhilarating to know that you are being mentally raped a hundred times a day.'

Retrospective cries of 'sexism' are unhelpful in this context. By making his character think these thoughts, Lodge is merely establishing an authentic atmosphere. Yet this, it transpires, is merely a modest form of middle-class contempt. By far the worst fictional misogyny of the period can be found in the novels of working-class life. There are the streams of abuse hurled by Callow's apprentices at young women who have the misfortune to pass them in the street (' "Jesus, she's pale – I bet she's got the jam rags on" ... "I bet her fanny's like a horse's collar" '), insults born of straightforward terror rather than sexual sophistication. To Machin in *This Sporting Life* (1960) all women, with the presumable exception of his mother, are 'tarts'. Like Jim Dixon and Billy Fisher he is keen to judge them by quite arbitrary standards. Female cigarette smoking is condemned on the grounds that ' "it looks obscene" '. Above all, Machin is appallingly and viciously rude. Encountering his mistress in the street, while out walking with a friend, he tells her: ' "You look bloody awful ... if you feel like a slut you shouldn't show it." '

Some idea of the wider environment in which Machin and his kind operate, with its routine ostracisms and dismissals, is provided by Arthur Haggerston in Chaplin's *The Day of the Sardine* (1961). Informed by his mother that she intends to accompany him on any excursion from the house, Arthur is horrified. Venerable rules will be infringed:

> You only walk with a woman when you're courting her; after the honeymoon she's on her own while you go out with the married men of your own age. I've seen characters push a pram and it's held against them for life – they never live it down.

Yet just as middle-class fictional notions of women are confused by the habit of regarding them as both ice-maidens and tarts, so the working-class view is complicated by the altogether ghastly idea of 'respect'.

Clegg in *The Collector* (1963) believes on the one hand that women are worthy only of casual duplicity. He has been advised by a fellow clerk that 'you shouldn't ever tell a woman you loved her. Even if you did. If you had to say "I love you" you said it jokily. You had to play hard to get.' On the other hand, poor entombed Miranda is 'not like some women you don't respect so you don't care what you do, you respected her and you had to be careful'. In the end, as we know, Clegg despises his victim both for her class superiority and her lack of malleability. The best of a very bad bunch is Sillitoe's Arthur Seaton, who in his more reflective moments thinks that:

women were more than ornamental and skivvies. They were warm wonderful creatures that needed and deserved to be looked after, requiring all the attention a man could give, certainly more than the man's work.

This might seem to reduce a woman to the status of a superior household pet, but it is somehow preferable to Clegg's 'respect' and Machin's cruelty.

A few, a very few, attempts are made here and there in male novels of the period to mitigate, or at least to explain, this atmosphere. One scapegoat occasionally trundled out to explain upper-class male behaviour towards women is the conditioning imposed upon boys by a public school education. Douglas-Home's *Hot for Certainties* (1964) and Benedictus's *Fourth of June* (1962), for example, convey the impression of good-natured and honourably-minded adolescents seduced into thinking that it is acceptable – in fact desirable – to treat women badly. In the latter novel, Phillips, a character for the most part presented sympathetically, starts a correspondence with a girl he has met in the course of a boating holiday. At this early stage their relationship is portrayed merely in terms of an adolescent crush. By the time Phillips invites Jill down to the Fourth of June celebrations, however, popular opinion has convinced him that women prefer to be treated rough. Naturally enough, the day ends disastrously. Jill's tearful recriminations – ' "Why have you changed so much, Tom, what have they done to you?" ' – are unanswerable.

Another explanation, of course, is that men treat women badly because women make them. A consistent theme of *Lucky Jim*, for instance, is that Jim in his relations with Margaret Peel is as much victim as oppressor. Despite Margaret's many unappetising qualities, it is hard to feel much sympathy for Dixon, who has had an opportunity to study her at leisure, and if he did not want the relationship could have prevented himself from being dragged into it. Conditioning, though, works both ways. The message of several female novels of the post-war period is that women were quite as capable of exploiting men, or at any rate cheerfully tolerating their behaviour. Jane Graham in *The L-Shaped Room* (1960), though patronised and sworn at by her boss, the public relations manager of a London hotel, approves of him on the grounds of broadmindedness. Similarly, the independent-minded young woman of the early 1960s novel was prepared to preserve that independence by means of male subsidy. Sarah in Drabble's *A Summer Bird-cage* (1963) makes what is a fairly typical remark: 'I could see that he was quite a nice sort of person to have dinner with from time to time, as one would be able to have all the expensive things on the menu, but as for marrying –.' Men want to sleep with women, but they don't really like them. Women, for their part, graciously consent to being bought expensive dinners.

However, the idea of the novel as a relentless and more often than not unsatisfactory sexual pursuit was being called into question. The relation between the novel and the society it affects to describe can never be exactly defined. At different times in English history it is possible to believe that fiction has mirrored the social climate, anticipated it, or lagged some way behind it. In the field of sexual relationships this juxtaposition is even more difficult to establish. Does the fiction of the 1950s, with its tentative adulteries and its discreet liaisons, provide a reliable guide to the sexual mores of the time? A large-scale comparison of fictional attitudes with contemporary surveys of sexual behaviour could doubtless be undertaken; one knows in advance how inconclusive the results would be. Some readers of *Scenes from Provincial Life* were shocked by the easy relationship enjoyed by Joe and Myrtle; others presumably marked it down as a 'normal' portrayal of contemporary, or near-contemporary (the novel is set in 1939), sexual life. At any time in the twentieth century one man's 'immorality' has been another's convention.

Two things, however, can be stated with confidence about the sexual climate of the early 1960s. The first is that some form of sexual revolution, embracing both pre- and extra-marital sex, had begun to take place; the second, authenticated by the Chatterley trial, the conviction that a greater degree of frankness was permissible, and in fact desirable, in the artistic treatment of sex. The coming together of these two already closely related strands is sharply apparent in the fiction of the later 1960s. The fictional man or woman of the time is immediately characterised by sexual involvement. No Margaret Drabble heroine of the 1960s manages to retain her virginity. For Clara Maugham in *Jerusalem the Golden* (1967) 'real life' means living in London and having affairs. John Fowles's *The Magus* (1966) is, after one detaches the pseudo-philosophical elements, not much more than a sexual promenade.

Simultaneously, the treatment of these sexual encounters became progressively more graphic. It would be tedious to recapitulate the censorship victories of particular years, or to demonstrate what it was, progressively, that the writer could get away with. The 1960s were full of 'daring' novels. As early as 1963 the blurb for David Benedictus's second novel, *You're a Big Boy Now*, could contain references to impotence, something that would have been unthinkable ten years before. By 1967 it seemed no more than routine for the opening chapter of Alexis Lykiard's second novel to supply clinical descriptions of the symptoms of venereal disease. A benchmark for the increasingly elaborate treatment of sex can be found in a comparison of the original version of *The Magus* with its revised edition of 1977. Fowles marks down the strengthening of the erotic element as 'merely the correction of a past failure of nerve'.

The consequences of these changes in focus and emphasis for both the tone and structure of the average English novel were profound. Though debarred from producing explicit sex scenes, many of the writers of the immediately pre-war period had contrived to deal with sex in a fairly realistic way, for example by emphasising its unappetising features as well as its allure. One thinks of Orwell's lovers frustrated by lack of money, contraceptives or sheer conviction. Even the seductions of so mannered a novel as Anthony Powell's *Afternoon Men* (1931) convey something of the lapses and incidental dissatisfactions that accompany the conventional sexual act. In contrast, the post-Chatterley trial novel's descriptions of sex seem faintly unreal. It is not simply that the sex is flawless, as it generally is, but that the preliminaries customarily associated with the sexual act have disappeared. Hardly anywhere, for instance, in the fiction of the 1960s will you find mention of contraceptives. Even Andrea Newman's *The Cage* (1965), a detailed account of teenage pregnancy, gives no clue as to what mischance was responsible. In this area David Lodge, always a writer with an eye for the less alluring aspects of sex, is something of a trailblazer. Jonathan Price in *Ginger, You're Barmy* actually buys a packet of Durex from an army barber. The eventual deflowering of his girlfriend, after a protracted courtship, is accomplished with maximum dissatisfaction on both sides. Lodge's *The British Museum is Falling Down* (1965), built upon Catholic attitudes to birth control, is another example of a novelist straying into a topic of consuming public interest rarely touched on by fictional commentators – how *not* to have children. Generally speaking, though, characters in the post-Chatterley novel simply meet, have sex and damn the consequences. The account of the precautions taken by Sam Beresford in Michael Blakemore's *End of Season* (1968) to avoid impregnating his girlfriend – *coitus inter-ruptus* – is startling not because of its explicitness, but because of its rarity value.

Sex in fiction was ceasing to be a moral problem, or rather it was becoming a different sort of moral problem, of whose consequences the majority of novelists were not yet aware. In retrospect the transformation from a fictional world in which female virtue, whether unmarried or married, was yielded up only after an extended moral *crise de confidence* to one of unbridled sexual licence was accomplished with extraordinarily little self-questioning. The attempts of Jenny Bunn in Amis's *Take a Girl Like You* (1960) to resist the attentions of Patrick Standish are made to look more than a little foolish. The thought that a young woman might have excellent reasons for not wanting to sleep with a vain and tedious womaniser like Standish scarcely surfaces. There is an odd and, in terms of the fiction of the time, almost unpre-cedented scene in *A High-pitched Buzz* in which Elizabeth, having been out on a date with Fenwick for the first time, apologises for the fact that she doesn't want to go to bed with him. ' "I'm good, you see, that's the trouble, and I've got so used to being good that I can't all of a sudden – " '. Fenwick continues:

> Then it struck us both, I think, how comically absurd it was that, after one conventional evening, a girl with good morals should be apologising to a man she had never met before for not committing what it is still possible to think of as a sin.

Longrigg's young lovers are resisting a social pressure. Longrigg himself is resisting what was even by 1956 an artistic pressure to get the hero and heroine to bed with minimum dispatch. Inevitably, these promptings were, over the next decade, to have a profound effect on fictional form. Instead of working up to the sexual climax fairly late on, contemporary fiction tends to start with the sex and then decline into a welter of adjustments and infidelities. *Take a Girl Like You*, consequently, is one of the last great courtship novels, a relentless 300-page stalking of its virginal heroine by the shiftless seducer. ' "Well, those old Bible class ideas have certainly taken a knocking, haven't they?" ' Jenny enquires at the novel's close, which, with its drunken forcing, leaves an unpleasant taste even now. ' "They were bound to you know, darling," ' Standish replies, ' "with a girl like you." ' But it was already becoming clear that the mechanisms that linked this type of novel to the society whose preoccupations it attempted to reflect were breaking down. According to Amis, *Take a Girl Like You* was designed to ventilate the question of whether nice girls should sleep with men. Several contemporary critics alleged that the question had already been settled in the affirmative.

If the courtship novel is dead, or changed out of all recognition, that other 200-year-old staple of English fiction, the adultery novel, is looking distinctly uneasy. On the evidence of a novel like *Day of Atonement* the novelist's handling of what was once a crucial fictional theme is deeply unsatisfactory. In this context, what the reader might think about adultery (is it a good thing or a bad thing?) and the incidence of adultery in society (is the novelist reflecting social mores?) are irrelevant: the problem is a functional one. For a man's wife to begin an affair with a smarmy gangster almost without reflection, for the man himself to knock off the gangster's obliging personal assistant, and for all this to affect husband and wife's relation both to the gangster and to each other, is not so much implausible as *technically* inadequate. For adultery to matter in a novel it has to impose a genuine moral dilemma which impedes or assists the development of the plot. Have characters jumping into bed with smarmy Mr Big or his lickerish assistant almost at the drop of a hat, and it loses its force.

Sexual duplicity, it might be said, is an effective fictional tool only when people care about it. Such confusion is not a new phenomenon in the novel. Wain's *A Travelling Woman* (1959) is an early example of the sexual merrygoround book in which the question of motive lags some way behind the interchange of partners. Iris Murdoch's *A Severed Head* (1961) uses a similar situation as a vehicle for abstruse existential jokes. Among contemporary fiction, something of this feeling – the thought of standards being imposed on a set of characters to whom these standards don't really apply – emerges from the novels of Andrea Newman (*Alexa, A Sense of Guilt* and so forth), which transfer from the printed page to the small screen with some success. Ms Newman specialises, it is fair to say, in middle-class sexual guilt. Her characters, people with names like Felix and Inge, each of them marching at the head of a tribe of ex-spouses, lovers and mistresses, simply meet and perform a sort of sexual quadrille with each other before falling victim to the sexual guilt. To make this point is not to criticise Newman's characters on moral grounds – to suggest that this is rather a feeble way of living your life – but to say that the force which is supposed to motivate them is merely inadequate. After all, there is little mileage in attributing sexual guilt to people who spend most of their time acting as if sexual guilt didn't exist. Adultery might have meant something, and meant something to a novel about, a 'New Woman' of the 1890s entombed in a loveless marriage with a sniffy little bore: to a thrice-married advertising executive hot in pursuit of 'sexual fluency' it seems pretty small beer.

At the same time, if adultery and the sexual act generally no longer seem an adequate driving force for the novel, providing only negligible tensions and pointless dilemmas, the way in which novelists write descriptively about sex is scant compensation. The post-Chatterley trial relaxation of constraints gave writers a hitherto unthought-of degree of freedom, but it also presented them with an obligation – to find an appropriate language in which descriptions of sexual activity could be conveyed. With a very few exceptions this obligation has been ignored, and the freedom to write about sex in whatever way you choose is generally agreed to have been an aesthetic disaster. Even at an early stage the omens were unpromising. The most scrupulous and realistic writers of the 1950s, for example, were capable of losing their heads when addressing their characters' attitudes to sex. In Philip Callow's *Common People* (1958), a painstaking and unsensational account of a working-class upbringing, there is an odd scene in which the hero, Nicky Chapman, saunters past a Mayfair prostitute: 'My heart pounded. A feverish excitement dulled my senses, like an intoxicant.' Confronted with his own sexuality Chapman is reduced to the status of a character in a romantic novelette. In the last thirty years this tendency has grown much more pronounced. Here, for instance, are extracts from three highly acclaimed literary novels published, respectively, in 1966, 1983 and 1988:

Her arms slipped round my neck and we kissed again, crushing each other. I slid a hand down her back, slipped the fingers inside the edge of the costume, appled a curved cheek, pulled her closer still, against the hardness in my loins, made sure she could feel it and knew she was wanted. Our mouths twisted, our tongues explored wildly, she began to rock against me and I could sense she was losing control, that this nakedness, darkness, pent-up emotion, repressed need . . .
John Fowles, *The Magus*

He put a hand under her white, accordion-pleated crêpe de chine skirt, feeling its incredible softness on the back of his hand at the same moment that he felt the incredible softness of the skin of her thigh underneath it. With the other hand round her shoulder, he now forced her face back, until they were squinting at each other, and then, with a groan, pressed his lips on hers. She gagged, squirmed, raised the leg that he was fondling. Then, all at once, she went strangely rigid and still.

'Christ, how smooth your flesh is!' He was babbling incoherently as his hand, venturing further, tugged at her knickers. 'Oh God, let me feel your cunt, let me feel it! Open your legs, open them, oh, please, please!'

She jerked her lips away from his. 'Careful. The servants . . .'

'Bugger the servants!'

He jumped to his feet, unbuttoned his fly and pulled out

his penis and testicles. Involuntarily, she stared. The penis was enormous . . .
Francis King, *Act of Darkness*

As I slid into her she brought her knees up level with my armpits and crossed her ankles in the small of my back. I already knew that was just about her favourite position, and it must have been a good one for her because she went into a string of orgasms so close together that it made me think of a crazy alarm clock that couldn't help going off every few seconds. As I worked my ramrod in and out, now fast, now slow, now thrusting it in to the last available millimetre, now deliberately allowing it to stay in the shallows for a while, a part of my brain remained detached enough to form thoughts, and the thoughts it formed were all to the effect that Vinnie was really something special.
John Wain, *Where the Rivers Meet*

Your initial reaction to any of these three extracts is, of course, to laugh – at the portentousness and the excitable language of wildly exploring tongues, but also at the sense of incongruity which invariably emerges whenever a novelist tries to write in a romantic context about essentially unromantic physical detail. There is also the weakness of the writing itself. Fowles, King and Wain are considerable stylists, each of their novels is 'well-written' in the accepted sense, and yet when describing the sexual act their prose descends into the lamest airport novel cliché. The worst culprit, perhaps, is Francis King with his incredible softnesses, incoherent babblings and implausible dialogue. Comparison with the average commercial novel is unavoidable and yet, queerly, it is a comparison from which the average commercial novel emerges with a certain amount of credit. The sex in a work by Jilly Cooper or Jackie Collins has an odd, tongue-in-cheek quality, so ridiculous and overblown that the author seems to be constantly looking over her shoulder and winking. In contrast, Fowles, King and Wain are deadly serious.

The most effective modern writing about sex consequently tends to avoid this gloating over physical detail and approaches the sensations of the sexual act from a more oblique angle. A. S. Byatt's account of the first occasion on which Daniel and Stephanie make love very properly concentrates on incongruity, awkwardness, an incidental comedy that is all the more telling in that the reader understands that the event is a matter of great significance to them both:

It was not very successful, a disorganised arrhythmic flurry, with both bodies constantly in danger of slipping off the bed, inhibited almost to the last by creaking springs and unanchored, slithering bedclothes. Daniel, overexcited and wild, did not know, half the time, whether he was in or out, coming or going. Stephanie, not habituated to piercing sexual pleasure, made no attempt to exact an orgasm and did not achieve one, a fact of which the floundering Daniel appeared to be unconscious, since he made no attempt either to induce one, to enquire whether one had happened, or to apologise for the apparent deficiency. This she found more comforting than not, because of the lack of embarrassment. They got hot, and wet, a little battered and confused. Daniel groaned and it was over.

Ian McEwan, describing the loss of his protagonist Leonard Marnham's virginity in *The Innocent* (1990), concentrates on a series of mental reference points:

Of what followed he remembered only two things. The first was that it was rather like going to see a film that everybody else had been talking about; difficult to imagine in advance, but, once there, installed, partly recognition, partly surprise. The encompassing slippery smoothness, for example, was much as he had hoped, even better, in fact, while nothing in his extensive reading had prepared him for the crinkly sensation of having another's pubic hair pressed against his own.

Again there is an underlying touch of comedy, which does not compromise the seriousness of what is taking place. The overriding note, as with Byatt, is realistic. John Fowles's characters are actors in a Hollywood movie, detached, airbrushed, stylised. Daniel and

Stephanie, Leonard and his German girlfriend Maria are actually having sex.

The implications of moral uncertainty, social change and an accompanying linguistic failure for the serious novel, the traditional evocation of manners and morals at which the English customarily excel, are wide-ranging. It is, inevitably enough, not entirely the novelist's fault: he or she is simply reflecting, or orchestrating, the moral chaos that lies around us, a society in which Christian sexual morality has largely disappeared and very little else emerged to take its place. But the consequences for the novel *as a novel* are similarly profound. Novels about sexual morality tend to flourish in a morally stable society, or one that is only beginning to break up. Take away moral prohibition, and the traditional novel of manners is robbed of most of its point. This, perhaps, is the reason why Andrea Newman's books seem unsatisfactory as pieces of narrative. They are about sexual morality, but the exact nature of the moral code which is at stake always eludes us. Predictably, the recent novels which have dealt best with 'morals' are those in which the prohibitive element remains. A good example might be Lodge's own *How Far can you Go?* (1980), which charts the progress of a group of 1950s Catholic teenagers for whom pre-marital sex is literally a mortal sin. The deliberate throwing-over of deeply held conviction is what gives Daniel's urge to sleep with Stephanie its seriousness, as Stephanie acknowledges:

Stephanie feared her own incapacity to deal with Daniel's morality. Sin, which she supposed it was, was a complex business. There must be some sense in which going to bed with her would be wrong, and the urgency of his intention to ignore this wrong excited her. It made the whole business serious and important in a way none of her Cambridge encounters had been, although it now occurred to her that it had suited her to flatten out all the responses of the young men to the automatic and everyday level at which she chose to behave herself. But this plunge into the unknown consequences of Sin alarmed her.

But there is another side to this decline which has little to do with the sheer vacancy of most fictional adulterers, or the sheer implausibility of most fictional descriptions of sex. The more the novel's detachment from this part of the social process continues, the more the novel loses a key aspect of its allure: the ability to subvert. For over a century the novel has chipped away at, refined and criticised bourgeois sexual morality. Now that morality is dying, it has no adequate response. Life has caught up with Art with a vengeance. A truly 'subversive' contemporary novel would suggest that monogamy was a cultural imperative, that adulterers are criminal lunatics, and be titled *The Woman who Didn't*. ' "I suppose sex has just ceased to be a moral issue," ' says a character in Bradbury's *Eating People is Wrong*, published immediately before the Chatterley bomb-blast. The majority of modern fiction exists in an uneasy limbo, occasionally inclining towards Bradbury's imperative, more often than not harking back to an older but increasingly invalidated sexual morality. We can believe that adultery was the great crisis of Emma Bovary's life. It is much less easy to believe it of a woman in a novel by Fay Weldon or Andrea Newman. With a few glamorous exceptions, sex in the late twentieth-century English novel has become a matter of routine, something which, for all its clinical detail, is perfunctorily outlined and takes no account of the moral or technical difficulties which the introduction of sex into a novel imposes. What the critic of a hundred years hence will make of this is anyone's guess, but it seems likely that he or she will regard it in the way that we now regard the death of Little Nell in *The Old Curiosity Shop* – overstated, curiously unaffecting, and rather too obviously ministering to a contemporary neurosis to be assisting the progress of a work of art.

I I

The Exclusion Zone

Normally there is this second go of life in a woman which is wasted.
She is energetic, though with much sexual disturbance and emotions,
and is liable either to feel completely frustrated or to interfere with
her children, if she doesn't get a job. So many undergraduates
with good degrees will get married (they are more attractive to
intelligent men than the uneducated ones) and knocked out of work
for ten years or more. But they mustn't be wasted for the community.

Naomi Mitchison, *Among You Taking Notes: The Wartime Diary
of Naomi Mitchison, 24 November 1942*

The seventies were a woman's decade, and there have been mighty
changes in women's lives – not least because women found each
other, personally and politically. There have been real changes in
women's expectations at work, in their personal lives, that can't
really be recorded and measured statistically ... the way that women
walk down the street, the way that women have insisted on certain
things now being part of their working lives.

Beatrix Campbell, in *The Writing on the Wall: Britain in the
Seventies* (1985)

The Second World War was widely believed to have multiplied
the paths of women's opportunity, not merely to have provided
employment for a contingent of hitherto under-utilised citizenry,
but to have expanded the scope of female horizons, and, in a
minority of cases, to have placed women on an equal footing with
men. The reality was markedly different. With a few conspicuous

exceptions, women's war work was manifestly low-level and routine. Women might have been permitted to infiltrate a number of
tightly guarded male environments, but positions of responsibility
or influence were largely denied them. The female operatives of
The Fancy (1942), Monica Dickens's account of conditions in an
aircraft factory, are pleased to be 'doing their bit', and proud of
their ability to undertake men's work, but they are aware that the
real decisions are still being made by the male-dominated works
committee: the best they can hope for is a sort of uneasy patronage.
The majority of characters in the women's fiction of the war and
the war's immediate aftermath, consequently, are habituated to the
mundane. Of the young women resident in the May of Teck Club
in Muriel Spark's *The Girls of Slender Means* (1963), set in the
summer of 1945, one is training to be a teacher of elocution and
another working as a shorthand typist in the Ministry of Labour.
A third, Jane Wright, is envied for her 'glamorous' job, which
turns out to mean devilling for a seedy publisher. The role of
women in winning the war might have been celebrated on screen
and in the popular press: its practical reward, in terms of future
opportunity, was severely limited.

Undeniably the war brought a certain freedom – the war novels
of Monica Dickens and Pamela Hansford Johnson are full of
young girls using the munitions factory as an excuse to escape
from stultifying familial hearths, meet men and have affairs, and a
feature of the May of Teck Club is the degree of sexual licence
enjoyed by its inhabitants – but it is easy to exaggerate the long-
term effects. The concept of young women living a relatively
unsupervised communal life in London, for example, was hardly
new. The May of Teck Club is an Edwardian foundation. An
earlier incarnation of the communal spinster life can be found in
the Burpenfield in Priestley's *Angel Pavement* (1930), where Miss
Matfield measures out her joyless evenings amid the coffee spoons
and aspirin orgies. Moreover, the minor relaxation of constraints
had little effect on attitude. Sheila, the *ingénue* of *The Fancy*, while
exulting in her release from paternal thraldom, transports her
assumptions about society and the people in it from the provinces
to London without so much as a second thought. The environment

may have altered, but the mental outlook is the same. What follows, inevitably, is a crash-course in wrecked illusions.

For a number of novelists, too, the war furnished an invaluable opportunity for authenticating much cherished notions of female subservience. Olivia Manning's *Balkan Trilogy* (1960–5), for instance, seeks to domesticate the war through the curious relationship that exists between Harriet Pringle and her husband Guy. Aloof and 'difficult', Guy antagonises his wife by his wish to preserve his own friendships and alliances in the midst of social and political confusion. Harriet feels that this betrays 'the concept of mutual defence which existed in marriage', and that this gives her 'just cause for revolt'. However, Harriet's rebellion is half-hearted and short-lived, and the novel's emotional message – wedlock as a defensive union against predatory external forces – is highly conservative.

The real-life Harriet Pringle was similarly hamstrung, both by her own timidity and by an institutionalised indifference to women which the incoming Attlee administration, with its single female cabinet member, did little to ameliorate. Women made scant progress towards an enhanced social status in the late 1940s. Equal pay in teaching and other professions was seen, at best, as an eventual possibility; the admission of a Jewish woman lawyer, Rose Heilbron, as a QC in 1949, and later to the judicial bench, regarded as an act of extravagant radicalism.

The war, with its focus on symbolic figures such as the Land Girl and the ATS, had at least encouraged an emphasis on youth: Spark's girls of slender means working as Ministry typists, Dickens's glossy-haired young women cracking their fingernails on the gun-casings. Fiction of the immediately post-war period tended understandably to concentrate on another type of heroine, the middle-aged and usually middle-class woman coping with changed patterns of existence and contemplating an apparently limitless series of emotional and practical readjustments. The two sisters in Rosamond Lehmann's *The Echoing Grove* (1953), warily reconnoitring each other after years spent apart; Laura Marshall in Mollie Panter-Downes's *One Fine Day* (1947) coming belatedly to realise what six years of conflict have done to a seemingly immutable way of life; Christine Cornwell in Francis King's *The Widow*

(1955) contending with children whose lives and ambitions have been irrevocably knocked out of kilter.

The middle-aged woman, living on capital, attempting to occupy herself with useful work though generally untrained for it, uneasily conscious that the tenor of the time is somehow inimical to her existence, is a feature of this type of book. One might take as a representative example the sisters Angela and Olivia Chesney in Rumer Godden's *An Episode of Sparrows* (1955). Living in a Pimlico square that has managed to preserve its gentility in the face of bomb craters and working-class encroachment, the couple are far from useless: Angela, trained as a chartered accountant, devotes herself to the administration of charities, and both have been brought up in the assumption that women are entitled to have careers. Even so, there are prerequisites for this type of existence, and depressingly conventional ones at that. As Olivia reflects bitterly, 'those premises . . . had rested on one thing, a man, and there had never been the vestige of a man for Olivia'.

Many of these readjustments, with their attendant social and financial pressures, were framed in a deliberate political context. The suspicion that they labour beneath the eye of a government that is fundamentally hostile to their interests animates many a female middle-class character of the time, and invests even the most trivial lament about changing circumstance with a high degree of political awareness. When Mrs Cornwell, the penurious victim of a fixed pension, suggests that the government should do something about rising rents, her daughter crisply informs her that she is a member of a class ' "about which the government is likely to do precious little" '.

In this atmosphere of relative privation and unease, sharply symbolical treatments of the shifting social and political landscape abound. The opening scene of Marghanita Laski's *The Village* (1952), for example, takes place in a Red Cross post on VE Night. Here convene the two wardens who have staffed the post for the duration of hostilities, the upper-class but increasingly impoverished Mrs Trevor, and her former charlady Mrs Wilson. Their outwardly innocuous conversation is barbed with the consciousness of a fragmenting social structure. The district's big houses are being sold or shut, the ancient county families are in retreat;

Mrs Trevor privately doubts whether there is anyone left in the village with the resources or the sense of occasion to open champagne to celebrate the war's end. The relationship between the two women is complex: a mixture of deference, solidarity and mutual awareness that a bomb has exploded beneath a bygone way of life. The whole is bound up in a series of unavoidable ironies. While Mrs Wilson still refers to the daughters of her former employer as 'Miss Margaret' and 'Miss Sheila', Mrs Trevor is already sweating over the possibility that the girls may fail the scholarship exam, in which case a decent education will be denied them. Mrs Wilson's son, it is concurrently revealed, earns more than the Trevor family's weekly income. Yet the women are united by genuine amity. At the end of the evening they kiss each other 'for the first and last time in their lives', an embrace which is entered into 'almost sacramentally'. The war has brought them together, but the effect of its conclusion and the apparent social conflict it has engendered is to break them apart. Subsequently Mrs Trevor departs to the area of the village 'where the gentry lived', while Mrs Wilson proceeds 'down Station Road, among the working classes'. Later passages find Mrs Trevor vainly trying to come to terms with an uncertain future and a domestic existence robbed of its former glory, obsessed throughout by 'angry thoughts about the contrast between her past and present life'.

For the most part these tensions are concealed, disclosed only to intimates or gestured at in a few loaded wisps of conversation. Occasionally they spill over into actual generational and political conflict. Kathleen Nott's *Private Fires* (1960), set in the bomb-cratered streets of South London, recounts the battle fought out between Mrs Hand, an elderly landlady, and an officious Welfare State, here represented by an interfering borough council, which wants to send round a sanitary inspector and refer her to the Rent Chairman. Mrs Hand's most convinced opponent is a woman council employee named Syd, an occasional frequenter of Communist Party meetings who feels that there must be somebody capable of dealing with this obstructive old lady. 'Exploiting classes, she thought, small rentiers, lumpenproletariat.' This is an unreflective mental shorthand, born of intermittent yet inadequate exposure to left-wing political thought. Syd's superior at the council offices takes a more exhortatory line: ' "Mrs Hand, if you knew what I knew, if I could make you see what I've seen, I think you'd want to co-operate instead of just sneering at other people who're only trying to do their best for the community." ' But Mrs Hand is determined to remain, however precariously, a free spirit. Such ambitions were assisted by financial independence. The fictional married woman of the immediately post-war era, economically constrained and wearied by the preceding years of struggle, tended to wilt beneath the consciousness of missed opportunities. The mother in Thomas Hinde's *Mr Nicholas* (1952) is a poignant example of a woman distressed by an indifferent family and a domineering (and eventually unbalanced) husband, who realises that she has forfeited a great deal of long-anticipated pleasure. She is aware that her children think her a fool. Her feelings towards Mr Nicholas are difficult to unravel. She loved him once, and perhaps still does. Moreover, she has a conviction 'that she should love and obey him which she held strongly, so strongly that it did not seem right to distinguish between it and something else which she really felt.' It is 'too simple', she thinks, to mark her husband down as merely another opportunity for martyrdom. All the same, Mrs Nicholas is forced to concede that 'it seemed so'; she remains uneasily aware that the Christian societies which she organises can be explained as a way of forgetting the failure of her happy family.

Middle-class fiction of the immediately post-war period occasionally appears to be taking place within a dim, twilit palisade, hedged about with economic and caste-based uncertainties. Its characteristic concern, perhaps inevitably, is the contrast between the inexplicably superannuated assumptions of the past and the novelty of a new but inchoate and threatening social framework. Though such transformations brought no real shift in political or social power, they were sufficient to colour the average refraction of national life of the kind achieved by Angela Thirkell with a sense of radically impaired prospects. For a certain positive energy, and for an awareness of the potentially liberating effects of social change, one is forced to look a little further down the social scale. The handful of novels of contemporary female working-class life, many of them written from the vantage point of a fifteen- or twenty-year hindsight (Maureen Duffy's *That's*

How It Was was published in 1962; Christina Stead's *Cotters'
England* appeared five years later), have a calculated, documentary
quality. Their purpose is to recount the passing of a historical
moment, as well as to record the ambitions and anxieties of the
people transfixed within it. Detail, consequently, is all, not simply
the minutiae of scene and milieu, but a conscious matching up of
attitude to prevailing circumstance.

Maureen Duffy makes this point with some force in an introduction to a 1983 reissue of the novel:

> A book is written not in a vacuum but at a precise historical
> moment which will affect not only the stylistic dress in which
> it is clothed but its moral and political underpinning.

The result, in the case of *That's How It Was*, is a meticulous re-
creation of a working-class war-time childhood, whose chief areas
of action are oddly remote from the progress of the war. While
Paddy, Duffy's narrator, is understandably affected by food shortages and the bombs that eventually demolish the family's seaside
lodgings, her real concern is with the ravages of her mother's
tuberculosis and the absolute necessity of winning a scholarship
to secondary school. The war is seen in terms that are at once
practical and personal. At its end, Paddy reflects that 'I ought to
be glad'. However, 'it doesn't seem to mean much. It means
nobody will be killed any more, and rationing will end.' Hanging
above the dreadful struggle to retain independence and integrity
in a family circle beset by privation and incurable disease, however,
is the scent of opportunity. ' "It's the one thing they can't take
away from you, your education," ' Paddy's mother tells her shortly
before she dies, in a scene as poignant as any in post-war aspir-
ational fiction. In this close, jealous, working-class environment
educational advancement has predictable consequences. The effect
of Paddy's scholarship is to set her even further apart from her
step-brothers: 'there was a new viciousness to Arthur's punches'.
But Paddy's progress is set squarely in the context of an upwardly
mobile trend. In a significant passage she contrasts the East End
community of the early 1960s with the milieu of her childhood.
Thirties people, she notes, were 'small and undersized, stuck to

their principles and their mates, hard-working and drinking. Their children's children are teachers and nurses and television play-wrights.'

The thought of an older world jogged forward into new patterns of existence re-emerges in Stead's *Cotters' England*, a compelling picture of working-class life in post-war England, seen largely through the eyes of the radical journalist Nellie Cook. Split between Nellie's home territory of south-east London and the ancestral family base in the North-East, the novel exposes a number of attitudes that seem ripe for superannuation. The casual sexism of old man Cotter's behaviour towards his womenfolk is in marked contrast to his daughter's hopes for less subservient female relationships with the opposite sex. Nellie's middle-class friend Caroline, recently emerged from a country vicarage and harbouring all manner of pious notions about the nature of working-class life, is roundly rebuked for her suggestion that a woman's best friend is a man (' "of all the goddam backward bourgeois attitudes" '). Elsewhere, there are ominous signs that time-honoured domestic arrangements are under threat. As a family unit the Cotters have begun to disintegrate: the younger members are restless and ill at ease in their native environment, daughters reluctant to undertake the care of their elderly relatives (' "what should I get up for?" ' Nellie's younger sister Peggy complains. ' "Two old invalids, that's a pleasure for a young woman?" ').

Despite its focus on lives lived out under pitiable constraints, the sense of precarious existences burrowing on through the com-post of the post-war landscape, *Cotters' England* preserves a note of optimism, notably in the figure of Nellie, with her copy of *The Ragged Trousered Philanthropists* and her promise of a world in which working men and women will come to occupy their rightful places in history. If the novel has a weakness it lies in Nellie's volubility, her very self-assurance. Reading her dialogues with Caroline, an adversary manifestly not up to her opponent's fight-ing weight, one is conscious only of the fact that one could never argue with her, such is her conviction of invincibility. But for all that she is a vital and, in the context of the English literature of the time, practically unique figure. *Cotters' England* can profitably be read alongside the social surveys of early 1950s working-class life, which demonstrate a shifting of traditional attitudes to issues such as male authority and female submission and, above all, a growing acceptance that questions of family size might be a matter of joint decisions. Women were having fewer children, having them earlier and subsequently returning to work. Yet Stead's novel is much less a refraction of a recognisable social scene than *That's How It Was*, and Nellie Cook a visionary rather than a social analyst. When she informs Caroline, during a discussion of the national past, that ' "the workers, pet, were walk-ons in all this glorious history, their play has got to begin" ', the reader is conscious of ulterior motive mixed with the genuine awareness of possibilities.

The partly emancipated girl allowed a slightly artificial period of war-time freedom, the middle-aged woman looking back regretfully to a vanished but more satisfying past, the working-class autodidact conscious of a changing world: these are all important figures from the immediately post-war women's novel. However, the characteristic post-war women's fiction, that was to reflect and in some cases to define the admittedly not always coherent ambitions of a generation, had scarcely begun to emerge. This might be described as the female diaspora novel, the account of the young woman who, prompted by educational opportunity or simply an inchoate desire for 'freedom', leaves her provincial fastness for London and the pursuit of a more rewarding life. The displaced female protagonist, contemplating the walls of her metropolitan bedsitter with a mixture of nervousness and rapture, is a staple of English fiction from the mid–1950s; her rise can be compared to the appearance of the 'New Woman' in the novels of the 1890s.

Two early examples are Susan in Brigid Brophy's *The King of a Rainy Country* (1956) and Ellie Parsons in Olivia Manning's *The Doves of Venus* (1955), ambitious, bemused, longing to exchange provincial gaucheness for city sophistication. The social origins of the diaspora heroine, who has only a handful of pre-war predecessors, are difficult to untangle – there are, alas, no reliable statistics for female mobility in the 1950s and 1960s – but they are probably connected to the greater availability of places in higher education and the gradual relaxation of constraints on young women whose careers seemed likely to remove them from the family hearth. The genuine novelty of the diaspora heroine can be gauged from the fact that there were at this time very few exemplars, fictional or real. A. S. Byatt points out in *The Virgin in the Garden* (1978) that, with the exception of a handful of film starlets, the majority of female role models of the period were, if not maternal, then definitely mature. The elevation of the very young girl, in her teens or early 20s, into a symbol of social change comes later, in the 1960s. The young ambitious woman bent on making her way in the world consequently occupies a distinctive niche in the novel from the outset, to the point where, a decade later, she is almost generic. Intelligent, restless, invariably reacting against her conventional middle-class upbringing, she is characterised by her aspiration: the exciting job, the most suitable man, a social life which affords glimpses of 'the real thing'. Curiously, apparently limitless general ambition can often exist side by side with a matter-of-fact appreciation of probable destiny. Raised during the war, the late 1950s and early 1960s heroine is usually all too conscious of the dampening effect of past austerity. Frederica in *The Virgin in the Garden* claims that war-time privations have stunted her aesthetic sense. Olivia Manning's Ellie puts it more simply: ' "I grew up during the war. I didn't expect much." '

In the field of professional opportunity this caution was wholly justified. The post-war years might have been a time when female employment reached unprecedented levels – nearly a third of the workforce by the end of the 1950s – but the prospect of real advancement remained limited. Fifteen years after the war's end fewer than 10 per cent of those designated by the census as 'higher professionals' were women. Aspiration, however, was seldom narrowly focused on a particular job. Conversely, the fictional women of the time are hot in pursuit of less concrete but potentially more enticing goals. Chief among these is a desire to break free from the straitjacket of a provincial or at any rate family-based existence. Ellie in *The Doves of Venus* is so desperate to escape a future serving in her mother's seaside restaurant that she simply decamps to London and accepts the first job offered to her. The largely introspective tone of Margaret Drabble's *Jerusalem the Golden*

(1967) is regularly set aflame by Clara Maugham's contempt for 'Northam', the provincial city of her birth. She hates her home town with such violence that she returns each vacation from university 'with an ashamed and feverish fear'. Northam's horror lies in its drabness, its cancelling out of the possibility of enjoyment or happiness. Its effect is to impart a largely undeserved aura of sophistication to those people with the good fortune to be born elsewhere. To the 18-year-old Clara, 'all people who were not from Northam seemed at first sight equally brilliant, surrounded as they were by a confusing blur of indistinct charm'. The fear of being forced to return produces a terrible resolve. Coming back in her early 20s on the occasion of her mother's terminal illness, Clara tells herself that she 'would survive'. Whatever happens, 'they would not get her that way, they would not get her at all'. No amount of maternal dissuasion has the slightest effect on Ellie's decision to forsake the enervated world of Eastsea.

The strength of this resolve is put into focus by the fact that the immediate prospects offered by the capital are generally poor. To inferior jobs and loneliness can be added a lack of appropriateness to milieu which only years of experience can overcome. Thus Susan in *The King of a Rainy Country*, so proud of her bohemian credentials, finds herself accused of snobbishness by her boyfriend Neale over her attitude to a photograph of a former schoolfriend she discovers in a pornographic book. According to Neale, she reacts ' "as if you didn't believe the girls you were at school with had bodies" '. Other drawbacks are more obvious. Ellie, let down by the middle-aged dilettante who has casually seduced her, realises that by coming to London and working in the studio of an antiques restoring business 'she had not moved very far'. Bright lights could easily be exchanged for humdrum solitude. Eugene's visit to the home of a former girlfriend in Shena Mackay's *Dust Falls on Eugene Schlumburger* (1964) describes what must have been a familiar reality. Eugene finds Florence in an Ealing bed-sit whose kitchen cupboards are crammed with tins, packets of soup and paper bags 'destined to become well-balanced meals for one'.

However, the heroines of the late 1950s and early 1960s were not merely reacting against milieu. In most cases their revolt had a personal focus: their parents. Convention suggests that this resentment should be paternal in origin: in fact it seems to be attached equally to mother and father. Pregnant Jane Graham in *The L-Shaped Room* (1960) has very definite reasons for declining the security of her father's protection:

He'd help, as he'd helped before, and, as before, I would be constantly aware of an ever-increasing debt to a man I didn't want to have to respect because he wasn't my sort of person.

Jane's resentment stems from a desire to avoid unwelcome obligations. In Margaret Forster's *Georgy Girl* (1965) the antagonism arises out of Georgy's dislike of her father's slavish devotion to his employer. Paddy in *That's How It Was* is motivated by vague notions of reparation, conventional day-dreams of revenging her mother's hurt: 'I hate him. He left you in the lurch. I'll make him pay.'

More often than not, however, the father is absent from these accounts of generational conflict: Clara in *Jerusalem the Golden*, Val in Andrea Newman's *The Cage* (1965), Olivia Manning's Ellie are the daughters of widows. Generally speaking the animosity reserved for this collection of fictive matriarchs is of an altogether higher order. No sooner does Ellie return to her mother's restaurant for the Christmas holiday than 'at once their old antagonism was alive between them'. Mrs Maugham is a terrible ogress, who seems to exist only to dampen her daughter's enthusiasms. Clara's main object in life, consequently, is somehow to put herself beyond her mother's grasp – a distancing process that is as much geographical as emotional. Clara's years in London strengthen her desire to live there for the rest of her life: 'while she was there her mother seemed, most of the time, to be no more than a dreadful past sorrow, endured and survived'. Occasionally the girl is sensitive enough to realise that much of the conflict is born of her mother's frustration, the consciousness that the opportunities now available to a younger generation were denied to its predecessors. There is a revealing scene along these lines in *Jerusalem the Golden* when Clara uncovers the mementoes of her mother's past life. Mrs Maugham, so long regarded as merely a capricious stumbling block placed in her daughter's path, is briefly revealed as a young girl with ideals and ambitions of her own. For this reason even maternal sympathy can be double-edged. Sarah's mother in *A Summer Bird-cage* (1963), for example, upbraids her daughter for not appearing to want a proper career. ' "I don't know what I would have given for the opportunities you've been given ... In my day education was kept for boys you know." ' Significantly, this complaint is followed by the reproach that Sarah spends insufficient time at home.

Bright, ambitious, articulate – if occasionally reduced by upbringing into a wary laconicism – the late 1950s and early 1960s heroine might claim an apparent sophistication. In fact she is remarkably ill-equipped to deal with a life taking place beyond known environments. A. S. Byatt, Margaret Drabble and Olivia Manning's women are distinguished by an almost culpable naivety. Clara Maugham, for instance, has no idea what an art gallery is or what goes on inside it. She finds the nature of friend Clelia's job 'obscure', but as her creator explains, 'the nature of most jobs was obscure to her'. It seems wonderful to Clara that people not only live in London, but that they live there long enough to appear in its telephone directories. Such ingenuousness has a decisive effect on attitudes to other people and, especially, the opposite sex. The early 1960s girl looks for expertise, knowledgeability, appropriateness to milieu, for people who will guide her into areas and situations where she would be reluctant to venture alone. Thus Quintin, the effete middle-aged roué with his bowler hat and his social dexterity, seems 'exactly right' to Ellie Parson's inexperienced eye. To Clara Maugham the physical unattractiveness of one early boyfriend is amply compensated for by his slight air of sophistication, 'the sense he gave of being connected'. Clara's search for connection is an enduring theme of *Jerusalem the Golden*. Her pronounced intellectual powers will always be compromised by the need for direction, authentication by somebody else. Taken by a man named Peter to a poetry reading, she admires her escort not only for concealing his opinions about the performance but 'even more for the sophistication of having them'. She is baffled by the stock Northam phrase 'I don't know much about it, but I know what I like' on the grounds that it suggests a deliberate preference. Clara, alternatively, is aware that without knowledge she has no means of liking or disliking.

Given this chronic impressionability, nearly every relationship is likely to take the form of an heuristic experience. Frederica in *Still Life* (1985) finds her boyfriend Nigel Reiver sexually attractive, but she is simultaneously fascinated by his links with hitherto unimaginable areas of modern life – in this case the City of London, a subject of which Frederica is altogether ignorant. Sex, though welcomed for obvious physical reasons, is inextricably bound up with the pursuit of knowledge. Ellie Parsons, having offered herself up to the fastidious Quintin, returns to her Chelsea bedsit where she dances excitedly round the room 'to celebrate the end of her virginity', but what Ellie is really celebrating is less the fact of physical release than the dawn of sophistication. Frederica's involvements with the young men of Cambridge have all the sedulousness of the laboratory technician.

The sense of everyone being involved in a play, a highly coloured entertainment in which suitability and appropriateness take precedence over emotion, is continual. This fragile atmosphere provides the fictional heroine of the time with little defence against the men with whom they come into contact: their inability to discriminate frequently verges on the painful. The briefest exposure to Quintin's insipid charm prompts Ellie to decide that 'this was the man she would have chosen for herself. That he should have sought her out still seemed unbelievable felicity.' Val in *The Cage*, made pregnant and married to an amiable nonentity, realises that she has been seduced by appearances: her husband 'only looked the part'. Clara Maugham, confronted with the gorgeous and married Gabriel, is another victim of the ideal. It is 'not in her to say no'. She has 'always been looking for such a man as Gabriel, so endowed, so beautiful'. Significantly, Clara enjoys being Gabriel's mistress more for the beguiling complexities such a liaison brings to her life, rather than the undoubted physical pleasure. This, however, is in line with a general attitude to sex which might be described as verging on the dispassionate. Early 1960s women often seem more interested in the prestige and cachet that sexual experience confers. Margaret Forster's Georgy, who anticipates simple pleasure – ' "I can imagine exactly what it will be like" ' – is relatively unusual.

As regards wider attitudes to sex, no moral generalisations can be made. Early 1960s fiction of the Drabble/Newman variety is occasionally paraded as a harbinger of the permissive society: in fact all that can be demonstrated is a kaleidoscope of experience confidently labelled 'normal' or 'abnormal' depending on the views of the participant. Such heterodoxy is broadly confirmed by contemporary sociological research. While the 1960s are commonly held up for inspection as a decade of unparalleled sexual licence, studies of sexual behaviour suggest that the permissive advance was comparatively restrained. In Geoffrey Gorer's survey of 1971, *Sex and Marriage in England Today*, 63 per cent of the women questioned were virgins at the time of their marriage. Virginity is not perhaps so highly prized by contemporary fictional heroines, but it is far from defunct. Georgy, for example, is still a virgin at 27. Rosamund Stacey in *The Millstone* (1965) manages to convey the impression of wide experience while remaining sexually inactive. Set against this are more practised hands: Georgy's flat-mate Meredith, for instance, who calculates that she and her boyfriend Jos have slept together seventy-two times in their three-month relationship (' "that's pretty impressive," Jos acknowledges. "I've never slept that much with anyone else, I bet" '), and bed-hopping Frederica. The thought that a great many contemporary sexual attitudes rested on pretence rather than actual experience is conveyed by Val in *The Cage*: 'It was the fashion to pretend to have gone further than you really had, but most important not to go too far.'

Some wider questions remained. Conditioned by books and hearsay rather than life, the average attitude to love and marriage tends to the bizarre. A. S. Byatt includes a long passage in *Still Life* outlining Frederica Potter's paradoxical views on the subject. Frederica 'longs' for a husband, partly because she is afraid that no one might want her, partly because she cannot decide what to do with herself before this problem is solved, partly because everyone else is looking for a husband. On one level she is naively romantic. At the same time she wishes to avoid the snares of her mother's generation, in which freedom and liberty were allowed only in a 'brief, artificial period before concession and possession'. Her relationships with men are typified by a contempt for her suitors which prevents her from taking them seriously. Her view of men is ingenuous, exemplified in her refusal to accept that they have feelings:

> Men were deceivers ever, the bad ones, and masterful, the good ones. The world was their world, and what she wanted was to live in that world, not to be sought out as refuge from or adjunct to it.

In short, Frederica wants simultaneously to be a romantic heroine and a free spirit accepted by men on their own terms. The literary reference is appropriate, as Frederica tends to derive most of her opinions about behaviour from books. Here, however, literature provides no satisfactory yardstick. The women in men's novels are unreal and unrealised; and the world has moved on since Rosamond Lehmann. So Frederica and her boyfriends battle on, as Byatt puts it, the men to be hopelessly devoted, Frederica to be both abject and free. Both, predictably, are 'puzzled and hurt' by these confusions.

Still Life is a good analysis of the pre–1960s feminist mind, vainly trying to reconcile romantic upbringing with an appreciation of broader possibilities. But the reaction of the new type of women's novel against the attitudes of a previous generation was most marked in its anti-domesticity. The early 1960s heroine is, for instance, conspicuously uninterested in having children. While the period produced a roster of pregnancy and illegitimate baby novels, for example *The L-Shaped Room*, *The Millstone* and *The Cage*, they tend to be concerned with the frustrations arising out of missed opportunities rather than the physical processes of childbearing. Jane Graham's immediate anxiety is the probable curtailment of her career in the publicity office of a West End hotel. Val in *The Cage* regards her unborn child as 'not a person but as an embarrassing encumbrance that was going to spoil my life'. The arrival of Rosamund Stacey's daughter in *The Millstone* is perfunctorily described in comparison to the meticulous analyses of mental states that occupy preceding chapters. Given the new freedom of expression that swept over the 1960s novel, one might have expected such books to contain epic descriptions of childbirth, awash in blood and emotion; only the account of Stephanie's confinement in *Still Life* – the rigours of a 1950s maternity ward painfully outlined – takes up this challenge. For Stephanie the experience of giving birth is epiphanic. Much more common is Meredith's reaction in *Georgy Girl*. Announcing the news of her pregnancy to Jos, along with the information that she has had two previous abortions, she declares that 'I can easily get rid of the baby. I've no tender feelings about it.' In the event Meredith decides to go through with the birth. However, the baby revolts her. 'She was supposed to bathe and clean and feed it for years and years. She couldn't do it. They would have to take it away.' Georgy's preoccupation with the child, whom she eventually adopts, is unusual for a 1960s heroine. In fact her straightforward interest in domestic life, her willingness to settle for limited goals – 'I just want to look reasonable,' she decides on a visit to an expensive hairdresser – emphasise her detachment from her contemporaries. So, too, does her decision to marry her father's widowed employer for reasons of financial security.

Elsewhere, the dire consequences of domesticity are sharply apparent. A. S. Byatt's novels are full of warnings about the pitfalls of early marriage. There is a nasty scene in *The Game* (1968) in which Julia, attending an Oxford dinner party convened by her sister, is introduced to a don's wife who has abandoned a promising academic career 'before childbearing overtook her'. Sylvia Redmon, having been publicly snubbed by her husband, tells Julia that she admires her books because they deal with a problem ' "nobody thinks anything ought to be done about. That is – women, intelligent women, who are suddenly plunged into being at home all day." ' Love for her children co-exists with days on which she sits down and cries over a knowledge of waste.

A variation on this theme occurs in *The Virgin in the Garden* when Jenny, Alexander's quasi-mistress, meets Wilkie and Frederica at a party. She finds their callow, gamecock bumptiousness infinitely distressing. Though barely older than she, their lives are full of beguiling ambitions: 'they saw themselves wheeling up, up and on'. Jenny's existence, conversely, is constrained by her husband, her baby and her husband's job. Even her part in Alexander's masque is a continual battle with domestic responsibilities. But this predicament is the result of an earlier confusion:

> She had known that she must solve the problem of marriage and child-bearing first, before she could identify any rational future. She had wanted marriage, without ever considering not wanting it, all through her degree ... She had no idea at all whether, if she had thought differently, she might have identified herself, seen herself brilliant and perhaps become it.

Yet the opportunity for self-definition has passed; the peacock chatter of Wilkie and Frederica is merely a reminder of her own impotence. Significantly, perhaps, her dislike is reserved not for Wilkie but for Frederica, whose crime is not so much to believe herself to be a genius but to express this conviction 'comparatively grossly and stridently'. That this judgement is a function of sex, Jenny is 'brilliantly aware'.

'One could not simply become invisible at twenty-four,' Jenny tells herself in an attempt at reassurance. Worse, perhaps, was the realisation that one could be both visible and unregarded. For all the incidental chatter about 'freedom' and 'liberation', the women of the early 1960s novel are still dominated by men. If a single characteristic unites Frederica, Rosamund Stacey, Clara and Georgy, it is their anxiety to please, to win male approval. Even an independent-minded young bohemian like Susan in *The King of a Rainy Country* is worried that she might bore her boyfriend. The 1960s, as many a feminist critic has pointed out, was a man's decade. Pinned down in a variety of literary and cinematic snapshots, from *The Collector* (1963) to Antonioni's *Blow Up* (1966), the women never flutter free. Their 'liberty', especially sexual liberty, is nearly always the liberty to be exploited by men. The connection between 1960s liberation and the burgeoning women's movement is made in several contemporary novels. Angela Carter's *Love* (1971), for example, looks back to a 1960s provincial bohemia – the world of Philip Callow's novels ten years on – of bed-sitter parties, dope and cheery antinomianism, its focus a middle-class girl who has her life ruined and her personality denatured by her husband Lee and his disturbed brother Buzz.

As an evocation of a particular messy, morally neutral late 1960s world, the novel is quite unsparing. The brothers, in particular, are classic pieces of contemporary flotsam. Residents of a decaying Northern city, they move disinterestedly in a floating environment centred loosely upon the art school, the university and the second-hand trade, making their impermanent homes 'in the sloping, terraced hillsides where the Irish, the West Indians and the more adventurous of the students lived in old decaying houses where rents were low'. Naive, confiding Annabel – ' "If you deceive me, I'll die," ' she tells Lee with evident seriousness – is unable to contend with her husband's routine duplicity, evasiveness and refusal to consider the consequences of his actions: his cheery detachment is a constant. When eventually she gases herself, the responsibility seems to extend beyond her immediate circle. Though the novel ends with the brothers squabbling 'as to which of them was more to blame', the implication is that Annabel was destroyed less by personal callousness than by the social structures of which she was a part.

If Lee can ever be said to meet his match, it is in the shape of the wife of his philosopher tutor, with whom he has a casual affair. A repository for fashionable female opinion (' "It's like screwing the woman's page of the *Guardian*," ' Lee tells his brother), his mistress combines a shrewd contempt (' "Of course, I can hardly expect you to be faithful to me" ') with a calculated vindictiveness (' "I could make things very unpleasant for you at the university" '). The phenomenon of a woman using a man for her own purposes was to become increasingly familiar in the fiction of the next decade. A more combative note enters English feminism at the beginning of the 1970s: *The Female Eunuch, Spare Rib*, the founding of Virago Press all date from around this time. Aggressive, literate, quintessentially middle-class, it found a characteristic platform in the novel, most obviously in a style of fiction that does not so much attack male iniquity and the system which perpetuates it as purposely subordinate the male role in social and sexual arrangements.

Doris Lessing's *The Golden Notebook* (1962), whose 'free

women' operate in a world without husbands, following marital collapse, is an early example on the grand scale, but the tendency is detectable throughout a whole range of more mundane but no less committed work. The three novels completed by Verity Bargate before her early death each depict a woman on the brink of psychological disturbance, whose response to increasingly alarming contingency is to construct a mental palisade from which the male sex is deliberately excluded. In each case the result is a tense emotional melodrama perpetually in danger of falling into a symbolist snare. Jodie in *No Mama No* (1978), with the infant sons whose gender she resents; Rosie in *Children Crossing* (1979), whose daughters are killed in a grotesque accident; the heroine of *Tit for Tat* (1981), betrayed and vengeful: Bargate's women can seem hopelessly overdrawn, their psychological quirks and obsessions blown up beyond any realistic measure. A relentless interior logic works to reduce this sensation. In particular, Bargate is careful to link the unravelling tragedies of her characters' lives to fundamental female experience. The pivot on which *No Mama No* turns is the birth of Jodie's second child. It is this that drives a wedge between husband and wife, and 'our failure to communicate became irreversible'. Her husband's belief that 'I was mad' established at an early stage, Jodie spends the remainder of the novel enacting an elaborate charade in which her sons Matthew and Orlando are passed off as 'Willow' and 'Rainbow', prior to their mother's eventual confinement in a psychiatric hospital. The downward spiral which gathers up Rosie in *Children Crossing* is precipitated by her husband's adultery.

Throughout, the attitude of Bargate's protagonists towards their men is not so much hostile as dispassionate. The indifference, insensitivity and occasional violence of the average husband is accepted as an inalienable fact, a source of disillusionment but in the last resort assimilable. Moreover, the condemnation of male attitudes is far from universal. Unexpectedly polite football supporters met on trains, friendly taxi-drivers – for a moment a faint scent of solidarity rises above the page; it rarely amounts to anything much. Even the scrupulous young doctor who befriends Rosie in *Children Crossing* has no hope of entering or understanding her inner life. At best men are well-intentioned but slightly foolish onlookers. If Bargate's novels have a weakness, it is that the schematics obtrude, that character is ruthlessly subordinated to the symbolic gesture. *Children Crossing* ends with Rosie offering herself to a Soho kerb-crawler. When the man subsequently enquires about payment, she neatly turns the tables on him by asking, ' "How much do I owe you?" ' *Tit for Tat*, a yet more uncompromising work, concerns a young woman who feigns cancer and endures successive mastectomies as a means of revenging herself on a faithless lover. But such schematisation is characteristic of a wide range of women's fiction of the past twenty years. Fay Weldon's novels, to take the work of a commercially successful practitioner, are notoriously pre-programmed, the victims of an altogether rigid determinism. The short pieces collected in *Moon over Minneapolis* (1991) are a good example of the thraldom exercised by Weldon's themes, the most cursory fragment of scene-setting providing an excuse for another salvo in the sex war. Thus a story set in Sarajevo, where the assassination of the Archduke Ferdinand precipitated the First World War, is hedged about with all manner of authorial injunctions not to forget the Archduke's wife. Amid these showy gestures it is difficult for the reader not to feel that the odds stacked against decent male behaviour are unacceptably high. There is something wearying about the protagonist of 'A Visit from Johannesburg' who, having married an outwardly exemplary left-wing county councillor, discovers the inevitable, fatal flaw:

> in fact he talked about his response and his feelings so much, and how he could best make amends for the sins of his gender, that she sometimes fell asleep before he got round to sex.

Invariably such symbolism works better in a working-class setting, where the issues at stake are not those of sexual guilt or bourgeois angst, but immediate problems of earning a living, surviving: an atmosphere in which female solidarity is demanded by hostile circumstance. Something of this feeling emerges from Pat Barker's graphic dramatisation of the Yorkshire Ripper case, *Blow Your House Down* (1984). To Barker's collection of prostitutes and ordinary women – an invidious distinction, perhaps – men are at once peripheral and, in the case of the Ripper himself, unavoidably central. At the novel's core, too, lies a connection between the specific violence here practised on women and the wider environment. Wandering by mistake into the slaughterhouse unit of the chicken processing factory where she works, one of Barker's women is rebuked by a male operative. ' "Killing's for the men," ' he explains. The point is well-made, but the grasp on the lapel is comparatively restrained.

Typically, women in novels of the Barker type find men, if not menacing, then appendages of rather limited value. In trying to construct their own destinies they are wary of partners whose initial allure is swiftly compromised by selfishness or simple inanition. Carol Birch's two novels *Life in the Palace* (1988) and *The Fog Line* (1989) explore this theme with considerable success. Battened on to by weak, conniving men, their protagonists are involved in an unyielding struggle to maintain their independence, to resist unreasonable demands, to preserve their integrity in a world where the exploitation of women seems to derive more from innate male feebleness than straightforward aggression. In each case the solution is final. Judy in *Life in the Palace* is saved from a destructive relationship with an unreliable drifter by his sudden and unexpected death. Gloria in *The Fog Line*, whose rape as a teenager has coloured much of her subsequent experience, ends up killing the emotional limpet who has had such a lowering effect on her adult life.

The struggle to repel, ignore or simply to diminish attracted some unexpected but welcome allies. Ian McEwan's first stories provide a notable example of a male writer sympathetic to the women's movement, satirical send-ups of male attitudes in which traditional bravado is subtly deflated. 'Homemade', which opens the collection *First Love, Last Rites* (1975), is a splendidly comic deconstruction of male fantasies of sexual initiation. The light, ironical tone is short-lived, however. The stories collected in *Between the Sheets* (1978) are altogether graver in their implications. 'Pornography', the most conspicuous engagement in gender conflict, ends with the castration of its protagonist by the two women whom he has simultaneously infected with gonorrhoea. By the time of *The Comfort of Strangers* (1981), in which the characters painstakingly ventilate their attitudes to patriarchy, the effect of this very genuine commitment was becoming rather stifling.

Of equal interest, if only because of the uncertainties of their position, are Nigel Williams's *My Life Closed Twice* (1977) and *Jack Be Nimble* (1980), two odd, offbeat novels in which largely unreconstituted men are driven back into the folds of rectitude by dominant feminist women. *My Life Closed Twice* features Martin Steel, a BBC producer who writes obsessively (and badly) in his spare time. Each of his unpublished manuscripts contains a thinly veiled portrait of a girl named Julie, with whom he was briefly and unsatisfactorily involved as an undergraduate. The novel moves into gear when Martin's wife Ellen, understandably distressed at being ignored in favour of these unrealisable literary and sexual ambitions, decamps. In a final showdown she presents Martin with an exhaustive catalogue of his personal failings, in particular his lack of interest in her involvement with the Labour party and the women's movement. ' "For you my political work is the equivalent of a Victorian lady's stint at the soup kitchen. Isn't it?" ' Worse, Martin is a bad writer. ' "Amanuensis to a Great Man's a bit of a sticky one," ' Ellen obligingly explains, ' "but Amanuensis to a mediocrity – sorry no deal." ' Confronted by this onslaught, Martin is forced to reappraise his position. His response is a resolve to cast aside the attitudes of what he identifies as male élitism and abandon the quest for literary glory: 'What we need now is more Real People,' he decides, 'men and women who are prepared to face life, not run away from it.' However, this is a flawed commitment. The novel ends with him seated covertly in the study poised to deflower yet another virgin notebook. 'Well, what are you waiting for Steel? Put the pen down. Go on, put the pen down.' For all the earlier expressions of solidarity, the reader is uncomfortably aware that Martin's twenty-second unpublished novel is about to follow the preceding twenty-one into the slush-piles of Bloomsbury.

The notion of fine male principles let down by defective practice is brought sharply into focus in *Jack Be Nimble*. Warliss, its picaresque, TV script-writing hero, goes so far as to create a series of different identities to steer him through his complicated emotional life. His wife Annie might know him by his real name, but to Lucy, the mother of his child, he is 'Luke Danby'; to the mid-European expatriate Nellie, with whom he conducts a spasmodic affair, he is 'Mr Jarlsberg'. Ultimately, when all three women and their various male attachments relocate to a sort of bourgeois commune in north London, Warliss is on the point of fleeing to suburban solitude. However, after a climactic scene in which Nellie gives birth to what is presumably his child in the presence of the house's inhabitants, he resolves to turn his back on his former self-absorption and acknowledge the advantages of the communal life. Like *My Life Closed Twice*, *Jack Be Nimble* has some conspicuous targets. Prominent among them is the average man's indifference to political issues. The commitment of Communist Annie, who by miscarrying during the course of a rowdy anti-racist demonstration loses her chance of ever having children, is in deliberate contrast to Jack's complacent acceptance of the status quo. To say something about politics is 'one of the major ambitions of his life'.

Male selfishness, too, is held up for fastidious scrutiny. At one point, for example, Jack remembers a letter dispatched to a discarded girlfriend (there is a similar passage in the earlier novel): 'A stylish letter, full of lines like . . . "I hope this isn't arrogant, or, even worse, humble, but . . ." you are an old slag, or words to that effect.' The problem, as Warliss recognises, is that women don't write graceful, agonised letters back. Their distress is of a more visceral sort: they ring you up and scream at you, jump out of windows 'or something equally tasteless'. Jack's mistress Lucy attempts to place this emotional divide in a class context: ' "you said you loved me but you didn't love me you didn't love anyone," ' she tells Jack during a particularly withering and unpunctuated tirade; ' "you're not capable of love you're all so clever and rich and beautiful you went to the right schools and the right universities." ' In the face of this and other assaults, Jack grows conscious that he has limited room for manoeuvre. Loitering in a pub he is aware that he doesn't 'have a group to belong to'. The women in his life 'wouldn't let him engage in anything so frivolous, time-consuming or essentially male'. An acknowledgement of personal guilt is not far behind, and Jack is forced to concede that he is 'a bore and a rapist and a lout who did not understand women or at best was unable to think of them as human beings'.

Meanwhile, the communal household begins to take shape, its advantages enthusiastically outlined by Lucy:

> Wouldn't it be marvellous? All of us living together and raising everyone's children together and the men sharing in it, and everyone you love there, just *there*, sort of equal and participating.'

Jack, evidence of whose intended getaway now comes to light, is made to see the error of his ways by a collective harangue. Like Martin Steel, he is damned on the grounds of immaturity, again viewed as the special prerogative of the artist. As one of his accusers puts it:

> 'You think that you're an artist or something. Or rather you're somebody who wants the privilege of being an artist without the responsibility . . . you're basically a fast-moving layabout, a sort of bloody child.'

To Jack, wavering between responsibility and the continuation of a selfish male existence, the birth of Nelly's child is an unignorable piece of symbolism:

> for the first time in his life, Jack could not have cared how he ought to be labelled and what role was expected of him. Instead, he found positive pleasure in the circle of faces, the confusion of parenthood that made the six, no the nine of them indistinguishable from a family, but not a family wished on him, instead an elected group, sustained by the delicate balance of affection.

By participating in childbirth, the implication runs, Jack has somehow been able to find himself as an individual, as well as to appreciate that he must treat women by the same standards that he would want himself to be treated.

The reader, though, is entitled to feel that this is something of a fake epiphany. Where, for example, in Jack's previous career is any indication that this new role can be sustained? The edginess of tone, too, is ominous. It is as if Williams, a humorist by disposition, rather feels that he might be guilty of insufficient gravitas. Many of the jokes consequently tend to be cancelled out by the awareness of a serious purport, and the result is an edifice that frequently appears to topple under the weight of authorial prescription. Like the premises of many a contemporary women's novel, *Jack Be Nimble*'s conclusions are pre-ordained, the vigour of its characters reduced by their thraldom to destiny, its claims to plausibility eventually anaesthetised by sheer good intentions.

12

The Literary Consequences of Mrs Thatcher

When Macaulay declined to review *Hard Times*, allegedly on account of its 'sullen socialism', he was expressing a commonly held belief that the only proper response by a novelist to anything outside the orbit of character and motive is a sort of supine quietism, lying low 'inside the whale', in Orwell's phrase. 'Commitment' has been a dirty word in English fiction for upwards of fifty years, disparaged equally by the small group of high-minded people who think it the writer's duty to remain 'above' politics – as if one could ignore the way in which one's country gets administered – and the much larger band of cultural saboteurs encouraging him to operate beneath it. Yet 'commitment', as we have seen, is not the exclusive province of fire-breathing Marxists or apoplectic neo-fascists, and *Brideshead Revisited* (1945) is quite as much a 'political' novel as *Love on the Dole* (1933). Scratch a writer who is held up as a model of apolitical detachment hard enough and he will generally turn into something else – after all, even quietism is a kind of politics by default. Kingsley Amis's praise of Anthony Powell as an 'uncommitted writer' seems ironic in the light of the opinions on post-war social arrangements expressed in *The Soldier's Art* (1966). The same point could be made of Evelyn Waugh, whose claim, made towards the end of his life, that he had always been 'a pure aesthete' co-exists with novels of flagrant political bias. For Waugh and Powell politics and aesthetics are inseparable: in fact, Powell's politics are conveyed by way of his aesthetic preoccupations, a matter of ironic concealment, the deft allusion and the pregnant hint. Nick Jenkins, despite the critical tendency to see him merely as an absence, is a sharp operator, and much of his sharpness emerges out of his social and political judgements.

Yet Powell and Waugh can seem models of detachment when ranked against the 'political' novelists of the 1980s, a time when the novelist's role as a political commentator seemed once more a matter of public interest. One of the side effects of the eleven and a half years of Mrs Thatcher's rule was the pressure placed on writers to take up positions on either side of the political barricade, however embarrassing or pointless the result. Ironically, though, this pressure came at a time when form was struggling with attempts to assimilate a highly predictable content. All art is propaganda, up to a point, and on the face of it writing about politics ought to be as straightforward a business as writing about adultery. But a number of factors have combined to render the novelist's engagement with the current political framework fraught with danger.

Something of these changed circumstances can be seen in a comparison of the political novels of the 1980s with Trollope's *The Prime Minister*, one of the greatest of all political novels, published in 1876. Trollope's novel relies for its psychological effects on the contrast between Plantaganet Palliser's sense of duty (combined with extreme personal diffidence) and the exalted social ambitions of his wife – ambitions which, to do her justice, Lady Glencora imagines will help her husband's position. Arriving at his country house in preparation for a political gathering, the Prime Minister finds that his wife has gone so far as to have the grounds redesigned. Questioning a workman over his instructions, Palliser realises that the man is ignorant of his identity.

This is a tiny incident, but it is enough to emphasise the gap between the political novel of the Victorian age (and the reality it reflected) and its modern equivalent – in so far as such a thing exists. Christopher Harvie's excellent study *The Centre of Things* (1991) charts what has been an inexorable decline. You couldn't write a novel like *The Prime Minister* in the 1980s, not perhaps because you were less skilled than Trollope, lacked his range or his awareness of the connections between public and private life, but because historical circumstance has changed. In the mid-nineteenth century novelists stood for Parliament (Thackeray, Trollope) or worked as parliamentary journalists (Dickens) and wrote vivid accounts of stump electioneering, for example in *The Pickwick Papers* and *Dr Thorne*. Perhaps the best worm's-eye view of Victorian politics is provided by the election scenes in *Ralph the Heir*, which reflect Trollope's own candidature for the notoriously corrupt seat of Beverley. But that age is dead. About the only realistic description of a parliamentary election in recent years occurs in Melvyn Bragg's *Autumn Manoeuvres* (1978), and Jimmy Johnston's constituency is far from being a microcosm. Its inability to represent what might be thought of as national opinion is, you feel, Bragg's point.

The decline of the conventionally framed political novel, in which ministries rise and fall and personal preoccupations intrude into the field of public interest, seems all the more curious in the light of the decade's highly charged political atmosphere. One might attribute the dearth of 1950s political fiction to the dampening effect of the Butskellite consensus, but the 1980s was a time of schism, crisis and drama. Why then did the decade fail to produce a satisfactory fictional re-creation?

The explanation lies in the great shifting of public authority, and public accountability, that has taken place in England in the last hundred years. The Victorian political novelists, Trollope and Disraeli, were interested in power, in who made decisions and how they were reached. Additionally, they were interested in the human consequences of these contingencies, the effect of what might be called 'accidents of power' – one thinks of Archdeacon Grantley in *Barchester Towers*, denied a bishopric owing to a change of ministry hours before his father's death. But to write in this way presupposes a knowledge of where public authority resides. Power in this country is at once highly concentrated and widely dispersed. We may think that we elect a House of Commons which, having divided up along party lines, eventually produces cabinet government. The reality is a small and covertly administered political executive, with wider industrial and economic authority wielded by an increasingly elusive oligarchy, a trail of shareholders and overseas connections that grows ever more faint.

Maurice Edelman, a politician and political novelist of an older generation, makes this point in *The Prime Minister's Daughter* (1964):

> Once you have parties, you get government by caucus. The democracy thing is as dead as Gladstone. What we've got in Britain is a kind of Venetian oligarchy and it runs right through the democracy.

This tendency is exemplified in Wilson's kitchen cabinet, in Mrs Thatcher's habit of dispensing with cabinet government altogether. The impenetrable aura of secrecy that this cast across decision-making and the exercise of authority might be bad for democracy, but it was disastrous for fictional analyses of the higher administrative process. Any analysis of power framed in the mid–1980s would consequently have to consider the psychology of a handful of people whose motives can only be guessed at. In this context the media, whose searchlight qualities are often made much of in the field of public accountability, is scarcely relevant. Television may have brought the faces of politicians nearer to us than they were in Trollope's day, when Plantagenet Palliser could go unrecognised by a workman on his own estate, but as people they are infinitely remote.

Yet the garish, phantasmagoric quality of the average politician is only a symptom. If the sentient modern elector is aware that executive government is uncomfortably remote, he is also likely to be struck by the feeling that public politics in the old sense has ceased to matter. The Victorian system of rigged elections, rotten boroughs and open bribery, in which seats could be bought and sold over the counter, was a swindle, but at least everybody knew it was a swindle. In the 1990s it is the pretence of democracy, the illusion that the country *isn't* being run for the benefit of vested interests, that sticks in one's throat. Sooner or later, whatever his or her private notions of self-determination, the late twentieth-century English citizen will be forced to admit that his life is ultimately governed by, on the one hand, the media, and, on the other, the international economy and the people who manipulate it, both of which are quite beyond his power to influence.

This air of unreality is mimicked by art. Taking its lead from political satire of the *Yes, Minister* variety, the straightforward political novel has degenerated into a kind of burlesque, dominated by a single gargantuan monster. The fictive Mrs Thatcher who appears shaking hands with James Bond in John Gardner's 007 retreads, who marches through Pete Davies's satire *The Last Election* (1987), who greets Parsons the Tory Home Secretary in David Caute's *Veronica, or The Two Nations* (1989) ('Today it was a terracotta outfit in two parts with a busy pattern of what looked all too like snakes and ladders') is no more than a caricature. Even a really subtle and imaginative spoof like Mark Lawson's *Bloody Margaret* (1991), in which the Prime Minister is seen through the eyes of innumerable hangers-on, security men and political small fry, can only invest her with a sort of blurred remoteness. But then the real Mrs Thatcher, brought to us by the televised walkabout and the photo-opportunity and groomed for us by the spin doctors of Central Office, was conspicuously in want of a third dimension.

If Mrs Thatcher was no more than the chief monster in an elaborate demonology, the dislike expressed by novelists of whatever image they happened to perceive was real enough. In fact the degree of writerly fascination with the Prime Minister is unique in twentieth-century history. In his day Harold Wilson might have inspired equally extreme reactions, but somehow he did not seem a fit subject for the novel. The carefully fabricated cult of Mrs Thatcher's personality, alternatively, let alone a roster of policies guaranteed to raise liberal hackles, was a consistent motivating force. The late 1980s were remarkable for the degree of unanimity among the literary community, and for the existence of a literary opposition more vocal and coherent than at any time since the 1930s. It was the time of Lady Antonia Fraser's June 20th dining club, which met in the incongruous setting of the late Sir Hugh Fraser's house in Campden Hill Square, the time of Salman Rushdie's 'Mrs Torture' and the public rebuke of Ian McEwan by the *Sunday Times*. Its characteristic charge was a supposed appeal to baser instincts, a shabby populism of self-interest. The words put into an imaginary Mrs Thatcher's mouth by Michael Dibdin in *Dirty Tricks* (1991) are typical:

You don't want a caring society. You *say* you do, but you don't, not really. You couldn't care less about education and health and all the rest of it. And don't for Christ's sake talk to me about culture. You don't give a toss about culture. All you want to do is sit at home and watch TV. No, it's no use protesting. I *know* you. You're selfish, greedy, ignorant and complacent. So vote for me!

Several cherished left-wing notions of the 1980s are contained in this outburst: the idea of Mrs Thatcher as a hectoring, Philistine bully, an unrelenting nanny ('I *know* you'), whose most dangerous whims were tolerated by a supine electorate. Such stridency was all very well when it came to making political capital; artistically it tended to have a wholly vitiating effect.

Ian McEwan's *The Child in Time* (1987), a projection of third-term Thatcherism in which presumed Tory policies such as family values, the ruination of public transport and the vulgarisation of television have been grotesquely extended, makes its points with the grace of a meat-cleaver. Livi Michael's *Under a Thin Moon* (1992), an otherwise convincing indictment of thirteen Conservative years, jars only in its coat-hook symbolism. At one point frail, vulnerable Wanda arrives at the flat of a loathsome couple who will ultimately exploit and rob her, in the middle of a prime ministerial television broadcast. ' "It's all monetarist policies," ' vile Kev helpfully explains, and there is a sense of iron filings leaping upwards to obey the magnet's call. No doubt Michael would argue that the connection is integral to her theme – that political realities have personal consequences – but in a work of hitherto unforced naturalism this sort of signposting can seem merely obtrusive.

Artistic creaking noises aside, if a single factor distinguished the literary response to Mrs Thatcher it was incomprehension, or rather a refusal to comprehend. The fact that millions of people had repeatedly voted for her seemed of little moment to a handful of left-leaning liberals whose favourite riposte was to regret Mrs Thatcher's 'vulgarity'. The mass-signature letters to the *Guardian* which typified the past decade do not, with hindsight, make edifying reading. Salman Rushdie's *New Statesman* rallying cry, written immediately before the 1983 General Election, seems particularly tired and petulant:

> I find myself entertaining Spenglerian thoughts about how there can be times when all that is worst in a people rises to the surface and expresses itself in its government. There are, of course, many Britains, and many of them – the sceptical, questioning, radical, reformist, libertarian, non-conformist Britains – I have always admired greatly. But these Britains are presently in retreat, even in disarray; while nanny-Britain, strait-laced Victorian values Britain, thin-lipped jingoist Britain, is in charge. Dark goddesses rule; brightness falls from the air.

Like many another left-winger of the time – Professor Stuart Hall is a notable exception – Rushdie makes the fatal mistake of not even trying to comprehend the basis of Mrs Thatcher's attraction or to appreciate the concerns of the constituency that brought her to power. There is an awkward silence, too, about the alternatives. Did Rushdie seriously believe that Michael Foot's fissiparous and diminished battalions were capable of filling the breach? There must have been several million electors who voted Labour in June 1983 – I was one – in the not quite conscious hope that Labour would lose. This ostrich-like refusal to face facts was endemic at the time. Until Labour woke up to Mrs Thatcher's appeal, it did not have the slightest chance of forming another government: such lessons were not easily learned in those bright, bitter days, when it was simpler to talk about vulgarity, Spengler, dark goddesses and brightness falling from the air.

Predictably, public hand-wringing over Mrs Thatcher's supposed excesses extends to the analyses of Thatcherism that begin turning up in the fiction of the 1980s. They find their dominant focus in the shape of the Thatcherite fictional hero, who makes his début somewhere around the middle of his mentor's second parliamentary term. Thatcher Man is a pervasive figure on the grim uplands of the late 1980s novel: self-sufficient, go-getting, entrepreneurial, he surfaces in Terence Blacker's *Fixx* (1989), Michael Dibdin's *Dirty Tricks* and Tim Parks's *Goodness* (1991). Occasionally he elevates himself to the high ground of national politics: Michael Parsons, the protagonist of David Caute's *Veronica, or The Two Nations*, is a Tory Home Secretary; Charlie Bosham in Julian Rathbone's *Nasty, Very* (1984) manages to capture a Labour marginal in the Tory landslide of 1983. More often than not, though, he is simply someone who through a combination of resourcefulness, guile and an eye for the main chance has managed to do well out of the 1980s. What is remarkable, perhaps, is the close relationship between these novels and the similarity of the personal lives held up for generally rather fastidious inspection. Their effect is to suggest that from the novelist's point of view the 'Thatcherite' was a distinctive and familiar animal, with recognisable social and psychological characteristics.

The shared social background is perhaps the most immediate feature. Fictional Thatcherites are, without exception, male, middle-class suburbanites. Bosham's father runs a precariously financed family business in the Orpington area. The Fixxes hail from Biggleswade. George Crawley in *Goodness* spends his early years in 'an ill-conceived semi-detached in Park Royal'. Such an upbringing, with its burden of latent anxieties and money worries, is enough to leave them with a slight, though abiding, sense of insecurity, and, more important, a ferocious dislike of the families with whom they were forced to share their early life. This manifests itself in all manner of subsequent slights and insults. Offered a partnership by his near-bankrupt father, the young Charlie Bosham takes the greatest delight in turning him down. Having left home to attend university, George Crawley records that he 'didn't go back home from one end of term to the other', and certainly not for 'such minor events as Grandfather's prostectomy or Aunt Mavis's suicide attempt'. When Mavis finally succeeds in killing herself, George declines to send flowers to the funeral ('What on earth was the point of a wreath of pinks for mad Mavis?'). Jonathan Fixx, the son of a celebrated war hero, contents himself with selling his father's medals.

Out of this tenuous foothold in the lower reaches of the middle class is born a terrible social uncertainty. The Thatcherite heroes are caught in a bleak, arid landscape, contemptuous of the shabby-genteel world they have left behind, doubtful of their ability to secure an entry into the grander circles to which they aspire. As

Fixx, remembering his childhood in the class-conscious 1950s, puts it: 'In the class war, we were stranded in No Man's Land. We talked in unconvincing accents, neither toff nor yob.' Attending minor public schools or the local grammar, the young Thatcherite is uneasily conscious of contending social strata and his comparatively humble position. Charlie Bosham might despise 'oiks' from the nearby council estate, but he is equally wary of the well-to-do. In later life Charlie will describe the upper classes as 'shits . . . they screwed you rotten with their faces turned away, but when they confronted you they were smooth as glass'. Despite his social aspirations, the Thatcherite hero tends to prefer people of his own sort, finding in them a greater awareness of the way in which the world works and the proper focus of human ambition. Michael Parsons, removed from his boarding school to a more plebeian establishment in the London suburbs, is not disheartened by what to some youths would be a social climb-down, as the new arrangements are much more to his taste; 'there was no idleness, no affectation . . . and no pretence that anything counted more in life than doing better than the next boy'.

Such single-mindedness is characteristic. As a human being, busily at large in the worlds of school, commerce or society, the Thatcherite hero is unlovely, venal, charmless – though quite prepared to use charm to dupe the foolish or further personal ambition. Above all, his entrepreneurial spirit is unquenchable. Even as a very young man he is generally regarded by his acquaintances as a 'fixer', someone who can get things done. Charlie Bosham arranges an abortion for his friend's sister. Fixx makes an early mark as proprietor of the school brothel. 'Sharp' rather than clever (Parsons is the only one to achieve academic distinction), often forced to rely on talented though subservient acolytes, they are distinguished by massive unscrupulousness. Fixx gaily shifts the blame for some of his depravities on to the back of a former associate and has him publicly exposed on a television programme. Bosham carefully contrives the removal of the prospective Tory candidate in the marginal seat on which he has set his sights. Though these activities might be thought to imply a certain amount of social skill, Bosham, Fixx and Co. are not sociable men, in fact rather the reverse: loners whose distrust of intimacy is a constant. As Crawley remarks, without apparent consciousness of the irony: 'When I'm outside the exhausting claustrophobia of family and intimate relationships, my personality shines.' Bosham, though troubled by aching loneliness, is constitutionally wary of unburdening himself to anyone.

Though arrogant, complacent and domineering, the Thatcherites are happy to defer to acknowledged superiors if there is something to be gained from this deference or the question of 'rules' is brought into play. There is a revealing episode in *Nasty, Very* in which Bosham, on holiday abroad for the first time, looks set to quarrel with a fellow hotel guest over the reserving of sun-loungers. Having had the 'rules' of the operation explained to him, Bosham is immediately and unnaturally quiescent. Elsewhere, the youthful Parsons happily characterises himself as his half-sister's 'devoted and obedient slave', the implication being that, forty years later, he enjoys a similar relationship with Mrs Thatcher. The hint of sexual subservience is unusual. Generally speaking, Thatcher Man is both voracious and domineering. He is also sexually precocious. We first see Bosham indulging in some schoolboy buggery, then in teenage fumblings with the daughter of a family friend. Fixx is seduced at the age of 12 by his nanny. To precocity can be added the hint of kinkiness. Fixx conceives an affection for a young woman who turns out to be his daughter, while Parsons's youthful relationship with his half-sister leads to a lifelong obsession with the literature of incest and, in his capacity as Home Secretary, to a self-destructive attempt to reform the incest laws. Extreme selfishness, always high on the personal agenda, takes on a special significance in the field of sex. Bosham takes a violent dislike to one girlfriend on the grounds that her enjoyment of sex is clearly superior to his own. Parsons decides that he would 'prefer an entirely frigid woman to one who derived more pleasure from me than I from her'.

A good adjective with which to describe the mental outlook of Bosham, Fixx, Crawley and their contemporaries would be 'petit-bourgeois'. Wary, envious, grasping, but without exception convinced of their own rectitude, they possess all the qualities necessary to launch themselves on their mercurial business careers. As might be expected, these are seldom located in the professions or traditional areas of commerce. The Thatcherite heroes are not accountants, solicitors or stockbrokers, but computer specialists, rack-renters, pop Svengalis. Their progress to 1980s prosperity tends to begin with involvement in the boom industries of the 1960s. Thus Bosham and Fixx start out in property, the former transferring to warehouse storage, the latter to 'Control Corporation Inc.', a South Africa based concern 'supplying third world governments with badly-needed security tools'. Crawley is in at the birth of a successful firm of computer software manufacturers. The parvenu north Oxford bourgeoisie of *Dirty Tricks* tend to be management consultants.

The advent of Mrs Thatcher's government imparts to each of these careers a glorious teleology, an expansive context in which all the enterprise of the Wilson years can be seen for what it was – the prelude to the long-overdue introduction of an environment which will encourage personal endeavour. The year 1979, Fixx believes, is an *annus mirabilis*, a time 'when with the long-awaited arrival of the businessman's government, we corporate tigers could at last break cover and roam the plains at will'. Parsons salutes the achievements of the Thatcher administration in class terms, the triumph of the self-made man over the vested interests of inherited wealth and organised labour: 'the class structure survived until our government was elected to place it on a sounder – because more rational – footing: initiative, energy, enterprise'. To Crawley, the 1980s, in contrast to the decade that preceded them, are a time when personal enterprise finally receives official sanction: 'you've got to remember that these were the bad old days, pre-Thatcher,' he points out, recalling the zeal with which he began his job at the computer firm, 'when enthusiasm, at least for work, was taboo'. Enterprise and initiative or social Darwinism? Dibdin's narrator, an ex-liberal whom *zeitgeist* has turned into a predatory go-getter, is in no doubt as to what has happened. His awareness sharpened by a long absence teaching English abroad, he notes that:

the attitudes and assumptions I'd grown up with had been razed to the ground, and a bold new society had risen in their place, a free-enterprise, demand-driven, fuck-you society dedicated to excellence and achievement.

Mrs Thatcher's triumph, apparently, had been to make the world safe for the businessman, but for a new type of businessman, one not overly concerned with commercial probity and prepared to use foul means if fair ones proved inadequate. Their success, however, in a world where sharp practice seems to have government sanction, is always liable to be compromised. While they can lay hold of material prosperity, their social aspirations are invariably confounded. It is the Thatcher hero's characteristic that he should be hated both by the class he has managed to leave behind and by the higher social stratum to which he seeks an entry. Bosham might eventually succeed in being selected as a prospective parliamentary candidate, but he does so in the teeth of undisguised hostility from the 'blue-rinse brigade', a collection of genteel Tory ladies who deplore his lack of gentlemanly qualities. The protean Fixx, emerging in the early 1970s in the guise of 'Jonty Fixx', property tycoon and pursuer of aristocratic heiresses, reflects on the difficulties of insinuating oneself into the English social élite: 'It's not easy becoming a nob. They close ranks, you know. They can sniff you out at thirty paces if you don't belong.' The distinction between old money or even jealously guarded bourgeois *amour propre* and these upwardly mobile parvenus is that of 'taste'.

The north Oxford *nouveaux riches* of *Dirty Tricks*, the management consultants and computer salesmen who imagine that money can somehow buy them social status, seem tawdry and vulgar when compared to 'the real right thing'. Typically, social distinctions reduce themselves to intangibles which can never be appreciated by the newly arrived, invisible barriers of knowing how to dress, how to decorate one's house and which music to play before dinner. At one stage Dibdin's narrator attends a party at the Boar's Hill residence of a socially ambitious management consultant named Carter. Unfortunately, Carter's ambitions are doomed to failure. 'It spelt money, but in a style which brought the denizens of North Oxford out in flushes of embarrassed superiority.' It is a proof of Carter's 'blissful ignorance' that he clearly has no idea that 'his swimming pool, fitted kitchen and high-tech appliances were as contemptible to the class whose values he so admired as the Parsons' Van Gogh prints and Dacron three-piece suite'.

If success was at best attainable only in material terms, the personal consequences of operating as a Thatcherite hero were yet more unfortunate. On the evidence of the fiction of the late 1980s, Thatcherism merely gave nasty people the opportunity to be nastier still, authenticating a whole range of dubious qualities under the banner of 'enterprise', 'initiative', 'freedom' and so forth. Bosham is a venal booby; Caute's Home Secretary a cold, arrogant, solipsist. Most frightening of all is the Thatcherite hero's separation from any kind of civilised values. Happiness is measured entirely in terms of possessions. Thus George Crawley, reflecting on the prosperity of his early married life, imagines that 'surely this was the good life, a triumph really of contemporary civilisation, busy young urban people, working hard, living well, faithful to each other, honest'.

But there is a darker side to Thatcherism than the spectacle of a series of *faux bonhommes* congratulating themselves on their ability to practise self-help. The personal creed of Dibdin's narrator, for example, leads directly to violence and murder. Bosham and Crawley are capable of astonishing callousness, even towards members of their own families. The supposed personal consequences of Thatcherism are perhaps best expressed in Tim Parks's *Goodness*, an almost Thackerayan depiction of a fool conscious only of his own rectitude. Crawley, an acquisitive 1980s go-getter – the new car, the foreign holiday, the philistinism – betrays the inadequacies of his moral position from one paragraph to the next. His fixation with material possessions is sufficient to turn the most delicate emotional crisis into farce. When his wife seeks to disguise her confusion over the possibility of motherhood by making a noise with the kitchen saucepans, he observes:

> I never objected to such purchases. On the contrary, I encouraged anything that would make her happy. I was always so relieved when there was something she actually wanted.

Saucepans, however, are a poor substitute for affection.

A similar note is struck on the occasion when his wife is provoked into leaving him. She departs in the family car, leaving him to reflect seriously that he will have to set the alarm earlier in case he has to travel to work by bus. George's immersion in the values of soap-opera is confirmed by Shirley's tearful return. The situation seems to him to possess a wholly admirable glamour. He imagines that 'we're really living now, really living: a modern life, with passion, with intrigue'. Even when Shirley gives birth to a severely handicapped child, George's tendency to place objects before people is not diminished. Listening to his brother-in-law's advice on childcare benefits, he is annoyed that the latter makes no comment on the pleasure of being driven in a new Audi.

Goodness ends with an exemplary 'practical' solution to the problem of the handicapped child. George resolves to start a fire which will destroy house and infant daughter alike, the whole cleverly stage-managed to resemble an accident. At the height of the blaze, however, his nerve fails him and he rescues the child from the flames, only for Shirley subsequently to dispatch her with an overdose. Once again a political philosophy, translated into a domestic environment, can be seen to have a cataclysmic effect on individual lives. Taken as a whole, the Thatcherite mentality as presented in the fiction of the late 1980s is virtually a casebook in psychopathology. Fixx, Bosham and the others are caricatures, but at the same time they are the flag-bearers of a distinctive style of thought: behind their absurdities and exaggerations lies the authorial conviction that they are representative of *zeitgeist*.

The connection between 'Thatcherite' fiction and the real Mrs Thatcher, her achievements and the attitudes she might be thought to have espoused is a great deal more tenuous. Three years after her political demise, the jury is still out on Mrs Thatcher: even the most dispassionate observers, though, are ready to proclaim her singularity. As Kenneth O. Morgan remarks of the mid–1980s:

> For several years, a sustained attempt had been made to inject the institutional and cultural life of the nation with market philosophies and business values, to galvanise national complacency with the short, sharp shock of enterprise.

One abiding difficulty was to assemble the structures that would define her in political terms. Here the road lay backward, far beyond – to take two recent versions of Conservatism – Heath's corporatism or Macmillan's paternalism. Milton Friedman, for example, thought her 'not a typical, classical Tory. She really is the closest thing there is equivalent to a nineteenth-century liberal, in British political terms, a Whig.' Mrs Thatcher's achievement, Friedman suggested, had been to overthrow the two contending 'aristocracies' – one composed of Labour, the other of the wise, wealthy and well-born – which had previously exercised political hegemony. But while Mrs Thatcher's economic views might not have varied very greatly from those of Lord Brougham, her social origins were markedly different. Like her standard-bearers in fiction, she had a petit-bourgeois upbringing, one of entrepreneurial, upwardly mobile, self-sufficient, middle-class neo-liberalism. Her election as party leader in 1975 represented a decisive victory for right-wing constituency parties over the consensus Toryism practised by Heath. Entrepreneurial, upwardly mobile, self-sufficient. For a moment Mrs Thatcher resembles a character out of one of the novels written to revile her. Subsequently the link between reality and its fictional representation grows more fragile.

Pre-eminently, there is the question of what Mrs Thatcher was supposed to have achieved. To the characters of the late 1980s novel, 1979 was the year when the world was made safe for business and 'initiative' ceased to be a sort of unmentionable personal foible. The Prime Minister appears as an unstoppable juggernaut, ploughing her way through the vested interests of state and labour to promote individual worth. While this view was promoted by Mrs Thatcher herself – 'I have changed everything,' she proclaimed at one point – in fact early forays into areas of potential controversy such as economic policy, social planning and labour relations were distinguished by an impressive pragmatism. Even in the mid–1980s, when the effects of the 'Thatcher revolution' were being felt across the public sector, local government and the educational establishment, their effect, queerly, was to promote the interests of the state at the expense of the individual. The ironies of Mrs Thatcher's administration are many, but the greatest, perhaps, is that a government publicly committed to personal initiative and freedom from bureaucracy should have presided over the most sustained exercise in centralisation since Attlee.

Moreover, if the idea that Mrs Thatcher brought personal self-determination scarcely bears close inspection, neither does the suggestion that the people who succeeded in the 1980s were created in her own image. The late 1980s hero tends to be a self-made man, bitterly opposed to inherited wealth, who wants to be treated on his merits. Neither Mrs Thatcher's immediate entourage nor the economic activity of the country as a whole confirms this pattern. Undoubtedly she brought into government entrepreneurs with practical business experience – Lord Young is an obvious example. At the same time she had a weakness for educated Tory gentlemen (Gilmour, Whitelaw, Hurd, Howe). Similarly, while the media, in search of commercial success stories, might choose to focus on a handful of charismatic individuals, many of whom had created their own companies from scratch, the true winners in the 1980s boom were the industrial giants and the financial institutions. It was the era of the small businessman, certainly, but it was also the era of the corporate dividend.

The Thatcherite hero who begins to populate the English novel towards the end of the Thatcher era has a curious grounding half in and half out of reality. In some cases novelists took recognisable aspects of Mrs Thatcher's upbringing or outlook and consciously sensationalised them. At other times they were content to perpetuate agreeable myths. Characteristic of nearly every novel written about the supposed Thatcherite ethos is the assumption that Mrs Thatcher introduced 'monetarism' to the management of the British economy. But monetarism began with the 1976 IMF crisis. In insisting on tight money, Mrs Thatcher was only continuing, if with greater persistence, the principles of Callaghan and Healey. Similarly, if she did not create monetarism, neither did Mrs Thatcher consistently apply it. By 1983 she was attracting criticism from former supporters such as Milton Friedman for not being tough enough over the budget: the subsequent spurt for growth, engineered by Nigel Lawson, killed off what had never been a very spirited animal in the first place. But the monetarist myth, like that of the self-made man and the commercial revolution, was pervasive. Each of these myths was sustained by a media with which the fiction of the time is inextricably linked. More so than in previous decades, political messages seemed capable of being reduced to tabloid headlines, their resonance confirmed by subsequent appearances in novels and social histories. It is significant that the triumphalist buzz-word used by the left-wing journalist who succeeds in exposing Michael Parsons should be 'Gotcha!' – a direct reference to the *Sun*'s notorious comment on the sinking of the *General Belgrano* during the Falklands War. Even Kenneth O. Morgan, in the passage quoted above, cannot prevent himself from intruding characteristic Thatcherite phrases such as 'market philosophies and business values' and 'the short, sharp shock'. If nothing else, this was a testimony to Mrs Thatcher's ability to dictate an agenda. That criticism should be framed in parodies of her own words or expressions associated with her is, perhaps, a proof of the power of the original.

Picaresque, ruthless, upwardly mobile, the Thatcherite hero is a dominant figure in the late 1980s novel: a myth, maybe, but one with which older styles of fiction, featuring older types of character, were usually unable to contend. The negative vitality of Fixx, Bosham and Crawley can lead to a certain amount of confusion. Intended as satires of Thatcherite values, novels such as *Fixx* or *Nasty, Very* frequently end up looking uncomfortably close to glorification. Set against them, attacks from the other side, novels which attempt to show decent people fighting against a sinister, free-market ideology, can often seem simply inadequate, a fictional world in which both sentiment and the character created to express it seem out of date. The English gentlemen in Tom Stacey's *Decline* (1991), which might be described as an elegy for old-style Tory paternalism, seem as remote and absurd as Sir Mulberry Hawk or Sir Tumley Snuffim: a straitjacket of burlesqued familiarity which the novel's good intentions and serious purpose can never quite shake off. One clue to this deficiency lies in the author's choice of names – 'Jumbo' Mainwaring (pronounced *Mannering*), the ailing captain of industry whose personal and financial degeneration the book outlines; 'Tibby', his son's ingenuous girlfriend; minor characters called 'Carstairs' and 'Anstruther' – but another lies in the high degree of authorial self-consciousness. It is as if Stacey *knows*, somehow, that to write about well-meaning aristocrats in the unfriendly 1980s is to court aesthetic disaster. 'Anthony could be so *namby*,' Jumbo's son reflects, after a choice pronouncement by one of his Eton friends. ' "How pompous you sound

Daddy," ' his daughter proclaims, after Jumbo has commended a particularly fine ham.

This may be realism of the most scrupulous sort, but decades of stylisation have reduced the fictional aristocrat to the level of drawing-room comedy. Jumbo himself may be an accurate portrait of a particular type of man, but regrettably the average reader is still going to laugh. *Decline*'s theme, too, emerges out of some hackneyed oppositions, though there is an up-to-date commercial twist. Sir James, first pictured in all his glory at a Guildhall dinner, is a man out of his time, worried generally about the new City morality, which seems to him to resemble sharp practice, and specifically by the prospect of having to sell the family firm to the Japanese. Commercial, or rather moral, uncertainty is reinforced by anxieties over his son Jamie, currently in his final year at Eton but fond of enquiring of his friend Anthony: ' "Don't you ever feel you have no substance? I mean, no substance of your own . . ." ' Thereafter, events follow a relentless parallel pattern. Jumbo, the wily orientals now installed on the Mainwaring board and the original factory founded by the first baronet in the hands of the receiver, is reduced to the role of an anguished figurehead. Jamie, after a formative experience with an aid agency in Mali, flunks out of Cambridge, concluding that only reparation to the sacked Mainwaring workers in Bradford can salve his conscience. Accordingly, he heads North, takes a job in an unemployed centre, gets involved with a drugs dealer, has his kneecaps broken by local vigilantes, and ends up in Pentonville on a charge of possession with intent to supply.

The whole should constitute an affecting lament for a political philosophy and a commercial morality – a threnody for an older England built on heavy industry, paternalism and social responsibility. Somehow it fails to do this. If the novel bears a resemblance to the work of another writer, it is to Piers Paul Read, some of whose understanding of the complicated mechanisms which bind together upper-class English life Stacey undoubtedly shares. Like Read, and unusually for a contemporary writer, he introduces a religious element, Jumbo's benign Anglicanism being contrasted with Jamie's creeping doubt. Like Read, too, he employs the technique of the 'incident', the crucial and initially overlooked event which has the effect of changing irrevocably a character's view of himself – in this case Jamie's apprehension of a burglar outside the Mainwarings' Eaton Square flat. All this is promising material, but in the end *Decline* is a novel constrained by the environment in which it is set. Compared to the vigorous, classless entrepreneurs who are supplanting them, Mainwaring and his kind seem frail, insubstantial ghosts. Eventually their protracted demise seems a finely judged piece of determinism, a flying in the face of historical circumstance that can only end in defeat. The evidence of other novels suggests that this is not merely an upper-class predicament. Livi Michael's *Under a Thin Moon*, for example, is a good example of what the past decade has done to the novel of working-class life, turning anger into inanition, resolve into a battered, worn-down weariness. Thirty years ago Alan Sillitoe and Sid Chaplin's heroes seemed to burn with a kind of desperate vitality. In contrast, Michael's protagonists have a much humbler goal, that of simply preserving their identity.

Decline is a protest from the disillusioned, patrician Right, *Under a Thin Moon* a lament from the old, communal Left: the literary opposition to Mrs Thatcher brought some strange alliances. Amid these accretions of hatred and ridicule, it is worth pausing to ask if the Prime Minister possessed any literary supporters at all. There are, naturally enough, Conservative novelists, though Kingsley Amis apparently came unstuck when he tried to present his idol with a copy of *Russian Hide and Seek* (1980), a dystopia which imagines a future England under Soviet control. To find support for Mrs Thatcher firmly associated with the university campus, the theme of Professor Ian Carter's combative study *Ancient Cultures of Conceit* (1990), is outwardly more surprising. Professor Carter's analysis of a large number of 'campus novels', coupled with an investigation of post-war higher education policy, allows him to reach two startling conclusions: first, that at the time of writing Mrs Thatcher's 'morally stunted economic liberalism' was attempting to destroy the generally accepted idea of the university; second, that university novelists were helping her to do it. The starting point for this examination, perhaps predictably, is *The History Man* (1975), which Professor Carter, as might be expected from a sociologist, heartily dislikes. Two hundred campus novels later (119 of them set in Oxford) he is in no doubt as to their animating spirit. British university fiction, he concludes, is timid, unreal, Oxbridge-biased, obsessed by its defence of an outdated, Arnoldian view of 'culture', steeped in the worst sort of Tory illusions, anti-science, misogynistic, xenophobic and anti-proletarian. As an exemplar Carter selects J. I. M. Stewart, author of the Appleby series of detective novels and a variety of cosy common-room fantasies in which elderly academics betray their inability to cope with the modern world.

Exploding the pretensions of the campus novel is not an especially difficult task. However, Professor Carter has a sturdier quarry in view. His assumption – a very reasonable one – is that there is a direct connection between official attitudes to higher education and the fiction that might be thought to reflect the workings of the average university. But the intellectual conditions in which the average university novel is produced are highly unpromising. Examining forty years of establishment musings on the purpose of higher education, from the views of university chancellors to government white papers, he concludes that the whole tenor of post-war thought on the university is merely élitist, built from an Oxbridge blueprint, fearful of compromised standards, and, as such, a prop to the Thatcher assault. But then, as Professor Carter winningly demonstrates, history played a dreadful trick. As well as discomfiting liberal Marxists of the *History Man* school, the Tory education secretaries of the 1980s imposed budgets which had the effect of pruning back humanities departments. Simultaneously, universities had grafted on to them a market philosophy 'radically different from, inimical to, that liberal humanism which university novelists thought they were defending'. The result is a utilitarian desert, of which Mr Gradgrind might have approved, and an obvious solution: our old notion of the humanities is dead, and 'the note of what constitutes culture must be transformed from that typical of British university fiction'.

As a conspiracy theory, of a sort, this simply fails to stand up. Professor Carter might be right about what 1980s Conservatism did to the universities – his own position seems to be that of a man who believes that higher education should be indefinitely extended, irrespective of the talent waiting to receive it – but he is entirely wrong about the role of the university novel. His chief weakness, apart from a fondness for phrases like 'Oxbridge hegemonies', is to take seriously something which does not take itself seriously. Doubtless it is accurate to say that Anthony Lejeune's *Professor in Peril* (1987) and Simon Raven's *Places where they Sing* (1970) are examples of right-wing prejudice, but such novels are generally riven with an irony that Professor Carter rarely seems capable of appreciating. The Oxford novel, in particular, is a deliberate fantasy land, a highly stylised genre largely derived from Beerbohm's *Zuleika Dobson* (1911) and Compton MacKenzie's *Sinister Street* (1913), most of whose exponents are simply amused by its conventions. To regard it as a conscious repository for social and political thought – a sort of touchstone of rightist opinion – is to give it a wholly unmerited significance.

In any case, there are more conspicuous villains. To draw attention to the occasional right-wing don is to ignore the fact that the attitudes of most library fiction, those quiet English novels which the younger type of critic likes to complain about, are implicitly conservative. Penelope Lively, for example, would no doubt deplore any attempt to categorise her as a 'Conservative writer', but the theme of a novel like *Next to Nature, Art* (1982) is unashamedly reactionary: know your limitations, don't cultivate unreasonable ambitions, don't be seduced by the attentions of phonies who talk about art. The victors at the end of Lively's novel are the sensible middle-class people who will return to their suburban homes and continue with their decent, useful lives; the losers are the collection of self-styled artists for whom the concept of personal responsibility is no more than a phrase, and whose emotional lives are always compromised by unappeasable vanity.

You could not call Penelope Lively a Thatcherite, but at the very least *Next to Nature, Art* is a triumphant defence of bourgeois values, and bourgeois values, it goes without saying, are the seedbed from which Thatcherism grew and prospered. Move a little further back to the popular novels of the last decade, the blockbusters full of sex, money and power (topics which, strangely, have not tended to occupy the 'serious' novelist), and you are left with the confused impression of a plot got up by Conservative

Central Office with the express intention of making people vote Tory. Arguably, the tribe of successful businesswomen who march through the pages of 1980s commercial fiction, with their entrepreneurial zeal, their voracious sexual appetites and their proud want of scruple, did as much to perpetuate the Thatcherite myth as Mrs Thatcher herself.

And that, perhaps, is the problem. Just as the existence of a few successful female entrepreneurs provided the model for a series of women in business novels with hardly any basis in reality, so a handful of catchphrases about Mrs Thatcher and English life in the 1980s formed the basis for a great many doubtful 'state of the nation' novels. The novelists of the 1980s, you feel, did their 'research' in the cuttings libraries of national newspapers: their 'observation' was of headlines and government statistics, their conclusions could be found in leader-page articles in the *Guardian*. Thus such a deliberate refraction of the national consciousness as Margaret Drabble's *The Radiant Way* (1987) swiftly reduces itself to the view from the Hampstead dinner table, sectional and stage-managed. The list of topics which its party guests discuss – AIDS, pension fund management, the steel strike – are, regrettably, simply lists, an inventory rather than a piece of art.

The same point, perhaps, could be made of David Lodge's *Nice Work* (1988), which juxtaposes the careers of a female academic and the male managing director of a Midlands engineering company. Constructed in acknowledged imitation of celebrated Victorian predecessors, the novel's oppositions – North and South, Commerce and Art, the life of the body and the life of the mind – are too obtrusive to allow the characters any life of their own. Such is the degree of schematisation that the reader finds himself approving the novel's undoubted cleverness rather than yielding himself up to the pleasures of a plausible, invented world. To say this is not to attribute blame. Stylisation was endemic to nearly every area of 1980s analysis. If our view of Mrs Thatcher's Britain was founded on a few strategically manipulated images and a handful of tabloid headlines, then it was perhaps unreasonable to expect novelists to investigate any further. Their grip on political reality might have been tenuous, but so was our own. More misleading, perhaps, is the way in which these myths extend backwards. The teleology behind the Thatcherite novels of Terence Blacker, David Caute and Julian Rathbone, for instance, demands the recapitulation of a great deal of post-war history. Its landmarks have a depressingly familiar ring: Suez, Profumo, the 'Swinging Sixties'. Frequently the protagonists exist on the periphery of these events: Bosham, for example, plays a minor role in the Profumo affair; Fixx is involved in the scandal of Lord Lambton's dismissal from government in 1973. The effect is to give the national life of the past forty years a lurid, pantomime quality. In this endless war-dance around a series of rather obvious totem poles, the reality of post-war national life has a tendency to be overlooked.

But if you wanted a sustained and thoughtful critique of our national life in the present era, where would you find it? Those novelists who have written most effectively about the great national 'issues' have tended to concentrate on limited areas where there is scope for specialist knowledge. The economic changes of the 1980s, for instance, and the subordination of the City of London to American capital and American know-how, are convincingly dealt with in Piers Paul Read's *A Season in the West* (1988), for all that the personal ramifications are experienced by a tiny redoubt of the English upper classes. Read's gaze even extends to Eastern Europe which, given the time, was a remarkable piece of prescience. Yet the image-mongering and the manipulations of the television age have meant that the true 'political' novel has detached itself almost entirely from the formal channels of national life. The modern political novelist sets his or her work in the council estate rather than the House of Commons chamber, and may not even mention a single politician by name. Carol Birch's *Life in the Palace* (1988), for example, which examines a group of late 1970s Waterloo tenement dwellers, is every inch a modern political novel – humane, understated, but always conscious of the wider forces working to govern the lives of its characters. Significantly, Birch's symbolism is inverted. At one point a national holiday is in progress, presumably that granted on the occasion of the Royal Jubilee of 1977, but it takes place off-stage, is simply a distant noise heard across the rooftops, and of scant interest to Birch's cast in the midst of their fragile, self-absorbed lives. The same spirit animates, or rather casts down, Michael's *Under a Thin*

Moon. Wanda, Valerie, Laurie and Carol, the inhabitants of a run-down Manchester tower block, are united not by class solidarity but by the battle to maintain some form of individual existence. Laurie, who sustains herself through shop-lifting, is careful to study her reflection in the mirror: without this stimulus there is a danger that she will forget what she looks like. To Wanda, with an illegitimate child and an unenviable destiny as the mistress of a seedy club-owner, petty theft seems an attractive option: what she regards as her own 'invisibility' will be an adequate hedge against detection.

Despite their passivity, a twilit state in which past and present dissolve into timeless brooding, Michael's characters are sharply aware that their present condition is an effect rather than a cause. Valerie, saddled with an alcoholic mother and an awesome neurosis, reflects that 'any choice she had ever made comes down to money in the end'. Laurie, limping in pursuit of her Giro, realises that she 'never knew before that you needed money to speak'. The absolute connection between personal security and cash is made plain in Wanda's hankering after 'peace and quiet: two commodities well out of her price range'. An immensely gloomy and distressing economic parable, *Under a Thin Moon* inevitably carries its own burdens of myth and overstatement, from 'monetarism' to the over-simplistic equation of entrepreneurialism and theft. In some ways their grounding in the tragedies of ordinary lives makes them more acceptable than the exaggerations and complacency of more formal inspections of the national destiny.

Epilogue

England Made Me

Social context is not everything. We read *Vanity Fair* for Becky Sharp and Jos Sedley rather than to admire Thackeray's skill as a cultural critic, and social histories of literature, with their chalk-line demarcations and their sense of everybody travelling unhesitatingly in the same direction, invariably have a slightly suspect ring. As John Gross puts it, a novel which can largely be reduced to the sum of its sociological parts can never have been much of a novel in the first place. At the same time, it would be a very cursory reader of Thackeray who did not appreciate that *Vanity Fair* takes place in a precisely evoked historical landscape and that, for all their individuality, Becky, old Mr Osborne and all the others are the representatives, if not the victims, of powerful social forces. To make this point is not necessarily to ignore the more prosaic reasons for which people read books, for our sense of a novel's aesthetic qualities and our awareness of its status as an historical artefact are intimately connected. If some of us occasionally feel that the literature of our own time is a debased and decadent animal, creeping along in the shadow of mighty ancestors, then we must also acknowledge the potent cultural forces working to undermine our traditional sense of what the novel consists.

This sea-change is especially notable in the field of character. Nineteenth-century novelists may share many of the preoccupations of their late twentieth-century successors – and there are enough definitions of liberalism in Victorian fiction to satisfy the most exacting modern political theorist – but their chief interest is in human quiddity. We may accept the art equals propaganda

equation, but simultaneously Plantagenet Palliser is more absorbing to us as a fretful husband than as a politician: in fact as a
politician, in terms of devising policy and carrying it through, he
scarcely exists. Built on prominent and predictable foundations –
the income, the politics, the religion – the great monsters of Victorian fiction simultaneously possess a defining individuality. The
absolute belief that the reader cultivates in the existence of a Becky
Sharp or a Paul Dombey gives their creators unprecedented room
for manoeuvre. Their characters are so securely rooted in their
world that they can allow them to behave apparently out of character while remaining true to the individual spirit that identifies
them. Perhaps the finest and most psychologically acute scene in
Vanity Fair occurs when Rawdon Crawley, unexpectedly sprung
from the debtors' prison, returns home to find Becky entertaining
the Marquis of Steyne. Suspecting his imprisonment to have been
deliberately contrived by his wife and her aristocratic lover to
assist their adultery, Rawdon assaults Lord Steyne, seizing a jewel
from his wife's décolletage and hurling it at the nobleman as he
lies prostrate. It is the ruination of all Becky's schemes, her plans
for social advancement, her career as Lord Steyne's mistress – from
now on her life will follow an inexorable downward path – but
she cannot help admiring her husband for his actions. The scene,
consequently, is vital to our conception of Becky and Rawdon as
people, causing us to acknowledge the complexity of Thackeray's
portraiture. Becky is a duplicitous, conniving schemer, who would
betray even her husband in pursuit of her own ends, but her
husband still has the capacity to move her, even while destroying
her ambitions. Rawdon is a witless half-pay officer who cheats at
cards and makes an income by fleecing young noblemen out
of their patrimony, but he retains, however narrowly, a sense of
honour. Dickens, you feel, would be incapable of this type
of subtlety, this imaginative exactness: in his hands Crawley would
simply be a caricature, Becky either sinister or comically
overblown.

There are dozens of similar scenes in Victorian fiction, episodes
in which the reactions of a set of characters to chance contingency
redefine or radically enhance our perception of them. A good
example of this group realignment comes in Trollope's *Phineas*

Finn, when the elderly Duke of Omnium conceives a desire to marry Madame Max Goesler. Such a marriage, particularly if it produces children, will naturally have serious implications for the Duke's nephew and presumptive heir, Plantagenet Palliser. As the proposal is made and mulled over, and the rumours accumulate around it, Trollope devotes several chapters to the reactions of the interested parties. Palliser displays his habitual aloof reserve: his uncle's private life is his own affair; the match may not come to anything; Madame Max is a woman of taste and discretion; a certain amount of surveillance may be appropriate. His wife, however, is seriously alarmed at the prospect of her son being disinherited and regards Madame Max as a scheming interloper. Eventually, when Madame Max declines the Duke's offer, the reader recognises the slight but subtle alteration in his view of all four characters. The Duke of Omnium becomes a foolish old man, slipping into his dotage; Plantagenet Palliser's diffidence is confirmed, even in matters relating to his own family, but also his sense of delicacy; the almost entirely favourable view we have hitherto taken of Lady Glencora is refined by this new evidence of toughness and manifest unfairness to Madame Max; while Mme Goesler herself impresses us by her objective consideration of the Duke's offer and her very sensible decision to decline. Significantly, the reader is neither elated nor cast down by this process of redefinition. Rather, his confidence in the author is renewed. We may not like Lady Glencora when she reflects, ' "What a blow it would be, should some little wizen-cheeked half-monkey baby, with a black brow and yellow skin be brought forward and shown to her some day as the heir!" ' but at least we can acknowledge that this is an understandable human reaction; Lady Glencora is more, not less, real to us as a result of it.

The reality card, of course, is a dangerous one to play in any discussion of the modern literary novel. In their feigning of felt experience, the major Victorian novelists created the illusion that their characters had lives of their own, an independent existence that is somehow never cancelled out by authorial trickery. In reading about David Copperfield, for example, one is aware of David Copperfield rather than the writer who stands behind him. The contemporary novelist's ability to mimic reality, alternatively, expresses itself chiefly in conscious manipulation. Keith Talent is a beguiling composite of the sinister and the comic, but he is not 'real' even in the sense that a Dickensian grotesque is real; always in a novel like *London Fields* (1989) you are aware of the author running into the room to arrange the furniture before the characters arrive. It is not that Keith doesn't possess an unmediated thought, but that Amis fails even to offer him the illusion of one, and the absence of the unmediated thought, the sense of any individual spirit, is Amis's point. In much the same way Vic and Robyn in David Lodge's *Nice Work* (1988), a novel seriously concerned with examining the national fabric, are entirely figurative, blocks of opinion put into suits of clothes and allowed to wander through their meticulously constructed playground; their every thought and sensation filtered through the consciousness of an omniscient creator.

Inevitably, one can overstress these distinctions. Thackeray and Trollope, to take two Victorian examples, are conspicuous presences in their texts, and Thackeray provides several early examples of the unreliable narrator, but generally they are concerned to sustain illusions rather than to undermine them; even Trollope's authorial interventions are ironic and short-lived. More important, Victorian displays of self-consciousness were never allowed to penetrate the carapace of personality. The self-consciousness of the modern novelist is everywhere remarked upon. Less widely apparent, perhaps, is the self-consciousness of the modern novelist's characters, those bright, uncertain creations who can't utter a sentence without reminding themselves of its banality, who can't enter a room without recalling other entrances in other rooms in other novels, and who sport their awareness of who they are like a rosette. This tendency occasionally reaches extreme heights. The late Richard Burns's *Fond and Foolish Lovers* (1990) contains a middle-aged man who compares himself to 'a paper cup on the stream of life', only to realise that this is 'a lousy image', and a pair of potential adulterers whose conversation is a deliberate parody of the speeches conventionally allotted to potential adulterers. Even the rain is 'slow fictional rain'. It is perhaps significant that the best passages in Burns's novel come when the cast can forget their own unreality for a moment: briefly and illusorily released from their authorial fetters, they spring dramatically to life.

These are easy criticisms to make, and one occasionally feels that the steady drip of newspaper articles about the post-modern world must at some stage reach saturation point. Even so, the spectacle of cultural pundits loftily asserting that 'romance' or 'belief' are moribund can frequently fall rather flat; such pronouncements rarely match one's own experience, let alone that of the great mass of the population who are scarcely aware that the world of literary in-fighting even exists. Amid these debates about the writer's role, and recriminations about the writer's inadequacy, the connection between novelists' sense of themselves and the wider socio-historical environment can often be overlooked. If we criticise modern novelists for self-absorption, reflexiveness, terrible uncertainty – in the last resort for not writing like their ancestors – then we must also acknowledge the powerful forces that are encouraging them to operate in this way. Cultural fragmentation, one sometimes feels, is not as widespread as intellectual orthodoxy maintains: even so it is impossible to gainsay the feeling – experienced, it must be said, by nearly every writer of talent – that many of the traditional foundations of the novel have disintegrated beyond redemption. Novelists struggle to write about 'value', for they inhabit a world in which there is no clear agreement on what 'value' means. The old axes of class and sexual morality grow steadily more rusty. What the writer of the 1930s knew as 'liberalism' is dead. The complexities and concealments of the wider landscape are more or less impenetrable. Denied these ancient standbys, writers rarely have much left beyond their technical awareness, their sense of how a novel works, and their own precarious relation to their craft. The final effect of these changes is, inevitably enough, to diminish further novelists' ability to perform what has always been considered their principal task – to create character. To say that when we read a modern novel we do so to admire the author's dexterity rather than to participate in the illusion of a fully realised interior life may seem hard on the average novelist, but to do so is to recognise the devastating effect of the last half-century on the average literary sensibility.

One might also say that English writers have nothing left but their Englishness, and that this is part of the problem. Certainly, the mainstream English novelist can sometimes seem constrained by environment in a way that the mainstream American or African – or, closer to home, the average Scottish or Irish writer – is not. The note of apology – a sort of chronic embarrassment about nationality and the shortcomings it might be thought to produce – rises above nearly all post-war domestic art. This type of defensiveness is a relatively new phenomenon. The concentration on nationality which characterises the Victorian novel is commonly seen as one of the more unpleasant by-blows of imperialism: in fact it has a much more positive function. To Dickens, for example, 'Englishness' can be identified with qualities such as gentleness, whimsicality, idiosyncrasy, 'decency': as a member of what Orwell called 'the non-military middle classes', the gallophobia of some of Thackeray's minor writings is quite beyond him. To any English writer born before about 1900 the notion that one should spend one's time apologising for the fact of one's birthplace would have seemed faintly ludicrous. There is a longish thesis to be written on the origins of post-imperial literary guilt: in any case, the symptoms are not in doubt.

If this tendency characterised the novels of the immediately post-war era, its emphasis has been redoubled in the fiction of the past twenty years. English art, English manners, English customs – and it is still 'English', hardly ever 'British' – all are damned for their reserve, their timidity, their fatal unwillingness to engage with the rigours of a modern world. The connection between the English sense of post-war diminishment and the creative arts has yet to be fully explored, but its consequences are everywhere apparent in the English novel, where 'English' remains a byword for hypocrisy, reticence, above all a sort of studied unfitness to act. Lucy in Nigel Williams's *Jack Be Nimble* (1980) sums up this assumption of inaptness very well when she informs Warliss:

> 'you're like all these terribly clever English people. You find it difficult to live, and what's the point of setting out to do all these good, brave and wonderful things when they only seem to make your hard heart worse?'

A question of upbringing, then. But there is more to it than this. Even climatic conditions, Doris Lessing's 'thin English sunlight', seem to have contributed to this dismal torpor, this gradual thinning of the blood, this slowing of the national pulse-beat. The English live tired, exhausted lives, inhabit a domestic environment typified by duplicity and lack of feeling (Warliss's foreign mistress thinks: 'these English people did not know what was a home and a family. They did not kiss or quarrel in public. They told cold little untruths to each other over the breakfast table . . . They had houses, these English, but not homes.') They send their children to boarding schools, Doris Lessing hints in her short story 'The Real Thing' (1992), because of their inability to communicate with them. Their cities, the clotted dreamscape of *London Fields*, David Lodge's grimy Midlands dust-heap, are collapsing about them. Their political system is driven by brutal self-interest rather than humane compassion. Interleaved with these expressions of contempt is an awareness of the failure of one positive national quality – English radicalism – to galvanise creeping post-war inertia. As another of Nigel Williams's fretful 1960s survivors puts it:

'Ten years ago we thought that a few marches and a few people setting themselves alight was going to sort out the whole of Western Capitalism. What we actually had in mind was a sort of Garden of Eden – a planned economy for hippies. What we're getting, ten years later, is lies and mess and muddle, with our private lives a mess and our public concerns in even worse shape.'

The revolution, then, was betrayed by amateurishness, lack of toughness, a belief that the citadels of power could somehow be stormed by sheer good intentions. Queerly, these complaints exist side by side with quintessentially English subject matter and preoccupations. *Jack Be Nimble*, for example, is a work of scrupulous ideological intent, with an inbred horror of anything that might be construed as 'sexist', but one of its strongest convictions is that foreigners are funny.

Ritual self-disparagement, consequently, often disguises a more innate superiority. Inevitably, some of the sharpest perspectives on

English life in the past twenty years are external, a product of the migrant's eye. Here the reader immediately runs up against the queer sense of promise unfulfilled, a naive belief in the possibilities of England brought down by bitter experience. Even those expatriates who profess to like the place are aware that they do so for slightly suspect reasons. Rosamund and Michael in John Broderick's *London Irish* (1979) are said to love London for 'its anonymity, its careless and infinite variety, its indifferent tolerance, the illusion it gave of still being the centre of the world'. The illusion, you note. In reality London is only the 'vast grey sink' descried by Paul Theroux's Hood in *The Family Arsenal* (1975), fatally wrecked, rife with the sour smell of decay.

The feeling of hope cancelled out by latent hostility or simple indifference, that cosy English self-absorption, is an abiding theme of the emigrant novel's view of England. The Chens in Timothy Mo's *Sour Sweet* (1982) are conscious that their tenancy of a council flat in the London Borough of Brent represents a type of usurpation:

> That English people had competed for the flat which he now occupied made Chen feel more rather than less of a foreigner; it made him feel like a gatecrasher who had stayed too long and been identified.

This feeling encourages Chen to enter into an unspoken complicity 'between himself and others like him, not necessarily of his race' – the West Indian bus conductor, for example, who deliberately undercharges him. In the Chinatown restaurant where he works, the waiters occupy their spare moments by discussing the idiosyncrasies of their English customers, their habit of not paying the bill, their incipient rowdiness. The mental distance is infinite.

At least the Chens are financially secure. The Nigerian narrator of Buchi Emecheta's *In the Ditch* (1972) finds her energies exhausted merely by coping with a pettifogging bureaucracy and an obtrusive Welfare State. Adah, struggling to bring up her children in the south London squalor of the early 1960s, as they wait for her husband to join them from Lagos, hasn't bargained for the social structure she finds in England. She expects to have to live frugally, but the difficulties of finding accommodation bewilder her. Neither does she imagine that she will have to live in conditions that would be intolerable back home. Her marriage crumbles, and even solidarity with poorer English people is denied her. As Emecheta puts it: 'She couldn't claim to be working class, because the working class had a code for daily living. She had none.' The horror of Adah's deracination is that it will not even admit the possibility of a routine.

The immediacy of Mo and Emecheta's observations has the quality of reportage. A broader framework, a long-term historical context in which the interloper is seen as a chronicler of older, fading patterns, is provided by V. S. Naipaul. Becalmed in a cottage on a Wiltshire estate which seems scarcely to have known the touch of the twentieth century, the narrator of *The Enigma of Arrival* (1987) – transparently Naipaul himself – becomes fascinated by the mysterious figure of his landlord (in reality the reclusive aesthete Stephen Tennant) whose achievement is to have retreated from life. To Naipaul, Tennant is a metaphor for the decline of Britain in the modern world, a disappearing empire and a fading past. The frail, delicate poems which the landlord occasionally dispatches to his tenant seem to him to evoke abandoned ideas of Edwardian England:

> a turning away from the coarseness of industrialism, upper-class cultural sensibilities almost drugged by money – my landlord's Indian romance partook of all those impulses and was rooted in England's wealth, empire, the idea of glory, material satiety, a very great security.

But it is a world as remote and faded as a cloche hat or a jar of hundreds and thousands. The sense of lost English time is continually present in the novel's opening section – Salisbury, Stonehenge, the Victorian Gothic of the village church, Jack, the narrator's neighbour in his ramshackle cottage, 'living in the middle of junk, amid the ruins of nearly a century' – yet it is a static past, inert, incapable of progress.

Ultimately Naipaul, a restless voyager from the colonial backwater of Trinidad, acknowledges that his idea of England as a

home has been replaced by the awareness that it is merely
a stopping point on a more elaborate trajectory:

> For years, in that far-off island whose human history I had been
> discovering and writing about, I had dreamed of coming to
> England. But my life in England had been savourless, and much
> of it mean ... And just as once at home I had dreamed of being
> in England, so for years in England I had dreamed of leaving
> England.

One searches amid these migrants' testimonies for some discussion of racial issues, a deeper immersion in questions of absorption and assimilability: it is rarely evident. Naipaul, for example,
is less interested in the question of race than the theme of the
colonial adrift in a post-colonial world, in which his own position,
quite as much as that of his former mentors, has been ineradicably
altered. Rightly or wrongly, race has still to occupy a prominent
place in the contemporary English novel: the emigrant remains
a fugitive, fleeting presence, patronised occasionally or brought
forward to illustrate some social theory, but largely invisible.

The same point could be made of the narrower literary preoccupation with 'pluralism'. We all know – anyone seriously concerned
with the state of modern writing knows – that the old boundaries
are fragmenting, that much of what constitutes 'English' writing
is distinctly un-English, in both its assumptions and perspective.
But while there may not be such a thing as 'the English novel'
any more, what might be called 'the novel of England' is far from
extinct, and though some of its exponents may come from the
Commonwealth and beyond, its preoccupations have scarcely
changed. Reticence, reserve, concealment, an obsession with a
faded and discreditable colonial past – the themes of a novel like
the Guyana-born David Dabydeen's *Disappearance* (1993) have
been endlessly rehearsed. In these cases 'pluralism' can turn out
to seem nothing more than a marginal tampering with a venerable
tradition.

The reader who sometimes feels that the novel and the novelist
who produces it are badly served by this and other types of
prescription is likely to be consoled by an examination of the

literary history of the last ten years. The tendency of the contemporary English novel is to the metropolitan, the slick and the contrived; conversely, many of the most satisfying novels of the past decade have embraced the provincial, the pastoral and the commonplace. A book like the late Don Bannister's *Burning Leaves* (1982), in which a university lecturer translates himself to a mundane existence in a Northern city, is a conscious retreat: its achievement to re-establish a connection between fiction and the ebb and flow of English provincial life, whose concerns are the concerns of the great majority of English people. J. L. Carr's novels bring off a similar effect. Though rooted in a sepia-tinted English countryside, riven with eccentricity and charm, they are never sentimental: rather their characters are seen to be making the best of things, forging emotional attachments that will give them satisfaction rather than the continual ecstasy that most modern fictional protagonists regard as an automatic right. Demonstrating the limits within which the average existence is lived may seem a very humble trick for the novelist, but in an environment where the average cultural commentator's detachment from felt life can verge on the alarming, the reader can occasionally wish that it is a trick more writers were able to perform.

Reading – and reviewing – the contemporary novel, one is frequently left with the sensation of staring at a world whose lineaments are quite unrecognisable, whose tensions and motivations have no connection with the landscape they are alleged to reflect. If there is a message for the English novelist in the debris of the past half-century it is that an awareness of 'Englishness' is at least as likely to enhance as to diminish the quality of English writing, and that by disparaging these tendencies in literature we disparage and undermine our own personal and collective identity. We have nothing to lose but our preconceptions.

Notes and Bibliography

Place of publication London unless otherwise stated

Introduction: Whatever Happened to Lucky Jim?

p. xvi 'It is over a century... complex social tissue': for Taine and Stephen, see John Gross, *The Rise and Fall of the Man of Letters* (1969), Chapter 4. Stephen's essay on Taine can be found in S.O.A. Ullmann, ed., *Men, Books and Mountains* (1956).

p. xviii 'breezily expressed... questions about society': see Simon Raven, 'Class and the Contemporary Novel', in Richard Mabey, ed., *Class* (1967).

p. xviii 'Malcolm Bradbury might hazard... spirit of modernism': see 'The Novel No Longer Novel', reprinted in *No, Not Bloomsbury* (1987).

p. xviii 'set against this... early twentieth-century novelists': see in particular Peter Keating, *The Haunted Study: A Social History of the English Novel 1875–1914* (1989).

p. xviii 'it was at least as much... book on Joyce': *James Joyce and the Revolution of the Word* (1978).

p. xxiv 'In his study of the conditions... nearly forty years': see Harry Ritchie, *Success Stories: Literature and the Media in England 1950–59* (1988)

1 Unconditional Surrender

p. 1 'The result of the 1945 General Election... a prodigious surprise': see Michael Davie, ed., *The Diaries of Evelyn Waugh* (1976), p. 629.

p. 2 'A more formal but equally deliberate... King's speech': for an account of Freeman's speech and its reception, see Anthony Howard, 'We are the Masters Now', in Michael Sissons and Philip French, ed., *Age of Austerity* (Oxford 1963).

p. 3 'In fact his comments... progressively more gloomy': Orwell's

London Letters to *Partisan Review* of Summer and Fall 1945 are reprinted in Sonia Orwell and Ian Angus, ed., *The Collected Essays, Journalism and Letters of George Orwell*, vol. iii: *As I please (1943–1945)*, (Harmondsworth 1968). The *Commentary* essay of October 1948 (pp. 343–49) is not included in the Collected Essays, but see Bernard Crick, *George Orwell: A Life* (1980), pp. 377–8.

p. 4 'Yet the potential for social revolution... the England of 1945': for social and political conditions in the period 1945–1951, see the essays collected in *Age of Austerity*; see also Kenneth O. Morgan, *The People's Peace: British History 1945–1989* (Oxford 1990), Chapter 2.

p. 8 'Move a little further... even more evident': a representative selection of the short fiction of the 1940s appears in Woodrow Wyatt, ed., *The Way We Lived Then: The English Story in the 1940s* (1989); for overviews of the literature of the 1940s, see Robert Hewison, *Under Siege: Literary Life in London 1939–45* (1977) and Andrew Sinclair, *War Like a Wasp: The Lost Decade of the Forties* (1989).

p. 9 'The concept of a "People's War"... impetus or vehicle': for a discussion of the People's War theme in fiction, see Alan Munton, *English Fiction of the Second World War* (1989), Chapter 2.

p. 11 'Consider, for example... Angela Thirkell': on Thirkell, see Margot Strickland, *Angela Thirkell: Portrait of a Lady Novelist* (1977), and David Pryce-Jones, 'Towards the Cocktail Party', in *Age of Austerity*.

p. 15 'This type of festering resentment... annoying the Labour Party': see Kingsley Amis's review of *Unconditional Surrender* in the *Spectator*, 27 October 1961, reprinted in *The Amis Collection* (1990).

p. 15 'After Waugh's intrigues... view of the post-war world': on Powell's war novels, see Munton, op. cit., Chapter 4; James Tucker, *The Novels of Anthony Powell* (1976); and Patrick Swinden, *The English Novel of History and Society 1940–1980* (1984), Chapter 4.

p. 27 'Something of this disquiet... Festival of Britain': see Michael Frayn, 'Festival', in *Age of Austerity*.

2 Figures in a Landscape

p. 52 'History as presented... neither glamorous nor consoling': see Margaret Scanlan, *Traces of Another Time* (Princeton 1990).

p. 61 'The American critic James Gindin... Wilson's early novels': see James Gindin, *Postwar British Fiction: New Accents and Attitudes* (Berkeley, Ca., 1962).

p. 61 'One remembers Orwell's comment... one of the symbolic figures of England: George Orwell, 'England Your England', reprinted in *Inside the Whale and Other Essays* (Harmondsworth 1962).

3 Cross-currents of the 1950s

p. 64 ' "Consensus" is perhaps too emollient a term ... political expediency': on the 1950s political background, see Morgan, op. cit., Chapter 4.

p. 64 'Evelyn Shuckburgh ... quantify this attitude': for a useful discussion of Britain's post-war Imperial role, see Peter Hennessy, *Premiership* (Oxford 1992).

p. 65 'The gulf between public portrayals ... influence in the world': see ibid.

p. 65 'A Mass Observation survey of 1949 ... a national obsession': see Arthur Marwick, *British Society Since 1945* (1982, rev. 1990), Chapter 2.

p. 66 'The mania for literary groupings ... a straightforward equation': on the literary background to the 1950s, see Ritchie, op. cit., and Blake Morrison, *The Movement* (Oxford 1980).

p. 67 'The novels of John Lodwick ... did not survive the 1960s': for Lodwick, see Walter Allen, *Tradition and Dream: The English and American Novel from the Twenties to Our Time* (1964), pp. 277–8; see also Anthony Powell, *To Keep the Ball Rolling*, vol. iii: *Faces In My Time* (1980), p. 44.

p. 72 'Reviewing Anthony Powell's *The Acceptance World* ... an exclusive group': the review, which originally appeared in the *Spectator*, 13 October 1955, is reprinted in *The Amis Collection*.

p. 80 'Coined by the political columnist Henry Fairlie ... on the City': see ed., Hugh Thomas, *The Establishment* (1959).

p. 81 'In reality novelists ... concerned by Suez': for the literary politics of the Suez crisis, see Ritchie, op. cit., Chapter 2.

5 The Day of the Sardine

p. 104 'Search for the proletarian literature ... a hole in the air': see 'The Proletarian Writer', a BBC Home Service discussion between George Orwell and Desmond Hawkins, broadcast on 6 December 1940 and reprinted in Orwell's *Collected Essays*, vol. ii: *My Country Right or Left (1940–1943)* (Harmondsworth 1968).

p. 105 'The clutch of late 1950s and early 1960s working-class writers ... are that much more homogeneous': on Sillitoe, see Ritchie, op. cit., Chapter 9; biographical details of Sid Chaplin can be found in the posthumous collection *In Blackberry Time* (Newcastle upon Tyne 1987).

p. 106 'No discussion of the working-class novel ... first published in 1957': see Richard Hoggart, *The Uses of Literacy* (1957); for a discussion of Hoggart's views and influence, see Marwick, op. cit., Chapter 8.

p. 120 'Harry Ritchie has pointed out ... an end to it': see Ritchie, op. cit., Chapter 9.

7 Scenes from the Class War

p. 151 'The election of 1964 was not 1945 mark two ... could accept that': on the Labour government of 1964–70, see Phillip Whitehead, *The Writing on the Wall: Britain in the Seventies* (1985), Chapter 1.

p. 152 'Writing over a decade later ... throughout the 1960s and 1970s': quoted ibid., p. 399.

p. 152 'This, at any rate ... Evelyn Waugh': Evelyn Waugh, 'I See Nothing but Boredom ... Everywhere', *Daily Mail*, 28 December 1959, reprinted in Donat Gallagher, ed., *The Essays, Articles and Reviews of Evelyn Waugh* (1983).

p. 158 'In a provocative essay ... catalogue prevailing attitudes': see Raven, op. cit.

8 The Search for Value

p. 169 'A. S. Byatt, for example ... in the language': see the introduction to *Passions of the Mind: Selected Writings* (1991).

p. 172 'Angus Wilson's *Anglo-Saxon Attitudes* ... human pursuit of truth': for a discussion of this theme, see Gindin, op. cit., Chapter 9.

p. 173 'In "Against Dryness" ... complexity and depth': Murdoch's essay is reprinted in Malcolm Bradbury, ed., *The Novel Today* (1970); Byatt's 'People in Paper Houses', which discusses similar themes, appears in the same collection and also in *Passions of the Mind* (see also the introduction to the latter volume).

p. 174 'As Carey acknowledges ... reserved for Catholics only': Orwell's review of *The Heart of the Matter*, which originally appeared in the *New Yorker*, 17 July 1948, is reprinted in the *Collected Essays*, vol. iv; John Carey discusses Greene's religious standpoint in *The Intellectuals and the Masses: Pride and Prejudice among the Literary Intelligentsia 1880–1939* (1992), Chapter 4.

p. 175 'it is difficult to dismiss ... moral and the aesthetic': see Rebecca West, *The Meaning of Treason* (1956).

p. 177 'In the 1950s and 1960s ... almost hectically ordered way': see A. S. Byatt's review of William Golding's *Darkness Visible*, reprinted in *Passions of the Mind*.

p. 178 'Examining the list of 1950s writers ... extremely confused': for a more detailed discussion of this theme, see Gindin, op. cit., Chapter 4.

9 Harold's Years

p. 194 'Though there have been several recent attempts . . . post-war era':
for a broadly sympathetic account of the Wilson governments, see
Ben Pimlott, *Harold Wilson* (1992); see also Ross McKibbin, 'Homage
to Wilson and Callaghan', *London Review of Books*, 24 October 1991.
The case against is memorably stated in E. P. Thompson's 'Yesterday's
Manikin', a review of Wilson's *The Labour Government 1964–1970*,
which appeared in *New Society*, 29 July 1971, and is reprinted in
Writing by Candlelight (1980). On the economic and political background, see Whitehead and Morgan, op. cit., Chapter 7 and 10
respectively.

p. 200 'William Clark's novels . . . British political establishment and
beyond': see Christopher Harvie, *The Centre of Things: Political
Fiction in Britain from Disraeli to the Present* (1991), Chapter 9.

p. 208 'Simultaneously . . . secondary education': on Crosland's time as
Secretary of State for Education, see Susan Crosland, *Tony Crosland*
(1982).

p. 208 'A feature of the late 1960s . . . higher education': on the 1960s
debate about educational standards, see Whitehead, op. cit., Chapter
10.

10 Sex and Sensibility

p. 219 'John Carey has suggested . . . food they eat': see John Carey,
Thackeray: Prodigal Genius (1977), Chapter 4.

p. 222 'The "New Woman" . . . Hill Top novel': for an account of the
rise of the 'New Woman' in Victorian fiction, see Keating, op. cit.
Chapter 3. Fictional examples of the 'bachelor girl' can be found in
Leonard Merrick, *The Man who Liked Women and Other Stories*, and
Alec Waugh, '*Sir, She Said . . .*' (1929).

p. 222 'George Moore . . . lurid and sensational work': Moore's polemic
against Mudie, originally published in the *Pall Mall Gazette*, 10
December 1884, and the correspondence it aroused are reprinted in
Pierre Coustillas, ed., *Literature at Nurse, or Circulating Morals: A
Polemic on Victorian Censorship* (1976).

11 The Exclusion Zone

p. 239 'The Second World War . . . equal footing with men': the social
background and statistical information on which this discussion is
based can be found in Morgan, op. cit., *passim*; Marwick, op. cit.,
especially Chapters 4 and 7; and Whitehead, op. cit., Chapter 16.

p. 241 'Olivia Manning's *Balkan Trilogy* . . . political confusion': see
Munton, op. cit., Chapter 4.

p. 253 'In Geoffrey Gorer's survey ... time of their marriage': quote in Marwick, op. cit.

12 The Literary Consequences of Mrs Thatcher

p. 266 'Christopher Harvie ... inexorable decline': for a discussion of the British political novel in the post-war era, on which I have heavily relied, see Harvie, op. cit., Chapter 9.

p. 270 'Salman Rushdie's *New Statesman* rallying cry ... tired and petulant': see Salman Rushdie, 'A General Election', reprinted in *Imaginary Homelands* (1991).

p. 278 'Three years after her political demise ... proclaim her singularity': for a discussion of Mrs Thatcher's first administration, see Whitehead, op. cit., Chapter 19; on Thatcherism as a political phenomenon, see Morgan, op. cit., Chapters 12 and 13.

p. 278 'Milton Friedman ... classical Tory': quoted in Whitehead, op. cit., p. 337.

p. 283 'There are, naturally enough ... under Soviet control': for an account of this episode, see Kingsley Amis, *Memoirs* (1991), p. 318.

Epilogue: *England Made Me*

p. 289 'As John Gross puts it ... in the first place': see Gross, op. cit., Chapter 11.

p. 294 'To Dickens, for example ... quite beyond him': Orwell's remark on Dickens occurs in 'Wells, Hitler and the World State', reprinted in his *Collected Essays*, vol. ii.

p. 297 'To Naipaul, Tennant is a metaphor ... a fading past': a fuller discussion of Naipaul's relationship with Stephen Tennant can be found in Philip Hoare, *Serious Pleasures: The Life of Stephen Tennant* (1990).

Index

Index

Index

Index

Mount, Ferdinand: *The Clique*, 42, 201–3
Munton, Alan: 20, 23, 225
Murdoch, Iris, xxiv, 50, 173, 177: 'Against Dryness', 173; *The Red and the Green*, 53–6; *A Severed Head*, 233; *Under the Net*, 51, 68

Naipaul, V. S.: *The Enigma of Arrival*, 297–8
Naughton, Bill, 106: *Late Night on Watling Street*, 111; 'A Skilled Man', 122
Newman, Andrea, 233, 237–8: *The Cage*, 154, 230, 250, 252–3, 254
New Statesman, 4, 120, 130, 135, 270
Nott, Kathleen: *Private Fires*, 243–4

Orwell, George, xiii, xiv, xviii, 3, 59–60, 73, 105–9, 130, 174, 265, 294: *Coming up for Air*, 4; *Homage to Catalonia*, 4; 'Notes on Nationalism', 33; *The Road to Wigan Pier*, 109

Panter-Downes, Mollie: *One Fine Day*, 6, 8, 29–31, 60–1, 241
Parks, Tim: *Goodness*, 271–2, 274–5, 277–8, 281
Powell, Anthony, 8, 10, 13–14, 27, 31, 52, 67, 90–1, 131, 158, 168, 265–6: *Afternoon Men*, 31, 230; *A Dance to the Music of Time*, 13, 29, 90, 211; *The Acceptance World*, 47, 72; *Books Do Furnish a Room*, 5–6, 11, 25; *Hearing Secret Harmonies*, ix, 204–5, 208, 211; *The Military Philosophers*, 6, 14, 22–3, 25; *A Question of Upbringing*, 90; *The Soldier's Art*, 7, 9, 15–20, 31, 265; *Temporary Kings*, 50; *Venusberg*, 31
Praed, Mrs Campbell: *Nadine*, 222
Priestley, J. B., 4, 10, 15, 21: *Angel Pavement*, 240; *Daylight on Saturday*, 10, 20, 225; *Festival at Farbridge*, 28–9, 36; *Out of the People*, 9
Pryce-Jones, David, 11

Rathbone, Julian: *Nasty, Very*, 272–5, 277–8, 281, 287

Raven, Simon, 81, 87: *Brother Cain*, 223; 'Class and the Contemporary Novel', xviii, 150, 158; *Close of Play*, 223–4; *The Feathers of Death*, 87, 155; *Fielding Gray*, 6, 24, 43; *Friends in Low Places*, 35–6, 83–4, 88, 161; *The Judas Boy*, 57, 206; *Places Where They Sing*, 208, 210, 285; *The Rich Pay Late*, 82, 88; *The Sabre Squadron*, 36–7, 42, 50, 155–6; *Sound the Retreat*, 56; *The Survivor*, 48–9
Raymond, Derek: *The Crust on its Uppers*, 157
Read, Piers Paul, 197, 282: *A Married Man*, 173, 200–1, 209; *The Professor's Daughter*, 198; *A Season in the West*, 287; *The Upstart*, 176–7
Ritchie, Harry: *Success Stories*, xi, xxiv, 67, 120
Rushdie, Salman, 270–1

Scanlan, Margaret: *Traces of Another Time*, 52, 54, 58–9
Scott, Paul: *The Raj Quartet*, 53
Shawcross, Sir Hartley, 2, 25
Shuckburgh, Evelyn, 64–5
Sillitoe, Alan 105, 129: *Saturday Night and Sunday Morning*, 5, 60, 105–9, 111–123, 125–8, 228–9; *The Loneliness of the Long-distance Runner*, 122
Sinclair, Andrew: *The Breaking of Bumbo*, 36, 82–3, 85, 88–9, 225
Smollett, Tobias, 103: *Roderick Random*, xix, 217–18
Snow, C. P., 4, 71, 83, 130: *Homecoming*, 130–1; *The New Men*, 77–8; *Strangers and Brothers*, 68–9
Spark, Muriel, xxiv: *The Girls of Slender Means*, 240
Stacey, Tom: *Decline*, 281–3
Stead, Christina: *Cotters' England*, 245–7
Stephen, Leslie, xvi, xx, 222
Stewart, J. I. M., 284
Storey, David, 106: *Flight into Camden*, 108, 111–12, 124–6, 154; *Present-Times*, 209; *This Sporting*